THE BETTENCOURT
AFFAIR

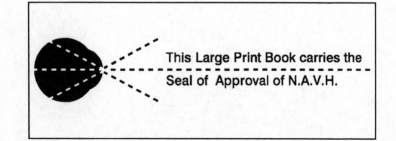

This Large Print Book carries the
Seal of Approval of N.A.V.H.

THE BETTENCOURT AFFAIR

THE WORLD'S RICHEST WOMAN AND THE SCANDAL THAT ROCKED PARIS

TOM SANCTON

THORNDIKE PRESS
A part of Gale, a Cengage Company

GALE
A Cengage Company

Farmington Hills, Mich • San Francisco • New York • Waterville, Maine
Meriden, Conn • Mason, Ohio • Chicago

Copyright © 2017 by Thomas A. Sancton.
Thorndike Press, a part of Gale, a Cengage Company.

ALL RIGHTS RESERVED
While the author has made every effort to provide accurate telephone numbers and Internet addresses at the time of publication, neither the publisher nor the author assumes any responsibility for errors, or for changes that occur after publication. Further, the publisher does not have any control over and does not assume any responsibility for author or third-party websites or their content.
Thorndike Press® Large Print Peer Picks.
The text of this Large Print edition is unabridged.
Other aspects of the book may vary from the original edition.
Set in 16 pt. Plantin.

**LIBRARY OF CONGRESS CIP DATA ON FILE.
CATALOGUING IN PUBLICATION FOR THIS BOOK
IS AVAILABLE FROM THE LIBRARY OF CONGRESS**

ISBN-13: 978-1-4328-4562-9 (hardcover)
ISBN-10: 1-4328-4562-4 (hardcover)

Published in 2017 by arrangement with Dutton, an imprint of Penguin Publishing, a division of Penguin Random House LLC

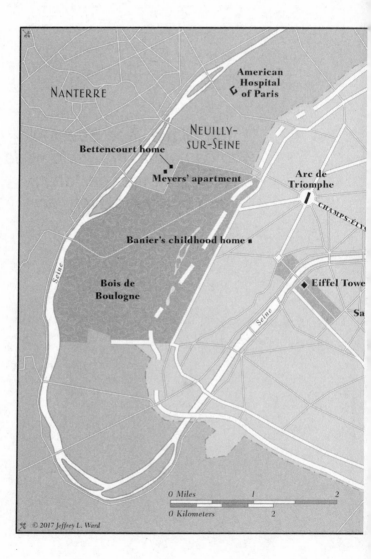

*For Maya Jane Sancton,
who came into the world while
this book was gestating,
and brightens every day*

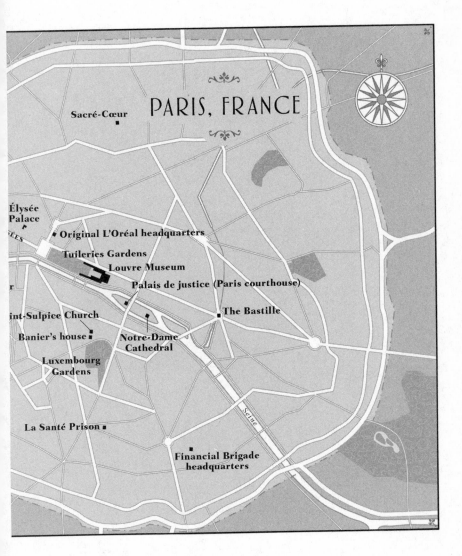

PARIS, FRANCE

Sacré-Cœur

Élysée
Palace

• Original L'Oréal headquarters

Tuileries Gardens

Louvre Museum

Palais de justice (Paris courthouse)

int-Sulpice Church   ■ The Bastille

Banier's house ■   Notre-Dame
                     Cathedral

Luxembourg
Gardens

La Santé Prison ■

            ■ Financial Brigade
              headquarters

Seine

Let me tell you about the very rich. They are different from you and me.

— F. Scott Fitzgerald,
"A Diamond as Big as the Ritz"

Happy families are all alike; every unhappy family is unhappy in its own way.

— Leo Tolstoy,
Anna Karenina

Do you think I'm going to go to court and plead against my mother, to add a public scandal to a private one?

— Thomas Mann,
Buddenbrooks: The Decline of a Family

CONTENTS

AUTHOR'S NOTE

A French friend of mine, a cultivated man passionate about theater and literature, asked why I wanted to write a book about "those people." By that, he meant the fabulously wealthy Bettencourt family, the brash artist who enchanted Madame Bettencourt and made off with a fortune, and the jealous daughter who tried to stop him. For nearly a decade, "those people" were fodder for a French media frenzy that often focused on gossip and scandal. *The Bettencourt Affair* is not a gossip book. It is an in-depth look at an intriguing set of characters whose intense relationships and clashing motives played out against the backdrop of wars, fortune, politics, and the arts — until the law intervened and led to one of the most dramatic court cases in recent French history. It is above all a rich human drama about money, class, seduction, and betrayal, very French in its forms but universal in its themes. In the end, "those people" might just tell us something about ourselves.

I have followed the Bettencourt Affair since it first erupted into the French headlines in 2010. As a former Paris bureau chief for *Time* magazine and a longtime resident of France, I had covered hundreds of stories about French politics, business, culture, and society. But I had never witnessed a drama quite like this — it was *Dallas, Downton Abbey,* and *House of Cards* rolled into one. I proposed a piece to *Vanity Fair* editor Graydon Carter, a friend and colleague from my days at *Time,* and got an immediate go-ahead. My 6,000-word article, entitled "Dangerous Liaisons," ran in the magazine's November 2010 edition. My interest in the case perked up again in January 2015 when it finally went to trial in Bordeaux. It was at that point that the idea of doing a book took shape — a book not just on the legal case but on the whole Bettencourt saga, from the founding of the L'Oréal cosmetics empire in 1909 to the bitter battle that tore the family apart and even threatened a president a century later.

A vast amount of research material existed already — including literally thousands of articles in the French press and at least a half dozen French books on the affair. Digging into the past of L'Oréal founder Eugène Schueller took me to the French National Archives, where the files on his alleged Nazi collaboration are housed. In addition to the written sources, I conducted more than sixty interviews.

Attentive readers will note that I gained direct access to François-Marie Banier and people close to him, including his partner Martin d'Orgeval and former partner Pascal Greggory. Despite numerous requests, however, I was unable to speak directly to Françoise Bettencourt Meyers or her husband, Jean-Pierre Meyers. This is deeply regrettable, but it was their choice. In the absence of face-to-face contact, I was able to talk to sources close to the Meyerses, including their lawyers, friends, and communications advisers. The five published interviews by Françoise Meyers between 2009 and 2012 gave me a good idea of her motivations and point of view.

As for the central figure in this drama, Liliane Bettencourt, my request to interview her for *Vanity Fair* in 2010 fell through at the last minute. Now it's too late: The ninety-four-year-old heiress is closeted in her mansion under the control of her daughter, deep into Alzheimer's, and obviously inaccessible. I was able to talk to a number of people close to her, including her guardian for legal matters, Olivier Pelat, a lifelong friend of the Bettencourts. In addition to a half dozen published interviews dating back to 1987, and two televised interviews, I was able to consult Liliane Bettencourt's prolific correspondence with François-Marie Banier between 1989 and 2010, two volumes of which are included in the court record.

One of the most useful resources was the thirty-five-volume investigative dossier. In addition to police reports and judicial documents, these files contain hundreds of depositions by witnesses ranging from principals in the case — Banier, Liliane Bettencourt, and Françoise Meyers — to the Bettencourts' domestic employees, advisers, family friends, medical experts, and the other defendants.

In pursuing the legal aspects, I carried out lengthy interviews with former prosecutor Philippe Courroye, who headed up the initial investigation, and Judge Isabelle Prévost-Desprez, who took over the case when Courroye closed his own probe in September 2009. I also met with a dozen lawyers representing the various parties, including one, Pascal Wilhelm, who ultimately found himself on the defendants' bench. Several lawyers also made their court briefs available to me.

On the political angle, I was unable to speak directly with ex-president Nicolas Sarkozy or his former campaign treasurer and cabinet minister Éric Woerth. But their depositions, published interviews, and, in Woerth's case, a whole book on the affair, provided useful insights. Interviews with two of Sarkozy's closest aides, former judicial adviser Patrick Ouart, and former chief of staff Claude Guéant, gave me a fascinating inside view of the case as seen from the Élysée Palace.

I am deeply grateful to all the above-named sources for their cooperation and assistance.

A note on monetary values: In general I have kept euro amounts in euros to avoid confusion. A euro is worth slightly more than a US dollar ($1.05 as of January 1, 2017). Rather than working out the precise conversion, readers may find it easier just to think of the euro as a "fat" dollar. I have converted the values of the French franc, predecessor to the euro, into dollars at their historic exchange rate.

— Saint-Germain-en-Laye, France,
January 2017

■ ■ ■ ■

THE BETTENCOURT
AFFAIR

■ ■ ■ ■

Prologue: Lost in the Fog

> Is it because she has no memory
> that she is so serene? Is it memory
> that causes pain?
> — François-Marie Banier,
> *Balthazar, fils de famille*

She is the world's richest woman, worth $36.1 billion at last count, but no one could envy her. Liliane Bettencourt vegetates in an armchair in her Art Deco mansion near Paris, surrounded by her servants, dogs, and caregivers. She is deaf and lost in the fog of senility. Medical experts have diagnosed Alzheimer's disease. One can only wonder what goes on in the old woman's head. Does she harken back to her childhood as the daughter of Eugène Schueller, multibillionaire founder of the cosmetics giant L'Oréal? Does she call to mind her late husband, André Bettencourt, and his illustrious career as a government minister, deputy, and senator? Does she think of Françoise, her only child, the serious-minded intellectual who preferred her books and piano to the grand dinner parties and receptions given by her parents? Does Liliane even remember François-Marie Banier, the seductive photographer, artist, and writer who became her closest friend and, according to Françoise, sweet-talked her out of hundreds of millions of euros? And does she know that her daughter's 2007 lawsuit against Banier triggered a judicial-financial-political earthquake whose aftershocks continue to reverberate?

It would be best for Liliane Bettencourt if she did forget that episode. For it poisoned her twilight years and exposed her private life, her extravagant finances, her free-spirited friendships, and her encroaching infirmities to relentless public scrutiny — which she denounced in her more lucid days as "the odious accusations that I read each morning." That was in 2010, the year the Bettencourt Affair exploded onto the front pages and even threatened to engulf French president Nicolas Sarkozy in what the press referred to as a "French Watergate." But long before it achieved such public notoriety, the conflict between mother and daughter and an audacious interloper was slowly brewing.

Perhaps it all started on a balmy July day in 1993. The scene was the Pointe de l'Arcouest, a promontory on the rocky, windswept northern coast of Brittany, where Eugène Schueller had built a grandiose vacation home in 1926. Liliane and her husband, André, loved to entertain there — presidents, ministers, movie actors, and famous writers had all enjoyed the Bettencourts' hospitality over the years. But on this day, the luncheon was a more intimate affair. Seated around a granite table in the front dining room, whose large windows offered a panoramic view of the English Channel, André and Liliane were joined by their daughter, Françoise; her husband, Jean-Pierre Meyers; and their two young sons. Also at their table that day was a somewhat eccentric houseguest.

François-Marie Banier, then forty-six, seemed to know everybody who was anybody. His conversation was peppered with the names of celebrities with whom he claimed to have intimate friendships — Salvador Dalí, Vladimir Horowitz, Samuel Beckett, Isabelle Adjani, Johnny Depp, President François Mitterrand, and on and on. With his loud voice and explosive laugh, Banier was impossible to ignore. He was witty, cultivated, amusing, seductive. But he also had a gift for getting on people's nerves. He often behaved like a child who was starved for attention — and he usually got it. Liliane Bettencourt, seventy years old and Banier's elder by a quarter century, was clearly fascinated by him.

As seagulls circled and cried outside the

open windows, Françoise, who had just turned forty, gazed at Banier through her heavy-framed glasses and watched her mother hang on his every word. Liliane, who suffered from progressive deafness since childhood, was all the more attentive in her effort to read Banier's lips. All her life, Françoise had craved, but rarely received, the kind of attention that Liliane was lavishing on this invasive stranger. He spoke, Liliane laughed. He smiled, she melted. He bragged about his latest photo exhibition, she gushed praise for his work.

As for poor André, seventy-four, a silver-haired senator and former cabinet minister, he had long since learned to put up with his wife's whims and caprices. Liliane was the heiress, the one who held the purse strings, bought his elegant suits and cigars, and financed his political career. If Banier made his wife happy, André had nothing to say. Besides, he also found this gay artist amusing. A persistent rumor had it that André had actually encountered and befriended Banier earlier, in a very different milieu, and that he was the one who introduced the photographer to his wife. Banier always denied it.

Jean-Pierre Meyers, forty-four, a bland-faced man with receding hair and arching eyebrows, observed the tense scene but said little. He was used to holding his tongue at these family gatherings. A practicing Jew, he well knew that the staunchly Catholic Bettencourts had not favored his marriage to Françoise, even though they brought him into the family firm. Someday, once his wife inherited the principal share of L'Oréal, he would be in a commanding position. Until then, he could afford to bide his time. But Banier's presence doubtless made him uncomfortable. Between the two men there were not six degrees of separation but three: Meyers had formerly lived with the sister of Banier's ex-partner, actor Pascal Greggory. Meyers's breakup with the woman had been followed almost immediately by his marriage to the future L'Oréal heiress. Excellent career move, but rather messy in human terms. Banier was a loose cannon, liable to bring up the awkward subject in the presence of Meyers's wife, his children, and his in-laws.

Banier did lash out that day — but Meyers was not his target. "He started speaking to my father with mocking, scornful and humiliating words," Françoise later recalled. "Right in front of him and in front of our children! I found his behavior completely odious." Françoise has never revealed the subject of Banier's tirade, but another witness claims to remember the scene quite well. Serving at the table that day was Pascal Bonnefoy, André's personal valet, a man so devoted to his employer that years later, after André's death, he would shed tears at the mere mention of his name. According to Bonnefoy, "Banier addressed Monsieur with irony, almost aggressiveness. He reproached him for the articles he'd published during the war in a collaborationist [that is, pro-German] newspaper. It was not a frontal attack but it was intended to wound. Monsieur was embarrassed. Madame didn't react. At times like that, she knows how to play on her deafness. Only her daughter tried to intervene. The others had their noses in their plates. The luncheon was ruined." (Banier remembers the scene quite differently, as an argument about musical preferences.)

The articles Bonnefoy referred to were anti-Semitic diatribes that André Bettencourt had written for a German-backed paper in 1941 and 1942, before he switched sides and belatedly joined the Resistance. Raising the subject on that occasion was doubly embarrassing, for Françoise's husband was the grandson of a famous rabbi who had died at Auschwitz, and the couple were raising their two sons as Jews. Lurking in the background of all this was an even bigger family scandal: Eugène Schueller, the revered founder of L'Oréal, had financed notorious pro-Fascist movements and was investigated for Nazi collaboration after the war.

Following the luncheon incident, Françoise told her parents she no longer wished to be in Banier's presence. But André and Liliane did not share her sentiments. The artist had been cultivating their friendship since 1987, and the Bettencourts, especially Liliane, welcomed his company. Flattered by Banier's attentions, and delighted to be introduced into his glittering world of artistic and cultural connections, she began to lavish extravagant gifts on him. Gifts that, on paper at least, totaled nearly a billion euros at one point — a staggering amount even for one of the world's wealthiest individuals.

But it was not just the money. As Françoise tells it, Banier so dominated Liliane's time that she found it increasingly difficult even to see her mother — though she lives across the street from the Bettencourt mansion in the posh Paris suburb of Neuilly. It seemed, she said, as if Liliane had been "pulled into a sect" by a "guru who cut me off from my family." Françoise looked on Banier as a sort of sibling rival, who attempted to insert himself into the family as a surrogate son and drive a wedge into the already troubled relationship between mother and daughter.

Things came to a head for Françoise shortly after André's death in November 2007, when one of the Bettencourt employees gave her some stunning news: She claimed to have overheard a conversation in which Banier insisted that Liliane legally adopt him as her son. "That was too much," Françoise re-called. "This man had denigrated my father, manipulated my mother, and shattered our family." On December 19, 2007, she filed a criminal complaint against Banier for *abus de faiblesse,* or exploiting the weakness of her aged mother.

Thus began the nearly decadelong drama known as the Bettencourt Affair. Before it was over, an illustrious family was torn apart, careers and reputations were ruined, an army of lawyers made millions, an eminent barrister and a senior police detective committed suicide, a witness tried to hang himself, a tarnished president lost reelection, one of France's proudest companies was threatened with a Swiss takeover, and François-Marie Banier, nearing the age of seventy, faced the prospect of three years in prison and a ruinous fine. The greatest irony was that Françoise, who had launched the whole legal battle, found herself under investigation for allegedly bribing a witness.

The Bettencourt Affair is a modern-day Greek tragedy based on jealousy, greed, vengeance, and retribution. It's also a story about money: the creation from scratch of one of the world's great fortunes, and the use and abuse of that fabulous wealth through three generations. The saga of the Bettencourt fortune has its dark chapters — the funding of pro-Fascist movements, the enormous profits made under Nazi occupation, a tide

of secret political contributions, illegal Swiss bank accounts, and tax-evasion schemes. On the positive side, the family firm is one of France's most dazzling industrial success stories, and the Bettencourt Schueller Foundation stands today as one of the country's leading philanthropies, pouring hundreds of millions into medical research, the arts, education, and housing.

For Liliane Bettencourt, the heiress who inherited it all, money has been the fundamental constant of her long existence. It paid for her mansions, her designer clothes, her travels, her army of domestic servants, even her own private island. Not least, it gave her the means to lavish gifts upon the charming artist who had opened the doors to a passionate life beyond the confines of the conventional bourgeois world into which she was born. And when her timid daughter finally rose up in protest, the Bettencourt billions were at the heart of one of history's great succession battles. But the deepest roots of the Bettencourt Affair stretch back to a silly war that broke out in the eighth decade of the nineteenth century.

PART ONE:
LIFE BEFORE BANIER

CHAPTER 1
THE FOUNDER

Charles Schueller never expected to be a soldier. Six months earlier, the young man had been a cook in his native Alsace, France's easternmost province. Now he was huddled with 15,000 Garde nationale volunteers in the town of Belfort, trying to defend its heavily fortified citadel against the far larger German force that had besieged them. More accustomed to wielding a frying pan than a rifle, Schueller, like his comrades in the ill-equipped and untrained band, mainly tried to survive until hoped-for reinforcements could arrive. Meanwhile, the Germans pummeled the citadel with their Krupp six-pound field guns, the long-range, rapid-firing weapons that had been decimating French troops ever since the Franco-German war broke out in July 1870.

The conflict had been triggered by a trivial diplomatic incident about which Charles Schueller, the twenty-two-year-old son of a shoemaker, understood nothing. What he did understand was that *la patrie* was being invaded by the Germans and his beloved Alsace was on the front lines. Like most German-speaking Alsatians, Schueller was a fervent French patriot who would rather die than live under German occupation. The Belfort volunteers — *les mobiles* — held out until February 18, 1871, three weeks after officials in Paris had capitulated and signed an armistice. Their commander, Col. Pierre Denfert-Rochereau, was thereafter hailed as "the Lion of Belfort" for leading the heroic resistance.

The Franco-German war had far-reaching consequences. Germany was unified under Prussian leadership. The Second French Empire collapsed when the dyspeptic Emperor Napoleon III, unwisely venturing onto the battlefield, was captured and imprisoned. Most important for Charles Schueller, the triumphant Germans annexed Alsace and Lorraine.

Schueller moved to Paris in 1871 in order to remain French. He knew no one in the capital, but soon met and wed Amélie Denisot, daughter of a toolmaker from Burgundy, who worked as a domestic servant for a baker. Shortly after their marriage, they bought a pastry shop on the rue du Cherche-Midi. It was there, on March 20, 1881, at nine a.m., that Amélie gave birth to Eugène Schueller in a back room. Eugène was lucky:

He was the only one of their five children who survived.

It was an inauspicious beginning for a man who was destined to build one of the world's great fortunes. "Life was very rude and very hard for us," he wrote in a biographical résumé, "and it's in this atmosphere of effort and work that I was raised, under the example of my hardworking parents." Before he went to school each day, he would rise early to help prepare the pastries, an apprenticeship that pointed to a future in the family business.

But the collapse of the Panama Canal Company in 1891 wiped out the couple's savings and forced them to move to the cheaper suburb of Levallois-Perret, where they bought another pastry shop. That turned out to be a big break for Eugène: His parents supplied bread to the nearby Collège Sainte-Croix de Neuilly, an elite private school, which agreed to admit the boy as a student.

Eugène earned top grades in all his classes before moving on to the Lycée Condorcet in Paris, another elite school. There again, he excelled in his studies. After taking his Baccalauréat degree — roughly equivalent to two years of college — he entered the Institute of Applied Chemistry, where, as he said with typical immodesty, "I succeeded brilliantly and finished first in my class." Following his graduation in 1904, he took a position as a laboratory assistant to Professor Victor Auger at the Sorbonne. That seemed to map out a respectable but hardly lucrative career as a university researcher.

But then something happened that would change his life. The owner of a large barbershop visited Auger seeking help in developing a synthetic hair dye. At the time, hair dyes were not widely used by Frenchwomen, largely because most of the lead-based concoctions that existed were toxic and irritated the scalp. The products were held in such ill repute that the Baroness de Staffe, a sort of nineteenth-century French Miss Manners, wrote in 1893 that their use "damages the brain and the eyesight." Schueller agreed to become the barber's technical adviser, working three hours each evening for 50 francs a month — a modest sum equal to about $260 today.

Even then the ambitious young man chafed at the idea of working under someone else's orders. He soon cut ties with the barber and struck out on his own. Starting with a capital of 800 francs — roughly $4,000 in today's money — he began experimenting with hair dyes in a rented space near the Tuileries Gardens, a vast park laid out in the mid-seventeenth century by the landscape architect André Le Nôtre, who also created the matchless perspectives surrounding the Château de Versailles. A photo from this period shows Schueller sitting next to some kind of mechanical contraption, looking studious with an open book in his hand, dressed stiffly in a black suit and bow tie, his dark wavy hair swept back from his high forehead, and sporting a black mustache. What doesn't show in the black-and-white photo is the intensity of Schueller's blue eyes, one of his most striking and defining features.

His first efforts were disappointing, and his attempts to sell his products to hairdressers got nowhere. "It was a very difficult time," he wrote. "I lived alone, cooked my own meals, and slept in a little camp bed in my laboratory, and when I think back on these days, I wonder how I got through it." But he persisted, continuing his experiments, changing formulas, even trying out the dyes on his own hair. "Finally, I had the good fortune, which I think I deserved, to obtain a product of excellent quality that allowed me at last to launch my company."

In 1909, he founded the Société française de teintures inoffensives pour cheveux — the French Company of Inoffensive Hair Dyes — a mouthful that he soon changed to L'Oréal. The new corporate name was a homonym for the brand of Schueller's first product, "Auréale," based on a popular hairstyle of the period and playing on the word *auréole,* or halo. He could not know it then, but his little business would in time become the world's largest cosmetics firm and generate the enormous fortune that his yet-unborn daughter would one day inherit.

Things moved quickly after that. The same year he founded L'Oréal, Schueller married a young piano teacher named Louise Madeleine Berthe Doncieux, better known as "Betsy." The couple moved to a larger apartment on the rue du Louvre, near the celebrated museum, where Schueller also set up his laboratory, his office, and his first store. An influx of capital from a new partner and the hiring of a full-time salesman — a former hairdresser for the Imperial Russian court — allowed Schueller to expand his activities. He created a hair-dyeing school, recruited representatives to market the product outside of Paris, launched a promotional magazine, and commissioned a well-known artist, Raoul Vion, to create his first poster: It depicted a blond woman whose hair took the sweeping form of a comet, the first graphic image of a brand whose reputation spread quickly around the country.

Schueller was an obsessive worker and a restless thinker. As if running his company was not enough to occupy his mind, he was forever probing new ideas about the organization of industry, the economy, and politics. In his early days, he dabbled with Socialist ideas under the influence of his friend Jacques Sadoul, an ex-schoolmate from the Collège

Saint-Croix and a future member of the French Communist Party. Around 1910, he became a Freemason, briefly immersing himself in the secret cult of intellectual humanism before leaving it three years later. (He would eventually become a visceral opponent of Freemasonry — along with Jews and republicanism.)

Schueller's philosophical ruminations, like his business activities, were rudely interrupted on August 1, 1914, by the onset of the First World War. Like his Alsatian father before him, Schueller was determined to fight for his country but, at the mature age of thirty-three, he was assigned auxiliary status. He volunteered for active duty in the army, but was offered only a post as a chemist in an armaments factory. He continued to demand a combat role and finally succeeded in joining the 31st Artillery Regiment of Le Mans. Sent to the front as a liaison officer, he distinguished himself at Verdun, l'Aisne, and other major battles. Schueller's wartime service won him five citations for valor, the Légion d'honneur, and the Croix de guerre, France's highest military decoration. One citation described him as a "peerless liaison officer" remarkable for his "vigor," his "boldness," and his "contempt for danger."

During Schueller's four-year absence from the helm of L'Oréal, his wife, Betsy, had run the company so capably that he found his business "flourishing" upon his return from the army in 1919. Her performance could have led Schueller to give her a more active role in the business. But he was a product of his times who considered a woman's place to be in the home, not on the shop floor or the corner office. (In France at that time, women were legally treated as minors who had no vote and only limited property rights.) So Betsy returned to her piano, her homemaking, and, before long, her childrearing: On October 21, 1922, she gave birth to the couple's only child, Liliane Henriette Charlotte Schueller, future heiress to one of France's greatest fortunes.

Meanwhile, the 1920s were roaring. In France, as in America, it was the Jazz Age, and women's styles were changing from the staid prewar fashions: Hemlines were higher, dresses more clinging, and, thanks largely to the influence of Coco Chanel, women started wearing their hair shorter. That was good news for Eugène Schueller: Shorter hair was easier to dye, and the emancipated spirit of the times freed women to change their color, something that in an earlier era was frowned on by respectable ladies. As the stock markets rose feverishly around the world, L'Oréal's business boomed. Its products were now exported to Italy, England, Holland, even crossing the Atlantic to the United States and

Brazil. By 1921, the company had permanent offices in London and New York, in addition to the Paris headquarters at 14 rue Royale, near the Madeleine church.

Emboldened by the success of his core business, Schueller began seeking opportunities in areas apart from L'Oréal. Shortly after his return from the war, a manufacturer of hair combs sought his advice on a way to increase production of celluloid. Thanks to what Schueller called his "opportune invention" to speed the manufacturing process, the celluloid company increased production tenfold and Schueller became a partner. After engineering a merger with a plastics firm in 1925, he became the director of the new Société industrielle des matières plastiques. Two years later, following a falling-out with his partners, he negotiated his departure in exchange for their shares in an American company, the Valstar Corporation, a manufacturer of paint and varnish. Schueller thus found himself the director and largest shareholder of Valentine, Valstar's French subsidiary. Around the same time, working with the Lumière brothers, the legendary cinema pioneers, Schueller created a Lyon-based firm called Plavic Film, which manufactured film for movie and still cameras.

Not all of Schueller's adventures succeeded as well as L'Oréal. Invited by the new Soviet government to set up a plastics factory near

Moscow, Schueller made several trips to Russia between 1926 and 1928, but the experience was a disaster: The promised factory site was far from the capital, the workers' unions interfered with production, and in 1932 the government took over the company. The experience left Schueller, despite his earlier Socialist leanings, with a profound distrust of unions and anything smacking of Bolshevism.

In 1928, he agreed to take over a failing soap manufacturer called Monsavon. But the French soap market was saturated with competitors at the time, and Schueller found it almost impossible to sell his product. At one point, he was spending 300,000 francs (worth about $1.5 million today) a month out of his own pocket and even had to mortgage his properties to keep the company afloat. Working with the fledgling Publicis advertising agency, created in 1926 by Marcel Bleustein-Blanchet, Schueller launched a massive publicity campaign, based on radio spots, posters, and newspaper and magazine ads.

In a pitch aimed especially at the rural population, Schueller added milk to the soap formula and circulated posters showing mother cows washing their calves with Monsavon and mooing: "There is nothing better than milk." Another sales tactic was to persuade the French that they were dirty and did not wash enough. Schueller instructed his sales force to "tell people that they're disgusting, they don't smell good and they're not beautiful." The image of the unwashed French multitudes apparently had some basis in fact. In his 1869 travel book, *Innocents Abroad,* Mark Twain complained that the people of Marseille, a soap-making center, "never . . . wash with their soap themselves." A report by the Rockefeller Foundation, which sent a mission to France to fight a tuberculosis epidemic after World War I, lamented "the indifference of public opinion on questions of hygiene."

The results of Schueller's campaign were impressive: By 1939, Monsavon was on the verge of becoming the biggest soap company in France. Schueller was way ahead of his time in his use of advertising, particularly radio ads, to sell his products. He hired composers and singers to create catchy jingles, created simulated conversations vaunting the merits of his products, and staged spectacular events like hanging a 10,000-square-meter canvas on the façade of a Parisian building, hawking L'Oréal's O'Cap hair lotion. Jingles for the company's Dop shampoo and Ambre Solaire suntan lotion became classics in the promotional genre. In 1933, Schueller created a slick monthly magazine called *Votre Beauté,* which he ran in his typical hands-on fashion, approving

45

the layouts, editing the articles, and even writing some of them himself.

Even as his affairs prospered, Eugène Schueller could hardly be reassured by the turbulence that swept over Europe in the 1930s against the backdrop of the Great Depression. In Germany, Hitler's Nazi Party came to power in 1933, reorganized the economy along authoritarian lines, and launched a massive remilitarization. In Italy, Mussolini, in power since 1922, consolidated his Fascist dictatorship and invaded Ethiopia. In the Soviet Union, a totalitarian Communist regime pursued its ruthless program of nationalization, collectivism, and central economic planning. In Spain, Franco crushed the Republicans in a three-year civil war and imposed his four-and-a-half-decade dictatorship. And in France, the Third Republic, the parliamentary regime that had followed the fall of Napoleon III in 1871, teetered on the verge of collapse.

President Paul Doumer was assassinated by a pro-Fascist Russian in 1932. Two years later, on February 6, 1934, violent clashes between police and far-right rioters on the Place de la Concorde left some thirty dead and two thousand wounded. In a country rocked by strikes, militant syndicalism, unemployment, and political instability — the revolving-door governments of the Third

Republic lasted an average of six months — the leftist Front populaire under Socialist Léon Blum won a parliamentary majority in 1936 and proceeded to carry out a number of sweeping reforms. Among them: the five-day workweek, graduated wage hikes, nationalization of the railroads and the Banque de France, and the introduction of two-week paid vacations for all workers.

The vacations, at least, were excellent for Schueller's business. All of a sudden Frenchmen and -women from all economic levels were thronging the beaches and basking in the sun. Sales of Ambre Solaire, L'Oréal's recently launched sun protection cream, skyrocketed. In spite of that boost to his bottom line, Schueller saw nothing good in the leftist policies of the Front populaire, the rising power of the unions, and the pernicious spread of "Bolshevism." For that matter, he had little use for democracy, which he believed only brought incompetent people to power and made them beholden to the whims of the ignorant masses. The fact that the Front populaire government was headed by a Socialist Jew did not raise his opinion of it. Schueller remained a French patriot, but when he looked at the example of Germany and Italy, he could not help admiring the authority, order, and efficiency that reigned there.

Starting in the mid-1930s, Schueller expounded on his economic theories in a series of books, articles, radio chats, and public lectures aimed at winning converts.

His main idea was the "proportional salary." Instead of paying workers an hourly or daily wage, he argued, their salary should be proportional to their production. He actually applied this principle, in part, to his operations at L'Oréal and Monsavon, and it received some attention from economists at the time. But the scheme never gained widespread support. Schueller's other main idea, a single tax on energy to replace all other taxes, also attracted some interest but never got anywhere.

Among the many French far-right groups that sprang up in the political ferment of the 1930s — ranging from archconservative Catholics and Royalists to ultranationalists and pro-Fascists — probably none was more radical than the Comité secret d'action révolutionnaire (CSAR). Known to the public as "La Cagoule" — the hood — this anti-Communist, anti-Republican, and anti-Semitic group was aimed at replacing the Third Republic with a dictatorship modeled on Germany, Italy, or Spain. Its leader was Eugène Deloncle, a brilliant and charismatic maritime engineer who called for "illegality" and "underground action."

Attracted by Schueller's ideas — and doubtless his deep pockets — Deloncle recruited him as a member of his group. Schueller provided financial support and made space available to the Cagoule in L'Oréal's offices on the rue Royale. There is no proof that Schueller himself was involved in the Cagoule's violent plots, but the organization that he was supporting and helping to finance was behind some very nasty business. Among the terrorist actions attributed to the Cagoule were a series of assassinations, the bombing of the French employers' association, and even an abortive coup d'état in November 1937.

Schueller and his fellow Cagoulards, as they were known, soon had the opportunity to observe German order at closer range. On September 3, 1939, France and Britain had declared war on Germany following Hitler's invasion of Poland. For eight months nothing much happened on the battlefield as French forces hunkered down along the supposedly impregnable Maginot Line and waited. This so-called phony war ended abruptly on May 10, 1940, when the Wehrmacht's armored divisions circumvented the French fortifications and invaded Belgium, France's northern neighbor. From there, the Blitzkrieg rolled into France, moved swiftly down the English Channel coast, and entered Paris unopposed on June 14.

By the time the armistice was signed on June 22 by Maréchal Philippe Pétain, the

World War I hero of Verdun, France's armies had been decimated: 90,000 soldiers killed, 200,000 wounded, and nearly two million taken prisoner. The armistice decreed a German occupation of the northern half of France with a nominally "free" zone in the south under the authority of Pétain's government in Vichy. (That fig leaf of sovereignty was ripped away in 1942, when German forces invaded the southern sector and put it under military administration.) The unprecedented collapse of the French forces in 1940 was a source of national humiliation and recrimination; for those of Schueller's persuasion, it was further proof of the failure of democratic government.

Under the Occupation, Schueller's writings and lectures became more explicitly pro-Nazi and anti-Republican. In his 1941 book, *La révolution de l'économie,* for example, he wrote, "I know full well that we don't have the chance that the Nazis did, coming to power in 1933, they had time. They could spend two years, three years, organizing themselves. We don't have the gift that the Germans had at this time. We don't have the faith of national-socialism. We don't have the dynamism of a Hitler pushing the world." Elsewhere in this volume, Schueller wrote, "We must rip from men's hearts the childish concepts of liberty, equality, and even fraternity," which can only "lead to disaster." He called for a "strong and durable government . . . independent of the whims of universal suffrage." It is worth noting that Schueller's book was part of a collection called "La Révolution mondiale" — The Worldwide Revolution — which also published a compendium of Hitler's speeches.

Following the German victory, Deloncle revived the Cagoule under a new name, Mouvement social révolutionnaire (MSR), which operated openly with the blessing of the Nazi occupiers and the collaborationist Vichy government. Deloncle described Eugène Schueller as "our future minister of National Economy, the most important man in the movement." It is highly implausible to think that a shrewd business tycoon like Schueller was unaware of the vile political leanings of the people he associated with and funded. The MSR's manifesto clearly trumpeted its pro-Nazi orientation: "We seek to construct the new Europe in cooperation with national-socialist Germany and all the other European nations liberated, like her, from liberal capitalism, Judaism, bolshevism and freemasonry . . . [We must] give the Jews who remain in France a harsh status that will prevent them from polluting our race . . . [and] build a young generation that is united, virile, and strong. We cannot make a revolution without revolutionaries." Deloncle's rabid anti-Semitism was not merely rhetorical. In the fall of 1941, Helmut Knochen, the powerful German commander of police and security for France, assigned Deloncle, along with SS officer Somer Hans, the mission of "blowing up the synagogues of Paris." The bombings were carried out during the night of October 2–3, 1941.

In February 1941, Deloncle merged the group with another pro-Fascist organization, the Rassemblement national populaire (RNP), headed by Marcel Déat, an ex-socialist turned Nazi sympathizer. From March to October 1941, Schueller served as president of the group's "technical committee of the general economy." He later claimed that he had never belonged to or financed the MSR or the RNP. Deloncle, he said, had lured him into a relationship by professing interest in his economic theories, then used his name in his propaganda.

But Schueller left some compromising tracks. In June 1941, at the group's first convention, he made this startling statement: "None of these three peaceful revolutions can happen without first of all a . . . preliminary revolution, of both purification and revival, and that one . . . can only be bloody. It will consist quite simply of quickly shooting fifty or a hundred important personages." At another meeting, in November 1941, Schueller declared that "the essential thing for us is a complete and definitive break with the recent past, with the men and methods of the Third Republic, with free-masonry and the Jews." He promoted similar ideas, along with his economic theories, in broadcasts over the German-controlled French radio.

Schueller had cause to regret his irresponsible words and dubious political associations once the German occupiers fled the country in advance of the Allied armies in 1944, taking with them Marshal Pétain, the quasi-senile figurehead of the Vichy regime, and Pierre Laval, his scheming, pro-German prime minister. The departure of the Germans and the collapse of the Pétain government fueled a bloody wave of reprisals and score-settlings known as the *épuration* — purification or purge. In the first phase of *épuration,* which began even before D-Day, Resistance groups and their hangers-on carried out summary executions of suspected collaborators, sometimes following hasty trials by people's courts but often without any attempt at legal niceties. Estimates of the number of extralegal summary executions range between a conservative 10,000 and an exaggerated 100,000 between 1942 and 1945. The second phase of *épuration* began in mid-September 1944 with the creation of special courts handing out death sentences and lesser punishments within a framework of due process. During this legal phase, military and civilian courts examined 160,287 cases, 45 percent of which resulted in acquittals, 25 percent in prison sentences, and 25 percent in loss of civic rights. In all, 7,037 death sentences were pronounced, but only some 1,500 were actually carried out.

These reprisals, legal and extralegal, were only the most dramatic manifestations of a country torn apart by the defeat of 1940, the Occupation, and the bitter internecine conflict between the forces of resistance and collaboration. During the postwar years and decades, the fault lines continued to run under the surface and the subject was so fraught that the first serious examination of French collaboration was the 1969 documentary *Le chagrin et la pitié* — The Sorrow and the Pity. It was only in 1995 that a French president, Jacques Chirac, officially acknowledged France's role in deporting Jews to Nazi death camps.

At the end of the war, Eugène Schueller was swept up in the net of the *épuration.* His troubles began when a disgruntled former employee denounced him as a collaborator in a report to the Comité régional interprofessionnel d'épuration dans les entreprises, an official body formed to investigate the wartime activities of businesses and companies and bring to justice "all those who favored the undertakings of the enemy, or hindered the resistance of the French people." On November 6, 1946, the Comité imposed professional sanctions on him "for advancing the enemy's designs by his public attitude during the Occupation." His case was sent to the Court of Justice of the Department of the Seine, where he was formally charged with economic and political collaboration.

On the economic question, a detailed accounting of wartime sales to the Germans by L'Oréal and Monsavon showed relatively modest levels. The investigating magistrate, Judge Marcel Gagne, ruled that Schueller could not be convicted for economic collaboration due to the "minimal percentage of German business and to the fact that the merchandise delivered was of no direct military interest."

As for political collaboration, the judge concluded that "Schueller showed a certain activity in favor of the ideas of Franco-German collaboration," and that he did in fact belong and contribute funds to Deloncle's MSR — in spite of his denials. (A 1942 police report stated that Schueller was "an influential member of the M.S.R." who "largely subsidizes the group's needs.") It would have been useful to have Deloncle's own testimony on Schueller's involvement in his far-right movements, but he was unavailable for comment: On January 7, 1944, Gestapo agents burst into his apartment and gunned him down because he was suspected of contacts with conspirators in the failed plot to assassinate Hitler. (Deloncle's son Louis, wounded in the attack, later joined the Spanish branch of L'Oréal — just one of many ex-Cagoulards who were welcomed into Schueller's company after the war.)

But Schueller had been able to call on various witnesses to support his claim that he had sheltered Jewish employees, aided staffers who resisted obligatory labor in Germany, and, not least, that he had secretly financed the Resistance. One influential witness on his behalf was his old schoolmate Jacques Sadoul, by then an important member of the French Communist Party, which had played a major role in the Resistance. Another was the Cagoulard turned Resistance leader Gen. Pierre de Bénouville. Not least among Schueller's defenders were future president François Mitterrand and Schueller's future son-in-law, André Bettencourt, both of them active in the Resistance. As a result, Judge Gagne recommended that all charges against Schueller be dropped. His case was closed definitively on December 6, 1948. Had he been convicted, Schueller could have been removed from L'Oréal's leadership, disgraced, and possibly jailed, while the company itself would have faced the threat of nationalization.

That judgment officially cleaned Schueller's slate and allowed him to remain at the helm of his businesses. But it leaves some important questions unanswered.

First, it doesn't explain how L'Oréal's sales nearly quadrupled between 1940 and 1944, from 56,899,862 francs to 208,862,574 francs. Even if the company did not record significant sales to the Germans, it is inconceivable that L'Oréal could obtain the necessary raw materials, energy, and transportation without the approval of the occupiers.

More important, what kind of business was Valentine doing with the Germans? Schueller officially ceased to be the director of this large paint and varnish manufacturer in October 1940, when a law issued by the Vichy government forbade any one individual to head more than three companies. But he remained on the board and continued thereafter to be a major shareholder with an interest in its sales and a significant voice in its decisions. Schueller was also instrumental in forging a partnership between Valentine and the German firm Druckfarben, which became a shareholder in the Valentine subsidiary Neochrome. The administrator of Neochrome was a German businessman named Gerhart Schmilinsky, a key figure in the Nazis' "aryanization" program to strip Jewish owners of their businesses and other property.

Schmilinsky worked closely with Schueller, whom he praised as "an ardent partisan of the Franco-German accord." Schueller and

Schmilinsky were also linked through a company called Alginates, a joint venture between L'Oréal and the German firm Goldschmidt AG, which derived chemicals from marine algae. By hiding behind these complicated corporate structures, Schueller was able to mask his involvement as an important supplier to the German war machine. For paint, unlike cosmetics and soap, is a highly strategic military product: No ship sails, no plane flies, no tank rolls without paint.

Valentine's official accounting records were said to have been destroyed during the Allied bombardment of June 24, 1944. But other archival documents, including an "internal journal" for 1941 to 1944 indicate that as much as 95 percent of the company's wartime tonnage was delivered to the German Navy, the Kriegsmarine. A 1945 French police report stated, "The company Valentine, of which Schueller is co-director, worked during the whole occupation for the exclusive benefit of the Germans, [who used] the paint for camouflage." According to the Reich's "Paint Plan," Valentine was listed since 1941 in the "first category" of paint suppliers. Thanks largely to his relations with the Germans, says French historian Annie Lacroix-Riz, Schueller "augmented his fortune considerably during the war." His tax returns for the period show that his personal net income increased nearly tenfold between

1940 (248,791 francs) and 1943 (2,347,957 francs).

Schueller's political collaboration was no less active. The postwar investigators noted his role as a financier and member of Deloncle's pro-Fascist movements, as well as his public declarations in favor of a National Socialist–type regime in France. But what completely escaped their notice was the extent of Schueller's direct contacts with German officials. Among them was the notorious Helmut Knochen, the commander of police and security for the Sicherheitsdienst, the SS intelligence service. Actively involved in the deportation of French Jews to the Nazi death camps, Knochen was responsible for the execution of several thousand French Resistance members and was an enthusiastic proponent of reprisal killings of civilian hostages. Interrogated by French intelligence services after the war, he listed Schueller among his "voluntary collaborators." In 1947, French investigators discovered a list of forty-five "agents of Knochen." Among them: "E. Schueller. Businessman."

"At the time I knew him," Knochen told interrogators, "he was seeking to get himself named Minister of the National Economy" in the Vichy government. "He worked for our Section III [specialized in economic questions] in order to obtain the help of the German services for his personal business and also to get the Services to support his ambition to become a minister." Schueller never won that coveted post, but he was designated as the future minister of "National and Imperial Production" on a list that Knochen drew up in 1941 to replace Prime Minister Pierre Laval's cabinet with more solidly pro-German figures. The plan was never carried out.

One other incriminating piece that did not make its way into his investigative file was a document signed by Schueller on the letterhead of Marcel Déat's RNP, an organization he claimed never to have belonged to. The letterhead identifies Schueller as the president of the Technical Committee of the General Economy and gives his address as 14 rue Royale — the same as L'Oréal headquarters. Dated July 29, 1941, it exhorts "all the members of the party . . . to enroll in the Légion des volontaires français" as the "only road" to "an honorable and perhaps glorious peace." The Légion des volontaires was a notorious unit made up of French collaborationists who went to fight alongside the Germans on the eastern front. The French unit was integrated into the Division Charlemagne of the Waffen-SS. Its troops swore allegiance to Hitler and fought in German uniforms. Schueller's support of this force was arguably an act of treason. Taken together with his role as a de facto agent of Helmut Knochen, this letter would quite likely have sealed his postwar conviction as a collaborator. But a combination of money, connections, and luck spared him that indignity — and perhaps even saved him from a firing squad.

Liliane Bettencourt, understandably, did not like to talk about her father's political dark side. And when she did, she attributed it to naïveté rather than any real conviction. "He was a man full of hope, pathologically optimistic, who understood nothing about politics," she told journalist Franz-Olivier Giesbert in 1996. "He was never in the right boat." It is surprising that a man with Schueller's acknowledged brilliance and vision as an industrialist could be so intellectually bereft when it came to his political choices. But such is the mythology of an adoring daughter.

CHAPTER 2
THE HEIRESS
AND THE CONSORT

In October 1927, Betsy Schueller died suddenly of an abscessed liver. Her daughter remembered the moment vividly sixty years later. "I was five years old. They came to get me in the middle of the night and I saw my father kneeling at the foot of my mother's bed . . . After she died there was no more music in the house."

Brutally deprived of her mother's presence and affection, Liliane fell under the influence of a father whom she came to adore to the point of obsession. "It allowed my father to raise me in his own way," she said. "A mother softens things. He thought of the life that awaited me." From that point on, it was the example of Eugène Schueller's energy and work ethic that shaped her character — along with the Dominican nuns who, for ten years, gave her a strict education based on religion, duty, obedience, and conformity.

In fact, Liliane did have another feminine presence in her life: Annie Grace Burrows, her English nanny. But she never regarded Annie, nicknamed "Nita," as a replacement for her mother. And when Eugène Schueller married the comely Nita (fifteen years his junior) in 1932, Liliane could look on her stepmother only as a rival for her father's love and attention. "She never, ever talked about her father's wife," says psychoanalyst Claude Delay, a close friend of Liliane's. "I find that extraordinary because this woman raised her, after all." After Liliane's mother died, "all her emotional potential was determined by her father. And she was the daughter of a father she admired. That counts enormously in terms of identity and identification."

"What shaped me," Liliane said in a 2010 interview, "was to be this little girl who adored her father. To have only a father is not always easy. He was always busy and surrounded by women. I remember — when I was seven or eight — looking not at my father, but at the man he was. A man rather short, with beautiful blue eyes, and such a look. And that changes everything." She describes their relationship in terms that almost suggest a courting couple. "He was very handsome, he made life beautiful. With me, he was not without a certain shyness. He gave me presents. I remember an Hermès handbag, navy blue with a silver clasp . . . I was like a little woman . . . Our relationship took all its force when we walked together."

In reality, those moments must have been rare. Schueller bragged of being a "6,000-hour" man — one who worked sixteen hours a day, seven days a week. According to one of his former secretaries, he would typically rise at five a.m. to pore over documents and prepare letters to dictate, head to his Valentine office in his chauffeur-driven Rolls-Royce, spend three hours there, then go across town to the Monsavon headquarters. He would gulp down a glass of grapefruit juice for lunch on the way to L'Oréal, where he would stay till nine p.m. Then he would return home with four briefcases full of papers and work until midnight. And before he even started his workday, he would go jogging every morning with his four dogs. Not much father-daughter quality time in that schedule.

During Liliane's childhood and teen years, L'Oréal was growing by leaps and bounds against the backdrop of a burgeoning fashion and glamour industry. The rolls of the great Paris couture houses, which had sprung up in the late nineteenth century, were expanding in the post–World War I years and changing the notions of feminine style with simpler, more modern designs. Schueller was acquiring and creating new brands for his group and growing his overseas markets, while his promotional magazine, *Votre Beauté,* joined *Vogue* and *Marie Claire* in the ranks of a nascent feminine glamour press.

These were exciting times for L'Oréal, and Schueller expected his daughter to be part of it all: During every summer vacation, he insisted that she work for several weeks as an intern at L'Oréal. "I had a tray full of labels and glue and we prepared the bottles," she recalled. "I was delighted because I talked to him about L'Oréal, the people who worked there, who impressed me, the products. It was wonderful to talk about all that. . . . I loved everything that brought me closer to him, everything that led us to talk even more. . . . I was his daughter and I clung to him. My father and I had the same language." It seems odd that a fifteen-year-old girl would be so thrilled to talk about business with her father. One gets the impression that it was the only subject that interested him and therefore the main channel open for communication.

Communicating with a brilliant but preoccupied father was hardly simple for a motherless child, as Liliane explained to her notary in 2009: "My father adored me, I adored him, but he had such a temperament, you see? For a little girl ten years old who was supposed to understand everything, it was difficult. But I never gave up. I always managed to understand his mental process, which was not easy." Another thing that made communication difficult — and not just with her father — was a serious hearing impairment resulting from a childhood bout of tuberculosis.

There was more to Liliane's early life than her Catholic school and L'Oréal apprenticeships. In 1926, when she was four, Schueller had built a granite villa on the Pointe de l'Arcouest in Brittany. Somewhat pretentious, with its colonnade, tennis court, and manicured lawn, it boasted a superb view of the sea and the Île-de-Bréhat. Some of the neighbors considered Schueller's twenty-five-room house pretentious, and frowned on his decision to enclose the whole property behind a high wall, something that was simply not done in those parts. But Schueller was accustomed to doing things his way.

It was at Arcouest that the Schuellers spent their vacations — though Eugène never stayed more than two weeks at a time and brought work with him. Liliane loved to swim, ride her bike, and take long walks along the rocky coast with her two Irish setters. And she cherished the privileged moments aboard her father's sailboat, the *Edelweiss,* in which they would sometimes go as far as the Isle of Wight, across the English Channel. Not content with leisurely excursions, the hypercompetitive Schueller would also enter the boat in local yacht races. "It was intense," Liliane remembered. "There were four or five of us in the crew, and he would really yell at us! It was serious, we had to win."

Schueller kept a jealous eye on Liliane as she began to mature and attract the attention of young men. "Have you seen those shoes?" he would snicker, causing his daughter to immediately lose interest in this or that suitor. Until one day in 1938 when André Bettencourt came to lunch at the family's sumptuous apartment on the Boulevard Suchet in Paris's 16th arrondissement.

Bettencourt, then nineteen, had been introduced to Schueller by a mutual acquaintance. Bettencourt was intrigued by the industrialist's economic ideas and welcomed the lunch invitation. That was the first time Liliane and André laid eyes on each other. She took little notice of him, and the young man was preoccupied by an animated conversation with her father. André later confided to a friend that he "didn't find her extraordinary, was intimidated by her gaze, and thought she wore too much makeup."

It is unclear whether Schueller had any thought then of André Bettencourt as a possible future son-in-law, but he was in fact an attractive prospect. Tall, handsome, and endowed with impeccable manners, he cut a fine figure. He had no fortune to boast of, but came from a prominent family in Normandy with some blue blood on his mother's side. For Schueller, the nouveau riche son of a baker and grandson of a shoemaker, André Bettencourt possessed a pedigree that would confer a respected social status on the future heiress.

Bettencourt claimed to be a descendant of Baron Jean de Béthencourt (c. 1359–1425), the discoverer of the Canary Islands. At the time André was born, on April 21, 1919, the family had been settled for four generations in Saint-Maurice-d'Ételan, a picturesque farming village located on a loop of the Seine in lower Normandy. His father, Victor, was a lawyer with the Paris Appeals Court, a member of the regional government council, and an influential member of the Catholic agricultural union. A fervent Catholic — André judged him a "saint" — he would walk from the family manor to the local church every morning to attend Mass. André's mother, Jeanne-Marie de Chalendar, daughter of a general, died of tuberculosis in 1924. Like Liliane Bettencourt, André was raised by a revered father.

The youngest of six children, André — known to friends and family as Dédé — was home-tutored until the age of nine, then attended a private Catholic boarding school in Le Havre along with his older brother Pierre. His strict religious upbringing was not limited to his formal studies: He took music lessons at a Dominican convent, where he sometimes donned monks' robes, and shared a private confessor with his brother Pierre Bettencourt. This devoted cleric, Canon Le Picard, came to their family home every two weeks and, according to Pierre, tried in vain to cure them of "the delights of masturbation."

According to his own account, André Bettencourt was a mediocre student: "Pierre was always first in his class, I was usually last." After elementary school, he was sent to a *collège*, equivalent to a US middle school, in the Alpine town of Thônes, then to a strict Jesuit boarding school in the northeastern city of Reims. He stayed there only a short while before he fell sick from some unspecified malady and returned to the family home in Normandy. That was the end of Bettencourt's schooling; he never received his Baccalauréat — the French high-school diploma — or pursued any form of higher education. At that point his father intervened to get André a job as secretary of the Jeunesse agricole catholique, an association for rural Catholic youth that was headquartered in Paris. And so it was that in 1938, armed with few qualifications other than his good looks and a respectable family background, André Bettencourt headed off to the capital.

In Paris he lodged at 104 rue de Vaugirard, a residence for provincial Catholic students run by the Marist fathers. His two closest friends there were François Mitterrand, the future president of France, and François Dalle, the future CEO of L'Oréal. Like most of their fellow students, they were swept up in the political ferment of the late 1930s — especially Mitterrand, who belonged to a group headed by Col. François de La Rocque, a leader of the nationalist far right. Mitterrand also frequented members of the notorious Cagoule but never actually joined their ranks.

Though none of them leaned toward the Royalist right, Dalle secured an invitation to visit the Comte de Paris, Henri d'Orléans, pretender to the French throne, at his château near Brussels in April 1939. A descendant of King Louis Philippe, ousted in 1848, Henri d'Orléans (1908–1999) was the titular head of a monarchist movement that was active on the French political scene before the war. (After the Liberation, Henri d'Orléans and Charles de Gaulle reportedly held secret talks about the possible restoration of a constitutional monarchy with the Comte de Paris at its head.)

The pretender's young visitors were all enchanted with the audience and impressed by the magnificent château and surrounding park. Mitterrand "talked all the time, quite brilliantly," Dalle recalled. But the thing that most struck André Bettencourt during their weeklong trip was a glimpse of a Hitler Youth camp just across the Luxembourg border. His admiring description of their discipline, fervor, and the physical beauty of their half-clad bodies is revealing in more ways than one:

> Coming from the pine forest and echoing through the valley, a song of extraordinary power and beauty, a song full of force, the expression of a whole people came to us in waves; and then, all of a sudden, at a turn in the road, we saw a hundred young men in their undershorts, their bodies bronzed by the sun, superb, their voices steady, marching in tight ranks at a steady pace . . . That day, I realized for the first time that next door to us, without our even seeking to know it, a great people was rising with the body and soul of their youth.

When the war broke out in September 1939, André, then twenty years old, somehow avoided being swept up in the *mobilisation générale,* the universal conscription that called on all able-bodied men to serve in the army. He claimed in his memoirs that he attempted to enlist in Normandy at the outset of the conflict but was rejected for reasons that are unclear. A second examination shortly afterward found him apt to serve but, according to Bettencourt, the French "debacle" prevented him from joining a unit or undergoing military training — an odd claim, considering that the army would presumably have wanted all the manpower they could get in that desperate situation. He said he tried once more in June 1940, this time in Brittany, but by that time the French army was collapsing in the face of the invading German forces and things were so disorganized that it was impossible to sign up. "I wanted to participate in the fight," he wrote, "but how?"

As the Germans proceeded to occupy the northern half of the country following the armistice of June 22, 1940, Bettencourt returned to his family home in Normandy. He found that the local commander of the German occupying force had requisitioned part of the house as his command post and flew a Nazi flag over the property. André's father, the village mayor, was forced to carry out German orders on all administrative matters. Meanwhile, André continued working for the Catholic youth organization, dividing his time between Saint-Maurice and Paris.

In February 1941, he also began writing for a paper, *La Terre française,* that was controlled by the German propaganda agency, the Propagandastaffel. His regular column, aimed at young readers, initially extolled the virtues of rural life and other harmless topics.

Starting in April 1941, inspired by his arch-conservative Catholic prejudices, André Bettencourt began to pen anti-Semitic diatribes of the worst sort.

"The Jews, hypocritical Pharisees, have no

more hope," he wrote on April 12, 1941. "They have no faith. . . . For all eternity, their race is soiled by the blood of the Just. They will be cursed by all. They condemned God, without even wanting to recognize or regret their ignominy. The Jews today . . . will be, and already are, vomited."

In addition to attacking the Jews, Bettencourt exhorted his young readers to become informers against those who opposed the collaborationist regime. "The young must be, in each village, the agents of the Maréchal [Pétain], I would even say the police of the Revolution . . . When it's necessary to accuse for the general good, there is no friendship that prevails. There is the duty: denunciation." In some of his columns, he explicitly praised the Nazis as harbingers of the "revolutionary current of the new Europe, of which Germany is the first point of crystallization . . . Let us not foolishly think that Christianity is opposed to National Socialism." Bettencourt's columns attracted little attention at the time — after all, there were dozens of collaborationist journalists writing similar things under the Occupation — but they would come back to haunt him decades later.

Meanwhile, Bettencourt's friend Mitterrand followed a different path. Mobilized into the army and sent to fight on the Maginot Line, the future president was wounded by a shell fragment at Verdun and imprisoned by the Germans in June 1940. After two failed attempts, he escaped in December 1941, returned to France, and got a job as a mid-level official with the Vichy government. In January 1943, disillusioned with the Pétain regime and perhaps sensing the tide turning against the Germans, Mitterrand entered the Resistance and cofounded the Rassemblement national des prisonniers de guerre (RNPG), an underground network made up of escaped war prisoners. Mitterrand enlisted Bettencourt in the movement, though André had never been a war prisoner or even served in the military. His role was to recruit Resistance members among the agricultural community.

On December 20, 1943, Bettencourt was arrested by the Gestapo while attending a Resistance meeting in the eastern city of Nancy. Though most of his fellow prisoners were deported to Germany, and several were ordered executed, he alone was released a month later for reasons that are unclear. He wrote to Eugène Schueller in January 1944 that "the experience of the cell, then of the shared barracks room alongside those who were about to leave for Germany, then the four days spent with those condemned to death, was somewhat hard, but excellent." Excellent? Bettencourt later said his liberation was due to "an intervention" by Marie

François, the Resistance agent at whose home he had been arrested. But François herself was jailed, tortured, and deported to the Ravensbrück concentration camp. How Bettencourt escaped a similar fate remains a mystery. In his memoirs, he attributed his deliverance mainly to the power of prayer.

After his release, Bettencourt passed clandestinely into Switzerland. Working in the Geneva office of the Conseil national de la Résistance, an umbrella group of the main Resistance organizations, he served as its liaison with Alan Dulles, the Swiss-based director of the US Office of Strategic Services, the precursor to the CIA, which funded the CNR. After the war, presumably at Mitterrand's behest, Bettencourt received an impressive collection of decorations: the Rosette de la Résistance, the Légion d'honneur, and the Croix de guerre, a rather extraordinary honor for a man who never served in the military or heard a bullet fired in anger, a man whose main wartime service was spent sitting behind a desk in a neutral country. No matter, André Bettencourt was now a certified war hero. What better credentials for a man who aspired, like his friend Mitterrand, to pursue a political career? To be sure, Bettencourt was hardly alone in switching loyalties: Many Frenchmen and -women who had initially seen Pétain as a national savior came to support the Resistance, actively or passively, as the war wore on.

Bettencourt's first step was to establish a regional base in his native Normandy. Using money inherited from his grandmother, he created in January 1945 a small newspaper called *La France agricole* that was aimed at farmers. He ran unsuccessfully for the National Assembly in 1946, but the following year won a seat on the Conseil général, an important regional government body. In 1948, he took over another local paper, a weekly entitled *Le Courrier Cauchois,* in which he wrote regular editorials on political matters.

Now it was time for Bettencourt to make an advantageous marriage. His friend Mitterrand had predicted, only half-jokingly, that since Bettencourt was "such a good-looking guy, he would marry a rich woman." Liliane Schueller more than fit the bill. And André was an attractive prospect in Eugène Schueller's eyes.

In addition to Bettencourt's other attributes — good looks, notable family, promising political future — Schueller was indebted to him for his help in beating his collaboration charges. Bettencourt had written letters on Schueller's behalf vouching for his aid to the Resistance. Mitterrand, meanwhile, had gotten his friend Gen. Pierre de Bénouville to testify that Schueller had actively aided his underground group from 1942 to 1944. Schueller never forgot a favor.

Ever since that first luncheon in 1938, André had kept in touch with Schueller. One January 1944 letter to Schueller makes it clear that the two men had met and corresponded "for several years now" and reveals a relationship that went beyond mere social courtesy. "You have spoken to me about your fears [concerning possible collaboration charges]," Bettencourt wrote. "Different conversations before my departure from Paris make me think that they are, unfortunately, fairly well justified. Be careful. You are terribly impulsive about all things . . ." When Bettencourt was working with the Resistance office in Geneva, Schueller offered to send money to cover his expenses. (Bettencourt politely declined.) Curiously, Bettencourt signed his wartime letters to Schueller "de Bettencourt," improperly adding the aristocratic particle to his family name — an affectation that could only enhance his status in the eyes of an ambitious nouveau riche billionaire with a daughter to wed.

In 1949, Schueller invited the young man to vacation with him and Liliane in the Alpine resort town of Évian-les-Bains. After emerging from a dip in Lake Geneva, Bettencourt began spitting blood. He was sent to a sanatorium hotel at Leysin, in the Swiss Alps, the very place where his mother had died of tuberculosis twenty-five years earlier. Liliane came to visit him twice a week, her "letters and presence . . . powerfully aiding the action of the antibiotics," as André's brother Pierre noted. During their long walks together, André and Liliane discovered that they had some important things in common. Both were products of a strict Catholic upbringing and education. Both had lost their mothers at age five. Both adored their dominating fathers.

But when André finally proposed, Liliane hesitated. Did she suspect then that André's sexual preferences were perhaps not focused on women? He was not, in any case, the only man in her life. When she was in her early twenties, she spent a long sojourn in Morocco, where her father, in 1943, had set up an office of L'Oréal Maroc. She fell in love with the country — the sun, the sea, the colors — and with the son of the powerful pasha of Marrakesh. They met by chance one night at a reception, and Liliane was swept off her feet. But after an intense (and secret) courtship, the relationship ended abruptly. "His mentality was too far from mine," she later confided. "After all, I am a Christian."

It was some years after the Moroccan romance broke off that she agreed to marry André. By her own account, Liliane did not dash headlong to the altar. "I was terribly frightened of marriage," she later explained.

"When I went to choose my ring I said, 'Above all, not too tight.' [André] had to use all his intelligence. Because I'm willing to hold on, but not to be obliged. I detest all the conventions of marriage, the 'you promise,' all these phrases that bind you and lock you into a role." Clearly this was a woman who valued her freedom. That was a fundamental pillar of her relationship with André.

The couple was married on June 8, 1950, in Vallauris, a picturesque village in the south of France noted for its ceramics and its association with Pablo Picasso, who lived and worked there from 1948 to 1955. Only nine people attended the family ceremony, presided over by André's older brother, Fr. Jacques Bettencourt, who had flown down in a private plane with the father of the bride. On the way to the church, Liliane ran ahead of everyone else, hoping it would all be over quickly. Whatever hesitations she may have had, Eugène Schueller must have been delighted to see his only daughter emerge from the church on the arm of this dashing young man — though Liliane later insisted that her father had not "pushed" her into the union.

Even after the wedding, Liliane kept up her ties to Morocco and for a time considered moving there for tax reasons. In December 1950, the newlyweds took a grand tour of the country organized by a certain Brahim el

Glaoui, described in André's memoirs as "a southern chieftan whom Liliane knew very well."

With his marriage to Liliane, André's fortune was made in every sense of the word. Schueller gave him a post in the management ranks at L'Oréal, though he had no diploma and knew nothing about business. And André's access to Liliane's wealth allowed him to make discreet political contributions to a wide variety of parties and political figures (continuing a practice begun by his father-in-law). As the saying goes, *il arrosait tout le monde* — he poured money across the political spectrum, left, right, and center. Among his more prominent beneficiaries were the Socialist Mitterrand and the conservative prime minister turned president Georges Pompidou, another close personal friend. Bettencourt's well-known largesse was one of the reasons why he was given cabinet positions, minor ones for the most part, under every postwar government until the election of Valéry Giscard d'Estaing in 1974. "Of course Bettencourt did political financing with his wife's money," says Georges Kiejman, a former Socialist cabinet member and Liliane's lawyer from 2009 to 2011. "Otherwise he would not have had the importance he had. He would not have been a minister. He was not an exceptional man."

■ ■ ■ ■

Liliane did not share André's passion for politics. "I was happy for him," she said of his political career. "As for me, I experienced other things." It is not clear what "other" interests Liliane was pursuing during these years, apart from her L'Oréal meetings, haute-couture shows, shopping trips, dinner parties, and tea with her close friend and neighbor Lucienne de Rozier, whom she telephoned every morning to gossip or complain about her health problems. Like many Frenchwomen of her class, she led a conventional and codified life. Though she funded her husband and accompanied him on certain high-profile occasions, she had little to do with his political activities. "At first, Liliane didn't want me to enter politics," André told a TV interviewer in 1992. "When I was first elected in 1951, she was so unhappy she cried. But she finally got used to it." The couple made a groundbreaking trip to China in 1970 — André was one of the first French officials received by Mao — but the main thing Liliane recalled was how Mao had flirted with her. "He really liked me. Maybe too much. It didn't go too far, but it was a marvelous joke. It was enormous for a woman."

"What could André Bettencourt have done

but politics?" says a former employee who knew him well. "He couldn't do a job — he had no qualifications, he never even completed his studies." Bettencourt's lack of diplomas led some malicious wags to call him *"Bête-en-long,"* a pun on the family name that translates loosely as "quite stupid."

The list of his cabinet positions is impressive on paper. From 1954 to 1973, he held nine portfolios in the ministries of Transportation, Industry, Culture, and Foreign Affairs (including a two-week interim as foreign minister). He was elected to the National Assembly in 1951 and the Senate in 1977, remaining until 1995. In all, fifty years of what he liked to call "political combat."

For much of his political career, Bettencourt was associated with the center-right group known as the Républicains indépendants, headed by Valéry Giscard d'Estaing. Former colleagues describe him as a man who acted through personal contacts and worked behind the scenes more than on the main political stage. Courteous, discreet, gracious, humble — such are the bland adjectives that people associate with André Bettencourt. But no one can point to a single law, political initiative, or reform that bears his mark. Nor did everyone in Bettencourt's own political family appreciate his political skills. When Giscard won the presidency in 1974, he pointedly did not include Bettencourt in his government. That snub reflected well-known tensions between the two men, even though André was a major financial contributor to Giscard's party. "I did not adore Giscard," wrote the normally cautious Bettencourt in his private memoirs. Giscard, after agreeing to be interviewed about Bettencourt for this book, changed his mind at the last minute because, as he put it, "I could only say bad things about him, and I don't wish to say bad things."

For all his financial contributions, Bettencourt showed little ability to influence policy. When Mitterrand became France's first Socialist president in 1981, André went to see him at the Élysée to complain about the crushing taxes levied on the wealthiest citizens. Mitterrand received him cordially, and in fact the two men continued to see each other on a personal basis all their lives. But on this occasion Mitterrand did not budge: "After all, André, you are not lacking for bread."

Bettencourt's political life was not limited to the national stage. From 1965 to 1989, he was mayor of his family fiefdom of Saint-Maurice-d'Ételan. (In France, it is legal, and common, for politicians to hold several offices simultaneously.) It is a traditional village (population 350) in Normandy nestled along the Seine between Paris and the port of Le Havre. Its narrow roads, muddied by tractors, are lined with old stone farmhouses and more recent suburban-style homes. At the village center is the fifteenth-century stone church, where several generations of Bettencourts lie buried. It was restored in the 1980s thanks to funding by André and Liliane.

The locals still speak of him with reverence. "With the people of the village, you know, he was very approachable," says Claude Herambourg, who replaced Bettencourt as mayor in 1989. "It was in his nature. He was a very pleasant man. He had a lot of class." As an example of his graciousness, Herambourg recounts that Bettencourt would have hot meals delivered to the poll watchers — even those of opposing parties — every Election Day. He would also stop in to chat with Herambourg or invite him to the local restaurant, sometimes even to the family manor, Belle Roche, for a meal. "He never drank wine, but he would smoke a cigar afterwards," says Herambourg, an exceptionally tall man with a Kennedy-esque shock of white hair, who, at eighty-three, still cuts a fine figure. For years, right up to the end of his life, André would call him almost weekly. "He just wanted to hear my voice," says Herambourg.

André spent most weekends in Saint-Maurice, arriving on a Friday in his chauffeur-driven Renault 25 and leaving on Sunday evening. On Saturdays, he would receive his constituents at Belle Roche, a handsome fifteen-room, three-story brick-and-stone mansion surrounded by hedges and shade trees. It was there that André and his five siblings were born. Liliane rarely accompanied her husband to Saint-Maurice. Like the world of politics, Saint-Maurice was André's domain, not hers. It was a place where he could feel his roots, see his hometown friends — and live his own private life.

From the time of his marriage to Liliane, André Bettencourt held a position at L'Oréal, eventually acquiring the title of vice president with a seat on the board of directors. But he never had any hands-on role at the company and was not consulted on management decisions. "To tell you the truth, I never felt he had any importance concerning business matters," says Jean-Pierre Valériola, former L'Oréal vice president in charge of public affairs.

When Eugène Schueller died in 1957, Liliane Bettencourt became the sole owner of L'Oréal. But there was never a thought of having her run the company. Her father had made it abundantly clear that he considered a woman's place to be in the home, and mocked the idea that the offspring of a *patron* — a boss — were competent to take over the helm. As he put it in a 1939 treatise on the economy: "One does not become a general because he is the son of a general. One does not become a *patron* because he is the son of a *patron*." As for André, even he admitted that he lacked the competence to head L'Oréal.

Schueller's handpicked choice as his successor was François Dalle, who had been a close friend of André's and Mitterrand's when they all lodged together at the Catholic student residence in Paris in the late 1930s. André could at least claim credit for bringing his friend into the fold by recommending him for a job at Schueller's soap company, Monsavon, in 1945. Dalle, in turn, lobbied to get Mitterrand hired as the editor of Schueller's promotional magazine, *Votre Beauté,* when the future president found himself jobless at the end of the war. Dalle quickly worked his way up to become head of Monsavon, moved to L'Oréal in 1948, and ran the company alongside Schueller. He took full command following the founder's death. A burly, round-faced bon vivant — the kind of guy you'd like to share a beef bourguignon with, says one source — Dalle expanded the company, developed new products, acquired new brands, and by the time he handed over the reins in 1984, had increased annual sales more than fortyfold.

L'Oréal was Liliane's passion, her link to her revered father's legacy, and the guarantee of the family's rank and privilege. As the group's principal shareholder, she held regular meetings with Dalle and his successors, kept up with *le chiffre* — the all-important financial figures — and was consulted on major decisions. She also held seats on the board of directors, the strategic committee, and the compensation committee. "On the really important matters, she's the one who had the final word," says Jean-Pierre Valériola. But Liliane's main job was to be an "ambassador" for the company. "She did public relations, she was the incarnation of L'Oréal, but she never had a direct role in the management," says a spokeswoman for the Bettencourt family.

Though she did not inherit her father's full powers, Liliane was sole heiress to his company stock, his immense personal fortune, and his real estate holdings. That included the villa in Brittany and Schueller's home in Franconville, eighteen miles northwest of Paris. Shortly after Liliane's marriage to André in 1950, Schueller built them a two-story, 1,500-square-meter mansion in the suburb of Neuilly. A one-square-mile enclave immediately adjacent to the western edge of Paris, sandwiched between the Seine and the Bois de Boulogne park, Neuilly is a residential town of tree-lined streets, posh apartment buildings, and imposing town houses. With a history dating back to the thirteenth century, it currently counts a population of some

60,000 souls and boasts the highest median per capita income of any French municipality: €46,000, compared with €25,830 for Paris. Among its illustrious residents past and present: painter Gustave Courbet; poet Charles Baudelaire; singer Édith Piaf; and film actors Jean Gabin, Jean Reno, and Jean-Paul Belmondo.

Unlike most of the neighboring town houses, the Bettencourt mansion is a free-standing beige stone edifice flanked by a one-acre lawn and garden lined with poplar, cedar, and oak trees. The property is bordered on the rue Delabordère by an eight-foot-high stucco stone wall that blocks it from the view of passersby. Security cameras over the dark-green metal gate surveil the entrance twenty-four hours a day. The opulent interior is decorated with master paintings by the likes of Picasso, Matisse, and Monet, and imposing furniture by the Art Deco cabinetmaker Émile-Jacques Ruhlmann, a personal favorite of Schueller's. At Liliane's insistence, a thirty-meter swimming pool was installed in the second basement to allow her to perform her daily laps. In addition to the Neuilly mansion and the villa at Arcouest, the Bettencourts acquired other properties along the way: a Fifth Avenue apartment in New York; a vacation home at Cap de Formentor on the Spanish island of Majorca; and, for a time, the private island of d'Arros in the Seychelles.

At home in Neuilly, they were waited on by a crew of fifteen to twenty servants. There were maids, valets, cooks, butlers, chauffeurs, bodyguards, nurses, secretaries, and laundresses. The Bettencourt household, in fact, resembled something out of *Downton Abbey*, with the servants vying for the favors of Monsieur or Madame, sniping at one another, forming clans, spying on their colleagues and their employers. Most were well paid, many received gifts from Madame Bettencourt — and more than a few spoke out when the time came.

Despite her humble family roots as the granddaughter of a baker and a domestic servant, Liliane had the air of a titled aristocrat. It was not just her immense wealth that created that impression, but the power inherent in her commanding role as L'Oréal's principal shareholder. She didn't lord it over people, but she had the regal manner of those born into money and privilege. "Liliane was a brilliant woman, who could be flippant and ironic in the knowledge that she belonged to the very wealthy class, and owed nothing to anyone," says her onetime lawyer Georges Kiejman. "She was not arrogant," observes actor Pascal Greggory, Banier's ex-partner, "but she had an imperial air — like, 'I know I'm a queen, after all.' People paid deference to her."

André Bettencourt was totally dependent

on his wife — and he knew it. It was Liliane's money that financed his lifestyle, bought his fine clothes and Havanas, and provided the cash he slipped to visiting politicians in discreet brown envelopes. Behind the impressive CV, he was a man who occupied what the French call a *strapontin* — a jump seat — in the worlds of politics and business.

And beyond. In 1988, he was elected to the prestigious Académie des Beaux-Arts, though his connection to the arts was rather tenuous: four months served as an interim culture minister, and the partial financing (with Liliane's money) of a contemporary art gallery near the Champs-Élysées, Artcurial. A more plausible candidate would have been his younger brother, Pierre Bettencourt, an immensely talented writer, painter, and sculptor. But André played his role to the hilt: At his induction ceremony under the cupola of the historic Institut de France, the country's preeminent learned society, he wore the traditional blue uniform with green brocade trim and ceremonial sword, joking in his acceptance speech that his wife had warned him not to cut his finger on the blade.

"He was anything but stupid," says Diane de Clairval, who assisted André with his memoirs. "Intelligence is not a matter of elite schools, but knowing how to take life. He chose this wife, introduced by his father-in-law, for whom he had great admiration. Once married, he could say to himself, 'With her means I can live as I want.' He had the intelligence to walk in Liliane's footsteps. And he enjoyed life. He had a great capacity for contentment." And that is perhaps the definition of André Bettencourt's true role: prince consort.

Liliane Bettencourt's marriage was not an entirely happy one. Her husband, though handsome, gentlemanly, and of good breeding, was also austere and extremely conventional. He was what the French call *terre à terre* — all on the ground level. His main interest was politics, which bored Liliane. Though they developed a closeness over the years, theirs was a marriage of convenience, not of passion. But dynasties need heirs. And so it was that on July 10, 1953, Françoise Isabelle Bettencourt, the couple's only offspring, came into the world.

CHAPTER 3
POOR LITTLE RICH GIRL

My mother is dead, but somehow I am still waiting for her, trying to see her face again.
— Liliane Bettencourt, 2005

At the heart of the Bettencourt Affair lies a tragedy whose roots go back to 1927. That was the year Liliane Bettencourt's mother died. The girl was five years old. She never experienced a mother-daughter relationship as a child, and lacked the fiber of maternal instinct as an adult. Her only parental role model was the strong-willed father she adored to the point of obsession. What a mother was, or should be, she hadn't any idea.

It would have been hard in any case for Françoise to forge a healthy relationship with such a mother, but her chances were skewed at the outset. Shortly after the birth of her daughter in 1953, Liliane suffered a relapse of the tuberculosis that had struck her and caused her deafness as a child. "She had to leave for a sanatorium and could not return to her daughter until she was three years old," says Lucienne de Rozier, one of Liliane's closest friends. "That can explain why she had trouble being close to her little girl, even though she adored her."

When Liliane returned home after her cure, Françoise clung to her, as she puts it, like "a mussel on a rock." But Liliane, smothered by her daughter's emotional demands, could not reciprocate. "I think that the relationship with her mother was terrible because of that," says Judge Isabelle Prévost-Desprez, who questioned Françoise in July 2010 regarding the Bettencourt Affair. "The child had an enormous need of love, which this woman, magnificent and terribly handicapped by her deafness, could not give her." Even now, Françoise gives the impression of a wounded child. Said Prévost-Desprez, "She has the gaze of a child, the laugh of a child. She is very touching. . . . You can see that this is a woman who is not in possession of her body. There is something about her that is, not exactly cold, but a bit, I'd say, disincarnate. This is not a woman who is bubbling over with life."

Not surprising: Her life was constrained from the beginning by the wealth and privilege that surrounded her. Every morning, a chauffeur took her to the Marymount School in Neuilly, a private Catholic establishment run by American nuns. She was constantly watched over by bodyguards because her parents feared that she might be kidnapped and ransomed by one of the far-left terrorist groups that were active in Europe in the 1960s and '70s.

In fact, it was Liliane herself who nearly became a kidnapping target. According to Alain Caillol, former member of a criminal band that in 1978 kidnapped Baron Édouard Empain, a wealthy Belgian industrialist, they originally had their eyes on Madame Bettencourt and even staked out her home in Neuilly. In the end, they decided against kidnapping a woman, because they weren't sure they could "manage her hygiene issues." Caillol, who spent eleven years in prison for the Empain caper, now believes it was a mistake not to grab Liliane, because they would have "had more means to exert pressure" in view of her personal fortune and her critical importance to L'Oréal. Empain, who spent sixty-three days sequestered in an underground tunnel and had his left little finger sliced off, was finally released without the 80-million-franc ($17 million) ransom payment the gang had demanded. "La belle Lili had a close call," Caillol said after his release from prison. "If we had nabbed her, we would have gotten the money with no problem."

Françoise likes to recount a happy childhood in which she and her parents "formed a close-knit family that loved to share the simple things of life." She and her mother adored visiting museums, traveling, and shopping together. She recalls happy family vacations at Arcouest — tennis games, sailing parties — and foreign trips with her parents, who let her choose the destinations: San Francisco, the Grand Canyon, Las Vegas, Haiti, New Orleans. "I was always very close to my parents, and perhaps even more so with my mother. My father was involved in politics and was often absent, but she bridged the gap. . . . She was always beautiful, yes, but I never felt the least rivalry. 'Jealousy' is a word that is foreign to me. Since she was always very elegant, I observed her with admiration. We have different tastes and personalities, yes, but is that an obstacle?"

Françoise's rose-tinted version is belied by Liliane's disdainful, often cruel words. "It's a failure with my daughter," she confided to a psychiatrist in 2009. "Françoise was heavy and slow, always one lap behind me." Liliane reflected on the relationship in a 2010 interview with *Paris Match* that shows, along with some harsh criticism, a certain tenderness mixed with regret. "I told you she was not happy, but that's not the right word," she said. "The word is unsatisfied. She never found what she wanted. . . . At age ten or eleven, she was still affectionate. Or was it me who remained passive because she didn't accept what I gave her? Perhaps." She reproached Françoise for not being more "magnetic": "With her everything remains in the moment, there is nothing to hook onto. That doesn't mean we're not touched or moved. There have been tears in our lives. . . . Nothing in this life makes one suffer more than love." Asked what Françoise blamed her for, Liliane snapped: "Not being a *maman gâteau*" — a mother who bakes cakes. "Even so, I interested her. I think she took a certain pride in me. But she didn't lift me or stimulate me. . . . She was timid, she never wanted to do anything or go swimming. She didn't go for it!"

But there was another side to the story. As Liliane recounted in dozens of letters to François-Marie Banier, dating back to 1989, she herself suffered from Françoise's lack of affection toward her, and from her limited access to her grandsons. "She never kisses me, she never holds my hand," she wrote in 1998. "Do you realize what that is for a mother? It's a total failure." In a 1997 letter she complained that her grandsons passed by her door "four times a day" but never stopped to say hello or give her a kiss. "She keeps them on a leash. Do you realize the lack of affection they show me? I really wonder if they are worthy of all that I'm going to leave them." In 2000, she complained that Françoise "has annihilated me, as far as her sons are concerned, I have no relationship. That's

96

what she wanted." In this tragically difficult mother-daughter relationship, the pain flowed in both directions.

One observer put the problem succinctly: "The mother massacred the daughter, then the daughter massacred the mother."

Françoise appears to have had an easier rapport with her father. Though he was often away on political (and personal) business, André Bettencourt felt a closeness to his daughter that Liliane did not share. In a way, he acted as a buffer between the two females — a "conciliator," as he put it — often appearing between them in family photos. Françoise considered him her "rampart." It was André, deeply steeped in traditional Catholic culture, who decided to name his daughter for St. Francis of Assisi. In his privately published memoirs, he described her as "joyous, docile, and emotive," endowed with a "strong-willed independence . . . Our daughter is probably more Bettencourt than Schueller," he wrote. Some have speculated that one source of friction between the two women was Liliane's jealousy over her daughter's close relationship with André. Perhaps. But there were many other reasons.

No woman could have been more different from Liliane Bettencourt than her daughter. While Liliane was social, outgoing, fashion conscious, and fiercely devoted to the family business, her only child was introverted and taciturn, drawn more to books and classical music than to fancy receptions or L'Oréal meetings. Though she was considered pretty when she was young — some compared her to Ali MacGraw — her looks as she grew older were no match for Liliane's scintillating beauty. With her unshaped mass of black hair and her heavy jaw often fixed in a frown, Françoise seemed to hide from the world behind the thick-framed tinted glasses that Liliane judged "hard to wear and hard to look at." Nor did her dowdy dressing style echo her mother's haute-couture elegance. Françoise suffered from the "syndrome of Nefertiti's daughter," says Georges Kiejman, Liliane's former lawyer, "sad because she was less beautiful than her mother. And it's true that there was a sort of rivalry between Françoise and her mother." As Liliane described the relationship in a 2008 letter to Banier: "It's a story of jealousy between women, it's the easiest thing in the world to understand."

Faced with a mother who was admittedly stingy with affection, Françoise found solace in her piano. Then, as now, she would practice for hours each day, with a special passion for Bach. "Music is my oxygen," she said. Though it was a mostly solitary pastime, she would sometimes play duets with her friend singer/actress/filmmaker Arielle Dombasle. "From the beginning, our common sensibil-

98

ity, our friendship was based on music," recalls Dombasle, who, as it happened, was also a friend of the young François-Marie Banier. "And I remember that Liliane absolutely adored our duos, especially one I sang for years, Offenbach's 'Grande Duchesse de Gérolstein.' "

Even if Liliane could enjoy her daughter's music at one time, she later came to see it as a shell into which Françoise retreated to block out the rest of the world. "I am too eccentric for her," Liliane wrote in 2007. "She does five hours of prayer [piano practice] a day, she's not interested by anything that is out of her sight. — Amen — I am just the opposite."

Dombasle offers an intriguing insight into the rift that developed between mother and daughter over the years. Françoise, who has the temperament of an "austere Carmelite nun," actively rejected the scintillating world of her wealthy parents and their friends. "Françoise was a somber little girl, rather reserved, and she could not abide their world of social conventions and superficiality. So she said that she must exist in her own way, on the enchanted island of her music. Her position as an heiress, her position as a rich girl, a powerful girl, all that is something she has always detested. Françoise did not like her mother's milieu at all." That temperamental difference with her mother, more than anything, drove a wedge between them.

According to Dombasle, the person Françoise liked and admired most was her piano professor, Yvonne Lefébure, a renowned performer and teacher who died in 1986 at the age of eighty-eight. Was she perhaps a surrogate for Françoise's grandmother, Betsy Doncieux Schueller, herself a piano teacher?

Françoise first laid eyes on Jean-Pierre Meyers one night in 1972, when he attended a preview showing of *The Godfather* in the Bettencourts' private box at the Garnier Opera House. Meyers, then twenty-three, son of a L'Oréal manager, had begun a promising career as a banker. He had a distinguished family background, but one very different from the Bettencourts and their circle. His great-grandfather had been the head rabbi of Avignon and Nice. His grandfather, Rabbi Robert Meyers, had died at Auschwitz, along with his wife after heroically saving dozens of Jews from arrest and deportation.

Françoise and Jean-Pierre got to know each other better at the Bettencourts' villa at Arcouest, where Liliane had invited the young man to vacation with the family — an invitation she may later have come to regret. Over the next decade, the friendship ripened into a romance, and one fine day the couple stunned their respective families by announcing their intention to marry. Jean-Pierre's parents, who had hoped to see their son wed a nice Jewish girl, initially opposed the idea. Nor were the fervently Catholic Bettencourts enamored of the match. As André noted in his memoirs, his daughter's marriage to a Jew "was not an easy thing to contemplate."

There was another problem. At the time, Jean-Pierre Meyers was living with Agnès Greggory, sister of the actor Pascal Greggory. Agnès, a widow, had two young daughters who looked to Jean-Pierre Meyers as a surrogate father. According to Pascal Greggory, Meyers just disappeared one day. "Agnès learned of the [impending] marriage between Françoise and Jean-Pierre through a notice in the *Figaro* four or five days after he left."

Françoise, in any event, was determined to wed Jean-Pierre, and the families eventually withdrew their opposition. "I wouldn't have prevented it, because I would have been too afraid of her reaction," Liliane confided in a 2001 letter to Banier. On April 6, 1984, they were married at Fiesole, Italy, in a small civil ceremony. "It was a marvelous wedding in all the sublime Italian colors," Françoise recalled, denying any family frictions over the mixed marriage. The couple moved into a duplex apartment — a gift to Françoise from her parents — located fifty yards from the Bettencourt mansion in Neuilly.

Apparently resigned to having Jean-Pierre for a son-in-law, Liliane and André asked him to quit his bank job and take a position at L'Oréal. André eventually developed a cordial relationship with Meyers, even calling him "an affectionate son," but Liliane never warmed to him. "She always blamed Françoise for marrying a man from a different social milieu," confided her friend Lucienne de Rozier. "She detests her son-in-law." Years later, Liliane described Jean-Pierre's courtship in these blunt terms: "He never lost sight of the prize: Money is money."

The couple had two sons, Jean-Victor, born in 1986, and Nicolas, born in 1988, and decided to raise them in the Jewish religion. It is tempting to see Françoise's choice of a Jewish husband, like the Jewish upbringing of her sons, as an act of atonement for a dark chapter in her family history: her grandfather's Nazi collaboration and her father's anti-Semitic articles. Of course, there is no way to prove this theory. It is even possible — though unlikely — that Françoise was unaware of that inglorious family history at this time. But it is a telling detail that she always avoided speaking of Eugène Schueller, much to her mother's chagrin. "In 50 years, my daughter has never talked to me about my father," Liliane wrote in 2008. "I think my father was too important for her." Important in what sense? Perhaps because Schueller's past was too heavy a burden for her to shoulder?

In any event, Françoise's marriage remains a striking symbolic act, one that found an echo in her 2008 five-volume study of the Bible, *Les trompettes de Jéricho* (The Trumpets of Jericho), aimed at fostering understanding between Catholics and Jews. In his review of the work, author Bernard-Henri Lévy wrote, "I suppose, since I know Françoise a bit, that she had personal reasons — biographical choices, the weight of past destinies — to undertake this task." Françoise's other published work, a 1994 study of Greek mythology entitled *Les dieux grecs* (The Greek gods), is no less symbolic. Its tales of jealousy, vengeance, and retribution, of parricides and matricides and ancient curses that tear families apart, seem eerily to foreshadow the events that would later befall the house of Bettencourt.

Today, Françoise Meyers still resembles the austere Carmelite described by her friend. She dresses most often in black pantsuits, their bleakness offset by large colored scarves. She eschews fancy jewelry and wears little makeup, apart from the black eyeliner that enhances her dark looks. "Françoise doesn't like luxury," says Arielle Dombasle. "She likes her Labrador, she adores her children, and she loves her husband."

There is little luxury on display in the Meyerses' apartment, which occupies two floors of a modern building on Neuilly's Rond-Point Saint-James, across the street from the Bettencourt mansion. The living room, with its two large picture windows, is modestly furnished with beige curtains, metallic bookshelves, and a few modern paintings — including a large black-on-black canvas by Pierre Soulages. The space is dominated by two grand pianos, a Steinway and a Yamaha, on which Françoise practices up to five hours a day. One visitor describes the décor as "frozen in the 1970s, sober and rather cold — the opposite of Liliane's elegance."

In contrast to the Bettencourts' lavish entertaining style, the Meyerses' social life consists mainly of quiet dinners at home with a few close friends. Though they have two domestics, it is Françoise who opens the door and pours the coffee. She appears to have few personal interests outside her music and her family, although she is involved with the Bettencourt Schueller Foundation and actively supports a research institute that has developed new cochlear-implant techniques to treat deafness — a condition that affects Françoise as well as her mother. Jean-Pierre, for his part, is deeply involved in supporting Jewish charities but, like his wife, flees the glare of public attention. Friends describe him in bland terms as "extremely polite," "nice," "simple," "warm, with a sense of humor." But it is difficult to get a fix on him as a personality — or as a businessman. At L'Oréal, says former public affairs chief Jean-Pierre Valériola, Meyers "never intervened very directly" in important decisions. Another L'Oréal veteran, former number two Pierre Castres Saint Martin, says Meyers is simply, like his father-in-law, "a prince consort."

For all her professed disinterest in wealth, Françoise and her family are sitting on one of the world's greatest fortunes. In 1992, to ensure the future of L'Oréal and the transmission of her estate, Liliane Bettencourt gifted the bulk of her company stock, nearly 172 million shares, to Françoise (two-thirds) and her grandsons (one-third) in the form of *nue propriété* — reversionary shares that will become theirs upon Liliane's death. At the time, the gifted stock was worth some €2.5 billion; today the value is more than ten times that sum. Liliane herself retained the voting rights over her shares and usufruct in the form of stock dividends that currently average over a million euros a day. Once she had taken care of her heirs, Liliane considered that she was entitled to spend her own money as she saw fit. As she put it in a letter to her notary in October 2002: "That's my margin of freedom, and I intend to preserve it." For her part, Françoise thanked her mother for the shares but added, rather tactlessly in Liliane's opinion, "If you had made this donation 25 years ago, we could have avoided all the complications."

Until the eruption of the affair, the Meyerses had lived under the same veil of discretion as the Bettencourts. Scrupulously avoiding publicity, neither family was fodder for tabloids or gossip columns. The Bettencourt name was associated with L'Oréal, with the foundation, with André's political positions, but their private lives passed under the radar. So it was surprising to publicist Seth Goldschlager when Françoise and Jean-Pierre Meyers contacted him some time before the suit was filed. "We're active in a lot of things, but nobody knows about us," Françoise told Goldschlager. She pointed, for example, to the couple's funding of cochlear-implant research. She told him she was preparing her book on the Bible, that she played the piano — she had even recorded a CD that was distributed privately to family and friends. When Goldschlager met with the couple, he found her "very headstrong and determined. She looked me in the eye and said, 'How can we exist?' They wanted to be known, you see? So we did a little work on her books and her piano, but frankly nobody was interested in that. The cochlear implants got a little play."

What motivated that sudden desire to attract attention? Was Françoise trying to send a message to her mother? Look at me, *Maman,* I can write books, and play piano, and do good works. I am not just the dowdy, reserved, timid daughter you are so ashamed of — I am somebody. Her initiative fell flat that time, but she would soon exist in a big way.

■ ■ ■ ■

Part Two:
Banier Enters
the Scene

■ ■ ■ ■

Friends in high places: Salvador Dalí and François-Marie Banier at Paris's Hôtel Meurice, 1971. **Alécio de Andrade, Adagp, Paris 2017**

CHAPTER 4
PORTRAIT OF THE ARTIST

Rue Servandoni is a narrow, cobblestoned street that spans two blocks from the neoclassical Saint-Sulpice church to the Luxembourg Gardens. Formerly called the rue des Fossoyeurs — street of the gravediggers — it has been part of Paris's urban fabric since the fifteenth century. It is a street steeped in history and literature. Alexandre Dumas's d'Artagnan, of *Three Musketeers* fame, was said to live here, as did a character in Victor Hugo's *Les Misérables.* Olympe de Gouges, author of the *Declaration of the Rights of Women,* lived at Number 20 — until she was guillotined in 1793. Twentieth-century residents include singer Juliette Gréco; literary critic Roland Barthes; and William Faulkner, who stayed at Number 26 in the fall of 1925. And today, behind a pair of tall, green doors, François-Marie Banier occupies the five-story town house that serves as his home, studio, and photo archive. The building also boasts a twelve-meter indoor swimming pool.

Granted an initial interview with Banier in September 2015, I passed through the remote-controlled doors and crossed a dank flagstone courtyard jammed with potted bamboo trees, azalea, and camellia bushes. An assistant accompanied me up the winding stairs to Banier's second-floor studio. He greeted me at the door and waved me to a loveseat that was spattered with blue paint. He was taller than expected, just shy of six feet, dressed all in black: black wool shirt, black trousers with fine stripes, black loafers. He settled down on a worn récamier, also paint-splotched. The vast room was filled with photographs, paintings, drawings — some framed and mounted on the walls, others scattered on the gray stone floor along with jars of paint, brushes, books, stacks of blank canvases.

Seated amidst the clutter, Banier calls to mind the portrait of Dorian Gray. His once-angelic face is now a web of wrinkles. The cascading curls of his youth have given way to thinning reddish-brown hair that prickles up from his scalp. The sensuous lips are now just a horizontal slash. The blue-gray eyes are tired but probing. When he talks, he moves constantly, waving his hands in the air, running them through what remains of his hair, clapping, sometimes shouting, sometimes whispering. His story spills out in disjointed episodes, like the scenes of a chaotic film, or rather scattered chapters of a novel. For Banier is a novelist, and he is his own main character. "The most important thing," he once said, "is to turn one's life into a work of art."

François-Marie Michel Banier was born in Paris, the second of three sons, on June 27, 1947. His father, Etienne, a Hungarian Jew who immigrated to France in the mid-1930s, beat him every day, and called him *"tordu"* — bent, twisted. His French-Italian mother, Madeleine, was eccentric and self-centered, a dispenser of rules and lessons but not the affection that her son craved. A childhood friend of Banier's remembers her as "a rigid bourgeoise" always accompanied by her yapping Chihuahua dogs.

Outwardly, his parents made an impressive couple, the kind whose elegance and beauty turned heads when they entered a restaurant. Though Etienne Banier — original name Banyaï — had started out as an assembly-line auto worker, he eventually prospered as an advertising executive, acquiring an apartment on the avenue Victor-Hugo, one of the most fashionable thoroughfares in Paris's tony 16th arrondissement, and a country home near Fontainebleau. But those trappings of bourgeois success only added to the boy's sense of malaise and alienation.

From an early age, he sought company and

affection outside the family. His mother would leave him for hours on end with the concierge of their apartment building, where he made friends with the Spanish maids. He enjoyed talking with a widowed antique dealer in his neighborhood — one of many older women in his life.

At the Baniers' country home in the town of Héricy, south of Paris, the young François-Marie spent more time with neighbors' families than his own. "He practically lived at our house," recalls a childhood friend, Douce de Andia. "If we pushed him out the door, he'd return by the window, almost insisting on becoming part of the family. He was funny, quick-witted, impertinent, and incredibly brazen."

Banier has undergone three psychoanalyses — all failures, he says — but it doesn't take a shrink to see all this as a search for surrogate parents in place of the real ones who had so deeply hurt and disappointed him. "François-Marie is someone who has a desire to be loved," says the actor Pascal Greggory, his former partner, who remains a close friend. "As a child he was beaten by his father and lacked affection from his mother. Because of this, he seeks love from others. He tests people — he can be aggressive, smother them with love, or say horrible things — to see if they accept his demand for love."

In his relentless quest for affection, the

young Banier was aided by exceptional physical beauty — a Cupid's-bow mouth, luxuriant chestnut curls, penetrating blue-gray eyes — and a natural gift for charm and seduction. On the street, where he spent much of his time, he could talk strangers into buying whole books of raffle tickets or his own early attempts at drawing and painting, inspired, he says, by the multicolored drippings of Jackson Pollock. "Your parents missed out on Modigliani," he would shout, "don't miss out on Banier." He claims that he would sell his works for 300 francs apiece, roughly $60, sometimes racking up the equivalent of $200 in a half hour — most probably an exaggeration. He was a mediocre student at the elite Lycée Janson de Sailly, but developed a passion for reading — Balzac, Stendhal, Proust, Flaubert — and a precocious flair for writing. All of which alienated him even more from his prosaic parents, who "believed in nothing, but they believed in nothing very strongly."

You can see the pain in Banier's eyes today as he relives this bleak childhood. He stops in midsentence and stares into the distance for a long moment. Suddenly he picks up his monologue again, but now there is a hint of admiration along with the hurt. "God knows I didn't get along with my father, but he was a remarkable man. He was in the Resistance

— he bombed bridges — but he didn't want that known. He was very, very discreet." That discretion did not prevent him from raining almost daily punishments down on François-Marie in the form of slaps, punches, belt-whippings, and worse. When he was especially angry, Banier says, his father would turn him upside down and beat his head on the floor. He once even threatened to put a cigarette out in his son's eye. Strangely, his brothers, Dominique and Nicolas, were never punished. Why was François-Marie the unique target of his father's wrath? "My interior world, my turbulence, my lack of respect for conventions, my big voice — my father had a weak voice — and my interest in people from nowhere." One day his father posed such unbearable questions about François-Marie's private life that the boy attempted suicide by downing tranquilizers from his mother's medicine cabinet. He was fifteen years old.

Banier describes his mother as an enabler, a vain woman so self-absorbed that she never intervened to protect her battered son. "She should have divorced my father," he says, "or taken me away, or called the police or done something. Instead, it was me they dragged to the doctors and psychiatrists as if I were insane. I was merely sensitive."

Gilles Brücker, a childhood friend of Banier's who later served as a medical adviser to Liliane Bettencourt, shares a revealing anecdote: "I remember one time, when François-Marie was about ten, Madame Banier came to visit my mother at our house. A storm was rising outside and there was a tremendous thunderclap. The phone rings, and it's François-Marie, calling to tell his mother to come home quickly — the chandelier has just crashed to the floor. His mother rushes back to see the disaster, but of course it was just a joke. He had this highly developed sense of fantasy and drama — it had to be the chandelier, not just a painting, falling down. And of course he was beaten."

Of course. Like a capricious child, which is what he was at the time, Banier was pushing the envelope to see where the limits were, calling attention to himself even at the expense of a whipping. That penchant for provocation, for temper tantrums, for outrageous behavior, remained with Banier even as he aged in years.

Childishness — which also embraces positive traits like curiosity, exuberance, and affection — explains a lot about François-Marie Banier. For example, his habit of talking and laughing too loud in public, or his attention-grabbing pranks. "When he comes here, he makes the whole restaurant laugh because he talks so loud," says Banier's friend Jean-Michel Ribes, director of the Théâtre du Rond-Point, a theater-restaurant near the Champs-Élysées. "He pushes the

117

door and rides his motor scooter right into the theater. Someone might have called the police, said he's crazy, he has no right, but it was pretty funny." François Bonduel, former owner of a restaurant on the rue Servandoni, recalls that Banier would secretly erase items from the chalkboard menu on the sidewalk. Bonduel thought it was one of the neighborhood children until his daughter spotted Banier wiping the slate. "I called him up and he said, 'Yes, it's me. I'm sorry.' He's like a big kid, you see?"

When the young man reached out for the affection he craved, he reached high. From his teenage years on, he managed to forge close, often intense relationships with an array of rich, famous, influential people who welcomed and encouraged his friendship. The first was Salvador Dalí, who often sojourned in Paris's majestic Hôtel Meurice on the rue de Rivoli. Banier was sixteen at the time, interested in drawing, and already imbued with a strong dose of chutzpah. He called the legendary Spanish surrealist from the hotel lobby and asked if he could show the master his drawings. Dalí invited him up and looked at his work. He apparently didn't think much of it — "Young man, your line is too large," he told him, adding a crude anatomical innuendo — but he took a shine to the brash and handsome youth and invited him back.

"His suite was always full of the most beautiful young boys and girls, but he always wanted to talk to me." Dalí was so fascinated by the young man's company that he would send his Cadillac to pick him up at his lycée and bring him back to lunch at the Meurice along with his wife, Gala.

Banier quit school at seventeen. Two years later, he left the family apartment and set out to conquer Paris like the social-climbing Balzac character Eugène de Rastignac, to whom he is often compared. After working in a bookstore, Banier landed a job as a press attaché for Pierre Cardin. From that privileged perch, where he remained for seven years, Banier made invaluable contacts in the fashion, society, and media worlds. One of the beautiful people he met while working at chez Cardin was the decorator Jacques Grange, two years his elder, who became his lover and long-term partner. It was with Grange that Banier bought his first apartment on the rue Servandoni in 1973 — a fourth-floor three-room flat — followed two years later by the purchase of a top-floor apartment with a skylight that had once served as a photographer's studio. Grange, whose wealthy clients included the shah of Iran, decorated the spaces lavishly with antique furniture, paintings, sculptures, and a library full of rare books. "They were one personality split into two halves," recalls

Banier's friend Valérie Lalonde. "Grange was all smiles . . . curing the wounds Banier inflicted. They made a marvelous pair."

Marie-Laure de Noailles was a well-connected socialite, art collector, banking heiress, and a viscountess by marriage. After meeting her at a book signing, Banier became a regular visitor to her sumptuous town house on the Place des États-Unis, a tree-lined square in Paris's 16th arrondissement that features a bronze statue of Washington and Lafayette and a monument to the American volunteers who fought with the French Foreign Legion in World War I. While admiring her Goyas, Picassos, Rubenses, and Delacroixes, Banier hobnobbed with the artists and intellectuals who attended her receptions. A patron of the arts, along with her husband, Charles, the eccentric viscountess — a descendant of the Marquis de Sade — had bought arms for the anti-Franco forces in Spain, financed Buñuel films, and delivered pâté-en-croute to the rioting Sorbonne students in May 1968 at the wheel of her Rolls-Royce.

In the spring of that year, Marie-Laure invited Banier to lunch with Bernard Privat, director of the prestigious Grasset publishing house. Banier impressed Privat with his precocious literary culture and asked if he could send him some short stories he had written. Ten days later, they met at the bar of the Hôtel Lutétia. Privat complimented the young man on his stories, but told him what he really wanted was a novel. Banier accepted the challenge and returned to the Lutétia one week later with the beginning of his manuscript. It consisted of only one sentence: "Monsieur Pélissier arrived every Saturday and spent his Sundays in Héricy." Privat told him to come back with more. During their weekly meetings at the hotel bar, they would go over Banier's writing three pages at a time. The result was Banier's first novel, *Les résidences secondaires* (Second Homes), published in 1969 to enthusiastic reviews. He was twenty-two years old.

The book is a satire of the affluent Parisians who flocked like lemmings to their weekend retreats in the village of Héricy, where Banier's parents had a home. The denizens of Héricy gossip and posture, lie and cheat, seduce and betray one another, and share a cultlike devotion to money and property. There are no heroes and no real plot. The characters are superficial, flippant, petty, and egotistical. As a microcosm of France's self-satisfied bourgeoisie, they made an excellent target for satire at a time when the upheavals of the '60s were throwing those values into question. At the same time, the young Banier shows a fascination with wealth, seduction, and rich old ladies that seems to foreshadow his future relationship with Liliane Bettencourt. One character experiences "the exaltation caused by the sudden possession of a large fortune." A young man who becomes the lover of an older woman is told, "You represented a lot of things in her eyes, you were youth, gaiety, freedom, everything that she no longer had." Fascinating themes in light of the scandal that would explode nearly four decades later.

Banier was basking in the glory of his early success. Affecting white linen suits and parking himself conspicuously in trendy Parisian cafés while he scribbled in his notebook, he contributed guest columns to leading newspapers, including *Le Monde,* France's equivalent of the *New York Times* in terms of reach and prestige, and *Le Figaro,* the major conservative daily. He became the darling of literary salons, the friend and protégé of famous writers and artists. "Everyone was at my feet!"

Among his admirers were press magnates Hélène Lazareff, creator of *Elle* magazine, and her husband, Pierre, founder of the popular daily *France-Soir,* who began inviting Banier to the Sunday luncheons that they hosted in the Paris suburb of Louveciennes. It was there that he first met Liliane and André Bettencourt in 1969. He was struck by Liliane's "very modern beauty," but recalls spending more time talking about literature with André. Banier continued to run into the Bettencourts at luncheons and dinner parties, but his close relationship with Liliane did not develop until many years later. A tenacious rumor claims that Banier had actually met André earlier, and had an intimate relationship with him before meeting Liliane. Banier has always scoffed at this story, even declaring in court that their relations were "without ambiguity." When Liliane was asked years later about a prior encounter between the two men, she replied vaguely, "I have absolutely no memory of that."

"I must show you something," Banier says suddenly. He gets up from the récamier, disappears into another room, then returns with a book whose pages are yellowed by time. It is entitled *Le paysan de Paris* (The Peasant of Paris) and bears an inscription: "To François-Marie, my extraordinary peasant from the Danube" — a reference to Banier's Hungarian roots. The author was Louis Aragon, one of the leading French poets and novelists of the twentieth century, a Resistance hero, and a lifelong member of the French Communist Party.

Banier met him by chance one night in 1968, oddly enough at the end of a James Brown concert at the Olympia music hall. It was raining and Aragon couldn't find a taxi. Banier introduced himself and offered to take the poet and his wife home in Jacques Grange's car. Aragon gratefully accepted.

123

Two years later, Edmonde Charles-Roux, editor of *Vogue* and a leading French feminist, took Banier to dinner at Aragon's apartment. The poet did not immediately recognize the young man who had driven him home from the Olympia, but he was impressed by the vivacity of his conversation and the fact that he was about to publish his second novel, *Le passé composé* (Past Tense), a dark tale of incest between a brother and sister. That was the beginning of an intimate friendship that lasted until Aragon's death in 1982.

The two men could often be seen dining together at well-known Parisian restaurants such as Maxim's, La Coupole, and La Brasserie Lipp, usually arriving and leaving on Banier's scooter, Aragon's long white hair flowing in the wind. Following the death in June 1970 of Aragon's Russian wife, Elsa Triolet, Banier was one of the people to whom the poet looked most for companionship.

Aragon's support proved invaluable. When *Le passé composé* was published in 1971, he penned a glowing review in his prestigious literary magazine *Les lettres françaises*. "[Banier] is the craziest, most generous, funniest person you will ever meet," Aragon wrote. "He has a fiery and disordered talent for conversation, he is an incomparable raconteur, and if he writes as he speaks, he will one day be the cruelest and gayest painter of his time." Extravagantly comparing Banier's writing to the likes of Stendhal and Turgenev, he hailed the young author as "a one-of-a-kind personage, one of that rare and troubling breed that bear the mark of the future."

The following year, Britain's *Sunday Times* magazine put Banier on its cover under the headline: "François-Marie Banier, Golden Boy of Paris." The photos showed Banier dining with Aragon, scribbling in his notebook, dressed in a white suit, drying his luxuriant hair while sitting, half nude, on the bed of Marie-Laure de Noailles. The accompanying article, while acknowledging Banier's burgeoning celebrity, cattily judged his talent to be "exaggerated by older admirers in whose company he is so often seen." For all the honor of the cover treatment, Banier was not entirely pleased with the piece. "It presented me as a dandy. Funny thing — generally dandies are lazy idlers. I work from morning to night, and I especially don't care about the impression I make." The *Sunday Times* article also signaled the danger of peaking too early: Banier's third novel, *La tête la première* (Headfirst), published in 1972, was a critical and commercial flop. He would not publish another novel for more than a decade.

Nicole Wisniak, editor of the avant-garde magazine *Egoïste,* taunted Banier about this hiatus over dinner at her apartment one night. "So tell me, joker, is it true you're not writing anymore?" she asked. "Everybody says you've given it up." With that, Banier took a felt marker out of his pocket and proceeded to write on the walls of her living room. His verbiage spilled out over the light fixtures and lampshades, the bookshelves, the fridge, and finally ended with four lines on the bathroom mirror.

Gleeful over his exploit, Banier sat back down and declared, "You see, I'm still writing."

Banier was in fact writing during that time — not novels but plays. São Schlumberger, wife of a wealthy French oil magnate, proposed to finance Banier's first play, *Hôtel du Lac,* in 1975. She reportedly put 350,000 francs (some $68,000) into the production and hosted a gala dinner at Paris's Grand Hôtel following the premiere. Among the two hundred guests were Salvador Dalí, Isabelle Adjani, Marisa Berenson, filmmaker Robert Hossein . . . and Banier's parents, who enjoyed the champagne and the attention but didn't seem to realize that the play was a satire of their conventional bourgeois world. In spite of Schlumberger's financial backing, the play failed, as did a subsequent theatrical effort by Banier three years later, *Nous ne connaissons pas la même personne* (We don't know the same person). Asked his opinion of

Banier as a playwright, his friend Jean-Michel Ribes, director of the Théâtre des Champs-Élysées, says diplomatically: "I'm not sure that the theater is the place where his talent is most effective."

Probably the best thing that came out of Banier's ill-fated sally into the theater world was his relationship with actor Pascal Greggory. They first met in 1974 at New Jimmy's, a hip dance club at Montparnasse favored by the gay crowd. "We danced together," Greggory recounts, "and suddenly he asked me, 'Do you have a car?' I said yes. He told me to follow his car. We arrived at his place on the rue Servandoni and he said, 'Here is where I live. Come have lunch with me tomorrow.' " At the time, Banier was looking for a young actor to play the lead in *Hôtel du Lac.* Greggory, who was then in acting school, was cast in the part — and immediately moved in with Banier.

The only problem was that Banier was still with decorator Jacques Grange. The three lived together for a time, then Grange finally moved out. "It was all done in an amicable way," says Greggory, who was Banier's partner for seven years and still lives in an apartment adjoining Banier's building. Banier's current companion, with whom he has a civil union, is actually Greggory's nephew, Martin d'Orgeval.

D'Orgeval, now forty-three, was eighteen

when he moved in with Banier, who is twenty-five years his elder. Today, the three remain exceptionally close. "In the homosexual milieu, families don't follow the schemas of classical families," Greggory explains. "We created a replacement family because what we expected from our real families was not offered."

Banier's ceaseless quest for affection led in many directions — gay, straight, young, old, beautiful, and, yes, even ugly. Madeleine Castaing was a true Left Bank character. She wore an ill-fitting wig, heavy red lipstick, false eyelashes, and a chinstrap attached to her wig by an elastic band on the theory that this would counteract the effect of gravity on her sagging skin. Castaing, a legendary decorator and antiques dealer, had counted Picasso, Chagall, and Modigliani among her friends. She was a passionate supporter of the Russian painter Chaïm Soutine, and served as his art dealer. She was feisty, opinionated, and unpredictable.

Castaing was seventy-five when Banier, then twenty-two, wandered into her boutique on the rue Jacob in 1969. Fascinated by this eccentric old lady and her links to the art world, Banier maintained a close relationship with her until her death at ninety-eight. But this Harold-and-Maude couple could also quarrel violently at times. After one dispute, according to the journalist Matthieu Galey, Banier bragged of avenging himself by secretly urinating in her teapot. (Banier denies this.) Another time, he allegedly snatched her wig and threw it in the open fireplace. (Ditto.) When Castaing refused to let him in the door after one of their spats, so the story goes, he got a ladder and climbed in the window. But their arguments were always followed by reconciliations. "We were two monsters," says Banier. "In other words, a real couple."

Castaing's family frowned on the relationship. Her grandson, Frédéric Castaing, claimed that Banier filched various objects from Madeleine, wheedled an apartment out of her, and even shoved her down the stairs. Banier sued for defamation in 2009 and won a judgment against the magazine that published these charges. He bristles at claims that he exploited Castaing or received money from her. "Madeleine was very stingy," says Pascal Greggory. "She once gave me a broken clock for my birthday."

Even if she didn't lavish gifts on Banier as Liliane Bettencourt later did, Castaing did become a patron of sorts by buying his photographs of the writer Nathalie Sarraute in 1989 for the hefty sum of 70,000 francs — worth about $14,000 at the time. It was his first-ever photo sale. She also contributed to his photo career by posing in her nightgown, wigless and bald, for what became one of his best-known pictures. Banier has been criticized for showing her in a demeaning way, but he insists that Castaing made him do it — and loved the result. When she later saw it hanging in an exhibition, she told Banier, "You're cheeky, but it's good, it's me."

Banier first met Yves Saint Laurent in 1968 while he was working as a press attaché for YSL's rival Pierre Cardin. The two became very close friends, but Pierre Bergé, Saint Laurent's business and life partner, looked on Banier as a boorish rival. It didn't help their relations that Banier referred to him, behind his back, as "the dwarf Bergé." In his 2003 memoir, Bergé recounts a restaurant scene where Banier, flashing on a young waiter, asked his companions in a loud voice, "You think he sucks well?"

Bergé's scathing commentary: "He wanted to be saucy, but he was embarrassing . . . [and] offensive." Elsewhere, he described Banier as a "pseudo-writer" whose "main quality is to seduce old people."

Part of Bergé's annoyance may stem from Banier's disputed claim to have invented the name of Saint Laurent's highly successful perfume, Opium, launched in 1977 with what fashion writer Alicia Drake calls "a *tour de force* of marketing, promotion and hype that had not yet been seen in the fashion industry." However, there is no doubt that Banier named Dior's Poison, which debuted in 1985, and earned some 10 million francs — roughly $2 million — from royalties over a ten-year period. It was largely thanks to that income, and his more modest book royalties, that in 1987 Banier was able to buy an eighteenth-century villa in the south of France along with his friend David Rocksavage (aka Lord Cholmondeley). A descendant of Sir Robert Walpole, Eton-educated Rocksavage is a peer of the realm, Lord Great Chamberlain to the queen, and sits on one of England's biggest fortunes.

Through his links to Saint Laurent, Cardin, and Dior, Banier gained a privileged entrée into the fashion scene during the 1970s and '80s. "The fashion world exploded at this time," recalls Judy Fayard, a former Paris-based editor at *Women's Wear Daily* and later Paris correspondent for *LIFE.* "Fashion designers were seen as culture heroes. The fashion world, the gay world, the party scene, it was all one." Hip clubs and bars sprouted like mushrooms — the Club Sept on the rue Sainte-Anne, Le Palace on the Faubourg-Montmartre, New Jimmy's on the Boulevard Montparnasse. Le Palace, a converted theater whose seats had been removed for dancing, was the epicenter of this nocturnal ferment. That's where the gay crowd, the fashion mavens, the beautiful people, and jet-setters rubbed shoulders with hippies, punk rockers, and anyone else who wandered in. "It was a total mix of everything that moved in Paris," says Fayard. "Money, women, gay, and straight. It was an all-night-long high-flying night life."

Naturally, Banier was in the middle of it all. Guy Marineau, a photographer for *Women's Wear Daily* who has published a photo book on Le Palace, remembers him well from those years. "Banier had become excellent in the art of creating friendships during fashionable events at Le Palace or at private parties." Usually dressed in a smart suit or dinner jacket, he would wander around looking for interesting people to meet. "He was both public and mysterious, with a Balzacian beauty that seduced certain women as well as men. I remember some evenings when he would arrive with Isabelle Adjani, Princess Caroline, or Françoise Sagan on his arm."

Looking back on those days, Banier says he didn't really like hanging out in "homo places" but he loved to dance — the twist, the hully-gully, the jerk. He recounts one wild evening at the Palace, where he danced with John Travolta and Maria Berenson and wound up with the two of them in Berenson's suite at the Plaza-Athénée. (He says he left before anything "happened.")

Between gulps of Coke Zero, Banier spews out the names of other celebrities that he has met, dined with, danced with, or in some cases, possibly slept with: Tennessee Williams, Truman Capote, Samuel Beckett, Andy Warhol, Gloria Swanson, Marlene Dietrich, Elizabeth Taylor, Richard Burton, Prince Charles, Ray Charles, Mick Jagger . . . He pulls out a picture of himself as a young man wrapped in the arms of Italian film star Silvana Mangano, with whom he had an intense though platonic relationship. He refers to pianist Vladimir Horowitz as his "real father," and claims to be the one who coaxed the maestro back onto the concert stage after a long hiatus. "Horowitz once told me, 'In the end I had only two friends — Rachmaninoff and you.' "

What explains Banier's uncanny ability to forge these high-end friendships? Was it relentless networking, calculation, and chutzpah, as his critics claimed, or was there something else involved? Banier runs his hand through sparse strands of hair and considers the question. "You know, these famous people, they came to me for the most part," he says after a long pause. "For certain people, at the time, I didn't have an ugly face. Or it was my vivacity, or my interest for them. I can't say why." How about charm, charisma, seduction? He scoffs at the suggestion. "I am not at all a seducer. I do not try. These things happen on another level, through dialogue."

Banier's elbow-rubbing with celebrities opened doors for him in unexpected places.

133

Pascal Greggory introduced him to film stars like Isabelle Adjani, Johnny Depp, and Vanessa Paradis, with whom Banier developed close friendships. Depp and Paradis, who considered him practically a member of the family, asked him to be the godfather of their first daughter, Lily-Rose, now a budding film actress in her own right. Banier's contacts in the cinema world eventually led to bit parts in a dozen films, including works of major French directors like Robert Bresson and Éric Rohmer. Arielle Dombasle, who gave Banier a walk-on role in her 1982 film *Chassée-croisé,* recalls him as "an absolute nonconformist" whose provocations were "always a little frightening. As soon as he grabs you he wants to kiss you."

In 1985, Banier reentered the active literary world with a largely autobiographical novel entitled *Balthazar, fils de famille* (Balthazar, Son of the Family). It is the first-person story of a sensitive but alienated teenager who is smothered, harassed, and misunderstood by his parents. He is bright, curious, and self-centered with a mixture of narcissism and self-loathing. Like Banier's own father and mother, Balthazar's parents are bourgeois arrivistes who live on the avenue Victor-Hugo. The father is a Hungarian immigrant who changed his name and initially worked on an automobile assembly line. Rigid and humor-

134

less, he regularly beats his son for real and imagined transgressions. The mother is flaky, full of nutty ideas for moneymaking inventions, forever dispensing lessons to her son and criticizing his laziness and lack of direction. Like François-Marie, Balthazar is a dreamer who gets bad grades in school, sells his drawings on the street, attempts suicide, and forms his strongest friendships with older men and women: a widowed antiques dealer, an elderly writer, and, most intriguingly, his wealthy godmother, La Marraine.

Though the book was published two years before Banier's close friendship with Liliane Bettencourt began, his description of this cross-generational relationship, and Balthazar's cynical use of it, bears a striking resemblance to the real-life story that was still to come. Balthazar charms and flatters the older woman, telling her what an "extraordinary personage she was" for him. La Marraine takes him under her wing, gives him money, presents, paintings, and brings him everywhere with her — dining, shopping, apartment hunting. He advises her on all her purchases, asserting his authority to the point where the salespeople realize that "she's the one who pays, but I'm the one they must please."

One passage seems to mirror Banier's relationship with Madame Bettencourt so closely that Françoise Meyers's lawyers would later cite it in their court brief as proof of a modus operandi based on intentional manipulation: "I saw in her falsely distracted eyes that I was starting to please her. I could take her out. She needs someone to pay the check even if she gives me the money under the table, someone to open the door for her, to give her his arm . . . call her a taxi, pay her a compliment, someone who gives her the impression that she is a desired woman and tells her thank you." What does Banier make of the remarkable parallels? "*Balthazar* is a novel."

Though Banier showed little interest in politics, one of his most surprising friendships was with François Mitterrand, the Socialist Party leader who was France's president from 1981 to 1995. Considered a cynic and opportunist by some — he had started his political career with the collaborationist Vichy regime before joining the Resistance — Mitterrand engineered an electoral alliance between the French Socialists and Communists that in 1981 brought the left to power for the first time since Charles de Gaulle founded the Fifth Republic nearly a quarter century earlier. Mitterrand nationalized leading banks and industrial groups on coming to power, later denationalized them, and endowed Paris with imposing architectural projects, including the modernistic Opéra Bastille, the Arch of La Défense, and the Louvre pyramid. Mitterrand was also one of the most charismatic and seductive figures of his time, a magnetic personality who could win the loyalties of men and the hearts of women with equal ease. His female conquests were legendary and mostly discreet — until he arranged to have his mistress and their love child play a front-row role alongside his wife and sons at his 1996 funeral.

Banier first met Mitterrand in 1972, when Françoise Giroud, powerful editor of the newsweekly *L'Express,* introduced the two men at a press conference. Banier was already known as a promising young novelist, and Mitterrand, who had a lifelong passion for books and literature, took a keen interest in his work. Their relationship blossomed after Mitterrand's election, when Banier became a regular guest at Élysée luncheons. Christiane Dufour, one of Mitterrand's secretaries at the time, recalls that Banier was at the presidential palace so often that he was practically "part of the woodwork." Mitterrand also brought Banier along on many of his state visits. Former foreign minister Hubert Védrine, who served as Mitterrand's chief of staff, was present at many of the president's meetings with Banier. "Mitterrand was amused by him," he recalls. "They would chat in his office, or go out to visit bookstores together."

Today, Banier still speaks of Mitterrand

with reverence.

Banier also owes Mitterrand an extraordinary boost to his photographic career. On one of his presidential trips, he introduced Banier to Hélène Ahrweiler, then director of the Pompidou Center, one of France's leading cultural showplaces. Reportedly at Mitterrand's urging, Ahrweiler offered Banier a retrospective exhibition of his portraits — an unheard-of honor for a photographer who had never even had a gallery show! Banier's 1991 exhibition, which featured portraits of celebrities and street people, drew record crowds and instantly put him on the map as a serious photographer.

The Pompidou show was the occasion for an even more important turning point in Banier's career: Liliane Bettencourt's decision to finance his work. Their acquaintance went back more than two decades, but the event that triggered their very special relationship was a single photo session in 1987. Nicole Wisniak, editor of the cult magazine *Egoïste,* landed a rare interview with Liliane Bettencourt and got her talking about the trials and tribulations of being France's wealthiest woman. Wisniak chose Banier for the photo shoot.

Banier didn't know what to expect when he arrived at the Bettencourts' mansion in Neuilly. "At the time, she was a very, very great beauty," he says. Liliane, though sixty-five at the time, still boasted the trim figure and high cheekbones of a film star. "I did her a lot of good because I was frank with her," he recalls. Indeed, Banier talked to her bluntly the way no one else dared: He didn't like her hairstyle — a bouffant helmet glued with L'Oréal hair spray — and insisted that she change her pants.

The resulting black-and-white photos betray an unspoken complicity between the photographer and his model. The first one, occupying a full left-hand page in the magazine, features Liliane seated on an ottoman with a long, elegantly manicured hand draped over her knee. She wears an open tweed jacket over a cashmere sweater and no jewelry apart from her wedding band. Her clear eyes stare straight into the camera with a seductive gaze enhanced by the half-smile on her lips. It's the kind of gaze that could rivet a man across a crowded room and make him wish that he, or she, were single. In the second photo, appearing on a right-hand page, Liliane wears a white blouse with gray trim and French cuffs. The full-cut woolen pants, pleated at the beltline, show off her slender waist and narrow hips. Her arms are folded in front of her, the face is tilted slightly forward, the eyes turned demurely downward. Compared to the come-hither look of the first photo, this one evokes modesty and mystery. But it too radiates a powerful sensual attraction.

At forty, Banier no longer had the Adonis-like beauty of his youth, but enough remained of his curls and tall, lanky stature to catch Liliane's eye. "The first time I saw you, I thought you were something special," she later wrote him, "that there was something unsaid and seductive." The proof of that, she said, was in the photos he took that day. She told him he reminded her of her father with his forthright gait. "It was an extraordinary encounter," Banier recalls. "After that, the relationship developed progressively."

Four years later, Banier ran into a problem while preparing the book that was to accompany his show at the Pompidou Center. Yves Saint Laurent, who took a keen interest in Banier's photography and had financed earlier projects, offered to pay the 250,000 francs (about $50,000) that Gallimard publishers were demanding to produce the book. But he had one condition: Saint Laurent wanted Banier to include a photo of his partner, Pierre Bergé. Banier howled. He was angry with Bergé at the time and said he'd rather not even do a book if it came to that.

After several unsuccessful attempts to find funding, Banier went to see Liliane Bettencourt. She immediately said yes. He returned to the Bettencourt home later to show Liliane and her husband a dummy of his book, *Photographies*. Liliane was fascinated by a certain photo — an old lady in a worn black coat and thick black stockings walking hunched over on a gray sidewalk and clutching a plastic bag. André said he didn't find it very interesting. Liliane slammed her hand down on the book, which fell on the ground, and shouted, "Well *I* find it interesting! Because it's life."

It was at that precise moment, perhaps, that Liliane Bettencourt decided to support the career of this little-known artist. Not only because she recognized his talent, but because he brought her something that she craved — *life.*

CHAPTER 5
SUCH GOOD FRIENDS

To Banier's critics, his only aim was to take the L'Oréal heiress for as much money as possible. Greed was doubtless part of the mix, but theirs was a profound and complex relationship. Whatever material interests motivated him, Banier had a deep and genuine affection for her. She apparently felt something stronger for him. As Liliane described the relationship in a 2008 letter to Banier: "With you, I am like a mother, a lover, all the feelings pass through me. It makes me tremble." Given the age difference and Banier's sexual preferences, there was apparently no physical intimacy between them — "good thing I never intended to sleep with François-Marie Banier," she quipped to her financial adviser. But according to Banier's confiscated notebooks (now part of the court record), Liliane longed for more physical closeness and wondered why they couldn't at least hold hands. For nearly a quarter of a century, they carried on a platonic love affair.

That Liliane was in love with Banier seemed obvious to several of her close friends. Lucienne de Rozier, her neighbor and friend for fifty years, said Liliane was like a *midinette* — a giddy teenager — when she was around Banier. "She fell in love with François-Marie Banier . . . She was fascinated by him to the point of stupefaction."

Banier's friend Gilles Brücker, who also developed a close relationship with Liliane, says she was "not only in love with Banier, she was someone who needed to have affectionate relationships and she was seductive with a lot of people. She flattered men with her words and gestures. She cultivated an image. She had an extraordinary physique for a woman of her age. She was a seductive woman who had a need to seduce." Her relationship with Banier, he says, was "real, affectionate, and loving."

Banier himself insists that Liliane was "never in love" with him, but it is difficult to deny that there was a powerful emotional attachment between them. The nature of their relationship is documented by the 500-plus pages of selected correspondence, ranging over two decades, that Banier's lawyers would later place in the court record. They write about literature, travels, art, movies, Banier's books and exhibitions, Liliane's health. On Liliane's side, there are numerous references to her father, criticisms of her daughter and son-in-law, and effusive words of affection for her dachshund Toma — "my beautiful child," she calls him, something that she would never say about Françoise. (Toma, by the way, was fed a diet of fresh fish and Volvic mineral water and sported a silver dog collar by Hermès.) There are frequent terms of endearment: Banier calls her *"ma petite chérie";* she writes "I kiss you tenderly."

Françoise's lawyers would later point to their voluminous correspondence — totaling in all more than two thousand letters and faxes — as proof that Banier was seeking to maintain his influence over Liliane through the sheer quantity of these exchanges and the flattering language that he often used. Jean-Pierre Meyers recounted that in 1995, while his family was vacationing with the Bettencourts at Arcouest, Liliane would often leave the swimming pool before lunch and dash into the house to check for new faxes from Banier. "That's when we realized that the relationship between Madame Bettencourt and Monsieur Banier was deepening." It was indeed, but it seems strange to reduce the exchanges to a simple vehicle of manipulation by Banier. After all, Liliane was writing him as often, perhaps even more, than he wrote her. The letters and faxes give evidence of a complex relationship that runs the gamut from affection, humor, and intellectual curiosity to flattery, jealousy, and, yes, self-interest. But above all, they are proof of a powerful bond between the correspondents.

For Liliane, it was far more than a friendship: It was a lifeline. Before she met Banier, her social world was confined to L'Oréal meetings, tea with the same old friends, and dinner parties with important people who tended to be business associates, bankers, or André's political connections. There was little to stimulate her curious mind, no one who shared her unformed but avid taste for art and literature. She was drowning in wealth and luxury, but she longed for something more. "Liliane was rich, she was beautiful, and she was bored to death," says her former lawyer Georges Kiejman.

Lucienne de Rozier recalls that the heiress was in a state of "grave depression" through much of the 1980s, often staying in bed and complaining of various illnesses "though there was nothing wrong with her." De Rozier thought her friend's maladies were psychosomatic, but to Liliane they were very real, particularly the back and hip pains that resulted from no fewer than four separate falls. "My health was bad for ten years," she later recalled. "I was very much alone and desperate after the fourth accident, fearing I would never walk again."

When Banier arrived on the scene, he immediately put some spice into her life. Brash, provocative, iconoclastic, he had none of the kowtowing deference that she was accustomed to. He would criticize her clothes, her hairstyle, playfully call her names at times, even as he flattered her and praised her beauty, her intellect, her sensitivity. Banier also talked to her about books and philosophy and art, things that were not part of André's dinnertime conversation. And he brought her out of her shell, introducing her to artists, writers, and actors, escorting her to art galleries, museums, theaters, auction houses. As Liliane put it, "he renovated me."

In the great Parisian tradition, they would spend hours talking together in cafés or dining in fine restaurants. Over twenty years, they frequented most of the capital's best-known establishments, but they had their particular favorites. Among them was Rech, on the boulevard des Ternes, founded in 1925 by an Alsatian who, like Eugène Schueller's father, had migrated to Paris after the First World War in order to remain French. Liliane especially liked Rech (now owned by superstar chef Alain Ducasse) because her father had often taken her there as a girl. Laurent, a former royal hunting pavilion located in a park along the Champs-Élysées, was another favorite, both for its elegant décor and its haute-cuisine menu. Not least among their regular eating spots was Le Grand Véfour, with its ornately painted walls and ceilings, nestled under the colonnades of the Palais Royal Garden. The sumptuous interior is virtually unchanged since the late eighteenth century, when the Véfour was a favorite meeting place of the capital's political and literary intelligentsia. One thing these three establishments have in common is a pricey menu, ranging from €100 to more than €300 per person. (Liliane usually paid.)

The downside of such places was the background noise, which made it difficult for Liliane to follow the conversation. It was partly for that reason that they often dined at home, either at Banier's place or at the Bettencourts', where they were usually joined by André. By all accounts, he and Banier had a cordial relationship — though there were times when even Liliane's reserved and mild-mannered husband lost his temper over his guest's verbal excesses, snapping on at least one occasion: "You do not raise your voice at my table."

Liliane had always loved to travel. As her relationship with Banier developed, she would invite him to join her and André at their vacation homes in Brittany, Cap de Formentor, or the Seychelles. Banier reciprocated by hosting the Bettencourts at Le Patron, his villa in the south of France, or at the palatial English country estate of his friend Lord Cholmondeley. Years later, after André's death, Liliane would come alone to Le Patron or travel abroad with Banier and his partner Martin d'Orgeval. In September 2008, they attended the International Film Festival in Venice, cruised on the Grand Canal, and danced on the famous Piazza San Marco. The following year, they flew to New York, where they shopped, took in the museums, and lunched with fashion designer Diane von Furstenberg, a longtime friend of Banier's, at her lower Manhattan shop. "She wore a bright orange scarf," von Furstenberg recalls. "She was happy, she looked very young. I'll always remember the first thing she said to me was, 'Is it easy to find good domestic help in New York?' "

What did Banier get out of the relationship? He was obviously attracted by Liliane's wealth, but it was much more than that. All his life, he had forged close relationships with older women, perhaps as surrogates for the narcissistic mother who never gave him the affection he craved. Banier insists that Liliane was not a stand-in mother for him: They shared an "adult" bond in which each party was on an equal footing. Their relationship, he says, was a "current" that passed between them. "Through me there was a vision, there was light," says Banier, "there was something that fulfilled her and pushed her."

Diane von Furstenberg offers this shrewd analysis of the relationship: "You have two people who meet, they both charm one another. He charms her with his intellect, he's funny, takes her to exhibitions. For the first time in her life she has fun, is stimulated intellectually. And she charms him with the only thing she knows. She couldn't compete with anything else but her money."

Liliane's "patronage" had begun with the 250,000 francs she paid for the photo book that accompanied his Pompidou Center exhibition in 1991. Though their friendship deepened over the next few years, the heiress did not offer him any more financial help until she came to lunch one day at Banier's place on the rue Servandoni. At that time, he owned three apartments in the five-story building, having bought out his former partner Jacques Grange in the mid-1970s. The first time Liliane came to lunch there, she was in a wheelchair suffering from debilitating back pains. Banier had since installed an elevator in the stairwell, largely to spare Liliane the four-flight climb to his dining room. She came two or three times a month, and the ritual was always the same: Her chauffeur would park in the delivery zone just across the street and open the rear door. Liliane, elegantly coiffed, impeccably dressed, would emerge from the car holding her purse in one hand and a small bag in the other. The bag contained the grilled bread and cheese that she always brought when she lunched with the artist — until he got fed up one day and told her it was rude to bring her own cheese.

One day in 1994, over a simple meal provided by Banier's cook, Liliane leaned back from the round wooden table and peered through the window at an apartment across the courtyard.

"François-Marie, you need more space," she said. "You like fine things; me too. I have the means to suit your tastes. And to start with, you're going to buy that apartment across the way."

"What for?"

"You'll need it. One day you will put your archives in there."

Good as her word, Liliane set up a *société civile immobilière* (SCI), a private real-estate investment company, and started to buy property for Banier, who was the titular co-owner. She later set up two other SCIs with Banier, providing the cash for apartments that were used by the artist for archives and studios. In 1997, she gifted her shares in the companies to Banier, making him owner of the entire building on the rue Servandoni, the same building where I would meet him almost twenty years later.

Between 1994 and 1999, Banier and Liliane cruised the galleries and auction houses in search of master paintings to enliven what he called her "sinister" house. Their purchases — paid by Liliane but chosen on Banier's advice — hung in the reception rooms, on the walls along the curved staircase, and in the upstairs bedrooms. The family's collection included other works inherited from Liliane's father, including a large Monet that Banier considered "hideous," but these more recent acquisitions had a special meaning for Liliane.

On February 23, 2001, she accompanied Banier to the offices of her notary, Jean-Michel Normand. In the downstairs hallway of Normand's building, just before entering the elevator, she told her friend the purpose of the visit. "I have decided to give you the paintings that we bought together," she said. "It's a road we have traveled together, it's our history."

Normand, somewhat surprised, proceeded to register the twelve paintings as *nue propriété,* meaning the heiress would keep and enjoy the works during her lifetime but Banier would inherit them. The collection, which included canvases by Picasso, Matisse, Léger, Mondrian, Braque, and Munch, among others, was valued at some €17 million at the time. (It is currently estimated at €90 million.) Liliane paid an additional 60 percent of the declared value in the form of gift taxes so that Banier would not be billed when the works came into his possession. Normand later said that he had no doubt Liliane was a lucid and willing donor: "She knew exactly what she wanted, and she stayed on course."

In a codicil to her will, the heiress called this extraordinary gift a "token of my gratitude for the moral and affective aid that François-Marie Banier has offered me. I will add that I would never have made this collection of paintings without him. I am indebted to him on an emotional level for his long and constant support — I have been through some difficult moments. As strange as it might seem, he has been a great help even on business matters."

Liliane's gratitude apparently knew no bounds. From 1997 to 2002, she named Banier in her will as the beneficiary on five *assurance vie* contracts. This type of contract is a sort of hybrid between a brokerage account and a US life-insurance policy. These instruments tend to gain value dramatically over the years, meaning that the potential payout to Banier down the line was in the hundreds of millions. (It did not endear him to Françoise that one of the contracts had originally been in her name.) Meanwhile, Liliane continued to provide Banier with millions of euros in cash and checks to "permit him to carry out his projects."

As always, she presented her gifts as a form of patronage to further Banier's artistic endeavors. But it was more than that. The money she gave Banier was the emblem of her personal liberty, her identity, her free will. Over two decades, she made it clear that this was her own decision and she drew enormous satisfaction from It. To Liliane, the fortune she gave Banier was not just money: It was an act of love that she could not express in other terms. It was also, perhaps, a means of punishing her daughter for her perceived shortcomings.

Liliane's largesse financed more than Banier's artistic activities: It enabled him to acquire a substantial amount of real estate in addition to his compound on the rue Servandoni. Between 1998 and 2003, he purchased four apartments on the rue de Vaugirard, a prime Left Bank location overlooking the stately Luxembourg Gardens, the fifty-six-acre park adjoining the Palais du Luxembourg, former palace of Queen Marie de' Medici (1575–1642) and currently the home of the French Senate.

In June 2007, Liliane cashed in a life-insurance contract worth €82.9 million (on which she paid €49.7 million in taxes) and gave the proceeds to Banier. He immediately put the funds into three new contracts, one in his name and the other two in the names of Martin d'Orgeval and Pascal Greggory. Using his own policy as a sort of cash machine, he drew large sums from it to buy artworks, a house in Marrakesh, and improvements on his villa in the south of France.

In addition to her personal support, Liliane arranged for L'Oréal to grant two generous contracts to Banier — one that sponsored his international photo exhibitions and books, another that paid him a hefty fee as an "artistic adviser." It was thanks to L'Oréal that Banier had twenty-eight photo shows from Tokyo, Rome, and Munich to Milan, Budapest, and Paris, among others, each accompanied by a glossy catalogue. Liliane and André would often attend the openings. The heiress looked forward to these events and even took tango lessons before flying to Buenos Aires for Banier's exhibition there in 2000. On that occasion she showed off her footwork in a *confitería,* one of the local pastry salons that offer tango dancing along with fancy sweets. That was a long way from the stuffy dinner parties she had known before meeting Banier.

The L'Oréal contracts, first signed in 1994, were eventually worth €710,000 a year to Banier. The business benefit to the company was questionable, but Lindsay Owen-Jones, L'Oréal's CEO at the time, went along with the sweetheart deal essentially to please Madame Bettencourt, on whom his job depended. "I make money for Liliane, and you make her live," he told Banier. When the contracts were renewed for ten years in 2001, Banier expressed his thanks to Owen-Jones

— known to his colleagues as OJ — in a rather fawning letter of October 24, 2001: "I am well aware that L'Oréal's aid is exceptional. Few artists in the world have, over such a long period, this boost, this tranquility, this freedom."

Banier's lucrative contracts with L'Oréal gave an ironic meaning to one of the company's best-known advertising slogans: "Because I'm Worth It." Was he worth it to L'Oréal? Not in any quantifiable way, though he claimed to "show that L'Oréal could be something other than a seller of mousse and hair spray . . . something more poetic." Was he worth it to Liliane? Apparently so.

Why did the heiress deem it so important to sponsor the work of this little-known photographer? Perhaps it was a means of self-validation. Liliane was fascinated by creative people, starting with her father. But she was not creative herself: She didn't write poetry or paint or play music, and in fact had only a secondary school education. When she latched on to Banier (and vice versa), she finally saw her chance to be creative: With her money and L'Oréal's sponsorship, she could "make" Banier as an artist. "What I want is for you to be known," she wrote him. His success would be her success, his creativity would be a projection of her own — to the point where she would tell friends "we" are putting on an exhibition when talking of

Banier's shows.

"She wanted him to succeed, she wanted to give him what he did not have, open the door to glory," says Liliane's friend Claude Delay. "She was intelligent enough to realize that she had never done much apart from inheriting from her father. She had a lot of good sense, and a need to exteriorize herself. Banier was her main means of doing that. She knows, at bottom, that she made him."

To a large extent, Liliane assumed the dominant role. Banier put it bluntly: "She's a woman who imposes her will on a man." That claim might seem baldly self-serving coming from a person suspected of manipulating the heiress like a guru. But it was corroborated by no less a figure than Jean-Michel Normand, the notary who registered all of Liliane's gifts to Banier and had many occasions to observe the pair up close at these critical moments. "It is Madame Bettencourt who takes the lead in this relationship," he insisted. "In spite of all Banier's gesticulations, this woman seems stronger than him." Though a man of the law, and not a psychologist, Normand offered up an insightful analysis of the relationship's underpinnings: "Each one got what they needed out of this situation. Madame Bettencourt had someone near her who liberated her from a very formal environment — a husband who was rather stiff, and a daughter with whom she had difficult relations — and Monsieur Banier drew considerable financial advantages while giving the impression that he felt protected by the presence of Madame Bettencourt."

Some of Liliane's close friends were astounded to see her shower such enormous sums on her protégé. They found it totally out of character in a woman who could be generous on occasion, but who was a notorious penny-pincher in her daily life. Monique de Libouton, who had known Liliane since 1942, described her as "stingy" and said it was always "a battle" to get her to accept the slightest raises for her employees. Lucienne de Rozier, another intimate, said, "Liliane was quite miserly. Whenever she had to give someone a wedding present, she was in turmoil. That's why I find the level of these donations staggering." Liliane herself, in her famous 1987 interview with *Egoïste,* admitted that she "detests overpaying" for anything. "It makes me ill. I don't like to waste money." Yet within a few years of giving that interview, she was shoveling millions into the open arms of an obscure artist. What happened?

It wasn't just that Banier stimulated her, flattered her, and made her laugh. And it wasn't just that he opened doors to the worlds of art and culture. Beyond all that, Liliane was enthralled by his person, his good looks, his quirky character, his scintillating conversation. She was impressed by Banier's early literary success and his exotic frequentations. Even his homosexuality must have intrigued and, in some strange way, attracted her.

The French have a colorful term — *s'encanailler* — which roughly means slumming, hanging out with rakish types from a different social milieu. That was undoubtedly part of the magnetism that drew her to François-Marie. "I don't like blandness, I like salt," she told *Egoïste*. "Naturally I like honest people better than dishonest people . . . But then again some unprincipled souls (*vicieux*) are very intelligent." She wasn't talking about Banier there — she hardly knew him at the time — and *vicieux* is too strong a word for his brand of iconoclastic nonconformity. But something in that remark suggests that Liliane was ripe for a walk on the wild side. Banier, who not only photographed the heiress for *Egoïste* but helped edit the interview text, must have taken note.

There was another thing that made Banier immensely attractive to Liliane: He reminded her of her adored father, Eugène Schueller. Over the years, the identification between Banier and Schueller became a leitmotif of their conversation and correspondence. Banier played on this, and even took to ending his letters "HLC" — an acronym for one of Schueller's favorite expressions: *"Haut les cœurs"* (keep a stout heart). "It's obvious that you're part crazy," she once told Banier. "So was my father. That's also a way to be far ahead of the others." In 2003, Liliane wrote to her notary: "I spoke to François-Marie as I spoke to my father — we went into deep things — which I needed."

At first glance, it would be hard to find two men more different from each other than François-Marie Banier and Eugène Schueller. Banier is tall and trim; Schueller was short and squat. Banier, at least in his youth, was an Adonis; Schueller, even young, looked more like Charlie Chaplin than a Greek god. Banier is an artist, writer, and romantic; Schueller was a scientist, inventor, and businessman. Banier is a homosexual half-Jew; Schueller was heterosexual, a staunch Catholic, and arguably an anti-Semite. Liliane might say that they were both creative types, but there is a vast difference between writing a novel or taking a photo and building a capitalist empire. Yet in Liliane's eyes, the two men had some fundamental things in common: a compulsive work ethic, an intellectual curiosity, a charismatic personality, and an outsize belief in themselves and their destiny. But the most important thing they shared was the blind admiration of Liliane Bettencourt.

As Françoise tells it, her idyllic relationship with her mother suddenly ended with the incident of 1993, when she says Banier insulted André Bettencourt over lunch at Arcouest, the family's villa in Brittany. After that, she told her parents that she no longer wanted to associate with the intrusive artist. As Banier insinuated himself more and more into the family life, Françoise found herself progressively shut out. She claims that it was only under Banier's influence that Liliane Bettencourt grew cool, even hostile, toward her daughter. "I got along very well with my mother until 1993. After 1993, things changed because Monsieur Banier took up more and more space. My mother knew that I did not appreciate him, and the subject became taboo."

Banier is baffled by Françoise's story. "There was no incident!" He says he got along fine with Françoise during his visit to Arcouest in July 1993. He remembers that voices were raised, but denies attacking André personally. It was an argument about music, he recalls. André, Françoise, and her husband liked French singer Charles Aznavour; Liliane and Banier preferred Serge Gainsbourg. So what? People disagree and argue all the time. If Françoise was so outraged, why did she agree to pull Banier behind her motorboat when he went water skiing that afternoon? And if André was so insulted, why did he continue to receive Banier in his house, invite him to the Bettencourts' private island in the Seychelles, and attend his photo exhibitions?

Clearly Françoise Meyers and François-Marie Banier saw the world through different lenses.

The two first crossed paths in 1981, on the set of Arielle Dombasle's film *Chassé-croisé,* in which Banier's then companion Pascal Greggory played the lead role and Banier himself had a bit part. Françoise was there as an adviser on Greek mythology, one of the film's themes. Banier made no particular impression on her at that time. She took more notice of him when he showed up at the Bettencourt home in 1987 to photograph Liliane for *Egoïste.* It was at that point that Banier's special friendship with Liliane began, though Françoise did not realize the extent of their bond for a long time. Françoise and Banier met again at Arcouest in 1990, apparently without any unpleasantness. Three years later, over what she remembers as a stormy lunch, the austere Carmelite quietly swore her enmity toward this brash infidel.

According to Françoise and those employees who later testified against Banier, the photographer was constantly hovering around the Bettencourt home, arriving unannounced and uninvited, often going directly to Liliane's room and even lying down on her bed when he felt like it. Although his visits became more frequent over time, it would have been difficult for him to impose his presence to that extent if only because Liliane Bettencourt's schedule was chockablock with meetings and obligations from morning till night.

On a typical day, the heiress would rise at seven a.m., have a bowl of muesli in her room, and peruse the morning papers. Then she would do some light stretches and undergo physical therapy sessions with her personal osteopath, followed by acupuncture treatments to ease her chronic back pains. After a visit by her hairdresser, she would meet with her chambermaid to choose her clothes from a well-stocked wardrobe, arranged according to color, that included dozens of silk scarves by Hermès, hundreds of cashmere sweaters by Loro Piana, ballerina flats and sneakers by Repetto, countless pairs of custom-made shoes, pantsuits by the likes of Yves Saint Laurent and Chanel, and more than fifty evening gowns by top haute-couture houses. One thing Liliane never wore was perfume — she was allergic to it and even forbade her staff to use it. Her aversion is more than a little ironic, since part of her personal fortune was based on the many perfume brands that L'Oréal had acquired over the years and relentlessly promoted.

At precisely 1:15 p.m., Liliane would take her place in the dining room and have lunch, usually with a guest and André when he was at home. The daily menu varied — generally fish, as Liliane does not eat meat — but her dessert was always a baked apple. After lunch she would walk for an hour in the nearby Bois de Boulogne, then return to her home for a marathon round of meetings with L'Oréal managers, bankers, lawyers, and financial advisers. She also spent several hours each day reading L'Oréal reports and documents. At dinner, the Bettencourts received friends, dignitaries, diplomats, politicians — usually no more than six people at a time, because Liliane had trouble following the conversations if there were too many guests at the table. And every Sunday, Françoise and her family came to lunch, a ritual that André apparently appreciated more than Liliane.

Banier's visits had to be sandwiched into Liliane's tight schedule. He says he would usually see her no more than forty-five minutes at a time and that most of his rendezvous were inscribed in her appointment book. "On average, I visited her four times a month. Over twenty years, there were not more than thirty or so impromptu visits." To be sure, he was a frequent luncheon or dinner guest, often in the presence of André, and was occasionally invited to join the Bettencourts at their homes at Cap de Formentor, Arcouest, and the island of d'Arros. And of course, he and Liliane found time to attend auctions, museums, and gallery openings.

The truth probably lies somewhere between Banier's modest claims and Françoise's charges that he was an omnipresent bloodsucker. What cannot be denied is that the photographer was a special, and welcome, friend in the home and life of Liliane Bettencourt. And to his mind, the attention he gave her was also a gift, part of the unspoken reciprocity that defined their relationship.

As Liliane's favors to Banier accumulated, one person looked on with increasing dismay. Claire Thibout had been hired in 1995 as an accountant for Clymène, the company that manages Liliane Bettencourt's investments. In reality, Thibout spent 80 percent of her time overseeing Liliane's personal affairs. In addition to handling Clymène's payroll, she managed all the Bettencourts' domestic personnel and kept the books on Liliane's finances, including her payouts to Banier. A hard-nosed woman with a helmet of blond hair that seemed to hide half her face, she was a powerful figure in the Bettencourt household, trusted by Liliane, feared by many of the employees, and looked on with suspicion by the photographer.

"Claire is someone who can be off-putting at first," says her lawyer Antoine Gillot. "She doesn't talk much. She's not someone who seems very warm." The mother of two young children and wife of a computer technician, she is the one who wears the pants in the family, says Gillot, who praises her rigorous "sense of duty."

Banier initially tried to win Claire over with a charm offensive. The first time they met, she said she had "never laughed so much." He would sometimes flatter her by asking her advice on various matters. But Claire was not moved. As she observed Banier's increasing influence — and the number of checks that flew into his pocket — she was frankly appalled. "They would go to restaurants, often the Ritz, or chez Laurent or other grand restaurants," she later recalled. "They would call either her secretary or her maid to make sure they put her checkbook in her handbag. It was a ritual. And he asked her for sums of money. There were lots of little checks for €100,000, €200,000. Sometimes they did dozens like that . . ." The accountant was not exaggerating the amounts. According to official court records, the total of Liliane's cash gifts to Banier between 1997 and 2005 alone totaled some €32 million — not counting the far greater value of the real estate, life-insurance policies, and outright gifts of artworks.

For a long time, Claire looked on silently and did her job. But she was in an awkward position, especially when she went over the

Bettencourts' taxes with André at the end of each year. André raised an eyebrow the first time he noticed the SCIs that Liliane had set up for Banier.

"What's this all about?" he asked the accountant.

"Oh, that's just some real estate operations, don't worry about it."

He shrugged and moved on to another item. It was his wife who had the money and made investments as she saw fit. His task was to look over the tax returns at year's end, but not to question Liliane's decisions. Moreover, Liliane had told Claire not to inform her husband about the details of her gifts to Banier. She also took care to register them with Jean-Michel Normand, the notary she shared with Banier, rather than the usual family notary so that André would not know the extent of her generosity. (In France, notaries are public officers who play a far more important role than US notary publics: They are trained lawyers who prepare deeds, wills, and other documents; register acts of sale; and advise clients on matters of civil law.)

"Monsieur Bettencourt did not know everything," said André's secretary Chantal Trovel. "Madame Bettencourt never talked to him about that." Even if he did know, or suspect, that Liliane was giving substantial sums to Banier, André was hardly in a position to protest. "After all," says Liliane's former lawyer Georges Kiejman, "wasn't he himself supported all his life by his wife? That made it difficult for him to tell her, 'You can't do what you want with your money.'"

But there were times when Liliane herself appeared to have second thoughts about the seemingly endless flow of gifts. On Monday, December 16, 2002, Claire telephoned Banier and asked to see him at his home. She was ushered into his sitting room at ten a.m. Banier was waiting for her, seated on a small red couch, surrounded by his precious collection of leather-bound books, paintings, and bric-a-brac.

"You must have guessed that I haven't come to give you good news," Claire announced with a forced smile. "Madame has decided to call a halt. That's it. No more."

Banier burst out laughing — that loud full-throated laugh that his friends found amusing, but to the accountant it was edged with mockery and intimidation.

"Why are you laughing?"

"Because you seem so distressed. It's of no importance at all."

Thibout stared at him, baffled.

"She can do what she wants," Banier went on, "give to whomever she wants, and she also has the right to stop giving. Let's just drop the subject."

As Banier recalls the scene, the accountant

suddenly slipped out of her "messenger of death" role and expressed concern for his future once the spigot was shut off.

"But what are you going to do?"

"Work, paint, write. Voilà."

That afternoon, Liliane called. She sounded upset, out of breath. "I'm not feeling well," she told him. "It's something internal that's not right."

Banier hopped on his motor scooter and headed for Neuilly. When he arrived at the Bettencourt home, he found the heiress in a state of near panic.

"My time is counted now," she said. "You told Claire you're going to work?"

"Yes."

"But we can't just leave you by the roadside."

He knew she would back down. And she did.

The following spring, Claire tried to block what she considered a new extravagance. Upon opening Madame Bettencourt's mail, part of her job, she stumbled upon a letter from the Cardif insurance company concerning a policy worth €253 million. Liliane had written the company on March 21, 2003, to name Banier as the beneficiary. Assuming it was an error, the accountant asked Liliane about it. The heiress confessed she'd made a mistake and asked Claire to help her "recover" the policy. Liliane wrote to the company on April 1, 2003, nullifying Banier's designation. But for reasons that are unclear, she changed her mind again and confirmed Banier's status as beneficiary on May 20, 2003.

Of all the things Liliane sought to give Banier, certainly the most exotic was the Seychelles island of d'Arros, a 1.5-square-mile oval of sandy beaches, palm groves, and limpid waters that formerly belonged to a nephew of the shah of Iran. Liliane and André bought the island in 1997 for $18 million, then poured some €50 million into upgrading its installations with new bungalows, an enlarged landing strip, and housing for thirty-five permanent employees. The couple visited d'Arros three or four times a year, often in the company of Banier, Martin d'Orgeval, and other friends. Françoise and her family were never once invited there.

Liliane's determination to keep d'Arros out of Françoise's hands was at least one motive behind the complicated transfer of ownership engineered by her business lawyer Fabrice Goguel. "In no case did she want the island to go to her daughter," Goguel explained. "She wanted to give it to François-Marie Banier." Along with a Swiss colleague, Goguel created a Lichtenstein-based foundation to which ownership of d'Arros was transferred in November 2006. Though the Bettencourts continued to rent the island from the foundation, its ultimate "beneficiaries" were François-Marie Banier and three medical associations run by his friend Gilles Brücker.

But Banier never did gain possession of the island paradise, which was finally sold in 2011 to a company owned by a Saudi billionaire. Apart from its monetary value, perhaps, Banier did not seem to be especially attached to the place. Questioned about his links to d'Arros in July 2010, Banier told investigators: "I detest this island, it is full of mosquitoes, it is tiny, and it's very humid. On top of all that, there are sharks. I hate islands."

CHAPTER 6
DARK ROOTS

Monday, May 6, 1991. Seth Goldschlager was awakened by an early phone call from Maurice Lévy, president of the Publicis advertising and media group. L'Oréal had been one of the company's main accounts since the days of Eugène Schueller, and Lévy was a close personal friend of the Bettencourts. Goldschlager headed the crisis management team at Publicis. And this was a crisis.

Had Goldschlager read the papers, Lévy asked. He had not. Lévy told him to hurry over to L'Oréal headquarters. "We're about two hours away from an international Jewish boycott."

Goldschlager hopped in a taxi and headed for the drab suburb of Clichy, just north of Paris. He was greeted in the corporate boardroom by a grim-faced trio: former L'Oréal CEO François Dalle; the current CEO, Lindsay Owen-Jones; and the company's chief outside counsel, Jean-Marie Degueldre. What they told him amounted, in Goldschlager's words, to a "total disaster" and "the beginning of a six-year crisis management job."

It all started in September 1987 when the recently retired Dalle joined forces with his friend Jean Frydman to form a film production and distribution company called Paravision. At age seventy, Dalle was a legend in the business world after his brilliant twenty-eight-year tenure at the head of L'Oréal. Frydman, then sixty-three, one of France's most influential figures in the audiovisual and advertising world, was a dual French-Israeli citizen with close ties to Shimon Peres and Yitzhak Rabin. Paravision was created as a subsidiary of L'Oréal, which put up 75 percent of the capital while Frydman provided the rest in the form of film catalogues containing the rights to some of the greatest cinema classics. Boasting an initial capital of $200 million, their aim was to become one of Europe's leading film distributors.

But the venture soon soured when the L'Oréal partners began to question the commercial value of the films that Frydman acquired, they said, at inflated prices. In the summer of 1989, the company announced Frydman's departure. The exact circumstances are unclear: Dalle said his former partner had left as part of a common agreement, but Frydman claimed he had been fraudulently evicted and that the L'Oréal side had even forged his signature on a bogus letter of resignation.

If Dalle and his associates thought they could get rid of Frydman that easily, they were seriously mistaken. Frydman had been a fighter ever since he escaped from a deportation train to Buchenwald as a teenager and joined the Resistance. He claimed that his ejection from Paravision was part of L'Oréal's effort to mollify the Arab League and avoid falling under their boycott of Western companies that did business with Israel or had Israeli citizens on their payroll. L'Oréal's 1989 acquisition of the firm of Helena Rubenstein, an American Jew and fervent Zionist of Polish origin, had already attracted the attention of the Arab League. As a result of secret negotiations with the Damascus-based organization, L'Oréal agreed to provide the league with the names and nationalities of its officers (thereby violating a 1977 French law forbidding companies to cooperate with the boycotters). It was in order to avoid the wrath of the Arabs, Frydman claimed, that L'Oréal faked his resignation and expelled him from the company.

Dalle denied this, but Frydman and his brother David doggedly pursued the matter. What they discovered was a bombshell that posed a serious threat to L'Oréal's worldwide image. The man who had engineered the Helena Rubenstein acquisition and, according to Frydman, orchestrated his eviction from Paravision was Jacques Corrèze, head of L'Oréal's American subsidiary Cosmair. Corrèze was a man with a very dark past — Frydman called him "the personification of horror."

Corrèze had been a hard-core member of the far-right Cagoule during the late 1930s, an assistant to its leader Eugène Deloncle, and allegedly the perpetrator of some of the group's bloodiest terror attacks. Arrested in 1938, he was released from prison at the onset of the war and drafted into a tank regiment under de Gaulle's command. Following the armistice of June 1940, Corrèze rejoined Deloncle and served as an officer in his collaborationist groups, the MSR and the RNP, alongside Eugène Schueller. Among other nefarious deeds, Corrèze took part in the expropriation of Jewish properties and businesses in the name of the RNP.

In 1940, Corrèze moved into Deloncle's 16th arrondissement apartment, where together they ran a lumber-purchasing operation for the Occupation forces — perhaps the origin of his nickname, "La Bûche" (the log). During this time, Corrèze carried on a more-or-less open affair with Deloncle's wife, Mercedes (whom he would later marry after Deloncle's assassination). Deloncle's apartment also hosted lavish receptions attended by German and Vichy officials, at which Corrèze liked to parade around in a German officer's uniform. Not content with such posturing, Corrèze finally put some real skin in the Nazis' game: As his friend Schueller had recommended in his circular of July 29, 1941, Corrèze joined the Légion des volontaires français that year and fought on the eastern front as part of the Charlemagne Division of the Waffen-SS. He swore allegiance to Hitler on October 5, 1941.

After the liberation, Corrèze was arrested on the Italian border and convicted in 1948 of cooperation with the enemy. He was sentenced to ten years at hard labor, but released in 1949 as part of a national reconciliation. Schueller, by that time cleared of collaboration charges, opened the doors of L'Oréal to his former comrade.

Hired on January 15, 1950, Corrèze started out as a salesman but soon moved into a management role, working with subsidiaries in Spain, South America, and finally the United States, where he became the president and chief stockholder of L'Oréal's American subsidiary, Cosmair, in 1961.

Frydman was outraged to learn of Corrèze's continuing role in the company, and allegedly in his own sacking. At the end of 1990, he filed suit against L'Oréal for racial discrimination. On March 28, 1991, French police searched the company's corporate headquarters and the homes of several

L'Oréal managers, including Dalle, as part of the investigation. In particular, they were seeking evidence of the company's co-operation with the Arab boycott, a violation of both French and US law. At that point, L'Oréal officials knew they had a problem on their hands, but a manageable one as long as the investigation remained secret.

No such luck. On May 6, 1991, the news-weekly *Le Point* published a scoop that was widely echoed in the French press. It reported on Frydman's suit, the police raids at L'Oréal, the company's illegal dealings with the Arab League, and the sulfurous presence of ex-Cagoulard Jacques Corrèze at the helm of L'Oréal's US subsidiary. For good measure, the magazine recalled Schueller's links to the Cagoule and other far-right groups during the war.

"Before we knew it," says Goldschlager, "we had a bunch of governments on our backs — the US, the UK, Israel. It became a big legal case." Dalle was dumbfounded. "How can this be happening?" he asked his colleagues, though he did not help matters by flippantly telling the press that Frydman was just trying to make money in the "Shoah business."

In a follow-up attack, Jean and David Frydman appeared on a popular French TV show and denounced what they called the "parallel L'Oréal": a list of former Nazi collaborators who had been hired by Schueller after the war. One especially despicable character on their list was Jean Filliol, an ex-Cagoulard who was said to have carried out more than a hundred assassinations. As an officer of the Milice — the pro-German French paramilitaries — Filliol had helped the Waffen-SS prepare their infamous 1944 massacre of the village of Oradour-sur-Glane that left 642 townspeople dead, including 221 women and 247 children. Fleeing to Spain at war's end, Filliol was hired by L'Oréal's Spanish subsidiary, Procasa. L'Oréal, said Jean Frydman, "systematically sheltered criminals in the service of the Nazis, murderers from the Milice, and Wehrmacht veterans who had one thing in common: They had all been friends of Eugène Schueller."

The list contained several errors, and some of the employees turned out to be children or relatives of the actual collaborators, but there were enough genuine Cagoule and MSR alumni to show that Schueller had given safe haven to some very unsavory characters. And the renewed spotlight on the founder's own ambiguous conduct under the Occupation was a serious blow to L'Oréal's reputation. "Schueller was a brilliant researcher and businessman who took a very bad course to finance a bunch of thugs," says a L'Oréal adviser who worked on the case. "The Cagoule were the storm troopers of the French pro-Nazis. That's always been the cloud hanging over L'Oréal and the Bettencourt family, haunting André, Françoise, and Jean-Pierre."

The scandal was an unexpected trial by fire for Lindsay Owen-Jones, who had taken over as CEO in 1988 and was still trying to make his mark. "When the affair exploded, he was stunned," recalls Jean-Pierre Valériola, then L'Oréal's vice president in charge of public affairs. "He's English, he knew nothing about Schueller's past or the events that had taken place during the war. We were all in the blue, engulfed in uncertainty."

Owen-Jones was a wunderkind who had joined L'Oréal in 1969, at the age of twenty-three, after completing his studies at Oxford University. He started as an attaché to Dalle, who took a personal interest in his career and groomed him for bigger things. Owen-Jones worked in France, Italy, and the United States, where his results convinced Dalle that he was "the booster of sales that L'Oréal would need after me." Following the transitional chairmanship of Charles Zviak (1984–1988), Owen-Jones became, at age forty-two, the company's fourth CEO — and the first who had not known Schueller personally.

An avid yachtsman, golfer, and Formula 1 racing driver, the strong-chinned OJ was a dashing and dynamic leader with a reputation as a ladies' man and a relentless pursuer of corporate profits. Publicist Seth Goldschlager describes him as "a bundle of energy, decisive, a man who never wavers but can show flashes of anger. He became the 'Hunger Games' champion of L'Oréal. He rose to the top by vanquishing the competition."

The last thing this ambitious young CEO needed was to see the company engulfed in a public-relations nightmare because of its dealings with the Arab League and its harboring of an ex-Nazi. Speaking at an angry stockholders' meeting in May 1991, and fearing the threat of an international Jewish boycott, Owen-Jones tried to downplay Corrèze's place in the firm. At seventy-eight years old, Corrèze "no longer played any operational role in the company but occupied a honorary post," Owen-Jones declared, seemingly convinced by Corrèze's claim that he had never committed "the slightest attack against the Jews."

But one L'Oréal official was not content to let the matter lie: Jean-Pierre Meyers, the son-in-law that Liliane scorned as a "man with no character." Accompanied by his uncle, Rabbi Charles Liché, himself an Auschwitz survivor, Meyers met secretly with the veteran Nazi-hunter Serge Klarsfeld and consulted his documentation on Corrèze's past. Meyers, acting with uncharacteristic boldness, told his in-laws and Owen-Jones that the head of their US subsidiary had to go. Under pressure from Owen-Jones and threatened with a possible expulsion order by US authorities, Corrèze signed a letter of resignation on his deathbed on June 26, 1991. "I cannot change what happened," he wrote. "Allow me simply to express my most sincere regrets for the acts that I committed forty years ago and for their consequences, even indirect." He died of pancreatic cancer several hours later.

At that point, the conflict appeared headed for a peaceful resolution.

Apparently at the request of President Mitterrand, who feared grave economic damage to this important French firm, Frydman and Dalle in December 1991 agreed to withdraw their reciprocal suits. But after Owen-Jones refused to pay him indemnities, and even launched a countersuit, Jean Frydman and his brother David pulled out the heavy artillery. Aided by Klarsfeld, they dug up all of André Bettencourt's wartime articles in the German-financed paper *La Terre française* and republished them in February 1994 in a brochure entitled *Pour servir la mémoire* (in the service of memory). This privately printed document circulated discreetly until *Le Monde* published a full page on its revelations in February 1995.

By that time, Liliane was deeply involved in her relationship with Banier. He was a frequent guest at her home in Neuilly and her vacation villas in Brittany and Majorca, often with Martin d'Orgeval in tow. Their regular restaurant luncheons and visits to museums and galleries provided welcome distractions from the unpleasantness of the Frydman affair, which Liliane followed from a certain distance, content to let Owen-Jones and his PR team deal with the fallout. In February 1995, she had invited Banier and d'Orgeval to join her and André at the K-Club, a luxurious beach resort on the Caribbean island of Barbuda favored by such celebrities as Princess Diana and Robert de Niro. It was an ideal getaway — luxuriant palm trees, white sand, turquoise waters stretching to the horizon — much like the Seychelles island that the Bettencourts would buy four years later.

But on this occasion there was no getting away from bad news. *Le Monde*'s exposé detonated like a land mine in the middle of the Bettencourts' beach party. Liliane was furious over the articles, which also spotlighted her father's grim past. André cut the holiday short and rushed back to Paris to defend himself. Expressing his "apologies" to the Jewish community, he attributed his columns to "youthful error . . . I regret these writings and especially twenty or so lines on the Jews. But how can one insinuate that I could be anti-Semitic?" By way of exoneration, he told journalist Stéphane Trano, author of a critical biography of Mitterrand,

"We knew nothing about the arrests of Jews, the deportations to the extermination camps. We could not imagine the horror." Probably his deepest regret, though, was over the damage done to his own reputation: "After fifty years of existence devoted to my country, the one thing that sticks is that I'm an anti-Semite and anti-Freemason? It's horrible!"

It was a mortal blow to Bettencourt's career. Even before *Le Monde* made Frydman's revelations so glaringly public, he had quietly resigned from L'Oréal's board of directors in December 1994 and was replaced by his son-in-law, Jean-Pierre Meyers. The fact that Meyers was Jewish could be read as a sign of atonement toward Israel and the international Jewish community.

Bettencourt signaled an end to his political life by declining to run for reelection to the Senate in 1995. But the affair's repercussions continued to haunt him. In February 1995, Serge Klarsfeld flew to New York to discuss the case with US officials. With Jean Frydman at his side, Klarsfeld held a news conference to denounce Bettencourt's wartime writings and called on the United States to place him on its "watch list," which bars former Nazis from entering the country. Even as the US Commerce Department fined L'Oréal $1.4 million for its compliance with the Arab boycott, the Justice Department opened an investigation into André's wartime activities at the demand of New York congressman Eliot Engel. The following year, the department concluded that "available evidence did not support the allegation that André Bettencourt was inadmissible to the United States under the US Immigration and Nationality Act."

That was slight consolation to André. His political career was over. His reputation was tarnished. Now in his late seventies, there was little left for him to do but look after family matters, tend to his correspondence, and, like many a retired politician before him, write his memoirs. Diane de Clairval, a communications specialist and author of children's books, was hired to assist him. Meeting with André weekly in 1998 and 1999, she took dictation, did archival research, and chose photos from the thousands that were scattered around the Bettencourt home. An experienced writer herself, she helped him shape the final text.

Privately published in two volumes, bearing the title *Souvenirs* in gold letters on its tan leather spine, Bettencourt's 369-page memoir was given to members of his family and a select group of friends, academics, and political figures. *Le Monde* published a scathing review of this "private" book, calling it "the story of an old man who, in the twilight of his life, wanted to repaint a rosy picture of it." The review dismisses Bettencourt, rather unkindly, as a man "without substance or ego [who] rubbed shoulders with princes for a half century without wielding the least influence. André Bettencourt resigned himself to his role as a financier of political life." Concerning his business career, said *Le Monde,* the memoir "fails to cite a single initiative taken during a half century to promote L'Oréal." On his wartime articles, the paper quotes Bettencourt's self-justifying explanation: "In the Catholicism of my childhood, the Jews had killed Christ. I didn't know any Jews, but I lived with this idea."

One wonders how satisfying that explanation was for his son-in-law and grandsons, whose ancestor and other relatives had died at Auschwitz. Looking back on this whole dark chapter, Jean-Pierre Meyers recalls it as "a very violent episode for my family that unquestionably had a psychological impact." Nor did the trauma end there: A decade later, the details of Bettencourt's and Schueller's inglorious wartime activities would resurface as the French media raked over the family history once again. There was no dye that could hide the family's dark roots.

Chapter 7
A Generous Man

I hope your future wife will have the financial means to help you, but not too much, because money is also the source of many complications.
— Victor Bettencourt,
advice to his son André

Among the Bettencourts' twenty or so domestic employees, some were closer to Liliane than others. Her longtime chambermaid, Dominique Gaspard, who cleaned her room, made her bed, prepared her medicines, and helped choose her clothes, jealously guarded her proximity to Madame. Christiane Djenane, Liliane's personal assistant, handled her correspondence, managed her appointments, and organized her travel and her relations with L'Oréal. Djenane often served as Liliane's intermediary for telephone calls, a trusted position that gave her an intimate knowledge of Madame's exchanges with Banier and others. Thierry Coulon, the Bettencourts' chef, met with Liliane daily to

185

go over the luncheon and dinner menus, an "important position," as he put it, since Madame paid particular attention to the quality of the cuisine served both to her guests and household employees. Probably her favorite was Enrico Vaccaro, the square-shouldered, sandy-haired bodyguard to whom she bequeathed an apartment and €1 million to take care of her dog after her death.

As for André, no employee was closer to him than Pascal Bonnefoy, the faithful valet who watched over "Monsieur" with a filial devotion for eleven years. It was Bonnefoy who chose the master's clothes, shined his shoes, cleaned his study — and shared many of his secrets. After André's death, Bonnefoy would play a pivotal and explosive role in what came to be known as the Bettencourt Affair.

Born in the central French city of Château-roux, Bonnefoy chose the profession of what he quaintly calls "servitude" because he was "in search of paternal recognition." His father, owner of a bar-restaurant, was murdered when Bonnefoy was twenty-one, leaving him to find his own direction in life. After moving to Paris and working as a waiter and barman, he was taken on by an agency that supplied servers for fancy corporate events. One day, he was sent to the home of the Bettencourts, who were seeking to hire a new valet for André. The trim, strikingly handsome young man immediately caught Bettencourt's eye. "You seem like a down-to-earth man, that's good," said Bettencourt, playfully adding, "I like your name." (Bonnefoy means "good faith" in French.) His contract was signed on June 1, 1990.

"I think André was seduced by the physical beauty of Pascal Bonnefoy," says Antoine Gillot, Bonnefoy's lawyer. "That's why he was hired in the beginning. Then a relationship developed over the years." It was apparently platonic — Bonnefoy is married and has a child — but the two were extremely close. André played a Pygmalion-like role toward this naïve and unsophisticated provincial, taught him elegant manners, how to speak and dress and conduct himself with a certain refinement. Bonnefoy was forever grateful for that.

The bond was interrupted in 1993. Disgusted by the rivalries and backbiting among the domestic employees, Bonnefoy took a job as personal valet to the Aga Khan. After crisscrossing the globe with "His Highness" — "the most demanding master there is" — he happily returned to the Bettencourts six years later. André welcomed Bonnefoy like a prodigal son. The faithful valet accompanied the couple on their regular trips to Arcouest, Formentor, and the Île d'Arros. The private lives of the Bettencourts held few secrets for him. He says the couple would even swim

187

nude in their swimming pool at Arcouest in full view of their domestics.

When they were home in Neuilly, Bonnefoy attended to André's every need. "André Bettencourt was an esthete, a refined dandy, as elegant in his clothes as in his words," he says. "He was horrified by dust. Everything had to be impeccable: his office, his clothes, his shoes — John Lobbs or Corthays. I shined them with a silk stocking. I chose his clothes according to the seasons and his daily schedule. He was always eventempered, the very embodiment of distinction."

After retiring from the Senate, André spent much of his time in his second-floor study, which Bonnefoy made sure to keep in order — and well dusted. It was a large room, bathed in light, lined with mahogany bookshelves, furnished with a large Empire desk, armchairs, a coffee table, and side tables. The bed in which André slept was nestled in an alcove. On one wall hung a large framed battle flag of the French Revolutionary armies. An alabaster bust of Dante stood on a pedestal. There were signed photographs of de Gaulle, Mitterrand, and Pompidou; portraits of Liliane, Françoise, her husband and sons. Among the bric-a-brac, one object stood out: a bronze statuette of an erect penis. When alert readers of *Capital* magazine noticed this curious item in a photo tour of the Bettencourt home, an ex-employee explained that it had been given to André by an old friend as a "humoristic gift, an allusion to their vigor in spite of their advanced age." Other interpretations are possible.

By far the most important object in André's study was the safe, which he kept stuffed with banknotes. Though discretion was de rigueur, all the domestics knew that Monsieur received many political personalities, especially during election season, and that they rarely went away empty-handed. "Madame et Monsieur were very much solicited," says Bonnefoy.

No employee knew more about that than Claire Thibout, the Bettencourts' personal accountant. It was Claire who made regular runs to the BNP bank on the avenue de la Grande Armée to withdraw cash for the couple's household expenses as well as André's political donations. It was a well-oiled routine: André would tell Claire that he needed a certain sum on a given day and she would prepare the cash in a brown paper envelope. Often, after a visit, he would call her back and say he needed more cash: "I've been drained dry."

"He didn't hide it," says Thibout. "He had always financed the right. It was a veritable parade of politicians at the house. They came especially at election time. Each one came to get his envelope. Some of the envelopes contained €100,000 or even €200,000."

Secret donations by well-heeled individuals like André Bettencourt were avidly sought by politicians because of the limits placed on funding by French campaign finance laws. There are no super PACs in France. No Citizens United. Political ads on radio and TV are strictly forbidden. Billionaires cannot blithely shovel tens of millions of dollars into campaigns under the guise of "free speech," as the Koch brothers, Sheldon Adelson, and George Soros do in the United States. Before 1988, French political parties were expected to be financed solely by the dues of their members — a woefully inadequate revenue source. As a result, they resorted to all sorts of shenanigans to fill their coffers: kickbacks and false billing from public contractors, municipal payrolls padded with fictitious jobs, corporate slush funds recycled through African cutout companies, and the like.

In an attempt to remedy these abuses, a reform law in 1988 set up a system of partial public financing of candidates and set caps on the total amount any campaign could spend. Subsequent laws forbade companies and organizations to make political donations, and limited individual gifts to €7,500 per candidate or party in any one election season. Under those circumstances, concealed cash was doubly desirable because it was not subject to caps on donations or to the overall limits on campaign spending.

That's why sugar daddies like André Bettencourt were avidly courted by politicians of all stripes.

Like Schueller before him, André had always cast a wide net, dispensing cash to parties left, right, and center, because a major French company like L'Oréal always needed friends in government regardless of their political color. Though he scattered his donations across the political spectrum, André naturally favored parties and candidates who shared his own conservative leanings. Liliane, who held the purse strings, never got involved in the process but gave it her blessing. "My father was already doing it before I was married," she said. "And one is not the wife of a politician in order to play marbles. You have to get on with it!"

As the laws got stricter, though, getting on with it could be a risky business. In 2004, no less a figure than former prime minister Alain Juppé was convicted of political financing violations, handed a suspended jail sentence, and declared ineligible to hold political office for five years. When Nicolas Sarkozy geared up his presidential campaign in 2007, prudence and discretion were de rigueur. But elections still cost money, and the support of willing, wealthy donors like André Bettencourt was most welcome.

CHAPTER 8
THE CHRISTMAS VISITOR

Tuesday, December 24, 2002. A man in a tan trench coat emerges from the Saint-Sulpice Métro station, crosses the square, and heads down the rue Servandoni. He stops in front of a pair of dark-green doors and presses the bell. A female employee escorts him to a narrow elevator that takes him to the fourth floor, where François-Marie Banier is waiting for him. The table is set for two. In the adjoining kitchen, Banier's cook prepares to serve lunch.

The visitor is an unassuming man of average height, sixty-six years old, with receding gray hair and wire-rimmed glasses. He could pass for an accountant, or perhaps an insurance adjustor. His name is Pierre Castres Saint Martin, but everyone knows him as Pascal because he was born on Easter Day in 1936. Today is the eve of another Christian feast day, but Castres is not here to bring tidings of comfort and joy. He is here to scare the hell out of Banier.

The two men know each other well. Castres is the financial adviser to Liliane Bettencourt and director of the family holding companies that manage her L'Oréal shares and investments. Before that, he spent two decades at L'Oréal, serving as legal director, financial director, and finally deputy director-general, the number two behind CEO Lindsay Owen-Jones. Since his retirement in 2002, he worked exclusively for Liliane Bettencourt. It was at her urging that Castres met periodically with Banier to advise him on how to manage the substantial funds she had shoveled his way. The two men had lunched together at Banier's home several times before.

Banier had even offered to give him one of his paintings. Castres declined. "It was a modern painting, enormous," he explains. "I didn't know what to do with it."

Castres knew that Banier had received numerous gifts from Liliane over the years, but he was unaware of the extent until the day that she asked him to examine her will and see that everything was in order. "Please show him all the documents concerning my succession," she wrote to her notary, Jean-Michel Normand. "I have absolute confidence in him and his discretion." When Castres pored over the papers at Normand's office, he was shocked to discover that Madame Bettencourt had made Banier the beneficiary on four life-insurance policies whose accrued value now reached some €625 million. Apart from the notary, no one, not even André, knew that the policies had been put in Banier's name. Castres dashed back to the rue Delabordère.

"Madame, this is madness," he told Liliane. "All of these dispositions will be contested." The day her will would be unsealed, he warned, her daughter's family would almost certainly sue Banier for *captation d'héritage* — illegally appropriating an inheritance. In place of the insurance policies, he proposed to offer Banier lifetime annuities, regular stipends for as long as he lived. That way, at least, the will would not be challenged. Castres proposed to talk to Banier and try to reason him into renouncing the policies. "She gave me her permission, and I went to discuss the matter with him."

No sooner than Castres sat down at Banier's table, he cut to the chase: "You're mad to seek such sums from Liliane."

Banier played innocent. "I never asked for anything. As far as the insurance policies are concerned, I wasn't even aware of them. I've just learned about it."

"One day Madame will be dead and you will be alone," Castres warned. "After she's gone, you will be sued over the succession."

But legal action was not the only threat. Nicole Gilbert, Banier's cook, recalled overhearing Castres's chilling scenarios of violent retribution. "He was trembling with rage as he spoke . . . Concerning the life-insurance policies, he said that the Mafia would be aware of what was going to be paid out to you and you will be obliged to give it all to them, that they would use whatever means necessary, first against those close to you, then to make you disappear they would plunge you into an acid bath." Banier says Castres told him he would wind up at the bottom of the Seine, alongside Martin d'Orgeval and Pascal Greggory, with their "feet in concrete."

Castres denies that he ever mentioned acid baths or concrete shoes, but he does admit making dire threats. "It's true I told him that he risked being threatened by the Mafia the day there would be a suit against him, because there were unscrupulous people who could be interested in recovering what he had obtained. Nothing more. I didn't go further than that." His aim, he says, was to "scare him" and "bring him to reason."

Castres succeeded in his immediate goal: His threats put the fear of God into Banier and nearly pushed him to the edge of madness. Banier immediately dashed off a fax to Liliane telling her what had happened. He was sure that Castres had been sent by Françoise and Jean-Pierre Meyers to frighten him into renouncing Liliane's gifts.

Liliane, who was vacationing on the Île d'Arros with André, sent a return fax urging Banier to keep calm. But she railed against her daughter and son-in-law, whom she suspected of being behind Castres's intimidation tactics.

"Castres told you he was linked with the Chapon," she wrote, using her favorite nickname for her son-in-law — a *chapon* being a castrated rooster. "You believe it or is it to annoy you a little more [?] I send you a big kiss, and please put this incident out of your head." In a separate fax, she wrote: "I see red when people don't behave well with me. . . . The jealousy of the other one [Françoise] is a gross jealousy, a real bitch of a jealousy, and badly expressed. So much the better. I send you a tender kiss. This is going to be amusing."

Banier was not amused. "This incident with Castres drove me mad," he says. "I went to the Bourdelle Museum one Sunday with Martin and I saw all the paintings advancing toward me, like in *The Exorcist*. And that's when I knew what madness is. I was so afraid that I wanted to throw myself in front of cars, I saw cars driving into my house, I saw abominable things." Banier was tempted to file a suit against Castres, but Liliane begged him not to, fearing a scandal that would damage the image of L'Oréal. The company, which had gone public in 1963, was by then the world's leading cosmetics firm, a flagship of the French beauty and luxury industry that carefully guarded its shareholder confidence.

Liliane's own countermove marked a dramatic turn in the conflict that pitted her devotion to Banier against the interests of her heirs. After her return to Paris in January 2003, she reaffirmed her testamentary gifts in a letter to her notary, citing "the affection that I have for François-Marie Banier and my gratitude for all that I owe him," and insisting that her legacies in his favor could not be "contested by anyone whosoever." She stipulated that if her daughter attempted to prevent the carrying out of Liliane's dispositions toward Banier, Françoise's share of the estate would be attributed 50-50 to Banier and the Pasteur Institute.

Meanwhile, she wrote Banier a reassuring letter about her intentions toward him and her daughter:

My dear François-Marie, I am leaving a considerable fortune to my daughter — and on top of that I have paid the taxes on it all. In no case should you feel indebted to her. . . . I am happy to have been able to help you in your work and in your life. From the day we first met, we have given enormously to one another.

And that has helped me a lot in difficult moments and even in business.

Liliane went further in arming Banier against a future attack by her daughter and son-in-law. "I am sending you the correspondence I have had with Normand," she wrote to Banier in January 2003, "and I authorize you to make use of it if my heirs have the bad taste to attack you." She closed, as she often did, with *"Haut les cœurs!"* When Banier received these precious documents, he carefully classified them in folders and kept them at the ready.

What is extraordinary in all this is that, long before the so-called Bettencourt Affair erupted, Liliane had assumed an adversarial position with respect to her own heirs. She correctly anticipated the likelihood that Françoise and Jean-Pierre would one day take action against Banier. And she clearly sided with Banier against them — even advising her friend to hire a lawyer to "secure" the donations. Moreover, it was Liliane who insisted that Banier formally accept the insurance policies in spite of Castres's attempts to intimidate him. And this at a time when no one questioned Liliane's lucidity or powers of discernment.

Under French law, the subscriber of an *assurance vie,* or life-insurance policy, is free to change the beneficiary by modifying his or her will. It is the testamentary document itself that identifies who will inherit the policy. But once the subscriber formally designates a beneficiary to the insurance company, and the beneficiary officially accepts the policy, it can no longer be changed. In order to "lock in" Banier's claim, Liliane declared him as beneficiary on two of the contracts that bore his name and instructed him to formalize his acceptance with the companies in March 2003. He immediately did so for one contract, but waited more than a year, after a chiding letter from Liliane, to accept the second. (Liliane's will also named Banier as the beneficiary of a third contract, though it was never declared to the company.)

As for Castres, his ill-fated attempt to frighten Banier led to his downfall. "I well understood that [Banier] had told Madame Bettencourt to get rid of me," he says, looking back on the episode more than a decade later. So in October 2004, he handed in his resignation. On the recommendation of Lindsay Owen-Jones, he was replaced by Patrice de Maistre, a L'Oréal auditor — a man who would play a major role in Liliane's inner circle, and not always for the good.

Before he took his leave, Castres made it a point to inform André of the exact circumstances of his departure. "I told him that I could not remain in the presence of someone like that who was too close to Madame Bettencourt." André "simply took note" but did not react. "He wasn't involved because it was Madame who managed her fortune. She

199

was the master of it, not him." As the years wore on, and Liliane's payouts mounted into the tens and hundreds of millions, André would be informed of the situation by more than one interlocutor. Not once did he react.

The Castres incident possibly marks the moment when Françoise and Jean-Pierre Meyers became more fully aware of Liliane's prodigality toward her protégé. Up until that point, they had no way to know about Liliane's real estate dealings with Banier, or the checks she cut him, or the paintings she had reserved for him in her will. Banier is convinced that Castres informed the couple about the four life-insurance policies (one of which had actually been switched from Françoise's name to Banier's) and was sent by them to intimidate him. "The real reason behind the suit against me is in the visit by Castres at Christmas 2002," he says. "He blackmailed me with a death threat so I would give up the insurance policies."

Castres admits that he was friendly with the Meyerses during his days at L'Oréal, but he denies acting on their behalf or even informing them about the policies. If only Banier had accepted his offer of annuities in place of the policies, he says, there wouldn't have been any suit. "He didn't realize the risk he was running, so I tried to make him understand. I know it's incredible all the things I told him, that he'd have the Mafia on his back and all that. I just said any old thing, but it didn't work."

Chapter 9
The Ambitious
Monsieur Sarkozy

One of Abraham Lincoln's biographers wrote that his "ambition was a little engine that knew no rest." The same could be said of Nicolas Sarkozy, except that in his case the little engine was a turbocharger. Like the diminutive Corsican Napoleon Bonaparte, Sarkozy, the son of a Hungarian immigrant, was an outsider who wanted desperately to break into France's political power elite and rise to its summit. Unlike most French political leaders, he did not graduate from the elite École nationale d'administration or the Institut d'études politiques de Paris (Sciences Po). Armed with a simple law degree — he financed his studies by working as an ice-cream vendor and gardener — Sarkozy made his way up the ladder not through the usual old-boy network but by his own relentless drive and ruthless calculation. It was said of him early on that, according to a popular French expression, he had *des crocs qui rayent le parquet* — fangs so long they scratched the floorboards.

Sarkozy started out in politics as a student activist handing out tracts for candidates of the conservative Gaullist movement. His method was to attach himself to powerful senior members of the party, advance on their coattails, and then, in more than one case, betray them. In 1983, at the age of twenty-eight, he outmaneuvered the Gaullist heavyweight Charles Pasqua, his erstwhile mentor, to get himself elected mayor of the affluent Paris suburb of Neuilly-sur-Seine. From that perch, he made it a point to get to know his most prominent constituents, particularly the wealthy ones who could be relied on for votes, influence, and especially campaign contributions. And his wealthiest constituents by far were André and Liliane Bettencourt.

Though Nicolas Sarkozy was never an intimate friend of the Bettencourts, he cultivated the relationship during his years as mayor of Neuilly and later as a member of Parliament and cabinet minister. It was not always easy. At one dinner at chez Bettencourt, while he was still mayor, Sarkozy was seated next to Liliane and struggled to converse with her in spite of her deafness. She remarked that she liked to swim. He replied diplomatically that he also liked to swim. She demanded that Monsieur Sarkozy be served again because he said he liked to eat. She had mistaken *nager,* "to swim," for *manger,* "to eat." For her part, Liliane was put off by the fact that Sarkozy's then wife, Cécilia, spoke on her cell phone throughout the meal.

Sarkozy became a faithful lieutenant of Jacques Chirac, another famously ambitious politician, and helped organize his losing presidential campaign against Mitterrand in 1988. When Chirac's ally Édouard Balladur became prime minister in 1993, he named Sarkozy Budget Minister then enlisted him in his own bid to eclipse Chirac as the Gaullist presidential candidate two years later. Balladur lost, and Sarkozy, considered a Brutus-like traitor by the victorious Chirac, was frozen out of the government until Chirac's reelection in 2002. Named Minister of the Interior, then Minister of Economy and Finance, he took over the leadership of Chirac's Union pour un mouvement populaire (UMP) Party in 2004 and emerged as the heir apparent.

To finance his 2007 presidential run, Sarkozy turned to his friend Éric Woerth. A former financial consultant and tax specialist with Arthur Andersen, Woerth was well versed in the game of political fundraising: He had been named treasurer of the UMP in 2002 and financial director of Chirac's successful reelection campaign the same year. As Sarkozy ramped up his own presidential run, Woerth organized an elite group of wealthy contributors called the Premier cercle. The cost of membership was a donation of €3,000 to €7,500, the legal limit for individuals. In exchange for their support, members were invited to monthly meetings at the five-star Bristol and other luxury hotels, often with Sarkozy himself in attendance. The group also held private dinners at the sumptuous homes of some of its wealthiest backers and hosted discreet fund-raising events as far afield as Geneva and New York.

Woerth was a man who wore many hats. In addition to his jobs as party treasurer and chief fund-raiser for Sarkozy, he was mayor of the affluent horseracing town of Chantilly and a member of Parliament. His dour mien, perpetual five o'clock shadow, and penchant for drab gray suits won him the nickname of "Croque-mort" ("The Undertaker") among his colleagues. But what he lacked in charisma he made up for in the persistent and methodical pursuit of his goals — not surprising for a man whose private passion was mountain climbing. Thanks largely to Woerth's efforts, the Sarkozy campaign received €9,125,105 in private contributions in 2007 — modest by US standards, but more than ten times the take of his Socialist challenger Ségolène Royal.

One of the Premier cercle's five hundred or so members was Patrice de Maistre. A descendant of Joseph de Maistre, the eighteenth-century antirevolutionary philosopher, he had served as an external auditor for L'Oréal before replacing Castres Saint Martin as Liliane Bettencourt's wealth manager in 2004. As such, he presided over the two companies that comprised the so-called family office: Thétys, which managed Liliane's L'Oréal stock; and Clymène, which received her dividends and handled her personal investments (one of which, a €30 million stake in Bernie Madoff's notorious Ponzi scheme, went up in smoke in 2008). In addition to those institutional roles, de Maistre acted as Liliane Bettencourt's financial adviser and managed little by little to insinuate himself into her personal affairs, including the hiring and firing of employees, legal matters, and tax strategy.

De Maistre was a distinguished-looking patrician with a fringe of silver hair, well-cut banker's suits, and an unctuous manner. He practiced the aristocratic hand kiss and identified himself on his business cards as "Count Patrice de Maistre." An avid yachtsman and hunter, he played golf and tennis with L'Oréal CEO Owen-Jones, stalked big game in Tanzania and Siberia, maintained a villa in Saint-Tropez, and belonged to the select Jockey Club and the Automobile Club de France. He also maintained a murky African network, with investments in Algeria, Cameroon, and Gabon. A millionaire in his own right, he was married to Anne Dewavrin, a wealthy heiress and ex-wife of LVMH president Bernard Arnault, one of the world's richest men.

"With high-placed people, or those who had money, he was affable and obsequious," says a woman who formerly worked with de Maistre. "With those he considered beneath him, he was haughty and scornful." His disdain even applied to André Bettencourt, whom he considered (not incorrectly) a mere prince consort. One day, de Maistre walked right past André without speaking to him. Liliane cut him dead. "You could at least say hello to my husband."

The Bettencourts themselves did not belong to the Premier cercle — the €7,500 entry fee was way below their level — but their wealth manager served as a willing intermediary. And in Woerth's eyes, de Maistre was a source worth cultivating. "Patrice de Maistre quickly attracted notice at the meetings that I hosted along with other political officials," Woerth wrote. "He was passionate about politics and obviously wanted to pursue a friendly relationship with me."

When they first met for coffee in January 2007, their discussion inevitably revolved around money and politics. According to de Maistre, André Bettencourt had asked him "to find out in what conditions the couple could finance the UMP and the future presidential campaign of Nicolas Sarkozy." On de Maistre's advice, they legally gave €30,000 to the campaign: €7,500 apiece to the party and €7,500 apiece to Sarkozy's campaign. But that was peanuts compared to the Bettencourts' means — and André's usual levels of support. By now, André, weakened by age and illness, had handed over his brown-paper-envelope functions to de Maistre. There were strong suspicions that at least one envelope handed to Woerth contained substantially more than the legal limit. What is not in doubt is that in March 2007, Éric Woerth wrote personally to candidate Sarkozy, then the interior minister, to recommend that Patrice de Maistre be awarded the Légion d'honneur — a coveted citation dating back to Napoleon I, awarded for "eminent merits" in the service of the nation. The request was approved on July 14, 2007. Woerth personally pinned the decoration on de Maistre's lapel on January 23, 2008.

On May 6, 2007, Sarkozy handily defeated the Socialist candidate Ségolène Royal to win the presidency. He celebrated his victory with a gala dinner at the glitzy Fouquet's restaurant on the Champs-Élysées, a traditional gathering place for film stars whose framed photos line its wood-paneled walls. The guest list was a star-studded mix of celebrities and wealthy friends, including venerable rocker

Johnny Hallyday, actors Jean Reno and Christian Clavier, industrialist Martin Bouygues, aviation magnate Serge Dassault, luxury-goods mogul Bernard Arnault, and reality-TV promoter Stéphane Courbit — a pal of Sarkozy's who would later be ensnared in the Bettencourt Affair. This high-profile partying just when he had taken over the helm of the Fifth Republic played badly in public opinion and set the tone for his presidency. It did not help matters when he and his family immediately embarked on a three-day Mediterranean cruise aboard a yacht belonging to wealthy industrialist Vincent Bolloré, leading critics to brand him as "the president of the rich."

Sarkozy's penchant for Rolex watches, gold neck chains, and Italian designer suits — not to mention his stormy divorce and subsequent marriage to singer-model Carla Bruni, ex-girlfriend of Mick Jagger and Eric Clapton — sealed his image as the "bling-bling" president. He was apparently sensitive about that label. Sociologist Michel Wieviorka recalls attending a private dinner during which the president pulled up his cuff and showed a new wristwatch to his guests. "Look at my watch," he said. "It's not bling-bling. Carla gave it to me. It cost four times more than the one I had before." Carla, though, reinforced the image by appearing in Bulgari ads with flashy emerald and diamond jewelry dangling around her neck. (Her Bulgari contract was reportedly worth €2 million.)

Among Sarkozy's first cabinet choices was Éric Woerth, named Minister of the Budget and Public Finances on May 18. Four months later, in what many saw as a payback for the Légion d'honneur, de Maistre hired Woerth's wife, Florence, as a financial analyst for Clymène. Starting annual salary: €140,000 with a €60,000 bonus. At that time, apparently no one involved saw a possible conflict of interest in the fact that a high official involved in tax collection was married to a woman who was handling investments for one of the country's biggest taxpayers. If there was ever a French version of *House of Cards,* Woerth's pas de deux with de Maistre would make a gripping episode.

CHAPTER 10
THE WHISTLE-BLOWER

Jiliane and André spent the month of August 2006 at Cap de Formentor on the Mediterranean island of Majorca. Their white stucco vacation home, nestled in a pine grove and surrounded by hydrangeas and oleander bushes, offered a spectacular, plunging view of the Bay of Formentor. The hilltop villa, purchased in 1958, was a far more modest affair than the family's colonnaded mansion in Brittany. Nor were the tame surroundings any match for the rugged force of Arcouest, with its frequent storms and heavy seas. "But one can't be shaken up all the time," said Liliane. "I have to breathe! I can't live with my father all the time and l'Arcouest is that for me."

This was meant to be a quiet and restful stay — al-fresco luncheons on the shaded patio, dinners at the four-star Hotel Formentor down the road, reading and napping in the poolside deck chairs, and of course the laps and calisthenics in the pool that were still part of Liliane's daily regimen at age eighty-four. But Liliane could not relax. She was gripped by anxiety, complained of muscular contractions, tightness in the "plexus," and insomnia.

On the night of August 24, alarmed by Liliane's agitation, André rushed to her bedside, tripped, and pulled her down with him. The maid was out dancing and the couple remained sprawled on the floor for several hours. The accident left André in acute pain — he had suffered a fractured shoulder — and threw Liliane into a state of panic and confusion. Over the next two nights, recalled her maid, Françoise Mauclère, the heiress awoke almost every hour, not knowing where she was and confusing André with her father. "She thought she was going to die," said Mauclère. "I think she was simply afraid, afraid of death after her husband's fall, afraid to wind up alone."

Rushed back to Paris in a private plane, they were met at Le Bourget Airport by Françoise and Jean-Pierre. When the door of the plane opened, the Meyerses were shocked to see André hobble down the steps followed by Liliane, her face pale and drawn with a lost look in her eyes — "completely haggard" in the words of her son-in-law. They both seemed ten years older. Jean-Pierre accompanied André directly to the American Hospital in Neuilly. Françoise drove her mother home to Neuilly. Liliane hardly spoke during the drive. Over the next few days she was so confused that she did not realize she was in her own home. "When are we going back to Neuilly?" she asked her secretary, Christiane Djenane. "Madame, we are in Neuilly," came the reply.

On the morning of Saturday, September 2, François-Marie Banier called the Bettencourt home at eight a.m. Liliane's chambermaid, Dominique Gaspard, answered with a laconic "Madame is sleeping."

"At eight a.m.?" said Banier. "That's strange."

"Madame Bettencourt had trouble sleeping last night," the maid replied. "She's going to sleep for a long time today."

Banier, who was at his villa in the south of France at the time, called back every hour and got the same answer: "Madame is sleeping."

Finally, around noon, he called his friend Gilles Brücker, a senior physician at the Pitié-Salpêtrière hospital. "You have to rush over to Liliane's house," he said. "She won't wake up. I'm very worried."

Banier and Brücker had known each other since they were kids. Their families were neighbors on the avenue Victor-Hugo. It was in the Brücker apartment that Banier would hide when his abusive father was on the warpath. They had lost touch with each other until one day in 1980, when they met by chance at the bedside of a dying friend of Banier's who was being treated by Brücker. Since then, their rekindled friendship deepened. Banier introduced Brücker and his companion, Christine Katlama, a leading AIDS researcher, to Liliane. The heiress took a shine to the couple and asked Brücker to be her regular doctor. A specialist in infectious diseases and a busy teaching professor, Brücker declined but recommended a colleague, Philippe Koskas, for the job. Brücker himself agreed to act as an informal "medical adviser."

At Banier's urging, Liliane had the family foundation invest a total of nearly €20 million in two associations founded by Brücker and Katlama, one to do research on an AIDS vaccine, the other to support AIDS treatments in Africa. (It was largely for funding this action that in 2001 Liliane was awarded the Légion d'honneur by Health Minister Bernard Kouchner, with whom Brücker had cofounded Doctors Without Borders in 1971.) Meanwhile, Brücker and Katlama became frequent guests of the Bettencourts and even spent two vacations with them on the Île d'Arros. Liliane gained such confidence in Professor Brücker that in May 2003 she named him her testamentary executor. Brücker, surprised but flattered, agreed to accept that role. He didn't know at the time that she had provided in her will for a €1 million honorarium.

Following Banier's phone call, Brücker dashed to the Bettencourt home on his Honda 650 motorcycle, arriving around half past noon. The heiress was still in bed, unable to wake up. "It was totally abnormal," Brücker recalls. "I said we couldn't keep her there. We had to put her in the hospital." He called Liliane's regular doctor, Philippe Koskas, who arrived at two p.m. The two physicians decided to admit the heiress to the American Hospital, close by her home in Neuilly, where she was treated for a "light coma" and "severe dehydration." During her forty-eight-hour stay, the doctors diagnosed "a confusional syndrome following an accidental fall and the consumption of painkillers." The heiress had suffered several mini-fractures of the ribs in the Formentor accident, hence the resort to painkillers that, according to Brücker, were too heavily dosed for a woman of her age — especially in conjunction with the potent sleeping pills and tranquilizers she was taking.

Liliane's hospitalization triggered a new flare-up of tension between mother and daughter. On the day she was admitted, the phone rang at Banier's residence. Martin d'Orgeval answered and heard the voice of Christiane Djenane, Liliane's secretary, literally shouting into the receiver: "Madame Meyers forbids Monsieur Banier to visit her mother." She added: "I hope there's no checkbook in her purse." Of course, Banier ignored the injunction. On the morning of Sunday, September 3, he sat at Liliane's bedside and read her pages from Stendhal's *La Chartreuse de Parme,* one of their favorite books. Her bodyguard, Enrico Vaccaro, who slept at Madame's hospital bedside, was amazed to see her sitting up in bed and laughing after Banier's arrival. Françoise, who avoided Banier's visit, later said she was "surprised" to find Vaccaro there: "The presence of a nurse would have been more justified than a bodyguard." Vaccaro, it should be noted, was one of the Bettencourt employees who got along best with Banier.

Françoise was no less annoyed by the arrival of Banier's friend Brücker while she and her husband were visiting. Not wishing to intrude, Brücker just stuck his head in the room to say hello. As soon as she saw him, Liliane perked up. "Gilles! Come sit next to me." Then the patient did an extraordinary thing: She asked her daughter and son-in-law to leave the room for ten minutes so she could be alone with Brücker. "She was transformed, radiant, perfectly lucid," says Brücker. "They say she was very fragile at that time, but that's totally false. She was tired from the accident and the overmedication, but afterward she was fine."

On September 5, the day of Liliane's return from the hospital, she invited Banier to lunch. She was livid over Djenane's phone call forbidding Banier to visit the hospital. "Christiane has betrayed me," she fumed. "I won't keep her." At the same lunch, according to Banier, Liliane asked him to formally accept a third life-insurance policy. This one, worth €262 million at the time, had already been attributed to Banier in Liliane's will in 1998. Now she was proposing to formally declare him to the insurance company as the beneficiary, which, following his letter of acceptance, would become definitive and immutable.

The paperwork was filed on September 14, just nine days after her return from the hospital. The same day, Madame Bettencourt wrote to her insurance company, Arcalis, instructing them to send all correspondence concerning the policy to the office of her notary, Jean-Michel Normand, "and in no case to my address in Neuilly." This was presumably to prevent André, Claire Thibout — and especially Françoise Meyers — from learning of the transaction.

The timing of this act would later be seen as a sign of Banier's manipulation of the heiress at times when she was particularly weak and vulnerable. Though she recovered physically from the effects of the fall, the incident appears to have marked an aggravation of her intermittent mental lapses. Many members of Liliane's entourage were alarmed by her confusion during the weeks and months that followed her return from Formentor. "She seemed to be going through a phase of dementia," said Lucienne de Rozier, her closest friend. "Her words were choppy and made no sense. She was in a deplorable state." Henriette Youpatchou, hired as Liliane's full-time nurse after her return from the hospital in September 2006, reported that the heiress "didn't know where she was. She asked me what country she was in." Bruno Lantuas, the Bettencourts' butler at the time, found her "shocked," "groggy," and "depressed," plunged in a state of "confusion" that he said lasted seven or eight months.

In this weakened and confused state, Liliane multiplied her largesse. On October 21, she gave €500,000 to the daughter of Brücker and Katlama to enable her to buy an apartment. On December 18, just three months after giving Banier the €262 million insurance policy, she declared an additional €33,519,852 worth of gifts to the photographer: two checks totaling €11,700,000 plus *nue propriété*, or reversionary ownership, of an African mask and statuette worth more than €7 million. (She had bought the pieces at auction six months earlier on Banier's recommendation.) On top of that, the heiress paid €12,960,000 in gift taxes. The same day, she informed Banier's companion, Martin d'Orgeval, that she was gifting him a painting by Max Ernst (€670,000) and a cardboard polychrome by Jean Arp (€478,602) as *nue propriété.* On those gifts she paid €551,329 in taxes.

This sudden surge of generosity was accompanied by a smoldering anger directed at Françoise. "I am in such a state of rage vis-à-vis Françoise that I'm making André lose ground physically," she wrote to Banier on November 28, 2006. "For years now, this coldness, her coldness, gnaws at me . . . She wants to crush me." The next day, André called Françoise and told her it was best not to try to see her mother for the time being. For how long? Françoise asked. "Weeks, perhaps months," he replied.

In April 2007, Françoise had an accident that required what her husband described as a "delicate operation." The night before the surgery, Jean-Pierre Meyers dined with his in-laws and explained the situation. André was very concerned and promised to visit his daughter in the hospital. But Meyers described Liliane as "completely absent." She had something else on her mind.

The next day, April 5, Liliane flew to Marrakesh with Banier and d'Orgeval to inspect a property that she wanted to buy as a vacation home for André. When she returned that evening, she was too exhausted by the 2,600-mile day-trip to go to the hospital. Françoise was terribly hurt, and blamed Banier for intentionally taking her mother away that day so she could not visit her ailing daughter following the six-hour operation.

Banier and d'Orgeval claimed, on the contrary, that it was Liliane who insisted on going that day and personally rented the private plane. When they met her at Le Bourget Airport that morning, they found her extremely fatigued — according to her bodyguard she had been heavily dosed with tranquilizers — and suggested she postpone the trip. "You stay here if you want," she huffed. "I'm going." In any event, the commotion of the whirlwind round trip left Liliane in a weakened and disoriented state, and, in the opinion of her physician Philippe Koskas, set back her recovery from the earlier Formentor episode.

Liliane's confusional episodes, often linked to overmedication, alternated with periods of lucidity during which she appeared perfectly normal. She was at her best in the mornings, but tended to flag in the afternoons as fatigue set in. In the months and years following the Formentor incident, her entourage reported bouts of alarming behavior: She would get lost on the way to her own room, call her black female nurse "André," cut up food in the dog's bowl with her own knife and fork, and once turned violently against a dinner guest, demanding to know who he was and what he was doing in her home.

At the same time, at least until the end of 2010, Madame Bettencourt kept up a busy schedule of meetings and social events, as shown by her confiscated datebooks. She attended L'Oréal board and committee meetings five times a year and met at least once a month with Lindsay Owen-Jones and his successor, Jean-Paul Agon, to discuss business matters. Throughout this period, her correspondence is perfectly lucid. As evidenced by numerous written exchanges, her husband deferred to her decisions on all matters concerning household and other expenses up until his death in November 2007.

Though Liliane followed an exercise regimen consisting of long walks and daily laps in her pool, her overall health was not good: She complained constantly of a tightening in the "plexus," anxiety, insomnia, weakness in the legs, and pains due to osteoporosis. She was also a hypochondriac who consumed as many as fifty-six pills a day, mostly homeopathic nostrums but also such powerful neurotropics as the somnifer Stilnox and the tranquilizer Lexomil. It was impossible to coordinate her health care, since she tended to practice what one physician called "a certain medical nomadism," changing doctors and medication frequently. Her address book contained the names of fifty-seven different doctors, plus ten acupuncturists and four astrologers.

Banier denies claims by some of Liliane's former employees that he sought to "control" the heiress's health care. The fact is that no one controlled it. One doctor that Banier introduced to Liliane, his friend Gilles Brücker, was appalled by the chaotic situation: "I saw that there were many doctors around her but no medical coordination. Prescribers unaware of who was prescribing what. My concern was to make sure the abundance of doctors and prescriptions was not excessive. My fears were not unfounded."

André had been in declining health for some time. Now eighty-eight years old, he was suffering from a spreading cancer that sapped his energy and often confined him to bed. He still got around with a cane, and sometimes swam in the basement pool and walked in the garden with Liliane. But his face was gaunt, his gait unsteady. Liliane's hostility notwithstanding, Françoise made it a point to come see her father every morning — but always before ten a.m., so as not to encounter the hated Banier.

On one such visit, in May 2007, she met Claire Thibout in the garden. "How's it going, Claire?" she said.

"Not so good," replied the accountant.

Françoise could hear the stress in Claire's voice, see the anger in her hard green eyes.

"Come have a coffee with me," said Françoise. "We need to talk."

In the Meyerses' duplex apartment, sitting face-to-face with Françoise across a coffee table, Claire abandoned her usual reserve and opened up. "I told her everything. I started with several small things, then I just let go. She was stunned. She had suspected that [Banier] was getting money, checks, but she had no idea of the extent of the donations."

The horror story that Claire related went far beyond a mere accounting of Liliane's gifts to Banier. There was his bullying behavior toward her, his omnipresence, his domineering attitude with the domestic employees, his disdain for André. Not to mention Liliane's confusion and memory lapses that were becoming more and more frequent.

One episode that had especially shaken Claire involved her employer's jewelry collection. Neither inventoried nor insured, it was kept in her safe-deposit box at the Société Générale Bank on the boulevard Haussmann, near the Paris Opéra.

Liliane had entrusted the key to Claire, who would occasionally go there, discreetly accompanied by a bodyguard, to fetch a necklace or brooch for Liliane to wear at some special event. At one point, toward the end of

2006, Liliane suddenly told Claire to remove the whole collection from the bank and bring it to the Bettencourt home.

Claire claimed that Banier was behind this surprising instruction, which was renewed every time he came to lunch with Liliane. The accountant dragged her feet and played for time. She was so stressed that she finally got a doctor's certificate prescribing sick leave for depression and sent it to Liliane by registered mail, along with a letter refusing to remove the jewels "for reasons of security."

Fearing that Banier would accuse her of stealing jewelry, Claire went to the bank accompanied by her lawyer, Antoine Gillot; Liliane's tax lawyer, Fabrice Goguel; and a court bailiff to photograph and inventory the whole collection. Liliane's "box" was actually a walk-in safe, nearly six feet high with a thick steel door. "It was Ali Baba's cave," says Gillot. There were diamond and pearl bracelets, necklaces, tiaras, rings, brooches, even gold ingots, the whole worth tens of millions. Over two or three hours, the collection was photographed and registered piece by piece.

But if Claire was thereby protected against charges of pilfering, the jewels were not yet out of harm's way. With Banier at her side, Liliane showed up one day at the office of her notary, Jean-Michel Normand, and told him she wanted to give the whole collection to the photographer. Normand refused, saying, "You have absolutely no right to do that" — not because it was illegal, but because he found it "indecent." At that point, Banier claims, he told Liliane he didn't want the jewels. Furious, Liliane lashed out at Normand, saying, "Very well. I'll throw them out the window, but I'll tell François-Marie to go down and get them."

When Claire finished her story, Françoise was on the verge of tears. "Would you be willing to testify if I decided to file a suit?"

Claire had not counted on this. A suit against Banier was a declaration of war. If she agreed to testify, she might find herself caught in the crossfire and lose her lucrative job. She asked for some time to think it over.

The next day, she went to see Antoine Gillot, a specialist in labor law. "What is going on there is not at all normal, and you would only be telling the truth," he reasoned. "Except that if that truth-telling costs you your job, you'd be taking a big risk. You're the accountant — how would you evaluate that risk?"

Claire had already worked it out. She earned €8,500 per month (later raised to €11,000), an extraordinary amount for a simple accountant. If she lost her job with the Bettencourts, the most she could hope to make at a private company was €3,000 to €3,500. According to her calculation, the lost

225

income over the ten years until her retirement would total €800,000 — more than a million dollars at the 2007 exchange rate. Her contract provided for indemnities in the event of termination. So Claire was willing to testify if Françoise agreed to pay the difference between her severance settlement (still undetermined at that point) and €800,000. Françoise summarized their understanding in a letter dated July 11, 2007: "We can imagine the delicate situation in which you find yourself and we are therefore grateful for your commitment to give us your cooperation when the time comes," she wrote. Meyers pledged to round Thibout's severance up to €800,000 in the event she was fired. She added: "It is well understood that this letter and its contents must remain strictly confidential."

Madame Meyers's agreement to pay a hefty sum to a key witness would later come back to haunt her. At the time, though, she saw it as the fulfillment of a vow made to her dying father to "protect Claire Thibout" in case she was fired. Said Françoise: "It was unthinkable for me not to respect the word of my father." To her, as to Claire, the promised money was not a payment for testimony but a professional indemnity that would apply only in the event the accountant was actually fired.

Yet there are indications that Claire Thibout was not an entirely disinterested employee. In 2001, she had received a donation of €50,000 from Liliane (actually a loan that Madame Bettencourt later converted into a gift). In March 2006, Liliane wrote to Banier: "François-Marie, you are going to laugh, but the accountant Claire Thibout has asked me for three apartments. I immediately refused. She won't have a tender spot for me in her heart, but she is already paid enough. I find that exaggerated. I am furious and annoyed." In spite of Liliane's professed displeasure, Claire Thibout wrote to Jean-Michel Normand on November 17, 2006: "As agreed, I am sending you the property titles to two apartments that Madame Bettencourt wishes to give me; one on rue Perret, the other on the Rond-Point Saint-James in Neuilly."

Thibout claims she never really intended to accept the apartments. It was all Banier's idea, an attempt to compromise her or buy her silence, for Claire knew more than anyone the extent of Liliane's gifts to the photographer. In Claire Thibout's scenario, Banier saw her as a risk, so he tried to neutralize her with enticing promises, alternately charming and harassing her. She claimed that he offered to set up a Swiss bank account to receive secret funds from Liliane. "He told me Madame Bettencourt wanted to give me two apartments and that I would be a fool not to accept them. . . . In order to shut him up, I sent two property titles to Normand and I never heard any more about it."

Thibout's story seems difficult to accept at face value. If she wanted to shut Banier up, she could have ignored his exhortations, or simply told him she'd dealt with the matter without actually sending the documents to the notary. It would have made no sense for her to forward the titles to apartments she had no interest in owning. "Let's say, for the sake of argument, that she might have been tempted at a certain moment of weakness," concedes her lawyer Antoine Gillot, "the fact is that she didn't do it. She doesn't have these apartments."

Assured by Madame Meyers's financial promises, Claire stood ready to testify on her behalf. But Françoise held her fire for the time being. She claimed she was reluctant to do anything that would upset her dying father. Or perhaps she feared that he would oppose the drastic legal action that she was preparing. For a long time, André had observed Banier's comportment, his influence over Liliane, his frequent presence in the Bettencourt home, but did nothing to counter it. Liliane had tried to keep him in the dark about the extent of her gifts to the photographer, but information leaked through to him over the years. Liliane's financial adviser Castres Saint Martin had told André as early as

2004 about what he considered Banier's predations and unhealthy influence over Liliane. But André didn't react.

During the course of 2007, several employees confided in André. Claire Thibout went to his room that summer and told him everything she knew about the Banier situation. André was in tears. "I didn't realize it was so terrible," he said. "We should have put her under guardianship some time ago. But I feel powerless against all that." He added: "My wife is sick. I'm going to go. She will be alone." André's secretary, Chantal Trovel, recounted that when she told him about checks that had been made out to Banier in April 2007, he replied "Ah, the bastard!" but said he "couldn't imagine imposing a double signature on Madame. That would kill her." Françoise herself told her father what she had learned from Claire Thibout. His reply, according to her: "Banier is a crook. One day there will be a suit."

André's valet, Pascal Bonnefoy, who was probably closer to him than anyone during his last years, recounts that "he did not react in front of the others out of respect for his wife. But I think in private he tried to curb things. Liliane Bettencourt always said 'we mustn't tell André.' People hid many things from him." In a September 2010 interview, Liliane said of her husband: "I think he sensed the problem that existed between

François-Marie and me, this material problem. But André didn't talk to me about it; he was with me."

Banier flies into a rage when anyone quotes André's supposed "deathbed" statements denouncing him. "It's shameful to make the dead speak," he fumes. If André was so disturbed by the relationship, why did he continue to receive Banier at his table, attend his exhibitions, invite him to restaurants? "If he had something to say, he would have said it and he would have acted. If he said nothing, and wrote nothing down, it's because there was nothing to say."

One can take Banier's protest with a grain of salt, but the questions remain: Where was André? What was he thinking? Why didn't he act when he could have, long before he was weakened by age and illness? This is one of the greatest mysteries of the Bettencourt saga. Was he a coward? Did he fear his wife would cut off his own access to her fortune? Was he somehow under Banier's spell himself? Or did he simply accept his wife's wishes? There are no clear answers.

At midday on Saturday, November 17, 2007, Pascal Bonnefoy took his leave of André. The faithful valet had been especially close to him the past few weeks, even sleeping in his room on a camp bed. Bonnefoy was alarmed by André's steady physical decline and that day found him totally exhausted. As he prepared to take off for the weekend, he told André to call him "if you need anything at all."

On Sunday morning, André managed to swim a few strokes with Liliane in their basement pool. That evening, they watched a movie. Then he told his wife good night and went to bed. He never woke up. Pascal Bonnefoy called on Monday morning to check on the master. He burst into tears when he learned of André's death. He had lost not just an employer but a father figure, a role model, and a mentor.

Banier was out photographing that morning, as usual. It was Martin d'Orgeval who got the 7:30 a.m. phone call from Liliane. "André is gone." D'Orgeval was stunned. He and Banier had dined with the couple Friday evening. André was very weak, but no one thought his death was imminent.

Liliane called back later and got Banier on the phone. She was fuming against her daughter, who had been hovering around André's bedside all morning. "Françoise has to see his body seven times," said Liliane. "Once is enough for me."

The atmosphere in the Bettencourt home was tense. Françoise and her mother clashed over the organization of the funeral and the reception that would follow. Françoise insisted that Banier should not be invited, and finally decided to hold a separate reception in her own apartment to make sure she would not run into him.

Even as André's body reposed in his upstairs study, the mother-daughter dispute came to a head. Pascal Bonnefoy claims to have overheard a bitter exchange between the two women.

"As long as Papa was alive, I didn't say anything," said Françoise. "Now I won't allow things to go on this way. I intend to take this to court."

"But you can't do that," Liliane protested.

"I've warned you. I will do what I have to do."

Liliane, distraught at her husband's death, was now pushed over the edge.

Bonnefoy recalls her confusion during the visitation. "The casket was in Monsieur's office. When Madame saw his body, she knew it was him. Thirty minutes later, or the next day, she did not remember he was dead." Olivier Pelat, a friend of the Bettencourts from childhood, says Liliane was "on her cloud" the day of the funeral. "She didn't understand what was going on. Which was fortunate because it would have been very difficult for her." Liliane's grandson, Jean-Victor Meyers, later testified that "she didn't understand why she went to the church nor why there were so many people there."

The funeral was held in Neuilly's Saint-Pierre

Church on November 22. Under the high vaulted faux-Gothic ceiling, as dappled light filtered in through the stained-glass windows and somber organ chords reverberated through the cavernous space, *le tout Paris* came to pay their respects to the former minister and senator. To the left of the aisle sat former president Valéry Giscard d'Estaing and former prime minister Édouard Balladur. Ex-president Jacques Chirac was ailing — allegedly touched by senility — but his wife, Bernadette, a close friend of the Bettencourts, was there.

Behind the political leaders sat André's fellow academicians from the Institut de France, along with an impressive collection of bankers, businessmen, titled aristocrats, and former associates from L'Oréal.

In the front pew to the right of the aisle sat Liliane, flanked by Françoise, Jean-Pierre Meyers, and their two sons. Behind them sat Liliane's twenty or so domestic employees, their clannish rivalries momentarily suspended. And of course there were Monique de Libouton and Lucienne de Rozier, Liliane's two closest friends. Before the communion, Pascal Bonnefoy, tears streaming down his cheeks, came forward and placed André's medals on a silk cushion atop the casket. At his side, Nicolas Meyers, the Bettencourts' youngest grandson, carried André's ceremonial sword from the Académie des Beaux-Arts.

In the very back row sat Banier and d'Orgeval. Banier did not attend the reception at the Bettencourts' home, because Françoise forbade it, but he dined with Liliane beforehand. He disputes the claims that she was confused on that occasion; in fact he has never admitted that she suffered from anything more serious than an occasional memory lapse. But that day marked a turning point in their relationship.

The consort was dead. Did Banier intend to take his place? Is that what Liliane wanted? "The day after [André's] death," recalled Monique de Libouton, "Liliane took off her wedding ring and since then only wears the ring that François-Marie Banier gave her." Banier denies this story, but admits to giving Liliane an expensive diamond ring he purchased at the JAR boutique on the Place Vendôme.

Pascal Bonnefoy was relieved and grateful when Madame decided to keep him on staff following André's death. He officially served as a part-time butler, but his main job was to maintain André's office as a shrine to his memory. "I wanted to preserve the presence of Monsieur Bettencourt in the house," he said. "My role was not to let anyone forget that Monsieur had existed. I had promised my allegiance to him. I became a sort of guardian of the temple. Every morning I knocked on his door as if Monsieur was still there."

But he was not. Liliane was now alone with her servants, de Maistre and his cabal of lawyers and notaries — and François-Marie Banier. According to some of the servants, the photographer was more and more present after André's funeral, even mounting the marble stairs and entering unannounced into Liliane's bedroom.

One day, not long after André's death, Dominique Gaspard was in Madame's bathroom preparing her morning medicines when she recognized Banier's voice in the next room. What she claims to have overheard left her breathless: "Concerning the adoption, we'll do a simple adoption. You will go alone to the notary." According to Gaspard, Banier added: "And if Françoise files a complaint, she can do nothing against us."

Gaspard immediately reported these words to Chantal Trovel, André's secretary, and Claire Thibout, the whistle-blowing accountant who at that point was still on the job. In no time, the news crossed the rue Delabordère. When Françoise heard about the adoption scheme, she was horrified. Coming just after the death of her father, she said, this adoption story was like "a dam that collapsed." Adoption would have made the hated intruder a member of the family, legally a sibling of Françoise with an equal right of inheritance. (Under French law, adoption of an adult is allowed, provided the adoptive parent is at least fifteen years older than the adoptee and that an administrative court grants its approval.) Banier and Liliane later dismissed the adoption claim as a malicious invention — "I never wanted to adopt a son, and certainly not someone who is over sixty years old," Liliane said. But to Françoise it was real. She could wait no longer.

In December 2007, she contacted several members of her mother's entourage and asked if they were willing to testify. In addition to Claire Thibout and Liliane's friend Lucienne de Rozier, six current and former Bettencourt employees agreed to provide affidavits describing Banier's alleged predations and the heiress's diminished mental state. On December 14 and 15, these witnesses were summoned to the offices of Didier Martin, Françoise's business lawyer, to submit their attestations. "There were six lawyers behind a big table," recalled de Rozier, with whom Liliane later severed relations because of her testimony. "Not one of them introduced himself, and so I greeted no one. There was one in particular who seemed to be in charge."

His name was Olivier Metzner.

■ ■ ■ ■

PART THREE:
THE BETTENCOURT
AFFAIR

■ ■ ■ ■

Showing the way: Liliane Bettencourt and François-Marie Banier at the Maison Européenne de la Photographie, 2003.
Horst Ossinger/DPA/AFP

CHAPTER 11
THE OPENING SALVO

On Wednesday, December 19, 2007, Philippe Courroye received a phone call from Olivier Metzner, one of the country's most famed and feared criminal lawyers.

Courroye was the *procureur,* or state prosecutor, in the Paris suburb of Nanterre. The two men had worked together on a number of cases in the past, saw each other socially, and spoke on a first-name basis — unusual in the formal context of French professional relations.

Metzner said he had a "sensitive" case to discuss with Courroye and wanted to bring the dossier to him personally. The twenty-minute drive from Metzner's Left Bank office just off the boulevard Saint-Germain took him through the open expanse of the Place de la Concorde with its imposing fountains and central obelisk stolen from the Egyptians by Napoleon. From there, his chauffeur-driven Jaguar headed up the Champs-Élysées and crossed the traffic-snarled circle around the Arc de Triomphe.

Arriving at La Défense, the Manhattan-like clutch of office towers just west of Paris, the car entered an underground tunnel that led to Nanterre. Ensconced in the backseat, puffing on one of his six daily cigars, half-height glasses posed on the end of his nose, Metzner paid no attention to the scenery. He was focused on the thick folder that lay in his lap.

Metzner, then fifty-eight, had risen to prominence through a series of high-profile cases that sealed his reputation as a shrewd and ruthless legal strategist, a master of the complex procedural tools of French justice, and a shameless manipulator of the press. Among his many headline-grabbing cases, he had defended rock singer Bertrand Cantat in the fatal battering of actress Marie Trintignant, daughter of Jean-Louis Trintignant (*A Man and a Woman*), in the Lithuanian capital of Vilnius in 2003.

Cantat, lead singer for a group prophetically named Noir Désir (Black Desire), had flown into a violent rage and rained nineteen blows on his lover, then left her comatose body in bed overnight. Flown back to Paris, she died four days later after an emergency operation. Metzner got Cantat an eight-year sentence for unintentional homicide instead of the fifteen years he risked for murder. (He was released on conditional liberty in 2007.)

His adversary in that case was his bête-noire, Georges Kiejman, who represented Trintignant's mother. Metzner had argued that the attack was triggered by the victim's "hysteria." Kiejman shot back, "The hysterical fury of women, that's the classic excuse of the machos who strike them." Since that face-off, the two men had barely been on speaking terms. Their courtroom encounters in the Bettencourt case would bring them close to fisticuffs.

No less spectacular was Metzner's successful defense of the dashing former prime minister Dominique de Villepin in the so-called Clearstream Affair, in which de Villepin was accused of trumpeting false claims of corruption against his bitter rival, Nicolas Sarkozy. Courroye thought the Clearstream case had caused his friend to "levitate" with self-satisfaction. "At that point, he left the land of human beings to join that of the gods."

But Metzner's previous exploits paled next to the juicy affair described in the dossier he was now holding: the bilking of the world's wealthiest woman, head of one of France's proudest industrial icons, by a flamboyant homosexual photographer, artist, and writer who had taken her for hundreds of millions of euros and counting.

Not that Metzner had anything against homosexuals — he was gay himself — but he knew a spectacular case when he saw it, and this one just might seal his reputation as the undisputed king of France's criminal lawyers. He also, secretly, looked on what would soon be known as the Bettencourt Affair as his last great case. Once it was done and dusted, he planned to retire to his private island off the coast of Brittany and indulge in his real passions: sailing on his yacht and contemplating the sea from his own rocky coastline. He was already a very wealthy man, and his new client, Françoise Bettencourt Meyers, had the means to pay him handsomely for the work he was about to do.

Philippe Courroye, a tall, slender man with thinning gray hair and tired-looking bags under his blue eyes, was a battle-scarred veteran of France's judiciary bureaucracy. He had started his career as one of the country's roughly five hundred *juges d'instruction,* the special magistrates that under the French justice system investigate cases and decide whether to send defendants to trial. Called "the most powerful man in France" by Napoleon (some say it was Balzac), the *juge d'instruction* has extensive powers to compel testimony, order wiretaps and surveillance, and put defendants in preventive detention for unlimited periods. He is assisted in his probes by an elite corps of detectives from the judiciary police. Once he completes his investigation and sends a case to court, it is up to the *procureur* to prosecute it before a panel of three judges, who preside over the trial and render the decision. (Juries are used only in cases involving violent crimes.) In France, all magistrates are civil servants.

Courroye had been an aggressive investigator earlier in his career, putting more than one corrupt official behind bars. But ever since he was named as the Nanterre prosecutor in March 2007, he had higher ambitions. For the prosecutors are part of the country's political power structure: Unlike the nominally independent investigating magistrates, prosecutors are directly responsible to the justice minister, who is responsible to the president. And Courroye, who nursed a burning desire to be named *procureur de Paris* — the absolute summit of his profession — had a powerful advantage in this quest: He was a personal friend of President Nicolas Sarkozy. His successful handling of a high-profile case, he reasoned, would almost assure him the appointment he craved.

The case that Metzner laid before him that day was a suit against François-Marie Banier, filed on December 19, 2007, for *abus de faiblesse* — abuse of weakness — committed against Liliane Bettencourt, then eighty-five years old, in the town of Neuilly. (Neuilly being part of the Hauts-de-Seine Department, the matter fell under the jurisdiction of Nanterre.) This was not a simple civil action to recover damages: It was a criminal case punishable by up to three years in prison and a €375,000 fine. Metzner's eighteen-page complaint accused Banier of having "knowingly abused the state of weakness of [Françoise's] mother in order to obtain considerable sums and values."

Courroye saw immediately that this was an important and highly sensitive case. And he was determined to keep it under his wing. Instead of assigning it to an independent magistrate, he decided to carry out his own *enquête préliminaire* — a preliminary investigation to determine whether the case should be brought to trial. Normally, such a probe would lead a prosecutor to hand the case to an investigative magistrate, who would then undertake an in-depth examination of the facts. Courroye's insistence on keeping the matter under his control later drew widespread criticism. But to his mind, this case was so important that he did not dare give it to anyone else. To assist him in his own investigation, he turned to the *brigade financière* — the unit of the judiciary police whose detectives are specialized in financial matters.

Metzner's dossier was "well supported," says Courroye, now fifty-eight, looking back on the case nearly a decade later. It contained the affidavits of Claire Thibout and seven other witnesses, medical certificates describing Madame Bettencourt's health problems, and a detailed accounting of the gifts Banier had allegedly obtained over the years. The total, according to Metzner's dossier, was more than €500 million.

The witness statements included in Metzner's file were devastating for Banier, whom they portrayed as a kind of guru bending Liliane to his will and milking her for millions. Dominique Gaspard, Liliane's personal maid, recounted a scene that had taken place on the Île d'Arros in December 2006. "Monsieur Banier harassed Madame Bettencourt for her to give him a check. When she refused, he did not want to have lunch or dinner with her. Madame Bettencourt was very unhappy, she was not herself. On Christmas Eve, he was with her when she was preparing to go hear the Christmas carols. I was present. He criticized all Monsieur and Madame Bettencourt's guests. When she was getting ready to put on her lipstick, he took it out of her hands and threw it against the wall saying it was not pretty. Madame was very upset; a half hour later, she had a malaise."

During the same stay on the island, Liliane's nurse, Henriette Youpatchou, claimed to have overheard a conversation Between Liliane and Banier. "That's much too much!" the heiress protested. "It's not enough," said Banier, to which Liliane replied, "André is going to find out!" Youpatchou declared: "Their discussions were almost always about money. He demanded a lot from Madame Bettencourt and he obtained what he wanted. I observed scenes where he demanded money with such insistence that she became ill and couldn't sleep. After each exchange with him, she was melancholic, very nervous. When she resisted (a little bit) his demands for money, he went into terrible temper tantrums."

Claire Thibout, the one who had first informed Françoise about Banier's predations, repeated those charges in her attestation. "At the end of 2005, Monsieur Banier telephoned almost every day to ask me to tell Madame Bettencourt that he loved her, that he cared a lot about her, but that he needed two or three million euros to pay for his swimming pool and other work. I remember that when he ran into me at the [Bettencourt] property, he asked for my advice: 'I'd like to go see Françoise Bettencourt to tell her that there is enough money for two.' I was staggered."

As presented in Metzner's file, these statements made a strong case against Banier. It was up to Courroye to determine whether they were borne out by other witness accounts and independently verifiable facts.

Courroye's investigative strategy revolved around two questions. "First, we had to verify that the gifts that were listed — life-insurance contracts, paintings, etc., had in fact been granted to Banier. Then there was the central question: Was Madame Bettencourt in fact in a situation of vulnerability? Because the gifts denounced by Françoise Meyers went back to 1997 — ten years earlier. So that meant that since 1997, Madame Bettencourt was in a situation of vulnerability. That had to be proven, because otherwise, she can do what she wants with her money."

Liliane's vulnerability was indeed the key issue. Article 223-15-2 of the French penal code defines the infraction in these terms: "The fraudulent abuse . . . of the situation of weakness . . . of a person whose particular vulnerability, due to age, illness, or infirmity . . . is apparent or known by the author"; or the abuse "of a person in a state of psychological suggestion . . . resulting from the use of heavy or repeated pressures, or techniques aimed at altering one's judgment" in order to lead this person "to an act or an abstention that is gravely prejudicial to him or her."

As Courroye and the Financial Brigade detectives launched into the investigation in early January 2008, Liliane Bettencourt was unaware of her daughter's legal action. She had another preoccupation at that moment. On November 19, the very day of her husband's death, L'Oréal CEO Lindsay Owen-Jones had sent her a letter that infuriated her.

Now that André was no longer there to serve as her "unofficial adviser," Owen-Jones proposed for Liliane to cede the "family representation" on the company's Management and Remunerations Committee to Jean-Pierre Meyers, her son-in-law, whom she suspected of trying to assert his control over the company and push her aside.

In 2005, Liliane complained to her notary, Jean-Michel Normand, that Meyers had pulled out an actuarial table and said that her "life expectancy was not more than five years! The absence of familiarity that has always characterized our relations excludes the possibility of a trivial or humorous interpretation." Six years earlier, she had written to Normand to recount a conversation between Owen-Jones and Jean-Pierre Meyers in which her son-in-law gave the impression that "he was merely awaiting my death in order to sell L'Oréal . . . I spoke about this with my husband, who told me that he is obviously waiting . . . He has been waiting for sixteen years." (With unintended prescience, André had suggested that she might become "gaga" well before her death.)

Now, apparently, Meyers was no longer content to wait. Before André's body was even cold, Liliane assumed that he had pushed OJ to write that horrid letter asking her, in effect, to kindly begin stepping aside. In her rage, she decided to change her will

and make Banier her *légataire universel* —
that is, her legal heir. Unlike adoption, which
would need approval by a judge, Banier's
designation as *légataire* was a simpler procedure that would give him succession rights
without bringing him into the family.

Under French law, dating back to the
Napoleonic Code, parents are required to
leave a certain portion of their estate to their
children. In the case of an only child, the
amount is one half. The rest — known as the
quotité disponible — can be left to anyone.
Liliane had already granted most of her
L'Oréal stock, comprising 92.6 percent of
her personal fortune, to Françoise and her
sons as naked, or reversionary, property. But
7.3 percent of her estate remained her exclusive property, to dispose of as she saw fit.
And on December 11, 2007, she officially
named Banier as the heir to that 7.3 percent.
(Martin d'Orgeval was named secondary heir
in case Banier should predecease Madame
Bettencourt.)

Apparently done out of spite toward Françoise and her husband, Liliane's designation
of Banier as her legal heir could have had
major consequences for L'Oréal. Among
other things, it put Banier in a position to
inherit those L'Oréal shares that had not
been designated for Françoise and her sons,
making the photographer the owner of 1.2
percent of the firm — a stake that would be

worth well over €1 billion today, according to Françoise's lawyer. Not to mention the buildings, apartments, jewelry, artworks, and liquidities that remained in Liliane's estate.

Banier's critics later accused him of manipulating Madame Bettencourt into taking this drastic step at a time when she was emotionally and mentally vulnerable. Jean-Michel Normand, the notary who was enlisted to draw up the act on short notice, considered it "stupidity" — *connerie* was the more vulgar term he used — and later sought to get it revoked. It was, in his view, "an act of pure violence toward her family," motivated not by grief over her husband's death but by "her conflict with her daughter."

Banier claims that he was unaware of his designation as heir until several days after the fact. "I was gutted. I told [Liliane] I'm not a punching ball between her and her daughter. I didn't need this war in a family I didn't belong to." Liliane's decision to make him her heir was "absurd" and "ridiculous," he said. "I'm not crazy and it would have been impossible to accept it."

Banier's after-the-fact protests are subject to caution. A week before the act was signed, he invited a lawyer and a notary to lunch at his house to discuss Liliane's "testamentary options" with a view to securing her gifts against any future legal challenges. Both of these jurists later told investigators that the

250

légataire designation was evoked on this occasion, yet Banier claims that he "never understood that I was to be [Liliane's] heir."

For the moment, Françoise knew nothing about her mother's testamentary juggling. And Liliane knew nothing about the legal whirlwind her daughter had just unleashed. Françoise was reluctant to tell her mother directly — partly for fear of encountering Banier in the house, and partly because her mother's deafness made verbal exchanges awkward. So on January 14, 2008, she wrote a letter informing her mother of her suit and the reasons for it.

Liliane tore open the envelope and read the first line: "I know ahead of time that you will be upset . . ." Françoise's letter went on to announce the legal action she had taken against Banier and, in a tone that Liliane found unbearable, presumed to lecture her mother on her choice of friends. There would be no problem if her relationship with the photographer were "truly friendly," wrote Françoise, "but that is not the case, considering what I have lived through personally, and what Papa endured deep down in his heart, discreetly confiding in me about his concern over [Banier's] intolerable behavior, which sooner or later must not be left unanswered. The one who pretends to be your 'friend' . . . has sought to separate you from us in order to control you for his own purposes . . . I

251

find it unbearable to think for a single instant that a so-called 'friend' can be so malicious towards you and our family." She signed the letter "your daughter who loves you, and because she loves you, I kiss you with all my heart."

The tender closing words left Liliane cold. "Your letter is absurd," she wrote on January 16. "Your problems with me do not date from a friendship with this or that person. Let's be honest, the friendship that you reproach me for has been essential to me and even did a lot of good to your father and me. I will not enter into the details — that concerns only me." Two days later Liliane wrote again. "Françoise, I really cannot digest your letter. You have no right to judge my relations and the choice of my friends . . . A suit against François-Marie is a suit against me. Have you thought of that?"

In a blistering follow-up letter, written as usual in green ink, Liliane threatened to launch a "revocation procedure" to claw back the L'Oréal stock that she had reserved for her daughter and grandsons. Defending her relationship with Banier, she wrote, "It's thanks to him that I did not remain locked in the conventional milieu that I seemed destined to by my situation and fortune . . . If all these gifts are the sign of my weakness, then what about the gift I made to you of my L'Oréal shares, considering that all the rest is quite modest compared to the value of that." In closing, she wrote: "This letter is a final warning."

On January 30, Liliane wrote directly to Courroye asking him to "put an end to this procedure." Her daughter's suit against Banier was "in reality a manifestation of jealously towards me." All her gifts to Banier were willingly offered "out of friendship" and "patronage," Liliane insisted. "If the amounts are substantial in the absolute, they are perfectly reasonable in relation to my fortune." For good measure, she sent the prosecutor copies of her irate letters to Françoise, along with reports from two doctors certifying her mental soundness.

Banier and d'Orgeval were off skiing at the chic Alpine resort of Courchevel when Liliane first learned of the suit. In the late afternoon of January 14, as dusk was descending on the mountainside, Banier had just finished his last run down the white-powdered slope and racked his skis. When he went to the hotel desk to fetch his keys, the clerk handed him a fax that had just arrived from Madame Bettencourt. That in itself was not unusual: He and Liliane sometimes exchanged two or three faxes a day. But this one sounded ominous. It announced a "disagreeable surprise" from her daughter.

Banier immediately called the Bettencourt

residence. Obliged by her deafness to use a maid as an intermediary on the telephone, the heiress avoided specifics but said she would explain everything upon his return. Banier and d'Orgeval wrapped up their Alpine holiday and headed back to Paris two days later. When they finally saw Liliane over dinner on Wednesday, January 16, she pulled out Françoise's letter and showed it to her guests, along with her reply. "I turned white as death," Banier recalls.

The next day, d'Orgeval went to see Liliane "to reassure her," as he wrote in his journal. She was still seething, and said she had slept badly because of Françoise's letter. "It's a story of mother-daughter jealousy," she told him. "She wanted to be Madame Bettencourt . . . What's sad is to do that just after the death of André."

Three weeks later, on February 6, police detectives descended on the rue Servandoni and rang Banier's doorbell at six a.m. "It was horrible," d'Orgeval recalls. "A dozen policemen searched the house for twelve hours." They were looking for documents related to Liliane's gifts, as well as Banier's correspondence with the heiress and his personal journals. D'Orgeval says they returned four or five times over the course of the investigation, and also searched Banier's country house in the south of France. "For the next five years, I went to sleep each night with the idea that they could return the next day."

Banier had actually done the investigators a great service by classifying all the relevant documents in color-coded folders. The papers they seized at his residences helped them determine the extent of the gifts he received. The detectives also discovered that the photographer had a complete record of Liliane's gifts to Françoise over the years, along with copies of correspondence between the heiress and her daughter. Banier later claimed that Liliane had insisted on giving him these documents so that he could defend himself if Françoise ever took him to court.

Banier was not the only one to receive a morning visit from the Financial Brigade. On Friday, February 1, detectives arrived at ten a.m. at the Meyers apartment in Neuilly to question Françoise about the facts surrounding her suit.

Why had she waited until André Bettencourt's death before taking steps to protect her mother? "I didn't want my action to further weaken my father, who had been very sick for months," she said. "My father knew many things about Banier. He even told me last June, 'He's a crook, and these things will be known sooner or later.' " She said she had finally decided to file the suit when Claire Thibout reported to her what Liliane's maid claimed to have overheard concerning Banier's adoption project.

Françoise called Banier "a professional of manipulation," who sought to "penetrate the intimacy of the family to the point of having a real control over my mother" and making himself "indispensable" to her. He worked to "isolate my mother from the rest of the family and from her friends" via a fifteen-year campaign of "denigration." Concerning her mother's vulnerability, Françoise described various episodes of confusion, memory lapses, and physical weakness over the years and accused Banier of trying to control her medical care in order to achieve his ends.

Under interrogation by Financial Brigade detectives, all the witnesses who had provided attestations in support of the suit repeated their charges against Banier and their claims about Madame Bettencourt's mental confusion. Other employees, however, provided contradictory accounts, describing Banier as a respectful and affectionate friend of "Madame" and attesting to her lucidity. Throughout the ensuing years of labyrinthine legal procedures, this dichotomy would persist.

On May 13, 2008, Courroye took the unusual step of personally accompanying the detectives when they went to interrogate Liliane at the Bettencourt home. "This was an elderly person, eighty-five years old at the time, quite elegant, who presented herself very well, in spite of the deafness she had suffered since childhood," he recalls. "She absolutely did not give me the impression of someone incoherent, suffering from Alzheimer's, and saying whatever popped into her head." The bottom line, says Courroye, was that she appeared lucid and had willingly bestowed gifts on Banier, but he "sensed a very strong conflict between mother and daughter."

Under Courroye's questioning, Madame Bettencourt described her relationship with Banier and her reasons for sponsoring him: "I have known Monsieur François-Marie Banier for twenty-five years. In the beginning, I knew the name. I knew he was an artist and that he wrote books. After two years, observing that this Monsieur was interested in art in general, a domain that is dear to me, I decided to help him financially."

When the prosecutor asked if she knew the total amount of her gifts to Banier, she admitted that she did not, but added: "The amount of the liberalities I gave him matters little to me in relation to my personal fortune. . . . The amount is certainly important but I must tell you that it gave me great pleasure to offer this money."

Why had she been so generous? "I wanted Monsieur Banier to be able to pursue his artistic activity and considered it normal to help him financially in order to provide the necessary means."

Did Banier ask for money? No, she replied

emphatically, "however when I saw him looking at artworks, I remembered them and sometimes I would buy them for him later. I never attempted to calculate Monsieur Banier's needs."

As for her relationship with her daughter, Liliane Bettencourt was scathing: "My daughter cannot abide Monsieur Banier. This animosity also results from her jealousy. She was jealous of the place that Monsieur Banier had at my side and of the friendship I had for him."

Françoise Meyers's suit presented a paradox: It sought to protect her elderly mother from exploitation, but the supposed victim loudly denied her victimhood.

Thus it became increasingly important to determine the state of Madame Bettencourt's vulnerability. During the May 13 interrogation, Courroye tried to convince Madame Bettencourt to undergo an examination by a neurologist. She flatly refused, saying she didn't "want to see a doctor just to give satisfaction to my daughter."

That became a constant refrain during the months and years that followed, and constituted the main stumbling block to the prosecutor's investigation. The conundrum was that Liliane's vulnerability could not be proven without an examination by a psychiatrist or neurologist, but there was no legal means to force her to accept that. And the people around her — Banier, de Maistre, and her lawyers — pushed her to resist an independent exam that might allow her daughter to put her under guardianship. The question of Liliane's mental health thus became a major battleground in the case.

The documents filed with the suit included accounts of Madame Bettencourt's mental confusion by the domestic employees and friends who had provided attestations to Françoise's lawyers. The nurse Henriette Youpatchou, for example, stated that "after her hospitalization at the beginning of September 2006, Madame Bettencourt was very confused, she was disoriented in time and space. She regularly thought she was in a clinic, or in a foreign country." Chantal Trovel, secretary to André Bettencourt, declared that during the same period, Liliane Bettencourt was "extremely fragile," "completely disoriented," and made "incoherent statements." Nicole Berger, a longtime family friend, recounted that after a two-week visit to the Bettencourt home in 2007, she left with "the feeling that [Liliane] had completely lost her head."

But these anecdotal accounts were of limited value to investigators without the backup of professional medical opinions that could prove her vulnerability. There was little doubt that Liliane Bettencourt had faced some serious health challenges in her life, going back to the childhood attack of tuberculosis that had originally caused her deafness (due to a bad reaction to the Streptomycin antibiotic used to treat her). She suffered a relapse of tuberculosis at the time of her daughter's birth, later underwent breast-cancer surgery, a colectomy (partial removal of the colon), and a double hip replacement that made walking difficult. In addition, she suffered from chronic osteoporosis that at times caused her excruciating pain. "My head is OK," she would say, "but my body doesn't follow."

The refusal of Madame Bettencourt and her entourage to accept an independent neurological examination made it difficult to determine the state of her mental health. But her medical record pointed to possible problems:

- In 2002, a brain scan revealed a "hemispheric leukoaraiosis," a relatively banal neurological condition affecting the white matter of the brain. Not uncommon in older people, it can cause cognitive difficulties in some cases.
- In 2003, Madame Bettencourt was hospitalized for the removal of a benign intestinal polyp. Some people in her entourage noted a bout of depression and memory lapses after the operation,

possibly due to overmedication. Claire Thibout told investigators that at this time "Madame Bettencourt was like a zombie . . . she trembled and did not speak."

- In September 2006, following the accident at Formentor, Liliane suffered a period of confusion attributed to excessive use of painkillers. At that time, Philippe Koskas, then Madame Bettencourt's regular doctor, noted "persistent memory problems" and recommended an MRI scan and other complementary exams, but there was no immediate follow-up. A scan performed in June 2007 noted "a diffused enlargement of the pericerebral spaces associated with a leukoaraiosis" — consistent with the findings of the 2002 MRI.

- On December 14, 2007, Dr. Michel Kalafat, a neurologist, examined Madame Bettencourt at the request of her daughter. Observing an "alteration of her mental faculties," he judged that the patient "needed to be advised and supervised concerning her civil acts and could under these conditions be placed under a regime of *curatelle*" — a limited guardianship requiring oversight of certain acts. Kalafat issued a certificate to that effect, which was included in the filing of Françoise's suit.

- In January 2008, at the initiative of Liliane's entourage, Professor Yves Agid, an Alzheimer's specialist, certified that she presented "no difficulties of intellectual strategy or language" and no "recent or long-term memory troubles."
- In September 2008, a contrary opinion came from Professor Philippe Azouvi, a neurologist solicited by prosecutor Courroye. His report, based on an analysis of Liliane's medical records but not a direct examination, pointed to "the possibility of an organic intellectual deterioration (Alzheimer's or mixed dementia)" and concluded that she showed "at least since September 2006, a probable vulnerability linked to an apparent degenerative neurological condition affecting her intellectual faculties."

Seeking to clarify these conflicting opinions, Courroye ordered an independent neurological examination in February 2009. Liliane refused, but instead underwent a half-hour oral examination by Dr. Hubert Rémy, a neurologist handpicked by her lawyer, Fabrice Goguel. Rémy declared that the heiress "disposes of her total will and discernment" and therefore, "needs no measure of protection." But Rémy's opinion was perhaps not disinterested: He was paid €1,000 for the thirty-minute consultation, which was attended by Goguel. Five months later, Goguel sought to obtain a new certificate from Rémy, but the doctor was appalled by the diminished state of the patient. He said she was "not the same person" he had seen in February and refused to provide the document. He subsequently destroyed all records of his consultations with Madame Bettencourt.

Hoping to avoid a public scandal that would damage the image of L'Oréal and the Bettencourt family, Liliane had earlier proposed a reconciliation accord with her daughter. In February 2008, she asked L'Oréal CEO Lindsay Owen-Jones, Publicis CEO Maurice Lévy, and Xavier Fontanet, a L'Oréal board member, to serve as mediators in a tripartite negotiation involving her, Françoise, and Banier. It is interesting to note that it was Jean-Pierre Meyers, not Françoise herself, who spoke for his wife's interests. The talks continued into the summer, resulting in several drafts of a proposed agreement. "With this odious suit, you are slowly killing me," Liliane wrote to her daughter in June 2008. "This protocol will give you an honorable way out."

According to one version dated April 2008, Françoise agreed to withdraw her suit on the following conditions: Liliane promised to grant Banier no more liberalities; Banier renounced any future adoption project; Liliane pledged not to give Banier a role at L'Oréal, the family holding company Thétys, or the Bettencourt Schueller Foundation; Liliane promised not to reduce the functions or status of Jean-Pierre Meyers and foreswore any future revocation of the L'Oréal shares gifted to her daughter and grandsons.

This version seemed to offer something for everyone. Banier could have kept everything he had gained up to that point and avoided a trial. Françoise would have succeeded in shutting off the spigot and preserving the family fortune. And Liliane could have continued her cozy relationship with Banier as a friend, but not as the object of her largesse. Most important, at least to Liliane and Françoise, the affair would be quietly settled before the press got wind of it and turned it into an embarrassing media frenzy. "I don't even dare imagine the risk of a leak, which grows larger each day," Liliane wrote to her daughter.

By the end of the summer, though, what had seemed like a promising reconciliation deal broke down. According to Maurice Lévy, there was a clause that called for putting Liliane under guardianship in the event her health declined. What shocked Madame Bettencourt, he says, "was the fact that the choice of guardian would be made by her daughter."

Another of the mediators, Xavier Fontanet,

pointed to a different source of the break-down: There was a clause guaranteeing that Madame Bettencourt could see her two grandsons, but "she only wanted to see Jean-Victor [the elder]. I don't know the reason why she did not want to see Nicolas." Liliane considered this "nonnegotiable." She called her younger grandson on his cell phone and told him, "Listen, I don't want to see you anymore, because every time I see you, you remind me of your mother."

Banier says he refused to sign his part of the agreement because Françoise's lawyers wanted him to acknowledge that "Madame Bettencourt had psychological problems and memory lapses," something that he never admitted. "I found that monstrous."

On July 1, 2008, in an apparent effort to convince Françoise to drop her suit, Banier wrote to her directly. "We crossed paths some fifteen years ago at Arcouest. But we don't really know each other, and furthermore I think that you haven't wished that." Seeking to explain his relationship with Liliane — and perhaps to launch a veiled threat — he wrote that "the hundreds, thousands of letters exchanged [between me] and Liliane will attest to the literary dialogue that we carried on. Your mother has told me to publish them." His relationship with André, he said, was "different, certainly with less complicity, but nonetheless very deep. Even though I sometimes wondered if he might have suffered from my proximity with Liliane, he assured me that our relationship had enlightened him." In conclusion, he wrote: "Your mother has too much personality for anyone at all to be able to influence her. . . . You are mistaken about her and about me."

On July 16, Françoise wrote a terse and unequivocal reply: "Monsieur, do not expect me to believe what you have written me. None of that is either true or sincere. As for me, I have confidence in the justice system that is now at work."

The time for reconciliation was over.

CHAPTER 12
SIBLING RIVALS

As one follows the tangled tale of the Bettencourt Affair, two characters stand out as the central adversaries in this bitter conflict: François-Marie Banier and Françoise Meyers. The pair deserve a closer look in relation to each other, since their enmity is the driving force behind it all. It would take a psychoanalyst to probe the complexities, but even a layman can see intriguing patterns emerging.

Banier and Françoise appeared to occupy opposite ends of the spectrum. He was gay, extraverted, provocative, witty, exuberant. She was shy, introverted, and discreet, avoiding contact with the world outside her small circle of family and friends. But in fact the two had much in common — including male and female versions of the same first name: François/Françoise.

Both had "mother problems." Madeleine Banier was self-centered and inattentive, more concerned with keeping up bourgeois appearances than showing her admittedly difficult son the affection he craved. Far from protecting Banier from his father's blows and insults, she would side with her husband and tell the trembling boy, "You will shed tears of blood if you don't do what your father says."

Françoise, who clung to her mother like a mussel on a rock, as she was fond of repeating, was met by an emotional pushback. Liliane told those around her that relations with Françoise were fine until the girl reached adolescence. What happened at that point? Did Françoise suddenly become rebellious, moody, and capricious like so many teenagers? Perhaps. But from Liliane's comments — in conversation, correspondence, and published interviews — it would seem that her daughter just didn't measure up to her expectations.

To hear Liliane tell it, as we have seen, Françoise was slow, passive, lacking in energy and initiative. Most of all, perhaps, Liliane was disappointed to see that her daughter showed little interest in the family business and almost never talked about her grandfather, the revered Eugène Schueller. For her part, Françoise said everything was fine between her and her mother until Banier came along. Believing that was easier than admitting a much more painful possibility: Perhaps her mother simply did not love her.

Banier's arrival on the scene did complicate things between mother and daughter, for Banier clearly enjoyed the affection and admiration that Françoise craved but never got from Liliane. That's why the adoption story — true or not — was so unbearable to Françoise. Deprived of his own mother's affection, Banier found a substitute in Liliane, as he had earlier done with Marie-Laure de Noailles, Madeleine Castaing, and Silvana Mangano. In Françoise's eyes, he was a cuckoo invading her family nest. "Our attachment is real," Liliane wrote to Banier in October 2008, "that's why [Françoise] can't tolerate it."

Banier always claimed that his bond with Liliane was an adult relationship, not a surrogate mother-son thing. That's not so clear. Liliane sometimes described herself as a "mother" to Banier. And in their correspondence, she would often badger him like a mother: Lose weight, get exercise, don't overeat, chew your food, use this kind of shampoo, get off your butt and promote your book. Banier, according to the butler Pascal Bonnefoy, would sometimes refer to himself as "the son she never had." Liliane's notary, Jean-Michel Normand, described her relationship with Banier as "quasi filial": "I had the impression that he was in a way the son she would have wanted."

■ ■ ■ ■

One indication of Liliane's maternal role was her harsh criticism of Banier's own mother, whom he had contacted in the 1990s after years of estrangement.

Liliane repeatedly lashed out at Madeleine Banier like a jealous competitor. "She is crazy," Liliane wrote in one December 1994 tirade. "She is total incomprehension . . . there is no hope . . . count only on yourself, accept nothing, nothing, nothing from her, there is nothing to understand." Her insistence on this point is revealing: It would seem that, in Liliane's eyes, "acceptance" is also an act of love; perhaps she saw Banier's acceptance of her own gifts in this light.

In July 2000, Liliane wrote: "Your mother makes me furious, she doesn't understand that it's too late." Five years later, the heiress lashed out again at Madeleine Banier: "I have no confidence in your mother. You don't wait till you're ninety years old to reach out to your son." Message: *Don't waste your time on this imposter; I'm your true mother, the one who really cares for you.*

Banier and Françoise resembled rival siblings, each competing for the warmth and comfort of their mother's breast. But this mother wasn't willing to share. It was like one of the biblical stories that Françoise knew

so well — Jacob and Esau, say, or the Prodigal Son — in which one child is favored over another. Banier was well aware of the rivalry, and profited from it. But contrary to Françoise's claims, he is not the one who originally poisoned Liliane's mind against her daughter. Though there are passages in the correspondence where Banier echoes Liliane's criticism of her daughter and son-in-law, particularly after the suit was filed, it is the heiress who takes the lead on this front and clearly needs no prodding.

In fact, Banier repeatedly urged her to reach out to her daughter and defuse the tense situation. In April 2010, in a written exchange with Liliane — they would often commit their conversations to paper because of her deafness — Banier wrote, "For 20 years I've been telling you to go sort things out with Françoise . . . [She's] your daughter! You should have said: I understand this, I don't understand that. Let's make peace."

Liliane answered vaguely, complaining of her daughter's lack of "continuity."

Banier returned to the charge. "Who abandoned the other? Isn't it you who abandoned her when she was little because she didn't follow you and André as quickly as you wanted, since you were accustomed to your father's dynamism?"

Liliane's reply was brutal: "You don't understand that I want nothing from my

271

daughter."

In another written exchange three weeks later, Liliane seemed to express remorse: "I think I eliminated Françoise — but without wishing to eliminate her. Perhaps out of incomprehension."

Banier's quasi-sibling rivalry with Françoise served his interests in one sense: The greater Liliane's hostility toward her daughter, the more she was inclined to pile gifts on him. But there was also great danger in this triangular face-off: As he put it, Banier had become an unwilling "punching ball" in the emotional battle between the two women. To punish her mother for preferring the usurper, Françoise had to destroy him. That was the psychological underpinning of her suit, even though the stated reason was to protect Liliane from abuse.

In his 1941 book *The Wound and the Bow,* the critic Edmund Wilson argued that suffering can be a powerful stimulus to artistic creation. Both Françoise and Banier fit this pattern. Banier in more obvious ways because he is an artistic workaholic, but Françoise is also an obsessive artist who spends three to five hours a day practicing her piano. It is a very private passion: She does not perform, though she has recorded a CD for distribution to family and friends — a compilation of Bach, Beethoven, Scarlatti, and Schumann

compositions, produced in 1992. Without hearing her play, it is difficult to judge the quality of her musicianship. Arielle Dombasle, herself a professional musician, actress, and filmmaker, says her childhood friend possesses "an extraordinary virtuosity and a surprising musicality." The praise is perhaps excessive. But it doesn't really matter whether Françoise is a virtuoso or a ham-fisted amateur. The wound-and-bow syndrome does not depend on the quality of the art.

Françoise and François-Marie have another thing in common: Both are published authors. Banier would howl at the notion that anyone could take Françoise seriously as a writer. Certainly, her attainment in that field does not compare with Banier's seven novels. But her two nonfiction books — five volumes on the Bible and a five-hundred-page tome on Greek mythology — are the products of long research and hundreds of hours spent putting words on paper. (Another interesting link between Françoise and Banier: Former Pompidou Center president Hélène Ahrweiler, who gave Banier his first major photo show, also wrote the introduction to Meyers's book *Les dieux grecs.*)

Banier always said that Liliane's family problems did not interest him. But there was a moment in court when he seemed to compare his own family drama to the one that tortured both Liliane and Françoise. "I talked to my father, who slapped me morning and night for twenty years," he said. So why couldn't Françoise "cross the street and talk to her mother," and why couldn't Liliane organize a lunch and work things out with her daughter and son-in-law? In a voice thick with emotion, he added: "For me, it's always the fault of the parents. I was a good little boy."

Who could say that Françoise was not a good little girl?

CHAPTER 13
SARKOZY JOINS THE FRAY

On Wednesday, November 5, 2008, a chauffeur-driven car entered the main gates of the Élysée Palace and crunched across the gravel courtyard. It is here that foreign dignitaries arrive between a double cordon of Gardes républicains with their polished helmets and red plumes to be greeted on the steps by the French president. There was no such ceremony today, for this was a private visit by Liliane Bettencourt and Patrice de Maistre, her unctuous financial adviser. Met by an usher in black tails, the pair was escorted up a white marble staircase to the second-floor office of Nicolas Sarkozy.

The president knew Madame Bettencourt personally, having dined at her home and, like many other politicians, visited her husband during election season. As for de Maistre, Sarkozy did not know him personally, though they had crossed paths at meetings of Sarkozy's fund-raising Premier cercle club at the Hôtel Bristol. (It happened that Jean-

Pierre Meyers was also a member.) The president had accorded this rendezvous as a courtesy to the leading shareholder in a major French company and a former constituent from his days as mayor of Neuilly. He was not informed ahead of time of the exact purpose of the visit.

As Sarkozy described the scene: "I see this grande dame arrive with an elegant man whom I don't know. I invite her to sit down. I greet her with some personal words, she asks about my family. I ask how she is and she tells me she has big problems with her daughter . . . who is trying to get her declared insane. I asked her what happened. She replied that she had made some gifts to friends and that had provoked a big mess."

At that point Sarkozy pushed a buzzer on his bronze and rosewood Louis XV desk and instructed his judicial adviser, Patrick Ouart, to join the meeting. A burly man with a boyish, meaty face, Ouart had held high positions in the private sector — including with the LVMH luxury goods group — before Sarkozy brought him into the Élysée. Skirting the normal chain of command, Ouart reported directly to the president and was charged with overseeing some of the government's most sensitive issues. Working behind the scenes, invisible to the press and the public, he was one of the most powerful and loyal figures in Sarkozy's constellation. Some said he was the de facto justice minister, the one who told the titular holder of that position what to do.

Ouart had no idea what to expect when he entered the presidential office. "The discussion was led by Madame Bettencourt, an elderly, deaf, and authoritarian woman," he recalls. "She gave us a summary of the affair, without consulting notes."

The reason Madame Bettencourt did not use notes was that she had learned by heart a speech that de Maistre had typed out for her. Dominique Gaspard, her chambermaid, had coached her on it until she could repeat it from memory: "I supported you for your election with pleasure, and I will continue to aid you personally. I have grave problems with my daughter that could have consequences for L'Oréal, and thus for the economy of the country."

As Ouart recalls the meeting, Madame Bettencourt then elaborated on the situation. She told the president her daughter detested her, and wanted to keep her from living her life freely. The whole affair, she said, had been whipped up by her son-in-law, who favored a takeover of L'Oréal by its minority partner, the Swiss food giant Nestlé. At that point, de Maistre jumped in and explained the danger for L'Oréal. If Madame Bettencourt were put under guardianship and declared legally incompetent, he said, Nestlé might be

277

tempted to set aside a shareholder stability agreement and seize control of the company.

"The president was very upset," Ouart recalls. "The idea of seeing this family tear itself apart publicly seemed preposterous to him." At the end of the thirty-minute meeting, Sarkozy offered to mediate between Madame Bettencourt and her daughter, and asked Ouart to meet with the lawyers for both sides in an effort to "calm things down."

It was highly unusual for a president to grant a personal meeting on short notice, and even more bizarre for a head of state to offer his mediation in what, at that point, was a family dispute. But L'Oréal was a major French company, the source of thousands of jobs and hundreds of millions in tax revenues for the state. If there really was a risk of a Swiss takeover, as Madame Bettencourt and de Maistre warned, then that was of concern to the president.

L'Oréal had come a long way since Eugène Schueller started tinkering with hair dyes in his kitchen laboratory. Under his brilliant successors, François Dalle and Lindsay Owen-Jones, the firm had grown vertiginously, acquiring dozens of brands and pushing into new markets on every continent to become the world's number-one cosmetics group.

Today the company boasts 82,000 employees in 130 countries, annual sales of more than €24 billion, and consistently strong growth rates. L'Oréal's recently renovated ten-story Clichy headquarters — with its atrium, landscaped gardens, employee restaurant, and in-house gym — is the hub of an international empire that includes twenty-eight brands. Among them, the cosmetics and perfume divisions of Lancôme, Helena Rubenstein, Maybelline, Yves Saint Laurent, Ralph Lauren, Cacharel, Vichy, the Body Shop . . . L'Oréal's stock is valued at some €90 billion, of which the principal share belongs to Liliane Bettencourt — or, more accurately, to Françoise Bettencourt Meyers and her two sons, who hold stock as reversionary property and will fully inherit it upon Liliane's death.

The firm's future seemed solidly in the hands of the founding family — until the Bettencourt Affair raised the specter of a foreign takeover. That fear had its roots in the politics of the 1970s. In 1972, Socialist leader François Mitterrand signed a pact with the then powerful French Communist Party calling for sweeping nationalizations of major French industrial groups and banks. Fearing a state takeover of L'Oréal if the left came to power, CEO François Dalle proposed a stock swap with the Swiss food conglomerate Nestlé, since a company with a foreign partner would be better protected from nationalization. The deal, which won the blessing of President Georges Pompidou and then finance minister Valéry Giscard d'Estaing, was signed on March 22, 1974. Under its terms, a Bettencourt family holding company, Gesperal, became the majority shareholder of L'Oréal. Fifty-one percent of Gesperal was owned by Liliane Bettencourt, and 49 percent by Nestlé. In exchange, Liliane Bettencourt was granted 4 percent of the Swiss company's shares. Less than a month later, Pompidou died after a long bout with cancer. In the election to succeed him, Giscard, the center-right candidate, defeated Mitterrand, and the nationalization fears subsided. But by then L'Oréal was tethered to Nestlé via a pact that froze the share ratio for the next three decades.

The arrangement functioned smoothly over the years, with each company holding seats on the other's board. But there were periodic worries that the Swiss giant, four times bigger than L'Oréal, might one day be tempted to swallow up the French firm. That seemed unlikely as long as the original pact remained in force. It was renewed for five years in 2004, and again in 2009, with the stipulation that neither side could sell its shares or increase its holdings until six months after the death of Madame Bettencourt.

But her daughter's lawsuit suddenly raised fears that L'Oréal might be put in play. The danger, Ouart explained to Sarkozy, was that if Liliane were found to be mentally incompetent, her votes on the L'Oréal board could be contested. She could also lose her voting rights over her shares, theoretically leaving Françoise free to sell them. In a more drastic scenario, under French law she could be declared "civilly dead," raising the question of whether the shareholders' pact with Nestlé would still apply.

How real were these scenarios? Liliane had always sworn that she would never give up the majority of L'Oréal as long as she was alive. Françoise repeatedly declared her own devotion to the family firm and denied any intention of selling to Nestlé. But de Maistre, Liliane's domineering financial adviser, harped constantly on the notion that Françoise and Jean-Pierre were dealing secretly with the Swiss firm and scheming to sell out. De Maistre even suggested that this was the real reason behind the suit. Knowing the depth of Liliane's dislike for her son-in-law and distrust of her daughter, de Maistre was able to play on this theme in order to increase his own influence over his employer's affairs. He also waved this flag repeatedly in his meetings with Sarkozy and Ouart.

Sarkozy's interest in L'Oréal went beyond jobs and tax revenues. L'Oréal was one of those companies known as a *fleuron,* or flagship, of French industry. There was something almost mystical about the state's relationship to these big, historic firms, particularly those with international reach. Apart from the economic power they wielded, they contributed to the nation's prestige and, in the case of a firm like L'Oréal, France's identification with beauty, style, and luxury. Cosmetics — like wine, cheese, and haute couture — were central to the national identity. Sarkozy put the matter crudely in a private meeting with his party's parliamentarians: "I don't want [L'Oréal] to piss off to Switzerland."

There may have been another reason for the president to take a personal interest in the case: If Sarkozy, as many suspected, had received illegal campaign contributions from the Bettencourts, it would be dangerous for investigators and the press to start digging through the family's financial records. Maybe there was a political time bomb lurking in there. For whatever reasons, the president apparently decided it would be better for all concerned if the case were shut down. He did not have the power to do that directly, but he did have at least two throttles that might slow down the machinery: Patrick Ouart, his trusted adviser, and Philippe Courroye, the ambitious Nanterre prosecutor, who had been a personal friend of Sarkozy's since 2001.

After that initial meeting with Madame

Bettencourt and de Maistre, the president instructed Ouart to ride herd on the case. Ouart met no fewer than five times with de Maistre, who had returned for a second Élysée meeting on November 13, and also huddled with Françoise's lawyers. "I quoted to both parties this aphorism that my grandfather liked to repeat: 'doing good makes no noise, and making noise does no good.' But I wasn't listened to. The war, which had very old psychological roots, was declared and was not amenable to reason."

As for Courroye, he had launched into the investigation so aggressively that it was hard to put on the brakes. "He had the instincts of a hunting dog," says Ouart.

Always with an eye on the top Paris prosecutor's job, Courroye had apparently assumed that the vigorous pursuit of this high-stakes case would help him clinch that prize. Now, nearly one year into his investigation, he started to hear a different message from the Élysée. Since the beginning of their friendship, Sarkozy and Courroye had lunched or dined together once or twice a year. Now, the pace of their meetings picked up dramatically. Over the period of Courroye's investigation, he met with Sarkozy at least eight times, sometimes arriving furtively by the Élysée's rear garden so as not to attract the attention of the press. He even dined with Sarkozy on November 5, the day of the president's meeting with Madame Betten-court and de Maistre.

What did the two men talk about? "Never about cases," Courroye insists. "What interested him was to gather ideas about judicial policy, the protection of minors, international judicial cooperation . . ." That strains credulity. Sarkozy is known to be blunt, often abrasive, rarely bending to rules and legal niceties when he wants something. And Courroye, who craved the Paris job, seemed unlikely to tell the president he wouldn't "go there" when asked about the case. In April 2009, in what some saw as a glaring proof of complicity between the two men, Sarkozy personally pinned the Order of Merit medal on Courroye's lapel. Speaking at the award ceremony, the president remarked, "People reproach the fact that we know each other, but that doesn't prevent him from doing his job, nor me from doing mine."

On December 1, 2008, the Financial Brigade sent Courroye a seven-page report that summarized their findings after nearly one year of investigation. Their accounting of Liliane's gifts to Banier dwarfed the amount cited in Metzner's original dossier: €993 million (worth well over a billion dollars) in artwork, real estate, cash, and life-insurance policies. The report's conclusion stated that "numerous interrogations" supported a "body of presumptions concerning the reality of an abuse of weakness committed by M. Banier." Courroye paid little attention to that judgment. "It was the opinion of a police officer, but it was in no way a judicial document," he explains. "It's always dangerous to offer an opinion, to say the subject is guilty of abuse — he's not authorized to do that."

Meanwhile, one of Liliane's worst fears came true: On December 18, 2008, following a leak on the satirical website Bakchich, investigative journalist Hervé Gattegno broke the story in the weekly newsmagazine *Le Point,* describing Courroye's probe into the "hundreds of millions of euros" given to Banier by the wealthy heiress. Gattegno, who clearly had access to some of the depositions, quoted several juicy witness statements describing Banier's pressures on the heiress and her moments of confusion.

How did the story suddenly hit the press after a year of radio silence? One suspects the hand of Olivier Metzner, Françoise's media-conscious lawyer, who liked to brag that his "instructions" to journalists were always "respected." Assuming Metzner was behind the leak, his likely motive was to pressure Courroye into completing his investigation and sending the case to trial. In any case, the genie was out of the bottle: The Bettencourt Affair soon became almost daily fodder for the French press in a feeding frenzy that even spilled over into such US publications as *Time, Vanity Fair,* and the *New York Times.* That was bad news for Liliane, now portrayed as a batty billionaire. Bad also for Banier, branded as a "gigolo," a "guru," and a "crook." Bad for Françoise, who was perceived as a jealous, vengeful, and ungrateful daughter. And bad for L'Oréal, whose image was tarnished by the spectacle of the founding family ripping itself apart.

For all her concerns over leaks, Liliane minced no words in the interview she gave the *Journal du Dimanche* shortly after the story broke. "What on earth has gotten into my daughter?" she asked. "Is she settling scores with me? In any case it's an act of sheer meanness. The funny thing is it doesn't touch me." She described Françoise as "introverted" and "closed in," gripped by jealousy over Liliane's close relationship with Banier. "He's an artist, and that motivates me." Her parting shot was laced with mocking cruelty: "I don't see my daughter anymore and I don't wish to. For me, my daughter has become something inert."

Most of all, perhaps, the press leak was bad for Nicolas Sarkozy, because of the political time bomb that was ticking under the surface. The media pile-on made it more urgent than ever to put a lid on the case before it did worse damage. There is no proof that the president explicitly told Courroye to quash the affair. What is obvious is that after waging a hell-for-leather investigation during the first year, the prosecutor now seemed to drag his feet — even as the press and the Socialist opposition called on him to assign the investigation to an independent magistrate, and Metzner demanded that the case be sent to trial without further delay. A staunch admirer of Napoleon Bonaparte, Courroye professed to be unmoved by the mounting pressures: "I am totally indifferent to criticism," he said. "I do not have to justify or defend myself." His job, he said, was to weigh the facts objectively and to base his actions on a strict interpretation of the law.

When the Financial Brigade finally handed Courroye their completed investigative files in June 2009, he stuffed the dossier into his briefcase and took it home to read over the weekend. "I studied all the elements of the dossier. What did we have? We had no medical opinion, we had the testimony of [Madame Bettencourt's] entourage, especially her personnel, and these accounts canceled each other out. That is, some people said Madame Bettencourt was sometimes tired but otherwise fine, others said she was not in good shape, and there was no way to decide between them." When he finished poring over the documents that Sunday evening, he says, he was "completely perplexed, because there was nothing that, in my view, permitted us to lean in one direction or the other." Returning to the office Monday morning, he gave the file to his assistant prosecutor, Marie-Christine d'Aubigney, and asked her to read it. She came back four days later and told him, "I don't see how you can send Banier to trial on this dossier." Courroye agreed.

But what about the hundreds of millions Banier raked in? What about his hovering presence around Liliane? His alleged manipulation? Liliane's confusion? "Let me tell you something," says Courroye. "Morally, sending Banier to trial, seeing him convicted, presents no problem for me. But we weren't dealing in morality, we were carrying out the law. The question was whether or not an abuse of weakness, a strict juridical qualification, was proven."

At that point, in early July 2009, Courroye phoned Metzner.

"Listen, Olivier, I wanted to let you know that the Prosecutor's Office has studied the dossier carefully and — I haven't taken the decision yet — but we're leaning toward closing the case."

Metzner had long suspected that the case was problematic. Without a smoking gun, or even an official medical report certifying Madame Bettencourt's vulnerability, he knew that convicting Banier was a long shot. But Olivier Metzner was a street fighter, and he was not about to give up that easily.

CHAPTER 14
METZNER'S END RUN

Philippe Courroye's investigation had dragged on for well over a year. Metzner, Francoise's lawyer, had pushed and prodded, gone on television, rattled the press about Banier's exactions and Liliane's vulnerability, but nothing seemed to overcome what he saw as Courroye's inertia.

Seeking a way around this roadblock, Metzner came up with a rarely used tactic: *la citation directe,* a petition presented directly to the court without passing through the Prosecutor's Office and obtaining an indictment. In other words, he would cite Banier as a defendant and, if the court accepted, take him directly to trial. The papers were already drawn up when Courroye informed Metzner that he was leaning toward closing the case.

On July 15, 2009, Metzner cited Banier before the 15th Chamber of the High Court of Nanterre. Its presiding judge, Isabelle Prévost-Desprez, a specialist in financial investigations, was only too eager to take the case. A former investigating magistrate with a reputation for stubborn independence, Prévost-Desprez had a long-standing rivalry — if not outright enmity — with Philippe Courroye. Some said the bad blood between them had its roots in a love affair gone sour, a rumor she dismisses with a contemptuous laugh.

Sitting behind the desk of her cluttered office in Nanterre's court building, Prévost-Desprez talks about the case with a mixture of humor, irony, and indignation. The judge, now fifty-eight, is a woman of average height, somewhat stout, with a round face, blond hair, large blue eyes, and bright-red lipstick. She laughs frequently and speaks bluntly, mixing legal terms with colloquialisms and an occasional obscenity aimed at her enemies.

Prévost-Desprez readily agreed to take on this high-profile case — not least because it would annoy Courroye. Which of course it did: The prosecutor filed several motions to nullify the proceedings but was systematically overruled. On September 22, Courroye finally closed his own investigation and grudgingly passed his files on to his nemesis — four volumes of depositions and documents in a state of total disorder. At this point, Prévost-Desprez changed all the locks in her office for fear that Courroye and his "spies" would come in and rummage through her papers and her computer. Suspecting the prosecutor of bugging her office, she would sometimes hold sensitive meetings in the office of her assistant. "I was under surveillance, it was totally crazy," she says with one of the nervous laughs that punctuate her conversation. Her paranoia was not entirely baseless, for Courroye did all he could to block her investigation.

When Banier got word of Metzner's petition, he flew into a rage. Up to that point, he seemed confident that Françoise's suit against him would collapse. "I thought it was a joke," he says. "I did nothing to defend myself." Largely because he genuinely believed he had done nothing wrong, and that there was no valid case against him. He had also been reassured by de Maistre's belief, based on his contacts with the Élysée, that Courroye's investigation would soon be closed down. Now the photographer suddenly learned that he would have to face charges in court. It was only at that point that he hired Hervé Temime, a top criminal lawyer, to defend him. Temime, who counted Roman Polanski, Catherine Deneuve, and Gérard Depardieu among his clients, also happened to be a longtime friend of Olivier Metzner.

At their first meeting in July 2009, Banier arrived in a state of uncontrolled anger at Temime's third-floor office on the rue de

Rivoli, the four-lane road that runs alongside the Louvre and the Tuileries Gardens and was a major access route for Allied tanks in the Liberation of Paris. Before he sat down, before he had even been introduced to Temime, Banier started shouting, waving his arms in all directions, railing against the injustice of the charges against him. Seated behind his desk, Temime silently observed this outburst and considered ending the meeting right there. The tirade lasted a long while — Martin d'Orgeval, who accompanied Banier that day, called it a catharsis — but Banier finally calmed down enough to tell the lawyer his version of the story. Temime was convinced at that point that the case contained no valid proof of Madame Bettencourt's vulnerability; failing that, he reasoned, she was free to spend her money as she chose. He was confident that he could win in court.

But the intensity of that initial meeting set their relationship at such a high emotional pitch that it was difficult to organize Banier's defense in a calm and dispassionate manner. "I had a confident and free relationship with Banier," says Temime, "but there were times when he couldn't control his emotions with me."

Meanwhile, in late June, Madame Bettencourt's advisers brought Georges Kiejman on board to represent her interests in the suit. Kiejman, then seventy-seven, a veteran of countless high-profile cases, was one of the most prominent members of the Paris bar. There was something intimidating about his beady eyes, set in a head as round and bald as a hard-boiled egg. His neatly trimmed mustache gave him the look of a 1940s film actor — someone who might have worn a French police uniform and stood next to Claude Rains in *Casablanca.* Apart from his intellect, Kiejman's most effective weapon was his tongue. With dazzling eloquence, he could construct his arguments and puncture those of his opponents with equal ease. A master of what *Le Monde*'s judicial correspondent called "oratory cruelty," he would mock and demean his adversaries with lacerating barbs.

Kiejman also specialized in networking and backroom negotiations. He knew the gears and levers of political power, having served as a three-time cabinet member under his friend François Mitterrand. Despite his Socialist leanings, he also cultivated his relations with conservatives like Nicolas Sarkozy and even handled the president's divorce from his second wife, Cécilia. Kiejman had also represented Mohamed Al-Fayed following the 1997 death of his son Dodi and Princess Diana, but finally resigned over the nuttiness of Al-Fayed's conspiracy theories.

When he was hired, Kiejman visited Madame Bettencourt in Neuilly to introduce himself and discuss the case over lunch. His first impression was of "someone brilliant and original" — and fully conscious of her charm. "During this first meeting, she told me, rather amusingly, 'Sir, you are an old man who hides his youth.' " Kiejman asked the heiress why she needed a lawyer. "She explained that it was unacceptable for her daughter to question what she did with her money," Kiejman recalls. "She also found it unjust to attack Banier." She said the suit was motivated by Françoise's jealousy over her relationship with Banier. Liliane knew she had given a lot to him, but assured Kiejman that every centime had been offered willingly and knowingly. "She never varied on that point."

That first encounter marked the beginning not only of a professional relationship but what Kiejman calls a "respectful friendship." Later that summer he was invited to visit Liliane at her Formentor vacation villa and spent the Christmas holidays that year on the Île d'Arros. Over one tête-à-tête luncheon, as she so often did, Liliane got to reminiscing about her adored father. Perhaps to be polite, she asked the lawyer about his own father. "My father?" said Kiejman. "You know, the last time I saw him I was ten years old. That's when they arrested him and took him to Auschwitz." There was an awkward silence.

The elephant in the room was the ghost of Eugène Schueller, who had praised the Nazis in his writings and speeches and was investigated for wartime collaboration. Liliane herself was not anti-Semitic in any strict sense — certainly not an active hater of Jews — but like much of the traditional French Catholic bourgeoisie she took note of who was and was not Jewish and judged accordingly. That she disliked and distrusted her son-in-law was common knowledge. She worried privately that her grandsons looked "too Jewish" and asked whether Françoise's lawyer, Olivier Metzner, was a Jew (he was not). Now here she was face-to-face with the son of a Holocaust victim. "Her milieu is not mine," says Kiejman, "but I regarded it without prejudice."

As news of the affair heated up in the press, Françoise Meyers gave an interview to the weekly newsmagazine *Le Point* on July 16, 2009. Up to that point, she had refused any public comment. Now, apparently prodded by the media-conscious Metzner and her professional communications advisers, she attempted to explain the motivations behind her suit, correct what she considered the distortions of the press, and project a more sympathetic image of herself.

"A daughter can't accept to see her mother subjected to such a situation of influence and isolation," she said. She claimed her mother's life was "entirely taken in hand and controlled by François-Marie Banier and people close to him. They have erected a veritable wall around her." Banier's real objective, she charged, was to "break our family bonds, to distance my mother from us and hold her at his mercy in order to take better advantage of her. I won't let him do that." Françoise adamantly denied any financial motivation behind her action. What finally triggered the suit against the photographer, she said, was the "stupefying adoption project that Banier evoked, with an incredible cynicism, shortly after my father's death. At that point, I said to myself that things had become too unbearable."

She mocked the claim that her mother's gifts to Banier were a form of *mécénat* — patronage of the arts. "Has anyone ever seen an artist 'subsidized' on the level of a billion euros? With a billion, you can build the Louvre or the Prado!" Asked why her father had not taken action against Banier, indeed a key question, she replied: "I think he was duped by the fact that François-Marie Banier seemed to amuse my mother. But little by little he came to understand this personage and his true motivations. When he felt that he was progressively kept apart from certain things, he confided his worries to me. In fact, he did not rule out the possibility that all that would one day wind up in court."

In September 2009, it was Banier's turn to

put his spin on the story in an interview with *Le Monde.* His conversation with journalist Michel Guerrin focused mainly on Banier himself: his artistic career, his books, his traumatic childhood, and his uncanny ability to forge friendships with the rich and famous — but also with bums and street people. "I am blessed with a gift for encounters," he said. "I'm profoundly interested in people I meet, whether they are known or just passing in the street. . . . I transmit a joie de vivre. I laugh a lot and I make people laugh." One senses a conscious effort on Banier's part to present himself as a charming, fascinating, and sensitive soul — with an intriguing dash of eccentricity.

When the subject finally got around to the suit, Banier exuded a serene confidence in the outcome of the case. "These gifts come from a woman who is totally lucid," he said. "What bothers people is that a woman of her caste can shatter the conventions. Two days ago, Liliane told me: 'My daughter will have a lot. But I still intend to live for another five minutes . . .' What really happened will be revealed in court. . . . The truth will explode." The adoption plan? "An absurdity! We never even discussed it!" Did he feel guilty about accepting so much? "Certainly not!" Banier snapped. "But it's a sad affair. This scandal has caused much pain to a brilliant and free woman. It is inhuman to do that to her in the twilight of her life."

Meanwhile, Banier continued to visit Liliane and dine with her regularly in Neuilly, though they curtailed their appearances at restaurants and other public places to avoid unwanted attention. In a December 2009 letter to Liliane, he lamented the suit's impact on their lives. "I understand that you are shocked by the revelations that are sprouting all over the media," he wrote. "I fear the publicity orchestrated by this affair will expose all your intimate family life and friendships to the public." Banier complained of the "truckloads of insults and calumnies" that he received each day in the press. For his own protection, he said, he would take his critics to court for defamation.

On December 1, 2009, Françoise petitioned a civil judge to put her mother under judicial protection and appoint a guardian to oversee her affairs — including her voting rights on the L'Oréal board and the family holding company Thétys. Seeking to explain her act to her mother, Françoise wrote what she hoped would be a mollifying letter. "My dear mother," it began, "as sad and painful as it is for you and for me, I wanted to write you these few lines . . ." Her act was necessary, she said, to protect her mother from the exploiters around her. "I already tried to do this nearly two years ago by launching the action that upsets you so, but alas that wasn't sufficient. That is why I believe I have no other choice today but to solicit your protection by the civil judge." In the absence of a medical certificate, however, the judge in question rejected the petition on December 8.

Three days later, Kiejman registered Madame Bettencourt as a plaintiff against her daughter's suit. It was an unusual move, since Liliane was not directly targeted by the abuse charges against her protégé. But as Kiejman explains, "It was the only way to express her categorical opposition to her daughter's penal action against Banier." The brief he filed on December 11, 2009, crackled with the irony for which the veteran lawyer was famous. He noted that Madame Meyers's complaint followed almost immediately upon the death of her father, who she feared "would never have forgiven this ignominious step." Speculating on Françoise's motives, Kiejman said it was either "a jealous reaction better treated on a psychoanalyst's couch" or "an act of cupidity" aimed at "recuperating several hundred million euros in order to rise out of her current state of abject poverty, since she merely holds a fortune of more than €10 billion given by her mother." Arguing that the daughter had no standing to attack an alleged abuse of her mother, since Françoise was not herself a victim, Kiejman called on Prévost-

Desprez to throw out the suit. He had few illusions on that score, however: He had earlier made a "courtesy call" on the judge, who told him curtly, "I don't always follow what the Prosecutor does." In other words, says Kiejman, the mere fact that Courroye had closed his own case was a compelling reason for Prévost-Desprez to pursue it.

At this point, Prévost-Desprez had not yet done any investigating on her own. She was operating on the basis of Metzner's citation, which contained the affidavits of Bettencourt employees and the files of Courroye's aborted probe. The question before her court concerned only the charge against Banier.

Before the hearings got under way, she huddled with the other members of her three-judge panel and voiced her view that Banier could not be convicted on the basis of Courroye's investigation. "I found that it didn't have the necessary elements," she says. "I was certain we could establish Madame Bettencourt's vulnerability, which was already proven in the dossier, but not the 'gravely prejudicial' aspect." In other words, if the amount of Banier's gains was not judged excessive in relation to Liliane's overall fortune, he could not be convicted of abuse of weakness under the terms of the law. "For Liliane Bettencourt, €700 million is not gravely prejudicial," says Prévost-Desprez. The only way to meet the gravely prejudicial requirement, she believed, would be to argue that Banier's hold on Liliane isolated her and deprived her of contact with her family.

That, in fact, was in line with what appeared to be Françoise Meyers's initial aim. Her original focus was not on the money: The 2007 complaint did not claim any monetary damages from Banier, nor even the return of the gifts he had received thus far. What she wanted was to free her mother of Banier's influence, get the photographer out of her family's life, and put Liliane under court-mandated guardianship. As the affair evolved, the monetary aspects would later come into play, but at this point even Banier's lawyer was convinced that money was not the central issue for Françoise. "In my opinion," says Hervé Temime, "the suit was motivated by the fact that Madame Meyers wanted all this to stop."

Whatever her ultimate aims, there were those who considered Francoise's action inexcusable because of the pain and embarrassment it caused her mother. "What I think is horrible is the daughter," fashion king Karl Lagerfeld told an interviewer from *Vanity Fair*. "You don't put your mother, in her late eighties, in a scandal like this. For me, that's unforgivable. Even if you're estranged from your mother, you don't do it. Her mother is allowed to give her money to whomever she wants. There's enough for everybody, so why not — if it makes her happy?"

That last point was echoed by the Comtesse de Gramont, a close friend of Liliane's for more than two decades. "Personally, I think that Madame Bettencourt's financial situation is beyond our comprehension," she said. "It's off the scale. When you have €20 billion, and your daughter is rich, what's a mere billion? . . . It's her own fortune and she can do what she wants with it."

Hervé Temime recounts that the affair became a hot topic of discussion at swank Parisian dinner parties during this time, and that opinion was divided into two camps: "People who stood to inherit money found [the gifts to Banier] abnormal, but the rich said you can do whatever you like with your own money and that if Madame Bettencourt acted freely, there was no problem."

After a series of preliminary sessions dealing with procedural matters, Prévost-Desprez scheduled a full hearing for July 1, 2010. This was to have been the day when Banier's trial began in earnest. But no one could have anticipated the bombshell that would explode on the eve of that event.

■ ■ ■ ■

PART FOUR:
THE NET
SPREADS WIDER

■ ■ ■ ■

The indiscreet butler: Pascal Bonnefoy,
Paris, 2014. **Alexander Guirkinger**

CHAPTER 15
THE BUTLER DID IT

Anyone who has seen *Downton Abbey* can imagine the level of intrigue, backstabbing, and rumor-mongering that reigned among the Bettencourts' twenty or so domestic employees. As chambermaid Liliane Hennion summed up the situation: "The atmosphere among the personnel in the house was not very good and tension was palpable." Liliane's nurse Alain Thurin called it "a basket of crabs."

The personnel were divided into clans and subclans by conflicting loyalties, jealousies, personal antipathies, and competing desires to win the approval — and favors — of their bosses. Some were closer to Monsieur, some to Madame. Some won bonuses and gifts; others did not. Some were allowed the use of apartments; others were not. Some, like the accountant Claire Thibout, were seen to have privileged access to, and influence over, Madame Bettencourt. And since Claire was also in charge of the domestic staff, there were naturally resentments over what some saw as an abuse of power.

Liliane's personal chambermaid, Dominique Gaspard, was similarly viewed as someone who took advantage of her position to lord it over the others and ingratiate herself with Madame. "Madame Gaspard often adopted a critical attitude toward a colleague and reported it to Madame Bettencourt," said former head chef Thierry Coulon. "She did everything possible to destabilize the personnel." One former colleague of Gaspard's, chambermaid Françoise Mauclère, went as far as to file a complaint against Gaspard for "moral harassment," describing her as "profoundly hysterical and jealous of her proximity to Madame Bettencourt . . . It was a permanent theater of daily threats and blackmail in order to be the only one close to Madame." While nothing proves that these charges were true, they illustrate the frictions that reigned among the staff.

On occasion, personal animosities could flare into physical violence. In May 2007, according to the Bettencourts' chauffeur, Jérôme Sarran, bodyguard Enrico Vaccaro showed up drunk one day and picked a fight with him. Result: Sarran's nose was broken and Liliane was forced to choose which employee to fire. In the end, Sarran got the boot and Vaccaro, one of her favorites, was spared.

Not all of the aggressions were aimed at

colleagues: Some went as far as to blackmail their employers. According to Banier's confiscated notebooks, one staffer reportedly threatened to tell the press that he saw André Bettencourt in the shower with a male employee unless he was paid three years' salary. A maid was rumored to have been paid €200,000 after wielding a similar threat.

Strategic calculations also came into play. The more recent employees eyed opportunities to eclipse or replace the older ones. After André's death, some concluded that the real power in the household resided not with Liliane but with Banier, and conducted themselves accordingly. For his part, Banier cultivated good relationships with some employees — the "charming" bodyguard Vaccaro was a particular favorite — and wrote others off as spies and *bonniches* (lackeys).

When Françoise filed suit, another rift opened up between those who sided with her and those who defended Banier. Claire Thibout, a partisan of the pro-Françoise clan, encouraged like-minded employees to provide attestations in support of the complaint against Banier. They paid dearly for that: Over the next few months, allegedly at the urging of Banier and de Maistre, Madame Bettencourt fired most of those who had originally testified for Françoise. Among them: Thibout, Gaspard, and secretaries Chantal Trovel and Christiane Djenane.

The one who landed on her feet, at least initially, was Thibout. When she was fired in November 2008, her lawyer negotiated a sizeable severance package: €400,000 — nearly three times her annual salary. According to the terms of their 2007 agreement, Françoise Meyers then paid Thibout an additional €400,000, bringing her total indemnity to €800,000. The accountant promptly invested the bulk of that windfall in real estate: an apartment in Paris and a large farmhouse in Normandy. As long as the details of her payoff remained secret — she didn't even report it to tax authorities — no one asked questions about the source of her funds or the nature of her relationship with Françoise.

Pascal Bonnefoy had not testified at that point, but as he watched his colleagues disappear one by one, he feared that he might be the next victim of the "witch hunt." Though he was devoted to serving Madame as a butler, his deepest attachment had been with André, whose office he continued to watch over like a shrine. He did not have the same close relationship with Liliane. And he knew for sure that he was not in Banier's good graces. He claimed that he had more than once caught the photographer urinating on the plants in Liliane's courtyard (which Banier adamantly denied). He also dared to criticize the language Banier used when addressing the heiress. On one occasion, he says, he heard the photographer call her *salope* — roughly the equivalent of "bitch" or "slut." Responding to the butler's reproach, Banier had reportedly said, "Don't you ever say *salope* to your wife?" Bonnefoy shot back: "Madame is not your wife."

Things came to a head in February 2009, shortly after Liliane's return from her vacation with Banier on the Île d'Arros. Her attitude toward Bonnefoy suddenly changed. "Madame frowned and ignored me," he recalled. "I no longer existed." A chauffeur who had driven Banier home told Bonnefoy the reason: The photographer suspected him of testifying on behalf of Françoise's suit and wanted him fired. On hearing this, Bonnefoy's blood ran cold. After serving dinner on the night of February 26, he took the heiress aside and tried to explain himself.

"Madame," he said. "I know you suspect me of testifying to the police against Monsieur Banier. I want to tell you that is not true." Without looking the butler in the eye, Liliane muttered, "I don't want to have any problems with François-Marie."

The next day, L'Oréal CEO Lindsay Owen-Jones came to lunch. After the coffee was served, Liliane and her guest retired to the Monet salon, so called because it features a large painting of water lilies by the famous Impressionist. Liliane sent for the butler. As soon as Bonnefoy arrived, Owen-Jones stood

up and interrogated him: "Madame Bettencourt needs to know if you testified before
the Financial Brigade. She must know if she
can have confidence in you."

Bonnefoy insisted that he had not testified,
but he knew Madame's trust in him was
broken.

Several weeks later, he bought a hand-held
Olympus digital recorder. His plan was to
capture Madame Bettencourt's private conversations with her advisers and Banier. "I
wanted to know what was going on. To
protect Madame from those who manipulated
her — and at the same time, protect myself."

Madame Bettencourt's meetings with her
advisers always took place in André's former
office. It was Bonnefoy's job to escort the
guests upstairs and serve them refreshments
— coffee, tea, Perrier, tea cakes. Since he was
the keeper of this inner sanctum, it was easy
for him to place his recorder, concealed in a
felt pouch, on a table behind Madame's
armchair. On Monday, May 25, 2009, Patrice de Maistre arrived at 12:15 and the first
recording began. Ironically the financial
adviser had earlier taken the precaution of
having security experts sweep the office for
hidden microphones, but apparently no one
thought of the possibility of a recording device.

Fearful of being caught in the act, Bonnefoy had a fit of nerves that first day. "After

serving the drinks, I closed the door and went downstairs," he recalled. "My stomach ached, I was sweating . . . I couldn't eat anything, I was too anxious. After one hour, I went back up and recovered the recorder with trembling hands. I slipped it into my jacket. Then, during my break, I went into an empty room to listen. I was horrified by what I heard."

Bonnefoy repeated this routine over the next few months, sometimes listening to parts of the recordings discreetly at his workplace, but more often in his car on the way to his apartment in Le Chesnay, fifteen miles west of Paris. The conversations he captured revealed not only what he knew — that Madame, handicapped by deafness, was often unable to follow the discussions and was subject to frequent memory lapses — but also showed that de Maistre and the other members of her entourage were wielding undue influence and exploiting her. There were also indications of tax evasion, secret Swiss bank accounts, political payments, interference in the case by the Élysée, and a conflict of interest involving de Maistre and Budget Minister Éric Woerth.

For the time being, though, Bonnefoy's concern was documenting the exploitation and mistreatment of his employer — and protecting his own skin. In January 2010, he decided to consult a lawyer. Antoine Gillot, who also represented Claire Thibout, agreed to see him. When Bonnefoy showed up at the law office near the Place du Châtelet, he pulled out his recorder, placed it on Gillot's desk, and pushed the Play button. "It was the atom bomb," Gillot recalls. After listening to several key passages, he told his client, " 'You know, Pascal, what you have done is a crime, it's violation of privacy that could cost you a year in prison and €45,000 in fines." Bonnefoy stared back at him wide-eyed. He knew he might be criticized for making secret recordings, but had no idea it was punishable by law.

"What do I risk if I give these recordings to the daughter?" he asked.

"There are two things that can happen," Gillot replied. "Either she decides not to make them public, and you risk nothing. Or she makes them public, and you will surely be charged with a violation of privacy."

The other advice Gillot gave Bonnefoy was to have the contents of his digital recorder backed up. If the device malfunctioned or was lost, there would be no trace of the conversations it contained. For this, Bonnefoy turned to Philippe Dunand, an information technician who had set up the Bettencourts' home computer system and had earlier given computer lessons to André. Dunand also happened to be the husband of Claire Thibout. Bonnefoy gave the recorder to Dunand and asked him to copy the files onto CD-ROMs, but without listening to the contents. Meanwhile, he bought a second device and continued to record Madame Bettencourt's meetings.

Bonnefoy could no longer claim ignorance of the law after Gillot's warning, but he felt compelled to continue. He was determined to capture the conversations of Banier, who had not yet appeared on any of the recordings apart from a brief telephone exchange. The photographer finally appeared in the office on Monday, May 11, 2010, nearly a year after the recordings had begun. Now that he had the evidence he was waiting for, the butler stopped his electronic eavesdropping.

When Dunand had finished copying the last of the recordings, he gave Bonnefoy the complete set of twenty-eight CD-ROMs. At that point, the butler had decided to give his notice. His attachment to the job had never been the same since André's death, and with the recent firings, all the employees he felt closest to were gone.

Besides, he had a project: Along with Christophe Loiget, a cook who had formerly worked for the Bettencourts, he planned to buy a seaside hotel and go into business. He negotiated a severance settlement with de Maistre — €215,000, equivalent to two years' salary — then called Françoise Meyers and requested a meeting.

On May 18, the butler crossed the rue

Delabordère and rang the doorbell of the Meyers duplex. He knew the family well. In happier days they came over for lunch every Sunday; Bonnefoy would also see them during their summer vacations at Arcouest. He had known the Meyers boys, Jean-Victor and Nicolas, from their childhood and still addressed them by the familiar *tu* form when he saw them privately. Today, the woman he referred to as "Madame Jean-Pierre" welcomed him cordially. She asked about her mother's health. "Not so good," said the butler. Then he produced the twenty-eight CD-ROMs and put them on the coffee table.

"What's that?" asked Françoise.

"These are conversations that I recorded at her home," he explained. "Whatever use you decide to make of them, I will accept the consequences."

"How did you get them?"

"Banier was threatening to get me fired. I wanted to defend myself so I decided to make these recordings in your father's study."

"What do they show?"

"That your mother was abused."

Bonnefoy asked Françoise to wait for his severance check to clear at the end of the month before she did anything with the CDs. As soon as he left, she called her lawyer, Olivier Metzner, and told him about her meeting with the butler and the stack of recordings he had left her. What should she do with them? "We have to be transparent and give it to the police," he said. But before doing that, he advised, they should make a copy and have the contents transcribed. The next day, they took the CDs to the office of Jérôme Cohen, a court-mandated bailiff (*huissier de justice*), and asked him to prepare transcripts of the roughly twenty-eight hours of conversations.

But Metzner, the self-proclaimed master of "communication," did not wait to have the complete text in hand before he began pulling strings. Once he learned of the stunning revelations, he called Judge Prévost-Desprez. It was essential to keep her hooked on the case, since he knew she had doubts. The judge could almost hear his lips smacking on the phone as he described the secret recordings made by Madame Bettencourt's butler.

"You will have them as soon as the transcription is done," he told her.

"What do they say?" asked the judge. "Do they support the abuse charges?"

"You can't imagine," replied the lawyer. "It's a gift from heaven."

On June 10, Françoise sent a courier to the headquarters of the Financial Brigade with copies of the twenty-eight CDs and a transcript of the first six. The brigade immediately contacted Nanterre prosecutor Courroye, who had them sent to his office. Though Courroye had closed his own investigation of

Banier, it was still his responsibility as prosecutor to examine this new evidence and determine whether it pointed to possible infractions.

The first violation he targeted was Bonnefoy's invasion of privacy. On June 15, he ordered the butler put under investigation, detained for forty-eight hours, and grilled about the circumstances surrounding the recordings. On June 30, Courroye ordered a complete transcription and technical verification by a specialized branch of the judiciary police. He apparently hoped to keep the contents of the recordings under his own control, but Metzner had also provided Prévost-Desprez with copies of the CDs and a partial transcription to make sure she was aware of the contents before the opening of Banier's trial on July 1.

Metzner's efforts to exploit the recordings did not stop there. On June 10, the same day his client sent them to the Financial Brigade, he bragged to the left-leaning intellectual weekly *Nouvel Observateur* that he would soon provide an "explosive document" to support Françoise Meyers's case. Shortly afterward, he offered to leak the recordings to Pascale Robert-Diard, judicial reporter for *Le Monde.* But Robert-Diard had ethical problems with the use of secret recordings and sensed that Metzner was trying to manipulate her for his own purposes. "Metzner had a reputation," she says. "He needed a lever, and the press was his lever." Robert-Diard turned the offer down. But on June 14, *Mediapart,* an influential investigative website, began publishing a series of excerpts from the transcripts, followed two days later by the website of *Le Point,* a leading weekly newsmagazine. These articles, widely echoed in the French media, had the effect of a bombshell. It was as if, in the United States, a story simultaneously made the covers of *Time, Newsweek,* and *People,* plus the front page of the *New York Times* and all the network TV news shows.

As Metzner had claimed, the recordings contained numerous demonstrations of Madame Bettencourt's vulnerability. But much of the attention now focused on the political angle — the fact that Sarkozy and his judicial adviser were apparently interfering in the case, the potential conflict of interest concerning Budget Minister Éric Woerth and his wife, financial adviser Patrice de Maistre's political payments, and what *Mediapart* editor Edwy Plenel called "the collusion between the summit of political power and one of the great fortunes of France."

It was against that backdrop that Banier's trial opened on July 1, 2010, in Nanterre. "The courtroom was as full as a beehive," recalls Prévost-Desprez. "It was horrible, the tension was unbearable." Banier, dressed in a tight blue suit and blue tie, seemed intent on mocking the whole procedure. Seated up front on the defendants' bench, he pulled out a large notepad and ostentatiously sketched a crude drawing under the title *"Ça m'est égal"* (I don't give a damn). Metzner and Kiejman, lawyers respectively for Françoise Meyers and Liliane Bettencourt, seemed more intent on insulting each other than defending their clients. Shortly after the proceedings got under way, Metzner taunted Kiejman. "Now he's looking for it," Kiejman riposted. "He'd better watch it or it will be terrible for him!" Metzner leapt to his feet. "Is that a threat? I demand that the court take note of this threat." Kiejman was livid. "Madame la Présidente," he said, addressing Prévost-Desprez, "tell Mr. Metzner not to rile me, because my left hook is formidable."

"I warn you, gentlemen, we haven't provided for an infirmary," said Prévost-Desprez, gaveling the pair to order. In view of the recordings, she said, the immediate question before the court was whether to order a *supplément d'information* — a supplementary investigation — based on the new elements they revealed.

Metzner, who had put the recordings before the court in the first place, predictably argued in favor. Hervé Temime, Banier's lawyer, opposed the idea of further investigation and complained that "the methods used by the plaintiff in this affair have surpassed an inviolable limit." Kiejman went even further. Denouncing the recordings as an act of "espionage" organized by Françoise Meyers, Liliane Bettencourt's lawyer demanded that the judge abort the whole procedure. "You can no longer render a credible decision," Kiejman thundered, glaring menacingly at Prévost-Desprez. The veteran barrister then turned the full force of his mockery on Metzner's client, "an aged little girl 57 years old" who had already received a fortune from her mother and was now whining, "my mommy didn't love me, she loved another more than me."

After hearing these heated arguments, Prévost-Desprez suspended the session and huddled with her two associate judges. Their ruling was not long in coming: Banier's trial would be adjourned indefinitely, *sine die,* while Prévost-Desprez herself headed up a supplementary investigation based on the fresh evidence contained in the recordings. To her mind this was a dangerous initiative, because she knew President Sarkozy wanted the whole affair shut down. "There I was, in a confrontation with Sarkozy," she says, "and Sarkozy doesn't mess around."

Chapter 16
Behind Closed Doors

The 518-page transcript of Bonnefoy's recordings provided investigators with a mother lode of information. But it's the fly-on-the-wall audio version that most dramatically penetrates the intimacy of the second-floor study where Liliane Bettencourt met with her advisers. More than the words themselves, it is the sounds that bring the scene to life. The clink of glasses when refreshments are served. The opening and closing of doors. The butler's footsteps. The yapping of Liliane's dog. The swish of turning pages as she reads over documents. The obsequious voice of Patrice de Maistre, alternately cajoling, flattering, and dominating the heiress. Kiejman's raspy baritone hurling ironic barbs at Françoise Meyers and the "little judge" Prévost-Desprez. Lawyer Fabrice Goguel's dry monotone explaining his convoluted legal maneuvers to the baffled heiress.

But it is Liliane's voice that is most striking — not so much the sound of it as the confusion it often conveys. Not only does she misunderstand much of what is said to her — she is, after all, very deaf — but even when things are repeated and explained, she often has trouble grasping and remembering. She can even be heard snoring on occasion. But there are also moments of lucidity and fierce determination. She clearly voices her resentment of her daughter and son-in-law, her concerns for the future of L'Oréal, her impatience over the drawn-out legal tug-of-war, and, yes, her fear of the demanding Monsieur Banier, even as she confirms her deep attachment to him. But the master manipulator in these sessions is not Banier, who appears only twice on the recordings: It is Patrice de Maistre.

De Maistre was at the center of Sarkozy's involvement in the case, the thing that caused the biggest sensation when the recordings were made public. It was de Maistre who first took Liliane to see the president on November 5, 2008, and thereafter maintained regular contacts with the Élysée. To hear him brag about it to his employer, one would think he had a dedicated hotline into the office of Sarkozy's judicial aide, Patrick Ouart. "I'm going to the Élysée this afternoon because Sarkozy's adviser called me this morning," he told Liliane on June 12, 2009. "He's following the affair . . . they are doing what they can."

On July 21, de Maistre gave the heiress some good news: "Sarkozy's adviser, whom I see regularly on your behalf . . . told me the prosecutor Courroye will announce on September 3 that your daughter's suit is not legitimate, and so he will drop the investigation." Not only was this advance tip-off to a party involved in a private suit highly improper; the fact that the prosecutor had apparently informed Sarkozy's office of his intentions pointed to an illegal collusion between the executive and the judicial branches. To many of the president's critics it seemed clear that he himself was pulling the strings — a charge that Sarkozy, Courroye, and Ouart deny.

De Maistre's optimism proved premature. Courroye did in fact terminate his preliminary investigation on September 22, 2009, but by that time, as we have seen, Metzner had craftily circumvented the foot-dragging prosecutor with his direct citation of Banier before Prévost-Desprez's court. Ouart continued to communicate about the case with de Maistre, but he admitted that the Élysée had less control over the independent-minded Nanterre judge. On April 23, 2010, de Maistre told Madame Bettencourt that "[Ouart] wanted to see me the other day and he told me, 'Monsieur de Maistre, the president continues to follow this case very closely. We can't do much more for you at the first trial, but we can tell you that in the appeals court, if you lose, we know the prosecutor very, very well.' " In other words, according to de Maistre, Ouart was suggesting that the Élysée could use its influence to quash the suit on appeal.

The appearance of high-level tampering in the case was bad enough for Sarkozy, but the revelations concerning de Maistre's cozy relationship with the budget minister at the time, Éric Woerth, who awarded him the Légion d'honneur in January 2008, heightened the president's political embarrassment. In September 2007 de Maistre had recruited Woerth's wife, Florence, as an investment adviser for Clymène, the family holding company that managed Liliane Bettencourt's stock dividends. De Maistre told the heiress that he hired her at the request of his "friend Éric Woerth." "Who's that?" asked Liliane. "He's our budget minister," de Maistre replied, baldly explaining the logic behind the hire: "He's the one who oversees your taxes, so I thought it wasn't a dumb thing to do."

After a time, though, de Maistre began to have regrets — not because of the questionable ethics of the relationship, but because he found Florence Woerth "pushy" and "tiresome." Finally, on April 23, 2010, he told Liliane that he was planning to let Madame

Woerth go because the press had gotten wind of the relationship and was asking embarrassing questions. "Since you're the richest woman in France, the fact that you employ a minister's wife, the newspapers say everything is mixed up," he explained, adding that Éric Woerth had originally "asked" him to hire her. Now the only solution was to let Florence Woerth go with a hefty severance "because it's too dangerous." (She was, in fact, allowed to resign two months later.)

As if that whiff of nepotism and back scratching were not enough, Woerth also had financial relations with de Maistre in his capacity as treasurer of Sarkozy's reelection campaign and of his UMP party. On the recording of March 4, 2010, de Maistre is heard instructing Liliane Bettencourt to sign checks of €7,500 each, the maximum legal limit, to Éric Woerth, Nicolas Sarkozy, and a UMP regional candidate. While Liliane signs the checks, only vaguely aware of what it's all about, de Maistre tells her: "You see, it's only 7,500, it's not very expensive. At this moment, we need friends." It is true that the legal limit, paid by traceable checks, did not amount to much in relation to the Bettencourt fortune. But that did not preclude the possibility of much larger gifts in cash-stuffed envelopes.

Another recorded reference to Woerth presents him, ironically, as an official who has complicated de Maistre's job by passing a law, effective January 1, 2010, requiring Swiss banks to report the accounts of French citizens. As de Maistre explains to the heiress in November 2009, she has three secret accounts in Switzerland, which he plans to transfer out of the country in a blatant and illegal tax-evasion scheme. "I am arranging to send [the funds] to another country, Hong Kong, Singapore, or Uruguay," he says. "Because if we bring this money back to France, it will be very complicated."

Ceaselessly attempting to extend his power and influence over the heiress, de Maistre convinced her to name him, along with Banier's childhood friend Dr. Gilles Brücker, as her future "protectors" in the event she was declared incompetent. His stated aim was to prevent Liliane's daughter from gaining legal control over her and her assets, but the result would have been to make de Maistre the ultimate arbiter of her fortune, while Brücker would have overseen her personal affairs. Throughout the discussion, recorded on September 7, 2009, Liliane's confusion is all too evident:

De Maistre: I have several things to discuss with you. The first is the protection mandate. You know what I'm talking about?

Liliane Bettencourt: Not really. A mandate? For me? . . .

De Maistre: The mandate states that, if you are not well in the future, you ask two people to protect you. . . . My thought is that, if you're not well one day, your daughter will immediately try to put you under guardianship. And that's what must not happen, in my view.

Liliane Bettencourt: That's obvious.

De Maistre: I have given this a lot of thought, and I say it's in your interest to sign as quickly as possible.

Two days later, Madame Bettencourt's notary, Jean-Michel Normand, arrives with the finished document for her to sign. She has no memory of the previous discussion:

Liliane Bettencourt: I sign at the bottom?

Normand: No, wait. I need to give you a word of explanation after all. We talked about this act in June. I presented it to you, you read through it, I gave you explanations, you asked questions . . . and so today, we regularize it.

[He gives the document to the heiress. Sound of pages turning, background conversation.]

Liliane Bettencourt: I can't go on like this, it takes too much time! I need to talk about it at the same time. You understand? . . . I prefer to take more time. In any case, I can't just sign like that.

Liliane's hesitations notwithstanding, and in the absence of a medical certificate on her mental soundness, the act was signed and notarized on September 23, 2009. In its final form, only de Maistre was designated as her future protector, with no further mention of Brücker. If a court had ruled Madame Bettencourt incompetent at that point, Patrice de Maistre would not only have managed her fortune but would have taken her seat on L'Oréal's board of directors and spoken for her as the company's principal shareholder.

The most stunning sign of de Maistre's manipulation, and the thing he will never live down, was his request that Madame Bettencourt buy him a sailboat as a "gift." In his most unctuous voice, he describes it as a "magnificent boat," a 21-meter, single-mast sloop dubbed the *Edelweiss* (which happened to be the name of Eugène Schueller's craft). He returns to the subject several times, describing the immense pleasure he gets from sailing. "When I cut off the onboard engine, I am happy in this simple, limited space," he gushes. "It's a simple life on the open sea."

Recalling her sailing days with her father, Madame Bettencourt tells him: "Oh yes, I understand. I adore the open air."

The money, he says, must come from one of her secret Swiss bank accounts to avoid detection:

De Maistre: Do you still want to offer me a gift? If you want to do something, it has to be in Switzerland, not here. And it would allow me to buy the boat of my dreams. . . .

Liliane Bettencourt: Very well. How do we do it?

De Maistre: I have to see how I can get the money sent here.

Liliane Bettencourt: You want to bring the money from Switzerland?

De Maistre: Right . . . I don't want anyone to know about it because you know I have signed something making me your [future] protector, so I can't do that. So it has to be a hand-to-hand thing. I don't want your daughter or anyone else to know about it.

De Maistre won Madame Bettencourt's assent, but finally gave up on the boat purchase because of the risk of tax and legal complications. The previous year, however, he had talked Liliane into giving him €5 million — "for my old age" — and paying an additional

€3.03 million in gift taxes. At the time, he was making €900,000 a year as director of the family holding companies, Thétys and Clymène — a fee that he had bumped up by 60 percent by pressuring Liliane to sign a revised contract after the first three years. The recordings thus underscored a situation in which de Maistre was taking advantage of the heiress — not on the same scale as Banier but in a way that, to some observers, appeared to make the two men objective allies in an effort to "pluck the feathers off the old girl," as one lawyer put it. Not that there was any camaraderie between the two men. *Au contraire:* De Maistre is heard on the recordings calling Banier an "imbecile" who "throws oil on the fire," while Banier, in private, is scathing in his comments about the financier.

As for Banier, though he himself appears only twice on the recordings — once on the phone and once in person — he is very much present as a subject of discussion. And almost always as a problem that Liliane's advisers must deal with. The most telling thing about these passages is the mixture of fear and affection he inspires in Liliane, who is extremely foggy about what she has already given him and apparently doesn't even remember naming him as her legal heir in December 2007. De Maistre broached this delicate subject in a conversation on March

4, 2010:

De Maistre: Your notary tells me you have made wills for certain people to whom you want to give money. For the rest, you have named Banier your *légataire universel* [legal heir] — that is, he will have all the rest.

> **Liliane Bettencourt:** *Légataire universel?*
>
> **De Maistre:** Yes.
>
> **Liliane Bettencourt:** Well, he can start by striking that out.
>
> **De Maistre:** Right. We agree.
>
> **Liliane Bettencourt:** But at the same time, we have to keep him in the will.
>
> **De Maistre:** . . . I think you have already given enough to Banier.
>
> **Liliane Bettencourt:** Yes, but don't overlook one little detail, that is, when he wants something, and especially when you're facing difficulties, as I have several times . . .
>
> **De Maistre:** Banier says: 'I agree . . . but this will must be changed' . . .

Eight days later, Normand, the notary, urges Madame Bettencourt to change her will, saying that even Banier agrees it was a folly to name him as her heir and wants that designation revoked. Liliane's confusion on the subject is one of the most glaring indications of her vulnerability at this point:

Normand: Banier wants you to change the dispositions you made in his favor. He prefers not to appear.

Liliane Bettencourt: As what?

Normand: As your *légataire universel.*

Liliane Bettencourt: . . . How much did I leave to François-Marie? What proportion?

Normand: *Légataire universel.*

Liliane Bettencourt: Which means?

Normand: Everything.

Liliane Bettencourt: Ah, no!

Normand: Yes. That's what you told me . . .

Liliane Bettencourt: Well, I didn't know that. I didn't know it any longer. . . .

Liliane's remarks about Banier reveal a mix of admiration and affection on the one hand, and irritation, even fear, over his excessive behavior on the other. On October 29, 2009, for example, Liliane tells de Maistre, "[Banier] is brilliant, but he doesn't know how to behave. . . . He has to bite." The financial adviser replies, "Yes, like a hunting dog, he has to catch something . . . and he bites hard. . . . There are very few people he really likes." On April 7, 2010, the heiress tells de Maistre that Banier "is someone that I like very much, he is very intelligent, but I just hope he doesn't kill me." It is clear from the context that she doesn't mean that literally; she means he sometimes wears her out with his incessant talk and hyperactivity. "He becomes too demanding," she says, "but he takes me to meet some very interesting people, and I just can't resist." De Maistre replies: "He doesn't know how to stop." Liliane adds: "He would devour everything. He has incredible stamina."

Some of the most convoluted discussions concerned the Île d'Arros, the private island in the Seychelles that the Bettencourts had bought from the nephew of the shah of Iran in 1998. At some point, as noted, Liliane apparently decided to give the island to Banier. In 2006, Liliane's lawyer, Fabrice Goguel, drew up papers transferring ownership to a Lichtenstein-based foundation whose "beneficiaries" were Banier and three medical associations run by Banier's friend Gilles Brücker and Brücker's partner, Caroline Katlama. Meanwhile, the island's manager, Carlos Vejarano, started hitting up Liliane for what looked like hush money because the island was never declared to French tax authorities. Concerning all these complications, Liliane remembered and understood almost nothing. The subject came up repeatedly in the recorded conversations, but this exchange of May 11, 2010, is typical:

Liliane Bettencourt: What island?

De Maistre: D'Arros. A priori it's going to go to François-Marie Banier one day. It's your decision. . . .

Liliane Bettencourt: But he's not ashamed to wind up with this island?

De Maistre: Yes, but you're the one who wanted that. You're the one who signed the papers.

Liliane Bettencourt: For François-Marie?

De Maistre: Yes. Through this foundation . . .

Liliane Bettencourt: Wait a minute. The foundation owns the island?

De Maistre: The foundation is the proprietor of the island.

Liliane Bettencourt: And the foundation belongs to whom?

De Maistre: Officially, to no one.

Liliane Bettencourt: And unofficially?

De Maistre: Unofficially to Banier.

Liliane Bettencourt: . . . I wanted to give him an island?

De Maistre: You decided to give him that.

This discussion is interrupted by Banier's arrival in the study. De Maistre had summoned him in hopes of straightening out the ownership mess surrounding d'Arros and getting the Lichtenstein foundation to finance its upkeep. Banier drags his feet, blames the problems on his Swiss lawyer, then abruptly changes the subject to the lawsuit against him. He wants de Maistre to provide him with details of Liliane's professional and social activities in 2006 in order to prove that she was lucid at that time. "For 2006, you have to find something," Banier tells de Maistre, sotto voce so Liliane can't hear. "She risks being put under court guardianship based on 2006."

That was the year of Liliane's accident at Formentor, at age eighty-four, and the period of mental confusion that followed. Banier's accusers would later pounce on this statement in an attempt to show that he was aware of her mental deficiencies dating from that time. Banier claims, on the contrary, that her active schedule proved that she was lucid, and that he was merely encouraging de Maistre to document that fact. For the moment, though, that legal debate still lay in the future.

Liliane, who had dozed off, suddenly woke up at this point and asked what they were talking about. Banier sought to reassure her. "No, I was just saying things will turn out fine, Liliane. Because in 2006 you saw many people. You just had some orientation problems like anyone can have. And that means strictly nothing." Earlier in the same discussion, he had told Liliane that her "breathtaking" correspondence with him between 2003 and 2007 would prove her lucidity: "With your letters, thanks to your ear, we'll win the trial, because you write so marvelously well that the reader is bowled over."

Banier's arrival in the office on May 11, 2010, was the thing the butler was hoping for: It was only after this session that Bonnefoy ended his yearlong eavesdropping and handed the recordings over to Françoise Meyers. Was it worth the wait? By themselves, certainly, his recorded words were not enough to convict Banier, but they demonstrated several important points: that he appeared to be aware of Liliane's mental lapses in 2006, a time when he benefited from substantial donations; that he was a participant, if indirectly, in the tax-evasion scheme surrounding d'Arros; and that he had a way of dealing with Liliane using excessive language that tended to support the notion that he sought to influence her through cajolery and flattery.

Beyond Banier's own words, the recordings made it clear that Liliane was confused and vulnerable to manipulation by those around her. Bonnefoy's CDs thus constituted a key turning point.

The recordings not only provided fodder for Prévost-Desprez's investigation, which focused exclusively on the charges against Banier; they also offered an opening for prosecutor Courroye to get back into the action. Though he had dropped his investigation of Banier in September 2009, he now opened a spate of new preliminary investigations. In addition to pursuing Bonnefoy for invasion of privacy, the new probes included publication of the illicit recordings, influence peddling (de Maistre's hiring of Madame Woerth and his Légion d'honneur medal), tax fraud (concerning the Swiss accounts and the undeclared Île d'Arros), and illegal political financing. For good measure, Courroye attempted to nip Prévost-Desprez's investigation in the bud, but his motion was rejected by the Versailles appeals court. Thus the prosecutor and the judge pursued their rival probes in tandem, using the same Financial Brigade detectives and often interrogating the same witnesses.

What might seem like excessive zeal on Courroye's part, or an effort to muddy the waters for his rival Prévost-Desprez, might also have been motivated by a desire to prove to his numerous critics that he was not out to protect his friend Sarkozy after all. "If [Sarkozy] had been spattered by illegal money payments during the campaign, he would have been treated like anyone else," says Courroye. "I couldn't have stopped the machine." Another possible interpretation is that, by carrying out these investigations himself, he was preventing the cases from being assigned to investigative magistrates who might conduct independent probes with unpredictable results.

Seen from the Élysée's perspective, though, Courroye's sudden judicial activism was most worrisome. The president's erstwhile ally now seemed to be wandering off the reservation. "At that point, everything spun out of control and nobody could do anything about it," says Patrick Ouart. So far out of control, in fact, that the press was soon talking about a French Watergate, and that Sarkozy, once out of office, would find himself under formal investigation.

CHAPTER 17
THE WOERTH AFFAIR

In the summer of 2010, Éric Woerth was a man on a tightrope. Switched from budget minister to labor minister in March, he became the spearhead for Sarkozy's boldest and most unpopular move: a reform of the national pension system. Its central measure was to delay the retirement age from sixty to sixty-two years, hardly draconian by American terms, but a risky move in a country where clawing back any kind of entitlement can send the masses yelling and screaming to the barricades. Bitterly opposed by all the major labor unions, the proposal sparked a wave of strikes and brought millions of protesters into the streets. This was the greatest challenge of Woerth's career: If he could successfully shepherd the bill through, he would be hailed by fellow conservatives as a tough and effective leader. There were rumors that Sarkozy might even name him prime minister in his next cabinet shuffle. If he failed, his high-flying ambitions would take a nosedive.

On June 16, just as the details of Woerth's pension bill went public, *Mediapart* began publishing excerpts from Pascal Bonnefoy's recordings. The online text version was accompanied by audio clips on which one could hear de Maistre's mellifluous voice bragging about his links to his "friend" Éric Woerth and telling Madame Bettencourt he had hired the minister's wife "to make him happy." *Mediapart*'s revelations, quickly followed by *Le Point*'s, touched off a media firestorm focused on Woerth's cozy relations with de Maistre. All that was bad enough for the minister, but a far more serious charge would be leveled at him three weeks later by a woman he had never heard of: Claire Thibout.

Thibout, the accountant who had first blown the whistle on Banier, now found herself ensnared in an aggressive investigation by Courroye. Madame Bettencourt's lawyer, Georges Kiejman, had filed a complaint accusing Thibout of stealing bank records and other documents after she was fired in November 2008. On July 5, 2010, Courroye had his detectives interrogate Thibout all morning at Financial Brigade headquarters, then sent them back to grill her at her own home well into the evening.

Kiejman's charge turned out to be totally false: Thibout produced receipts from Liliane's tax lawyer proving that she had returned all the documents in question. Among them were the bank books in which she recorded all the cash she withdrew and gave to Monsieur and Madame Bettencourt. "That's when the affair turned political," says her attorney Antoine Gillot, "because these books showed regular weekly cash withdrawals of €50,000 that were mostly given to André Bettencourt, who as everyone knew, gave money to certain political figures."

Angered by Kiejman's charges and the grilling she had received, Thibout vented her spleen in an interview with *Mediapart.* The investigative website put it online July 6 under the sensational headline THE ACCOUNTANT ACCUSES. Thibout described the Bettencourts' system of political donations, in which she played a key role by withdrawing cash from the bank and handing it over to André Bettencourt — or Dédé, as she called him. "There was a veritable parade of politicians in the house, especially at election time. Everyone came to get his envelope."

Then the accountant made a claim that transformed a family dispute into what the French call an *affaire d'état* — an affair of state. As quoted by *Mediapart,* Thibout declared that "Patrice de Maistre, who then dealt with the politicians because of André's illness, asked me to go to the bank and withdraw a sum three times greater than usual — €150,000." She pointed out that her cash authorization was limited to €50,000 per week. De Maistre's reply, according to Thibout: "Listen, it's to finance Sarkozy's presidential campaign! I have to give this money to the person who manages his campaign finances, Éric Woerth. And €50,000 is not enough.' "

Told by the bank that a €150,000 withdrawal would trigger a money-laundering alert, Thibout took out only the authorized €50,000. She said she gave the cash-filled envelope to Madame Bettencourt, who immediately handed it to de Maistre in Thibout's presence. (Confirmation of that meeting on January 18, 2007, was subsequently found in the date books of all three participants.) Thibout supposed that the financier got the remaining €100,000 he wanted from one of Liliane's secret Swiss bank accounts. She later testified that de Maistre had told her, "Sometimes it is useful to have accounts in Switzerland."

In the French context, Thibout's story was sensational. Though €150,000 seems like a pittance compared to the millions that super-rich contributors pump into US contests, it is twenty times more than the legal limit under France's strictly controlled laws on campaign financing. To say that Éric Woerth received illegal funds on Sarkozy's behalf was one step short of accusing the president himself. Prompted by *Mediapart*'s questioning, Thibout took that final step.

"Nicolas Sarkozy also received his envelope," she was quoted as saying, referring to the period before his election as president in May 2007. "Everyone in the house knew that Sarkozy also went to see the Bettencourts in order to get money. He was an habitué. On the days when he came, as was the case with the others, [André Bettencourt] asked me just before the meal to bring him a kraft envelope, which he took with him. I'm not stupid, after all, I didn't need a little drawing to understand what was going on."

The publication of Thibout's interview triggered a near panic in the Élysée Palace. Furious at becoming a target of what the press was now calling "the Woerth-Bettencourt Affair," the president lost his temper and at one point snapped at his labor minister, "I'm starting to get sick and tired of all this." He was determined to strike back. For that, he turned to his chief of staff, Claude Guéant, an ex-director general of the National Police and longtime Sarkozy ally.

Upon arriving in the Élysée in 2007, Guéant had organized a nucleus of hard-core Sarkozy loyalists to help him respond to the president's critics. Their job, he says, was to "light counter-fires." Like John Erlichman and H. R. Haldeman of Watergate fame, Guéant and his colleagues could be ruthless in defense of their embattled president.

On July 6, 2010, the day *Mediapart* put Thibout's interview online, Guéant called an emergency meeting of Sarkozy insiders in the Élysée's green room, next to the president's second-floor office. One participant suggested accusing the investigative site of "Nazism"; another proposed to compare *Mediapart* editor Edwy Plenel to Joseph Goebbels, Hitler's ruthless propaganda chief. Finally, it was UMP party leader Xavier Bertrand who publicly blasted *Mediapart* for using "fascist methods," triggering a defamation suit by Plenel's website. (*Mediapart* lost the 2013 ruling.)

That was just the beginning. Furious over Thibout's implication of his friend Sarkozy, Courroye ordered his detectives to reinterrogate the bothersome accountant. On July 7, they tracked her down at her cousin's house in the south of France, where she had gone to hide from the media, and grilled her until two a.m. As she would do in all her subsequent interrogations, Thibout firmly maintained her story about the €50,000 for Woerth, but she modified her statement about Sarkozy. Claiming she had been misquoted by *Mediapart,* she now said only that it was "possible" that Sarkozy had received cash envelopes at the Bettencourt home. Guéant seized on that partial retraction to issue a triumphant communiqué, claiming "the real truth comes out!"

Early the next morning the detectives escorted Thibout on a train back to Paris, where they interrogated her all day at the Financial Brigade headquarters. That afternoon, investigators confronted her face-to-face with Patrice de Maistre, who called her a "liar" and denied that he had ever asked the accountant for cash or spoken to her about political donations to Éric Woerth. "I felt they were treating me like public enemy number one," said Thibout.

"My client, who has ceaselessly told the truth, and always says the same thing, is the witness who must be destroyed," Thibout's lawyer told me in July 2010, two weeks after the *Mediapart* interview. "Why? Because she tells truths that disturb a lot of people. She disturbs Monsieur Banier and his friends, who have plundered Madame Bettencourt for years. She disturbs the president, because he got involved in this affair and because his name was cited among the visitors of Monsieur and Madame Bettencourt. She disturbs the prosecutor Courroye, who is close to the Élysée and tried to quash the whole case."

As the pressure on Sarkozy mounted and his poll numbers continued to dip — a mere 26 percent approval rating in July 2010 — the president took to the airwaves on July 12 in a carefully scripted primetime interview

344

on the state-owned France 2 television network. The setting was calculated to present Sarkozy in a majestic pose: The president sat face-to-face with anchorman David Pujadas on the rear terrace of the Élysée Palace, the classic eighteenth-century mansion that formerly belonged to three Bourbon kings and was a home of the Emperor Napoleon before becoming France's presidential residence in 1874.

Under Pujadas's softball questioning, Sarkozy defended himself against the "calumnies" of critics who were plotting against him. In the face of rising demands for Woerth's resignation, he praised his labor minister as "an honest man, who has all my confidence." The charges of illegal political financing, he insisted, had been whipped up by those who opposed his reform policies. "They present me as someone who, for twenty years, would go visit Madame Bettencourt to collect envelopes. It's shameful! That's just one more lie." Sarkozy's one concession to his critics was to "recommend" that Woerth drop his position as his party treasurer, implicitly acknowledging the ambiguities stemming from his double role as fund-raiser and cabinet member. Woerth did so the next day.

Meanwhile, Woerth's wife, Florence, resigned on June 27 from her lucrative job as an investment manager for the Bettencourts' Clymène holding company, saying that she had "underestimated the conflict of interest." Though Patrice de Maistre said repeatedly that he had hired Florence Woerth at her husband's request, she told a different story when she was interrogated by the Financial Brigade on July 21. She claimed that she had approached de Maistre in the spring of 2007 to propose financial products on behalf of the investment firm she then worked for. In June 2007, she said, de Maistre contacted her again and offered her a job investing Liliane Bettencourt's L'Oréal dividends. In September 2007, she signed a contract for an annual salary of €200,000, including the bonus. But there were frictions from the beginning, stemming from an apparent personality conflict with de Maistre. The financial adviser didn't think much of her work and, as noted, told Madame Bettencourt in April 2010 that he thought it best to let her go with a big severance payment.

A headstrong woman driven by social and professional ambitions — de Maistre called her "pushy" — Florence Woerth did not make things easy for her husband. Indeed, some of his colleagues in the UMP saw her as Woerth's "Achilles' heel." After Woerth was elected mayor of the affluent town of Chantilly in 1995, Florence could often be seen at its famous racetrack dressed to the nines and sporting elaborate hats like the queen of England at Ascot. In May 2008, she joined forces with a group of wealthy women to form Ecurie Dams, an association created to buy, raise, and race Thoroughbred horses. Presented as "an original and trendy way to enlarge women's influence," the group also served as a lucrative tax shelter thanks to a measure launched by Sarkozy, and supported by Woerth, that offered hefty tax deductions for investments in the racing and betting industry. In June 2010, Florence Woerth was elected to the supervisory board of Hermès, reinforcing her image as a woman enamored of wealth, luxury, and privilege.

Woerth had been suffering a Chinese water torture since the middle of June, when the steady drip of allegations had begun to erode his public image as an efficient technocrat and replace it with that of a sneaky political insider. The creases in his face deepened and his five o'clock shadow seemed darker than ever. His public statements on the subject were peppered with indignant denials of wrongdoing and whining complaints about being the victim of a "mediatic lapidation" and a "manhunt" aiming to "kill" him. Woerth's petulant remarks did little to endear him to the public. His was the face of the hated pension reform; his critics enjoyed watching him squirm.

Suspected of involvement in illegal political financing and influence peddling, Woerth was interrogated in his Labor Ministry office for eight hours on July 29, 2010. He admitted to several casual meetings with de Maistre, but denied having asked him to hire his wife or accepting cash from him. As for de Maistre's Légion d'honneur medal, Woerth insisted that he had played no role in initiating it. That claim was belied in mid-August when investigators discovered a 2007 letter that Woerth had personally written to Sarkozy recommending Patrice de Maistre for the prestigious decoration.

A further embarrassment for Woerth concerned Liliane Bettencourt's taxes. On June 30, 2010, the satirical weekly *Le Canard Enchaîné* reported that Liliane Bettencourt had received a staggering €30 million refund in March 2008. The reimbursement was made in all legality under the terms of the *bouclier fiscal,* or tax shield, a measure Sarkozy had passed to cap the total tax burden on high incomes at 50 percent. But the effect on public opinion was devastating for Sarkozy and Woerth, since it underscored, at a time of widespread economic hardship, the cozy relationship between the power elites and the moneyed class. The impression that the Bettencourts were receiving special treatment reemerged when Claire Thibout told *Mediapart,* correctly, that the family's tax returns had not been audited a single time in the fifteen years that she had served as their accountant. Insistent questions from the media and the Socialist opposition prompted an investigation by the Inspection générale des finances, the government's internal auditing agency, to determine whether Woerth had intervened to give favorable tax treatment to Madame Bettencourt. The in-house report released July 11, 2010, cleared him of any such suspicions.

Nonetheless, the Sarkozy team was circling the wagons. The president was furious over the relentless string of press revelations that entangled Woerth more and more deeply in the labyrinthine Bettencourt case. One leak in particular made him go ballistic: a long article in *Le Monde,* dated July 18–19, 2010, that contained verbatim excerpts from a deposition of Patrice de Maistre concerning his relations with Woerth. Sarkozy ordered chief of staff Claude Guéant to track down the source of the leak. An examination of phone records revealed multiple contacts between the author of the *Le Monde* article and an obscure Justice Ministry bureaucrat named David Sénat.

Though nothing proved that Sénat had given any documents to the newspaper, he was removed from his Justice Ministry post in July 2010 and assigned to a dead-end job in Cayenne, capital city of the steamy Atlantic island of Guiana that formerly served as a French penal colony. Judge Prévost-Desprez was right: "Sarkozy doesn't mess around."

CHAPTER 18
FILTHY RICH

The publication of the illicit recordings in June 2010 was devastating for the image of Liliane Bettencourt. Once admired as the main shareholder and a board member of the world's leading cosmetics firm, a philanthropist via her family foundation, the wife of a government minister, and an elegant grande dame perched at the top of France's social ladder, she now appeared as a senile old lady with more money than she knew what to do with. That unflattering view was embodied by "Mamie Zinzin" — Nutty Grandma — a marionette featured on the popular satirical show *Les Guignols de l'info.* Created in 1988 by the Canal+ network, the *Guignols* took the form of a mock news broadcast that pilloried politicians and celebrities to the delight of its millions of daily viewers. Starting in the summer of 2010, the figure of Mamie Zinzin emerged as a gaga octogenarian handing out banknotes with cheerful abandon — mostly to President Nicolas Sarkozy.

One skit showed Sarkozy's allies ringing the Bettencourt doorbell dressed in Halloween costumes. When Mamie Zinzin answers the door, grinning hideously and trembling with palsy, they shout "trick or treat." She thrusts wads of €500 notes into their hands, squealing, "Aren't they cute!" Sarkozy meets his henchmen at the street corner and grabs the cash. "That's for my 2012 campaign," he says, and sends them back for more. "Mamie Zinzin will forget you were there two minutes ago."

Such skits were a not-too-subtle stab at Sarkozy's alleged campaign gifts from the Bettencourts. But the main target was Liliane herself, for reasons that say a lot about French attitudes toward wealth. American audiences might sympathize with an elderly woman who is expropriated by unscrupulous plunderers. To the popular French mind, though, such a figure is more likely to be the object of scorn precisely because she is rich. Money is traditionally a taboo subject in France. Those who have it try to hide it, or at least be discreet about it, while those who don't tend to resent and envy those who do. Even within the Bettencourt family, the subject was avoided. "At home, we didn't talk about money," said Françoise Meyers. "It was not a word we pronounced easily."

In stark contrast to the United States, where John Kennedy could ride into the

White House on his father's money and a billionaire real estate mogul named Donald Trump could tout his personal fortune as a qualification for the presidency and win election, French politicians have traditionally sought public favor by denouncing wealth as antidemocratic and money itself as a source of corruption. "My only adversary, and that of France, has always been money," the conservative Charles de Gaulle famously declared in 1969. At the other end of the political spectrum, the Socialist François Mitterrand unleashed his most eloquent indignation against "money that corrupts, money that buys, money that kills, money that ruins and rots the conscience of men." François Hollande solidified his popularity among leftist voters by bluntly telling a TV interviewer in 2006: "I don't like the rich." Six years later, Hollande defeated outgoing president Nicolas Sarkozy, whose "president of the rich" image and bling-bling style played badly with the French public.

The reasons for France's money taboo have long roots. In a country whose population was largely agricultural until the mid-twentieth century, the peasant tradition of hiding one's money to avoid attracting the attention of thieves and jealous neighbors was widespread. *Pour vivre heureux, vivons cachés,* says an old French dictum — to live happily, live hidden. Another powerful source is the weight of Catholicism, with its stress on aiding the poor and the Gospels' camel-through-the-eye-of-a-needle view of the rich.

France's political history reinforced the anti-rich bias in multiple ways. The French Revolution began as a revolt against the privileged wealthy classes that didn't pay their share of taxes. Egalitarianism, central to the republican ideology that followed the collapse of monarchy, did not sit well with the accumulation of huge fortunes. The Marxist philosophy that inspired the French left equated wealth and profit with capitalist exploitation.

All this contributed to a popular view that, even today, tends to look on the wealthy with a mixture of hostility and suspicion. In one 2012 opinion poll, 72 percent of the respondents felt that the rich are "badly viewed" in France. "There is a reticence to talk about money," says sociologist Janine Mossuz-Lavau, author of the 2007 study "L'Argent et nous" (Money and us). "In the US, it's common to ask total strangers how much they make. Never in France! People who are willing to talk to me in detail about their sex lives will storm out of the room when I ask them about their salaries."

What made the Bettencourt Affair so explosive in terms of public opinion was the perceived collusion between private wealth and political power. "For those who wanted to show that political power is corrupt, this was the perfect demonstration of a link between power and money, a link that was deemed unacceptable and despicable," explains sociologist Michel Wieviorka, referring to the Bettencourts' suspected campaign payments to Éric Woerth. Woerth himself realized, too late, that it was a grave mistake for him and his wife to be associated with the Bettencourts because of the toxic image of money in the eyes of the French. If he had it to do over again, he said, he would never have let his wife take a job investing Liliane's stock dividends. "We did not fully appreciate the extent to which this family, though discreet and hardly ostentatious, embodied in the collective imagination the supreme symbol of excessive wealth."

Which is why there was so little public sympathy for Liliane Bettencourt, though she was depicted by her daughter as an elderly victim of an insatiable exploiter. Liliane herself was widely seen as an idle heiress who had done nothing to earn her wealth, while Françoise was perceived as a rich girl battling mainly to preserve her own inheritance. The publication of the butler's recordings, with their revelations about the Bettencourts' secret Swiss bank accounts and their undeclared island in the Seychelles, reinforced the view of Liliane as rich, privileged, and unethical to boot. And the news of her €30 million tax rebate, though in no way illegal, was greeted with a mixture of irony and indignation. One website invited users to compare their annual salaries with Liliane's dividends. A salary of €100,000, for example, would be equaled by the heiress in ninety-one minutes, a statistic sure to cause envy and scorn among the French. Interestingly, though, French consumers did not take their resentment out on L'Oréal, which continued to report healthy profits throughout this period.

The public's demonization of money and wealth also besmirched Banier, who despite a certain Robin Hood image, was widely seen as an unscrupulous gold digger. "They massacred François-Marie through a well-organized press campaign," says attorney Richard Malka, who defended Martin d'Orgeval and, indirectly, Banier himself. "They said he stole 500 million from an old lady. It's very hard to recover from something like that. For certain French people, gaining money is worse than pedophilia."

Liliane Bettencourt was sensitive about her superwealthy image long before the affair hit the front pages. Money was the main subject of her 1987 interview in *Egoïste,* the one for which François-Marie Banier first photographed her. "A rich woman," she said, "the term itself is disagreeable. It's an ugly word. I prefer fortune. A rich woman is locked into a certain status by her wealth. She is weighed down. Trapped in a definitive idea of herself. That's what is so annoying about this kind of stereotype they saddle you with: They rein you in and park you." No one was objective about wealth, she lamented. "Once you reach a certain figure, everybody derails."

She went on: "There are a lot of jealous people . . . wealth irritates them. How can you justify yourself? There is no justification in life, for anything. Either you accept your inheritance or you don't . . . Yes, you always have to excuse yourself when you have money; the French don't understand the industrial phenomenon. They say, 'Too much is too much.' "

Ever wary of wealth's negative image in France, Liliane Bettencourt in 1987 created the Bettencourt Schueller Foundation to support worthy projects in the arts, science, and medicine. Entirely funded by the Bettencourt family, the foundation devotes more than half its annual spending to medical projects, with particular attention to AIDS research. In the cultural domain, it awards annual prizes for choral singing — a particular interest of Liliane's, in spite of her deafness — and French craftsmanship.

The foundation also supports the restoration of historic sites, publications, and films it deems worthy of public interest, including

Jacques Perrin's award-winning 2001 feature on bird migrations, *Le peuple migrateur*. In February 2010, just as the Affaire Bettencourt was becoming an embarrassing subject of French media attention, Liliane donated €552 million to this family endeavor, bringing its total capital to some €750 million and making it the country's wealthiest private foundation. Message: Liliane's fortune could serve the public good in addition to enriching a little-known artist beyond his wildest dreams.

Madame Bettencourt's good works had in fact been recognized in 2001, when Minister of Health Bernard Kouchner pinned the Légion d'honneur on the jacket of her Chanel suit. The award recognized the foundation's leading role in AIDS research and Liliane's "43 years of social and professional activity." As it happened, the decoration provided the occasion for yet another mother-daughter dispute: Françoise had suggested a small family reception attended by a dozen close friends; Liliane overrode her and invited five hundred people to a high-profile ceremony in the gilded halls of the Health Ministry. Françoise's ruffled feelings were hardly soothed by her mother's choice for master of ceremonies: François-Marie Banier.

CHAPTER 19
BANIER'S *ANNÉE TERRIBLE*

On Tuesday, July 6, 2010, a helicopter bearing François-Marie Banier landed near the Bettencourt compound at Arcouest in Brittany. Banier alighted and entered via the rear gate, hoping to elude the paparazzi, who had been stalking the walled property. Other paparazzi, armed with powerful telephoto lenses, were crisscrossing the Bay of Bréhat in motorboats in hopes of snapping Liliane on her colonnaded front porch or in her garden.

Waiting by the saltwater swimming pool behind the house, the heiress greeted Banier with a peck on each cheek and walked with him to the side porch, away from the seaborne cameras. The whole country was in the grips of a record-breaking heat wave — *la canicule,* the French call it — but here in the shade, with a sea breeze blowing in from the bay, the air was quite pleasant.

The couple sat together in deep conversation. As they often did, they wrote down their exchanges. Their words flickered from subject to subject — Banier's new photo books, her recent TV interview, L'Oréal business, memories of André. Banier alluded to the passage from the illicit recordings where Liliane said of him "I hope he doesn't kill me"; they both laughed at Metzner's claim that Banier was literally out to murder the heiress. "At least that helps [the lawyer] make money," she quipped.

Banier confided his fear that Liliane would "drop" him when the suit was first filed. "I acted as I wanted," she replied, then turned to the fraught relationship with her daughter: "Françoise is one train behind me. I don't see how she can change. She could change her lack of kindness. I should say affection, but that's too important a word for her."

"Your daughter will see you again when you stop seeing me," Banier wrote. "Her lawyer said so."

"I guess that means it's official," Liliane ironized.

As things turned out, it was indeed "official": Banier would never again lay eyes on Liliane Bettencourt. When he called her a week later, after returning from a trip to New York, a servant told him that Madame was not available. Banier called again and was told that Madame "did not wish to speak" to him. He wrote her on August 17, thanking her for her "tender and dear" friendship. She never responded. He finally understood that it was over. No more talks. No more letters. No more luncheons at the Bettencourt mansion, no more dinners at fancy Parisian restaurants. No more sojourns on the Île d'Arros. And, of course, no more gifts.

When Banier thinks back on that bitter moment, he regrets that he "didn't batter down the doors of the rue Delabordère to tell her, 'I'm here!' " Refusing to believe that Liliane herself decided to cut him off, he assumed that the people around the heiress told her that Banier didn't want to see her anymore. He did not know it at the time, but a process was under way that would have major consequences for Liliane, Françoise, the Bettencourt fortune, and the future of L'Oréal. And there was no place in that scenario for François-Marie Banier.

For Banier, losing contact with Liliane was the cruelest blow in what in all respects was an *année terrible* — a terrible year. The publication of the butler's recordings in mid-June took some of the immediate heat off him as attention focused on the political angle involving Woerth and Sarkozy. But once Judge Prévost-Desprez's new investigation cranked up in July, the steady drumbeat of leaked testimony smeared him as a manipulative predator and worse.

"The summer of 2010 was extremely hard

for Banier; he took it very badly," says Hervé Temime, his defense attorney at the time. "We had completely lost the media battle."

It was at the end of that summer that Banier parted ways with Temime — "we had become toxic for one another," says the attorney, explaining that both men were too high-strung to carry on a calm working relationship. At that point, Banier put his defense in the hands of the veteran criminal lawyer Pierre Cornut-Gentille, backed up by his long-time copyright lawyer Laurent Merlet.

Whereas Françoise Meyers had a whole PR firm working for her and gave four high-profile interviews between July 2009 and July 2010, Banier had no media adviser at all. Temime had actively discouraged him from speaking out publicly, preferring a dignified silence to blow-by-blow ripostes — not least because he considered Banier "uncontrollable." Since the beginning of the affair, Banier had given only one interview, which ran in *Le Monde* in September 2009. In the wake of the recordings, however, he decided he had to defend himself and granted an interview to Christophe Barbier, editor of *L'Express,* France's leading newsmagazine, founded in 1953 and modeled on *Time.*

In his wide-ranging exchange with Barbier, Banier talks about his work, his special friendship with Liliane Bettencourt, and the evolution of her patronage over the years. He praises Liliane for her beauty — "like a second Ava Gardner" — her "unexpected vocabulary," her "culture," her "psychological acuity," her "desire to forge ahead." Above all, he says, she is motivated by love for "her child" — not Françoise, but L'Oréal. "Liliane lives with L'Oréal day and night." Why was she attracted to Banier? "She likes atypical people," he says. "I don't let people sleep, I want to know their truth." Why did she give Banier so much money? "Reverse the question," he says. "Why did I give her my time, when I had books, photos, and paintings to do? Because she's a woman who surprises me every day. Her generosity is intentional, decided, and calculated."

Banier denounces the "ignominy" of the daughter's suit against him. The adoption story? "It's grotesque, insane! Our relationship is a sensitive one, we have no age when we speak. To make me [Liliane's] son would be to underscore the generation gap between us. My own mother was living until three weeks ago, and I would never have renounced my name." The billion euros? "That's a round figure everyone is fixated on. It bears no relationship to reality." His alleged attempts to isolate Liliane from her family? "Does Madame Meyers-Bettencourt forget that she lives across the street from her mother in Neuilly?" The real reason for her action against him, says Banier, is not to protect her mother but "a banal struggle over money."

Whatever cathartic effect the *L'Express* piece may have had on Banier's morale was short-lived. He had discussed plans for the interview at his last meeting with Liliane, but by the time it was published on July 14, the heiress — or her entourage — had cut off all contact with him. And not just physical contact: On July 13, just one week after Banier left Arcouest, Liliane received her lawyer Georges Kiejman at the villa and, at his urging, gave him a handwritten letter nullifying Banier's designation as her *légataire universel.* Announcing the revocation to the press on August 28, Kiejman explained that Madame Bettencourt "understood that too much is too much and that she had already given a lot to Banier." Though Banier had always claimed not to want the *légataire* status, he could not have been heartened by the timing of Liliane's act and the publicity given to it by her attorney.

In September, Liliane echoed Kiejman's words — "too much is too much" — in a *Paris Match* interview that read like a farewell letter. Though she talked about how much Banier had amused her over the years, she said she must now turn away from him. Why did she give him so much money? "Because he asked for it!" With a seeming reference to Banier's Jewish roots, she added, "I imagine that it's an ancestral deformation with him! He's someone who wants always more, always bigger." Was this the end of their relationship? "With him, I realize that I can't breathe," she answered. "It's a shame after so many years, but he has become too exhausting . . . François-Marie won't change. He's unlivable. To him friendship is exclusive, demanding, and above all possessive. . . . This summer, I have thought things over. And I know that the biggest mistake at this time would be to see him." It is impossible to know whether those harsh words expressed Liliane Bettencourt's true feelings, since she was coached and edited by a media consultant hired by her lawyers. But the fact is that she would never see Banier again. The affair — *their* affair — was over.

There was more bad news for Banier. On September 20, L'Oréal announced that his contracts, worth €710,000 a year, had been terminated because "the media noise surrounding François-Marie Banier" was "prejudicial to L'Oréal." The company's decision had been prompted by a suit for "misuse of corporate assets" filed in July by a small shareholder and joined by more than fifty others. The complaint cited two contracts between L'Oréal and Banier's company, Héricy, signed in 2001 and scheduled to run until 2011. Héricy, devoted to the sale and promotion of Banier's photos, was chronically in deficit; only the L'Oréal stipends kept it afloat.

Following the cancellation of the contracts, Banier liquidated his company in May 2011. The disgruntled shareholders weren't the only ones who opposed Banier's sweetheart deal with L'Oréal: In February 2007, Françoise Meyers had personally telephoned Jean-Paul Agon, then the company's director general, and urged him not to renew Banier's contracts.

A further blow came in October with the cancellation of a scheduled photo show by the Maison européenne de la photographie (MEP). Banier had been preparing the exhibition for months and looked forward to the opening on November 8, 2010, as an occasion to occupy the spotlight as a photographer and artist rather than an accused exploiter of old ladies. But MEP director Jean-Luc Monterosso feared the opposite effect: "The current climate is not favorable for showing Banier's work. The public would come not to see the photos but to see a protagonist of the Bettencourt Affair." The same reasoning led the Bibliothèque François Mitterrand, France's biggest national library, to cancel a planned Banier show and prompted the Ghislaine Hussenot gallery to drop him unceremoniously from its artist roster.

Though Banier's critics would argue that

he brought it all on himself, the cumulative effect of these blows on his large but fragile ego was devastating. In addition to the pressure of the pending trial and the daily media battering, he felt increasingly isolated, abandoned by former friends who now avoided him. How far he had fallen from the "Golden Boy of Paris" days! "He tries not to show it, but he is greatly affected," Pascal Greggory told *Le Monde* in October 2010. "Especially by those who have forgotten him. One morning he told me: 'Last night, I prepared a rope and I wanted to hang myself.' " Looking back on that bleak period, Banier confirms that he was indeed on the verge of suicide.

What shocked Banier most was the realization that what he had taken as a game was in fact deadly serious. "He placed himself in a kind of theater in which he did funny things, played the buffoon," says actor and stage director Jean-Michel Ribes, a close friend of Banier's. "He was immersed in the unreality of that world because the world of money is unreal. It's a world that forces you not to be yourself, where all your points of reference are shattered. Then someone enters who is not part of that family, who in fact breaks up the game and has fun, and those people become crazy." Ribes spins an intriguing metaphor: "It's as if an actor played an assassin in a play and when he leaves the stage people say, 'We're going to arrest you.

You killed someone.' He says, 'What? I didn't kill anyone, it was a game.' It was theater, fantasy, the money had no reality to him. At a certain point it means nothing, whether he had 500 million or 2 billion, he doesn't care."

No, but Françoise Meyers cared. The judges cared. And in the end, even Banier had to care. One way or another, the curtain was about to fall.

CHAPTER 20
THE FIXER

For Patrice de Maistre, the publication of Bonnefoy's recordings signaled a "descent into hell." Not only was the financier personally implicated in tax-evasion schemes, political payments, and a humiliating request for the "boat of his dreams," but his employer was shown to be fragile, confused, often unable to follow the details of the complicated legal schemes concocted by her advisers. In short, the situation of Madame Bettencourt in the face of her daughter's suit was becoming untenable. In June 2010, de Maistre turned to the one man he knew who might be able to fix the mess: Pascal Wilhelm.

Wilhelm, then forty-nine, had been de Maistre's personal lawyer since 1996. Their professional relationship was amicable, but there was no real friendship between them. They came from different worlds: The financier was a patrician, hunter, yachtsman, and member of France's most exclusive clubs; the lawyer was the self-made son of a Jewish clothier from the Paris suburb of Nogent-sur-Marne. His favorite sport was not sailing, but judo — the art of using an opponent's strength against him.

A specialist in conflict resolution, Wilhelm boasted a list of blue-chip clients and contacts that made him one of the most influential members of the Paris bar, though he rarely appeared in a courtroom. His method was to make deals, solve problems, and reach settlements. Short of stature with slightly graying black hair and intense black eyes, he likes to describe himself as a man of "strong temperament." A passionate student of French history — he published a biography of the Revolutionary pamphleteer Camille Desmoulins in 2015 — Wilhelm had already played an indirect role in the case by recommending Georges Kiejman to defend Madame Bettencourt's interests. Now de Maistre was appealing to him to find a way out of the morass that was engulfing the house of Bettencourt.

In early July 2010, Wilhelm met with the eighty-seven-year-old heiress for the first time in the central reception room of her home in Neuilly. Known as the *salon rond* because of its semicircular shape, the room looks out on the garden through three glass doors framed by tan draperies. It is furnished with a large beige sofa and matching armchairs, a grand piano topped with family photos, and Art

Deco furniture by Ruhlmann. The polished wood coffee table is covered with art books, two black stone bird sculptures, and a large bouquet of sunflowers that recalls a Van Gogh painting. There are no actual Van Goghs on the walls, but Wilhelm was impressed by the Picasso, Braque, and de Chirico works on display, as well as the tall Matisse drawing that hung alongside the stairway.

As soon as Liliane descended the curved stairway, Wilhelm was struck by her regal bearing — "majestic like the queen of England."

Liliane sat next to him on the sofa and got right to the point. "Voilà, Monsieur. What should we do?"

"Madame," said Wilhelm, "your biggest problem is the Swiss bank accounts and the Île d'Arros. You have to regularize all that immediately."

"Can you take care of it?"

Of course he could. Wilhelm contacted the Finance Ministry and began a discussion aimed at settling Liliane's dodgy tax situation with the least possible damage. At the same time he managed, with great difficulty, to dissolve the foundation in Lichtenstein that legally controlled the Île d'Arros and transfer the ownership back to Madame Bettencourt, declaring that exotic asset to French tax authorities for the first time. In all, he brought €101 million in Swiss-held funds back to France. Taxes and penalties amounted to about half of that amount, but Wilhelm managed to avoid criminal charges and fines for tax evasion.

Then came the hard part: how to deal with Françoise Meyers's legal challenge. In mid-July, Liliane invited Wilhelm to Cap de Formentor to discuss the case. As soon as he was ushered into the heiress's hilltop villa, he was struck by her solitude. Apart from her domestic servants and her dog, she was completely alone. André was gone. Banier had been banished from her life, along with Martin d'Orgeval, for whom she had a tender spot. Her grandsons were uninterested in Formentor. As for Françoise and Jean-Pierre, God forbid . . .

Madame Bettencourt and the lawyer shared a light luncheon on the rear patio overlooking the swimming pool. Wilhelm sensed that his host was almost as grateful for the company as for the legal advice he could give.

"I can't continue with this situation," Liliane told him. "How can I work things out with my daughter? I don't have a life."

"Madame Bettencourt, you must begin by threatening her, and afterward, if she wants to discuss it, reach an agreement. It's imperative."

"Threaten her? How?"

"Threaten to take back the L'Oréal shares you gave her."

The idea had been bandied about earlier between Liliane and her advisers, but was considered too complicated legally. Now the heiress seemed to embrace this tactic. She asked Wilhelm to prepare a letter that threatened, in effect, to disinherit her daughter. But when she read Wilhelm's draft text, she found it "too violent." "I've thought this over," she told him. "It's too dangerous for L'Oréal." As an alternative, Wilhelm proposed to reach out to her daughter's lawyer and work out a deal. The heiress assented.

In late August, Wilhelm contacted Didier Martin, Françoise's business lawyer, and proposed to negotiate a peaceful settlement between mother and daughter. Martin agreed that it was the right solution, but said it was "too soon" — he would need time to bring his client around. Discreet discussions continued and the two men finally launched into an intense phase of negotiations, meeting several times a week, either at Wilhelm's posh headquarters overlooking the Parc Monceau or more often at Martin's offices on the Faubourg Saint-Honoré, two blocks from the Élysée Palace. The talks were carried out in such strict secrecy that both Olivier Metzner and Georges Kiejman, the rival criminal lawyers for Françoise and Liliane respectively, were left out of the loop.

Meanwhile, de Maistre sought Wilhelm's help

in devising a media strategy to counter the devastating "Mamie Zinzin" image resulting from the illicit recordings. In June 2010, they contacted two communications specialists: publicist Laurent Obadia, a friend and client of Wilhelm's; and Marion Bougeard, a crisis-management expert who had previously advised Kiejman. Working together under the aegis of Obadia's company, Opus Conseil, they set up a series of TV and print interviews aiming, in Obadia's words, to show that "the recordings did not reflect the true state of [Madame Bettencourt's] health." For their services, Opus Conseil received a whopping monthly fee of €80,000.

The results of this pricey campaign were mixed. Because of her deafness and memory lapses, Liliane had to be primed for the interviews with questions and answers prepared in advance by the media team. Marion Bougeard got directly involved in editing the taped TV interviews, telling the journalists where to cut and splice to make Madame Bettencourt seem more "punchy." On the print interviews, Bougeard admitted that she herself "reworked and amended" the texts.

The attempt to make the heiress appear spontaneous and dynamic backfired badly in some cases. For example, her media advisers contacted *Le Monde* on June 17 to offer up an interview. The paper sent one of its top reporters, Michel Guerrin, to Neuilly the next day. But Guerrin was abruptly ejected after twenty minutes by Patrice de Maistre, who was annoyed by questions concerning the undeclared Île d'Arros. "Madame is not interested in that," he snapped. "You can't get into those details." Marion Bougeard then stepped in and told Guerrin to email his remaining questions so Liliane could reply in writing. But the completed text she sent back to the journalist was largely written by Bougeard herself, with Madame Bettencourt supposedly "looking over [her] shoulder" while she typed. *Le Monde* published the interview the next day with a full account of the bizarre circumstances that surrounded it.

The televised interviews posed a special problem. The questioners had to sit directly in front of the heiress and speak slowly so she could read their lips. Her answers were hard to understand because of her soft voice and laborious articulation. One high-profile interview, with TF1's star anchorwoman Claire Chazal, was marred by Madame Bettencourt's constant head-turning to look at someone who was apparently standing off-camera to her right. It was later revealed that this was the network's news producer, prompting her answers from the sidelines.

The main thing most viewers retained from the TF1 interview, conducted at Liliane's Ar-couest villa, was her baffling use of a German word associated with the Occupation and the persecution of the Jews: *Raus!* ("get out of here," as in *Juden Raus!*). That interjection came in response to a question about the astronomical sums she had given Banier. "So what?" she said. "You want me to take it all back? You can't always count everything. The only thing that counts is people who work. As for the others, *Raus!*" Her incongruous use of that word lit up the Internet with tens of thousands of reactions and inevitably recalled the dark past of L'Oréal's founder. "Liliane Bettencourt must have taken German lessons along with her father Eugène Schueller," commented one contributor to a Jewish web forum, who went on to recount Schueller's wartime support of collaborationist groups and André Bettencourt's anti-Semitic articles. Not exactly the kind of image buffing that the heiress and her entourage had in mind.

Meanwhile, Nanterre prosecutor Courroye and Judge Prévost-Desprez pursued their parallel — and rival — investigations. During her interrogation of Françoise Meyers on July 20, 2010, Prévost-Desprez first learned the details of her secret financial arrangement with Claire Thibout: the €400,000 paid to the accountant in accordance, she said, with her father's wishes. Meyers explained that she considered this part of Thibout's severance indemnity, not a payment for her cooperation.

Prévost-Desprez, who admits having a certain sympathy for Madame Bettencourt's ill-loved daughter, explained to her that the so-called indemnity "poses a problem, because everybody is going to say you paid for her testimony." Françoise seemed not to grasp the full reality of this risk. "I sensed there were moments when I had to bring her back to planet Earth," says the judge.

Eight days later, a police search of the Meyers apartment turned up the famous letter of July 11, 2007, in which Françoise promised to round up Thibout's severance package to €800,000 if she was fired. In the event, the indemnity paid by Liliane's lawyers in December 2008 was €400,000; as promised, Françoise paid her an additional €400,000. Once the news of this deal filtered out, Banier's lawyers filed a complaint against Madame Meyers on September 20, 2010, for suborning a witness.

By this time, the jurisdictional battle between Prosecutor Courroye and Judge Prévost-Desprez was moving toward a climax. Courroye's ally in this combat was Georges Kiejman, who shared the prosecutor's aim of getting the "little judge" yanked off the case. On September 1, 2010, Kiejman phoned Courroye and railed about an article that had just appeared in *Le Monde.* The afternoon newspaper had just published a well-informed account of a police search of the Bettencourt home, carried out earlier that day on orders of Judge Prévost-Desprez. This and other *Le Monde* articles contained investigative material that could only have come from the judge, fumed Kiejman, who immediately filed a complaint for "violation of professional secrets."

Courroye, only too eager to confound his nemesis, ordered police to search the phone records of the journalists in question. The probe, of questionable legality, turned up fifty-seven text messages between Prévost-Desprez and one of the *Le Monde* reporters. Armed with that information, Courroye launched a formal investigation against the judge.

At this point, government authorities stepped in to put a sudden end to the catfight between Courroye and Prévost-Desprez. As Sarkozy's judicial adviser Patrick Ouart puts it, "the Nanterre tribunal had become a boxing ring." In early November, Justice Minister Michèle Alliot-Marie, prodded by Sarkozy, ordered all Bettencourt-related investigations moved to a neutral jurisdiction. On November 17, 2010, the cases were transferred from Nanterre to Bordeaux "in the interest of a good administration of justice." Prévost-Desprez still seethes over her removal from the case. "Why did they do it?" she asks rhetorically. "So I would stop the investigations that were poisoning the life of Sarkozy and Courroye, so that, finally, there would be no more Bettencourt Affair."

Courroye and Kiejman had finally succeeded in ejecting Prévost-Desprez from the case, but Courroye himself was disgraced and humiliated in the process. Not only were his own investigations snatched out of his hands; his very career was compromised and ultimately derailed: On August 3, 2012, Courroye would be demoted and sent to Paris, not as chief prosecutor, as he had always hoped, but as a subaltern in the Prosecutor's Office. Prévost-Desprez, for her part, was later cleared of the charges against her and promoted in August 2016 to the post of first deputy vice president of the Tribunal de Grande Instance in Paris, where she currently oversees antiterrorism cases.

The transfer of the case to Bordeaux spurred Pascal Wilhelm and Didier Martin, attorneys respectively for Liliane and Françoise, to accelerate their pursuit of a mother-daughter accord. The talks had hit a speed bump in October when Françoise suddenly filed a new petition to put her mother under guardianship. Wilhelm retaliated with a complaint against Françoise for "psychological violence" against his client. The exchange was hardly conducive to reconciliation, but Wilhelm's message was clear: "You want war, you'll get war." Liliane "was in combat mode at that point," he explains. "It was out of the question for her to be put under guardianship."

But the change of jurisdiction, with a brand-new team of investigators and judges, disrupted the strategies of both parties. Moreover, the litigation had just been made more complex by a second citation filed by Olivier Metzner on November 3, this one accusing de Maistre and Liliane's tax lawyer, Fabrice Goguel, as well as Banier, of abuse of weakness. The parties were now looking at a much longer procedure, with the possibility that Liliane Bettencourt, who had just turned eighty-eight, might die before it was resolved in court. Under these circumstances, both sides came under pressure from L'Oréal management to end the conflict that they feared might damage the brand.

In mid-November, Didier Martin informed Wilhelm that his client was ready to move ahead quickly. But both sides would have to make concessions. The Meyerses (for Jean-Pierre was totally involved in the process) had to give up on the idea of imposing a guardianship on Liliane and recovering all the liberalities given to Banier; Liliane had to sacrifice Patrice de Maistre — Françoise demanded his ouster — cut off ties with Banier, and grant the Meyerses an important role in L'Oréal's management, along with a substantial transfer of capital into their hands.

"Your daughter is like Prince Charles," Wilhelm explained to the heiress. "She could die before you, without ever having the attributes of power. So you have to rectify that by giving her access to your fortune before your death, and access to power within L'Oréal. That's the basis of the deal. We're going to negotiate your freedom against power and money." Liliane's two main concerns at that point, says Wilhelm, were "family coexistence and keeping L'Oréal in the family."

Liliane took no direct part in the talks. On December 1, 2010, she mandated Wilhelm to negotiate on her behalf. His interlocutors were not the Meyerses, whom he saw only four times during the process, but Didier Martin and Olivier Metzner, who had been brought into the talks in late November. It was Metzner's task to negotiate separate settlements with Banier, de Maistre, and Goguel.

On Monday, December 6, 2010, mother and daughter signed their agreement, each in her own home. That evening, the whole family gathered in the Bettencourt mansion to celebrate over champagne. Though Françoise reported that her mother was "very happy about the reconciliation," one can wonder how much the old woman actually understood about the terms. Indeed, Dr. Christophe de Jaeger, who examined Madame Bettencourt on December 17 at her daughter's request, judged that the heiress was "not apt to perform legal acts" or "manage her affairs" because her "cognitive faculties . . . were clearly altered by a cerebral malady of mixed origin."

The eight-page protocol contained a preamble, followed by ten articles and five annexes. The main points:

- Both women agreed to put a "definitive end to all procedures and investigations" in the case and to withdraw all their legal actions and claims.
- Pascal Wilhelm was named Liliane's *mandataire de protection future,* giving him authority to act on her behalf in the event that she was deemed incompetent to act on her own. This was considered a "softer" alternative to the court-ordered guardianship — *tutelle* — that Françoise had originally sought. Patrice de Maistre's earlier designation as protector was thereby nullified, while a separate agreement between Françoise and de Maistre removed the financier from all his other functions in exchange for a severance check of €1,913,600, plus €500,000 for his legal fees.
- Madame Bettencourt was guaranteed freedom of action in her "personal sphere," including her travels, expenses,

choice of domestic staff, and the "management and use of her personal assets."

- Jean-Pierre Meyers was named director general of Thétys and Clymène, giving him ultimate power over the two holding companies that controlled the family's stock and investments. (Annual salary: €1 million.)
- Liliane, who had hitherto received 100 percent of the dividends on the family's L'Oréal stock, was reduced to a 55 percent share, with 20 percent going to Françoise and the remainder staying in the treasury of Thétys. Through a complicated calculation, this provision actually resulted in a stock buyback that gave Françoise €300 million in cash. (To date, for reasons that Jean-Pierre Meyers and his family refuse to explain, Liliane has not received a dime in dividends since 2011.)

Like de Maistre and Goguel, Banier signed a separate agreement with Françoise Meyers. But there wasn't much room to negotiate, say his lawyers. The central points were take it or leave it: Banier gives up the two insurance policies on which he was the designated beneficiary; Banier and d'Orgeval can keep all the other gifts they received from Liliane up to the date of the protocol but can accept no more; both parties withdraw their reciprocal suits and all related legal actions.

In the interest of ending the conflict and avoiding a trial, Banier agreed to sign. But he first wanted a guarantee that his surrender of the insurance contracts was at Liliane's request. Once reassured on that point — Liliane's explicit demand was inserted into the text — Banier gave his OK. He was giving up more than €600 million on paper, but in fact he had little choice: Liliane, or her agents, could have cashed in the contracts at any time, effectively nullifying Banier's status as beneficiary.

On the afternoon of December 6, Nicolas Huc-Morel, Metzner's associate, hand-delivered the final text to the Left Bank office of Banier's lawyer Laurent Merlet. Sitting at a white marble conference table, Banier gave the seven-page protocol a cursory read, then signed with a black felt pen. Martin d'Orgeval took photos to mark what they all thought was the end of their ordeal. To celebrate, Banier, d'Orgeval, and Merlet went out that evening to take in a performance of *My Fair Lady at* the Théâtre du Châtelet. But their minds were not focused on Henry Higgins and Eliza Doolittle. "We talked more about Liliane than about the musical comedy," Merlet recalls. "Banier kept saying, 'Liliane did that to have peace.' "

L'Oréal's PR firm, delighted over the apparent end to the conflict, issued a press release celebrating the return of "family harmony" and "serenity." But as the terms of the supposedly confidential agreements became known, some observers questioned the lopsided nature of a deal deemed far more advantageous to the daughter than to her mother. Attention focused, in particular, on the €12 million that Françoise exacted from Liliane to pay her own lawyers for their services since 2007. This was not actually included in the text of the December 6 protocol, but was stipulated in a separate letter. As Wilhelm tells it, the demand had come from the Meyers side and caught him totally by surprise.

"Didier Martin called me one evening and said we had not yet talked about honorariums for the legal teams. I said each side pays their own fees. He says, 'No. Madame Meyers wants Madame Bettencourt to pay her fees.' I said, 'I'll ask her, but that's not what we agreed on. How much are we talking about?' He says, 'Twelve million.' " Wilhelm recounts that when he put the question to Liliane, "she laughed out loud." But in the end she paid.

One jurist who bitterly criticized the deal was Georges Kiejman, who had represented Madame Bettencourt since July 2009 but was left out of the negotiations. "I was in a rage, an absolute rage," he told me, denouncing this "scandalous" protocol that ran "completely counter to Liliane's deepest wishes. The people who rule over her life today are the very ones she detested before." Kiejman was especially miffed over the €12 million paid mostly to his bête-noire, Metzner — ten times more than he himself billed Liliane over the eighteen months that he worked for her. But his sharpest criticism of the accord was that Françoise and her lawyers had been shouting from the rooftops since 2007 that Liliane had lost her reason, so "how could she sign this protocol in 2010?"

"It's incomprehensible," says Richard Malka, lawyer for Banier's partner, Martin d'Orgeval. "Liliane Bettencourt gave up everything to her daughter and son-in-law. When she gives to her daughter, that's OK. When she gives to others, it's an abuse of weakness." This line of argument was hardly limited to the pro-Banier camp. Sarkozy aide Patrick Ouart privately questions the validity of accepting the signature of "an elderly lady" who had supposedly "lost her discernment."

One of the harshest criticisms of the deal comes from the man who helped negotiate it: Pascal Wilhelm. "I think those people [the Meyerses], from beginning to end, did not seek family reconciliation, they wanted money and power," he says. "If they thought Madame Bettencourt wasn't lucid, they shouldn't have asked for the 12 million. If they say she was in a state of weakness, then that was an abuse of weakness."

Wilhelm's objectivity may be subject to caution, not only because he negotiated the deal for Liliane but also because Françoise Meyers later took him to court. But the question remains valid: How could the Meyerses maintain that Madame Bettencourt was mentally incompetent and at the same time accept her signature on a document that gave them substantial advantages?

When a lawyer for Wilhelm later put that question to Jean-Pierre Meyers, his answer was as contemptuous as it was laconic: "No comment. That's the only answer I will give to your question." Françoise herself always hid behind the lawyers when asked about the circumstances surrounding the accord, denying that she had played any direct role in the negotiations or made any demands "concerning the financial conditions."

Nicolas Huc-Morel, one of her lawyers, defends the validity of the accord on the grounds that Liliane had legally mandated Wilhelm to negotiate on her behalf. "The family never considered that she was in a state to sign such a protocol — that is, in a state of perfect consciousness," he told me. "That's the reason she had a lawyer and that the discussions were carried out exclusively with this lawyer, who was charged with defending her interests." Liliane's interests were effectively served, says Huc-Morel, by restoring the "family peace," expelling "all the predators," and allowing her to "recover the life-insurance contracts." Concerning the last point, it is worth noting that one of those two contracts was signed over to Françoise (who partially cashed it for €93,900,000) and the other to Françoise's two sons, so the direct financial benefit to Liliane was zero.

Nor were all the so-called predators banished. If the agreements of December 2010 indeed removed Banier and de Maistre from Liliane's entourage, they enabled a new operator to take charge of the heiress's affairs: Pascal Wilhelm. In addition to his status as Liliane's legal representative and future protector, the lawyer replaced de Maistre as her money manager and became her testamentary executor on December 16, 2010. In those multiple roles, Wilhelm managed to oversee her spending and investments, her choice of personnel, her dealings with L'Oréal, and even modifications of her will. Starting January 2011, he says, "I assumed most of these tasks on my own . . . No expenditure was made outside my control."

Wilhelm argues that all those actions came under his responsibility as Liliane's future protector — where the "future" began was not entirely clear — a service for which his firm billed €200,000 per month. The problem was that he managed her business in a way that was often beneficial to him and raised questions about conflicts of interest. After convincing Liliane to designate her two grandsons as her legal heirs, for example, he attempted to block their access to their share of the family fortune and the insurance contracts until their fortieth birthdays (they were then twenty-two and twenty-four, respectively). During that long interval, Wilhelm was to manage the capital and receive regular fees for that service. When he was later questioned about this in court, Wilhelm claimed it was Liliane herself who insisted on this time frame — but nothing confirmed this in writing.

The biggest apparent conflict of interest concerned Wilhelm's intervention on behalf of businessman Stéphane Courbit, a pioneer in French reality TV. A client of Wilhelm's — and a personal friend of President Sarkozy — Courbit was then looking for investors in his online betting company. When several potential partners begged off, Wilhelm arranged for Liliane Bettencourt to invest nearly €150 million in a scheme about which she apparently understood nothing. (After her brief meeting with the boyish-looking and perpetually tanned Courbit, she mistook him for a pop singer and asked Wilhelm to send her a tape of his latest recordings.) The initial agreement with Courbit was signed on December 17, 2010 — the very same day that

Dr. de Jaeger examined the heiress and judged her incapable of performing legal acts.

Wilhelm and Courbit later faced legal action for making this deal with a clearly vulnerable party. But the irony is that Liliane actually made money on it — €15 million by the time Courbit paid back her original investment. "I was blamed for making the deal with a client of mine," says Wilhelm. "But financially it was a good investment." And incidentally, not a bad deal for Wilhelm, who billed Courbit's company €150,000 for his services.

In imposing his control over Liliane's affairs, Wilhelm found a valuable ally in Alain Thurin, who had served as her personal nurse since 2009 and was her most trusted employee. Thurin acted as a conduit between the lawyer and the heiress and, according to his accusers, attempted to isolate her from her family and other employees. In effect, Thurin rode herd on the heiress's personal life, while Wilhelm managed her business interests.

Communicating via email, Wilhelm would send Thurin the texts of letters that Thurin would then print out and dictate to Madame Bettencourt. The heiress would dutifully copy the documents on her personal stationery and sign them in her own hand. (This resembled a pattern whereby, according to Banier's accusers, the photographer would purloin her letterhead stationery and dictate self-serving letters to her — a practice that he denied, and was never proven, though the suspicions remained.)

Thurin, who actually slept in Liliane's bedroom, developed such a close relationship with his employer that he would speak to her in the familiar *tu* form — not even Banier dared do that. "Alain Thurin's role went beyond that of a simple nurse," said Wilhelm. "Madame Bettencourt insisted on his presence around her." Thurin's attentions did not go unrewarded: In August 2011, allegedly at Wilhelm's urging, Madame Bettencourt revised her will to include a €10 million gift to her nurse. (Thurin later claimed that he only learned of the legacy via the press and immediately asked the heiress to rescind it.)

Looking on all of this in horror, Françoise Meyers began to wonder if she hadn't exchanged one set of parasites for another. The December 6 protocol, which was supposed to bring the family back together and protect her mother, had accomplished neither goal — despite its material concessions to the Meyerses. One way or another, she knew she had to banish the new interlopers and establish full control over her mother. But for the moment, her hands were tied by the agreements she had signed.

Then a strange thing happened. The three

Bordeaux judges to whom the Bettencourt cases had been assigned kept working in spite of the peace pact, and in spite of the local prosecutor's call to end the investigations. How could that be? Under French law, the withdrawal of complaints by opposing parties does not necessarily end a procedure if the magistrates suspect that infractions may have been committed. In this instance, the Bordeaux-based investigating judges decided to carry on. The Bettencourt Affair was far from over.

For Georges Kiejman, though, it was over. Furious about the protocol, he quarreled with Wilhelm — "one of the moths who circled around the flame" — and was severed from Liliane's legal team. "They made her fire me in order to have a free hand," he says with some bitterness. The professional tie with Liliane was broken, but the friendship remained. In January 2011, shortly after Kiejman ceased to represent her, Liliane invited him to lunch in Neuilly. It was on that occasion that he realized, sadly, that her mind was indeed slipping. "At one point, she looked at me and said, 'You must be nice to your father,' " Kiejman recalls. "I replied, 'But Liliane, I told you my father was assassinated at Auschwitz.' "

■ ■ ■ ■

Part Five:
The Endgame

■ ■ ■ ■

Eye of the storm: François-Marie Banier mobbed by journalists at the Nanterre courthouse, July 1, 2010. **Reuters/Benoit Tessier**

CHAPTER 21
BORDEAUX

Bordeaux lies 320 miles southwest of Paris
— just over three hours on the high-speed
TGV train — but it is another universe. A
proud provincial city that was once enclosed
behind fortified walls, Bordeaux has always
marked its difference with the rest of France.
It was ruled by England for three centuries,
from 1152 to 1453. During the French
Revolution, Bordeaux, capital of the Gironde
Department, was a bastion of the so-called
Girondist opposition to the more radical Ja-
cobins of Paris, who ushered in the Reign of
Terror and guillotined twenty-two Girondist
deputies to the National Convention in 1793.
Among their alleged crimes: hatred of Paris
and "federalist" demands to give more power
to provincial cities like Bordeaux. The rivalry
with Paris continued long after the Bourbon
Restoration under King Louis XVIII in 1815.
Whereas Paris was always the center of political and financial power, Bordeaux, with its
bustling port on the Garonne River, was a

major commercial hub. Its considerable wealth was rooted in shipping and trade, exporting the prized vintages of the surrounding wine-growing regions and, until the French slave trade was abolished in 1818, sending black bodies to the West Indies in exchange for sugar and coffee.

Today, despite modernization projects that have replaced the old riverfront warehouses with parks and installed a new tramway system, Bordeaux remains marked by a past that weighs as heavily as the gray stones and wrought-iron balconies of its eighteenth-century façades. The narrow cobblestone streets of its old quarters recall the medieval city, as does the magnificent eleventh-century Cathédrale Saint-André at its center. But the building that most concerns us, lying only a stone's throw from the cathedral, is the Palais de justice, the neoclassical courthouse where the Bettencourt Affair was destined to play out.

When Sarkozy's justice minister, Michèle Alliot-Marie, ordered the Bettencourt case moved to a neutral jurisdiction, Bordeaux was not the first place she or her boss had in mind. That choice was made by the Cour de cassation, France's highest tribunal. It was not welcome news for the rightist president and his entourage. For Bordeaux, though a traditionally conservative city, is considered the country's most left-wing jurisdiction because of the presence there of the École nationale de la magistrature, the national school for French judges, which has strong links to a leftist professional union. "Bordeaux has always been a snake pit," says former Élysée aide Patrick Ouart. "It is by definition the jurisdiction most strongly marked by the left in all of France."

But the investigative judge assigned to oversee the case, Jean-Michel Gentil, then fifty years old, was anything but a left-wing activist. The son of a Mercedes dealer from the western city of Saumur, Gentil was considered by some to have conservative leanings, but politics were not his main concern. He was above all a stickler for law and procedure, with zero tolerance for corruption. Colleagues described him as aloof, independent, intransigent, and highly competent. In his previous postings, he had busted up a prostitution network in Paris and gone after the lawyer of Yvan Colonna, a Corsican assassin who was a popular local hero — a bold and dangerous move on that violent island where more than one French official had been gunned down by the separatists. Bordeaux, where Gentil was transferred in 2004, should have been a quieter assignment, but the Bettencourt Affair put him at the center of the hottest case of his career.

Arriving early to work sporting a black

leather jacket and clutching a thick briefcase, he would barricade himself in his basement office behind opaque glass doors and spend his days poring over the hundreds of dossiers contained in his armored steel file cabinets. Short and small-framed, with narrow black eyes, Gentil would interrogate witnesses in a manner some described as haughty, aggressive, and intimidating. There was no small talk with Judge Gentil — whose name, ironically, means "nice" in French — and even his assistant judges, Cécile Ramonatxo and Valérie Noël, kept a respectful distance. Gentil was not impressed by power, as President Sarkozy would soon find out, and cast a cold eye on people like Banier, whose immense fortunes, ill-gained or not, were a veritable insult to France's hardworking and underpaid magistrature. (Starting salary for a French judge: about $33,000 a year.)

Picking up where Courroye and Prévost-Desprez had left off, Gentil and his associates proceeded to interrogate witnesses, order searches, and sort through the thousands of pages of documents that had been forwarded from Nanterre. One of their first challenges was to untangle the hydra-headed jumble of investigations that had sprouted from Françoise Meyers's original suit. On January 27, 2011, they divided them into eight separate cases, the most important of which was the abuse of weakness charge against Banier, de

Maistre, and eventually eight other defendants. The remaining cases concerned, among other things, influence peddling, illegal political financing, invasion of privacy, and defamation. All of them were handled as discrete investigations by Gentil and his two colleagues, who would later send some cases to trial and drop others for insufficient evidence.

Though the protocols of December 2010 failed to halt the judicial investigations, the agreements themselves remained in force. Between January and March 2011, Françoise Meyers, Liliane Bettencourt, François-Marie Banier, and Patrice de Maistre officially withdrew their respective complaints (abuse of weakness, subornation of witnesses, invasion of privacy, and so on). But the boxing match was not over, even though the combatants had withdrawn to neutral corners.

A key stumbling block for investigators had always been Liliane's refusal to undergo a court-ordered medical examination to determine the state of her mental health. In June 2011, in a major breakthrough, Gentil finally obtained Madame Bettencourt's acceptance of such an exam. Accompanied by the judge and two police officers, a team of five neutral experts — specialists in legal medicine, audition, psychology, and neurology — arrived at the Bettencourt home at eight a.m. on Tuesday, June 7. They were expected. A butler let them in and served them coffee in the kitchen while nurse Alain Thurin prepared Madame for the visit. After a quarter of an hour, they were taken upstairs.

Professor Sophie Gromb, the team leader, was the first to enter the bedroom. She found Madame Bettencourt in bed, propped up with pillows, in a state described as "awake but sluggish." Gromb spent a half hour explaining the nature of the examinations to Liliane. The eighty-eight-year-old heiress, who appeared neither surprised nor particularly upset by the visit, responded with polished politeness. "She accepted the exam," said Gromb. "She even seemed happy that we were looking after her."

Gromb noticed that the room was fitted out with a hospital bed, a vaporizer, and other medical equipment. Thurin explained that "Madame" had recently suffered a fall. (In fact she had been hospitalized for two months and treated for a fractured hip and a pulmonary infection.) The other experts were then admitted to the room one by one to perform their exams, always with the hovering presence of Thurin, who often had to relay their questions to the heiress due to her hearing disability.

The experts' report, delivered to Judge Gentil on September 23, 2011, left no doubt about the heiress's presumed vulnerability. She didn't know exactly where she was —

possibly in Switzerland, she said — and could not even tell her own age. Her deafness was near total, with severe hearing loss estimated to date back to the 1970s, significantly affecting her "possibilities of communication and conversational comprehension." Neurologically, the heiress evidenced "cognitive troubles . . . temporal disorientation, memory loss, and reasoning problems." Diagnosis: "Madame Bettencourt shows signs of Alzheimer's disease at a moderately severe stage, with a possible vascular participation" — in other words, a double whammy of Alzheimer's and hardening of the arteries — "indicating a process of slow and progressive cerebral degeneration."

The report's most significant, and controversial, conclusion was that Madame Bettencourt's "most apparent troubles" dated back to the "confusional episode of September 2006," in the wake of the Formentor accident. Significant because this provided an official starting date for Liliane's presumed vulnerability, and controversial because the report's critics hotly disputed the validity of this retroactive diagnosis. Another point of controversy emerged when it was learned that Sophie Gromb, a specialist in legal medicine and the report's main author, was a personal friend of Judge Gentil and had been a witness at his marriage. (Demands by Banier, de Maistre, and others to nullify the report on these grounds were later rejected by the Bordeaux appeals court.)

Françoise did not wait for the experts' report before making her next move. On June 7, the same day the medical exam was carried out, she filed a petition to investigate Pascal Wilhelm's conduct as Liliane's protector. Three weeks later, she followed up with a demand to revoke Wilhelm's mandate and put her mother under guardianship. This was technically in violation of the peace accord of December 2010, which had specifically mandated Wilhelm and guaranteed Liliane's autonomy in her "personal sphere." But Françoise justified her initiative based on new information about Wilhelm's activities that ran "contrary to the interests" of her mother. The petition was handled by Judge Stéphanie Kass-Danno, a civil magistrate (*juge des tutelles*) who specialized in matters of protection.

When Kass-Danno questioned Liliane on July 11, 2011, the heiress told her she wanted to keep Wilhelm as her protector. Why? "That's how it is," she snapped, "and I agree with myself." What about her daughter? "My daughter scares me. She is distant. You can't convert people like that. She's completely blocked; we disagree on everything." Whatever mental lapses she suffered during this period, the heiress seemed perfectly determined on this point: She did not want to fall under her daughter's control.

On October 17, three weeks after the medical experts filed their report documenting Liliane's mental incompetence, Kass-Danno handed down her decision: Wilhelm's mandate was withdrawn; Liliane was placed under the joint guardianship of Françoise Meyers and her two sons for management of her financial assets; Jean-Victor Meyers, the elder son, was named guardian for his grandmother's personal affairs.

Three days before this decision came down, Liliane gave an interview to the *Journal du Dimanche,* France's main Sunday paper, voicing her fears of guardianship and her extreme bitterness toward her daughter. "I raised her and yet she is the opposite of me," she said. "You know, between a mother and a daughter, when the heart no longer speaks, all is lost." Using a scatological epithet, she called Françoise *"une emmerdeuse"* (politely translated as "a pain in the ass") who "wants to take my place." With an eye to the impending decision, she said that her "worst nightmare would be to depend on Françoise . . . I wouldn't even want to live any longer." In that case, Liliane vowed, she would flee the country. "If my daughter gains control over me, I'll smother. If it's her, I'll leave." Françoise always claimed that Banier was the cause of her problems with her mother, but at the time of this interview, Liliane had not seen or corresponded with the photographer for well over a year. At this point, Banier was totally out of her life. The problem was between the two women. Its roots were old and deep. "All this goes far back," said Liliane.

That was Liliane Bettencourt's last public utterance. Once the decision came down the following Monday, she no longer had any independent life, no power of decision, and no freedom — that precious commodity, worth more than all her riches, that she had fought so hard to preserve until senility and legal wrangling snatched it away. For years, she had lived in fear of this moment. Françoise claimed that Liliane's entourage had stoked her apprehensions in order to retain control over her. Perhaps. But the fear was real.

When Jean-Victor Meyers first visited his grandmother as guardian of her personal affairs, he found her trembling in an armchair.

"What's the matter, *Grand-mère*?" he asked.

"I'm terrified," the heiress replied. "I'm waiting for someone who's going to put me in prison."

"*Mais non,* it's me, Jean-Victor."

"They told me that Françoise was going to take away my dog, my airplane, prevent me from buying haute-couture clothes."

"No, *Grand-mère. Au contraire.*"

The heiress studied the young man for a moment. "Do you get along well with Françoise?"

"*Grand-mère,* Françoise is my mother."

On October 21, Judge Kass-Danno named real estate developer Olivier Pelat, a lifelong friend of the Bettencourts, as Liliane's *tuteur ad hoc* — the person who represents her in all judicial matters and acts as her stand-in in court. Pelat, Liliane Bettencourt's godson, was a childhood playmate of Françoise's. The circle was complete.

CHAPTER 22
HARDBALL

Back in Bordeaux, Judge Gentil had his eye on three big fish: Banier, de Maistre, and President Sarkozy, whom he suspected of soliciting large, and illegal, political donations from the Bettencourts. Sarkozy would have to wait: As long as he occupied the Élysée Palace, he enjoyed immunity from prosecution. But there was an election coming up in 2012 and the polls were not looking good for the incumbent. Banier and de Maistre were easier targets.

Monday, December 12, 2011, six a.m. In the predawn darkness, two official cars turn onto the rue Servandoni, their headlights cutting through a fine drizzle. They stop in front of a five-story town house. Four Financial Brigade officers sporting police armbands emerge from the front vehicle; two uniformed gendarmes from France's military police force climb out of the second. Police Captain Cyrille Rongier rings the doorbell. After a long moment, a groggy male voice answers the intercom. "Police, open up!" says Rongier, waving his badge before the security camera. Once the officers are buzzed in, they wait in the dark, damp courtyard for someone to unlock the door to the building.

Upstairs in their fourth-floor bedroom, François-Marie Banier and Martin d'Orgeval begin to stir. His eyes still adjusting to the light, d'Orgeval steps into the adjoining bathroom and splashes water on his face while Banier sits on the edge of the bed and starts to dress. The two men are neither surprised nor anxious, just fed up with the early-morning police visits that have occurred periodically since the beginning of the affair. They assume that this is yet another search for documents or artworks. The intercom buzzes again. "Open up the door," barks an impatient officer.

Martin takes the elevator to the ground floor and unlocks the front door. He is surprised to see six officers waiting in the courtyard — two men and two women from the Financial Brigade, plus the two gendarmes. He recognizes Captain Rongier from previous visits. Tall and trim, with a gaunt face and glasses, Rongier shakes Martin's hand with a formal courtesy. "Good morning, Monsieur d'Orgeval," he says. "We're going to go upstairs and explain why we're here today."

As he led the officers to the elevator, Martin noticed one detail that was different from the earlier encounters with Rongier: Today he was wearing a bulletproof vest. Had he expected a violent reception?

D'Orgeval escorted the group to the fourth-floor dining room, where they were soon joined by Banier. With a gesture that was almost Kafkaesque in its chilling banality, Rongier pulled out an arrest warrant and announced that the two men would be taken into custody and escorted to Bordeaux on the orders of Judge Jean-Michel Gentil. Then, as if to soften the blow, Rongier admired d'Orgeval's photos of boxed butterflies that hung on the dining-room wall. "They weren't here the last time," he remarked.

This made no sense, thought Martin. If the judge wanted to interrogate them, why didn't he simply issue a summons? They would have willingly traveled to Bordeaux. But Gentil was playing hardball. His intention, Martin guessed, was to show the couple that he was in charge and had the power to do whatever he wanted with them.

Banier and d'Orgeval hastily packed overnight bags with toiletries, a change of clothes, and a few books. Both men were frisked for "dangerous objects" — there were none — and escorted to the waiting vehicles. They were bundled into separate cars and driven to the headquarters of the Financial Brigade, a modern ten-story concrete-and-glass building near the bustling Chinatown sector of eastern Paris. The address seemed ironically fitting: 122 rue du Château des Rentiers — a *rentier* being someone who lives on unearned income, like rent, interest, or dividends. During the twenty-minute drive, Martin pulled out his cell phone (which would soon be confiscated) and canceled the flight to New York that he and Banier were scheduled to take later that day.

The two men were put into separate holding cells on the sixth floor of the Financial Brigade Building. Martin stretched out on his narrow bunk, began to read the book he had brought — *Images de pensée* by the German philosoper Walter Benjamin — then fell into a deep sleep. Banier, meanwhile, exercised his right to request a medical exam; after a ten-minute visit, the doctor declared him fit for detention and prescribed tranquilizers. Angry and depressed, Banier waved away the midday meal.

Martin was awakened shortly afterward by the arrival of a cellmate, a burly black man in his midtwenties with arms as big as hams. He said he had been arrested at six a.m. for using counterfeit credit cards. What was Martin in for?

"Abuse of weakness."

The other man scowled. "What's that?"

Martin gave a succinct explanation.

"So the daughter was jealous? And the mother, how many zeros did she give you? She gave you a lot, four zeros?"

"Something like that," said Martin.

At two p.m. the pair were driven to the Palais de justice on the Île de la Cité, the oblong island in the middle of the Seine that includes some of Paris's most visited sites: the Notre-Dame Cathedral; the Sainte-Chapelle, a world-renowned marvel of Gothic architecture and stained-glass artistry; and the Conciergerie, the legendary prison where Queen Marie Antoinette was held before her beheading in 1793. During the French Revolution, the Conciergerie was considered the antechamber to the guillotine; very few prisoners got out alive.

Fortunately for Banier and d'Orgeval, their destination was the more prosaic Dépôt, the underground cell-block complex for prisoners awaiting court appearances. After a short stay there, they were handcuffed, tethered, and led separately through the labyrinthine warren of passageways known as the *souricière* — the mouse nest.

They were escorted to the office of a judge who formally remanded them into custody and ordered their transfer to Bordeaux by a special unit of the gendarmes on December 14 — two days away. In the meanwhile, they would remain incarcerated in Paris.

The detainees, still handcuffed, were hustled into an armored van flanked by two motorcycle escorts with sirens blaring. Destination: La Santé, Paris's oldest and most notorious prison. A lugubrious hulk of stone and brick built under the reign of Napoleon III, La Santé — it means "health" in French — was the site of countless beheadings until capital punishment was abolished in 1981.

Banier and d'Orgeval were kept in the so-called VIP wing, away from the hardened criminals who dominate the inmate population. But not that far away: The cell next to Martin's was occupied by Ilich Ramírez Sánchez — alias "Carlos the Jackal," the Venezuelan terrorist who had masterminded some of Paris's bloodiest bombings in the 1970s and '80s. Banier's neighbor was more genteel: He was Vicomte Amaury d'Harcourt, then eighty-seven, scion of one of France's most aristocratic families, who had helped a friend arrange for a gardener to murder his wife with a sawed-off shotgun in 2008.

"It was a violent experience," recounts d'Orgeval, who was accused in his own right of obtaining gifts worth more than €3 million from the heiress. "You're in prison, they take away your shoelaces and belt so you won't hang yourself. The hardest thing was the arbitrariness of it all. We weren't sure when they would let us out. It could have been months." The only peaceful moment, he recalls, came late at night, when he heard "in the middle of the grave silence a supernatural, spiritual chant, a beautiful male voice, the prayer — the muezzin — which I realized could only have one effect on us prisoners: to save us. I understood the influence of Islam in prison."

On December 14, after two nights in jail, the two men were taken to Orly Airport. Escorted by six uniformed gendarmes and handcuffed like common criminals, they boarded a commercial Air France flight for Bordeaux, much to the amazement of their fellow passengers. Once arrived at the Bordeaux courthouse, the detainees were obliged to hide their faces with blankets to avoid being snapped by the gaggle of paparazzi who awaited them — obviously tipped off by the authorities.

After another long wait in holding cells, they were called separately before Judge Gentil. Banier, who went first, recalls that the judge was hostile from the beginning, hectoring him in a "high, grating voice" and berating him for placing his coat on an empty chair. To each man in turn, Gentil read out the charges — fraud, abuse of confidence, abuse of weakness, money laundering — and informed them that they were *mis en examen,* that is, formally placed under investigation for suspected wrongdoing, one step short of a criminal indictment. Banier was ordered to put up bail in the amount of €10 million; d'Orgeval's payment was a comparative bargain at €1 million.

Never one to hold his tongue, Banier protested before the judge "the extremely brutal way" that he and Martin were imprisoned, contested all the charges, and denounced the whole procedure as a "scandalous machination." Looking back on the incident, Banier's lead lawyer, Pierre Cornut-Gentille (no relation to Judge Gentil), says there was "absolutely no reason" to arrest his client. "He wasn't a fugitive from justice, he was in his own home." The flight to Bordeaux in handcuffs was intended to "humiliate and intimidate" the two men, says the lawyer, still bristling with indignation. "You can't do that in any democratic country." He tells me Banier's legal team is planning to bring a case against France before the European Human Rights Court for "violation of liberty."

Things had gone downhill for Patrice de Maistre since he was unceremoniously fired from Madame Bettencourt's employ after seven years of devoted service. His ouster had been one of Françoise Meyers's key demands when the reconciliation pact was being hammered out in the fall of 2010. "Either you become an obstacle, or you lie down and take it," Pascal Wilhelm told de Maistre at the time. The financier had little choice but to lie down. At Liliane's insistence, he was paid a generous severance, plus €500,000 for his legal bills. But the episode left a bitter taste in his mouth. "I was on the wrong side, I was no longer wanted," he said. "I took that with a lot of resentment."

But his troubles were just beginning. Not only was de Maistre suspected of exploiting Madame Bettencourt and engaging in quid-pro-quo deals with Éric Woerth; he was presumed to be the main conduit for political payments to President Sarkozy. When Nanterre prosecutor Philippe Courroye was still in charge of the original abuse case, he had apparently bent over backward to make sure de Maistre was not interrogated, even though he was Liliane's closest adviser and one of the people most deeply involved in her affairs. According to Courroye's rival, Isabelle Prévost-Desprez, the prosecutor had specifically instructed the Financial Brigade detectives to leave de Maistre out of the investigation. She and other jurists involved in the case were convinced that Courroye was thereby attempting to protect his friend Sarkozy.

In fact, Courroye did have de Maistre briefly detained and questioned in July 2010, but that was in the context of his investigation into suspected tax evasion, which had no link to the president. In any event, de Maistre enjoyed no special treatment once the affair was transferred to Bordeaux. On the contrary, Judge Gentil was gunning for him.

Wednesday, December 14, 2011, 6:50 a.m., Air France 977 touches down at Charles de Gaulle Airport after a seven-hour flight from Libreville, Gabon. The Boeing 777 taxis slowly to Terminal F. Patrice de Maistre, carrying a black canvas satchel, disembarks and treks with his fellow passengers down the long corridor toward the passport control area. Exhausted by the overnight flight, he is eager to get home after this quick round trip to attend a board meeting of one of the African companies in which he has interests.

Led by Commandant Didier Cheneau, three detectives from the Financial Brigade intercept the financier and present him with an arrest warrant issued by Judge Gentil on December 9, the same day as Banier's warrant. Following the same scenario, they load him into a waiting van and take him to a judge, who certifies his detention. Like Banier and d'Orgeval, de Maistre is then locked up behind the grim walls of La Santé to await his transfer to Bordeaux.

Fortunately for de Maistre, he had to spend only one night in prison, and he was spared the handcuff treatment on the flight to Bordeaux. But his reception by Gentil on the afternoon of Thursday, December 15, was no more cordial than Banier's. The judge laid out the charges against him — abuse of weakness, complicity in fraud, abuse of confidence, and money laundering — then put him under formal investigation. In addition, he was placed under judicial supervision and ordered to pay a bail of €2 million.

Three months later, de Maistre was back behind bars — but this time it was no overnight affair. On March 23, 2012, under the guise of pretrial detention, Judge Gentil had him locked up in Gradignan Prison near Bordeaux and kept him there for an excruciating eighty-eight days. It is hard to see why the sixty-three-year-old financier and yachtsman, alone among the Bettencourt defendants, warranted such a prolonged incarceration. He was hardly a menace to society. What Gentil really wanted, it seems, was to squeeze de Maistre until he coughed up the information that could nail Sarkozy.

The president sensed the danger. On December 14, 2011, the day de Maistre was first detained, Sarkozy summoned his key advisers to an emergency meeting to weigh the latest developments in the Bettencourt case. According to one attendee, Xavier Musca, who had replaced Claude Guéant as the Élysée's chief of staff, Sarkozy was worried about the press campaigns seeking to implicate him in the scandal and sought advice on how to organize his defense. A key subject of discussion at this and two subsequent meetings was the arrest and interrogation of Patrice de Maistre. Would Gentil manage to extract anything incriminating out of the financier?

There were several reasons why a judge like Jean-Michel Gentil might have had it in for the president. One was Gentil's hard-line stance against corruption. Another was Sarkozy's crusade to abolish the whole corps of *juges d'instruction,* the five hundred or so investigative magistrates who, in the president's eyes, were too independent and often abused their far-reaching powers — mainly by going after politicians like himself. Sarkozy's proposal to replace them by government-appointed prosecutors was met by angry protests from the magistrates' unions and finally put on the shelf. But Sarkozy's verbal sallies against the judges, like his aborted attempt to obliterate them, fed what the *Nouvel Observateur* called a "hatred of rare intensity between the magistrates of France and the Élysée." Thus the transfer of the Bettencourt dossier to Gentil and his two fellow judges was seen by many in the profession as their chance to exact revenge on a president who had declared a veritable war against them.

Gentil wanted to know whether de Maistre had given political money to campaign treasurer Éric Woerth or directly to Sarkozy, in spite of the financier's repeated denials. According to accountant Claire Thibout, as noted, Madame Bettencourt had handed de Maistre an envelope containing €50,000 on January 18, 2007. On the morning of January 19, de Maistre and Woerth met in a café near Sarkozy's campaign headquarters. Did de Maistre slip the cash to Woerth on that occasion?

Shortly after this meeting, de Maistre began to draw far greater sums from Madame Bettencourt's Swiss accounts. On January 30, 2007, he had flown to Geneva and instructed René Merkt, Madame Bettencourt's Swiss lawyer, to have €400,000 in cash delivered directly to the family mansion in Neuilly. Merkt called on the services of COFINOR, a Swiss company specializing in discreet cash transfers. On February 5, 2007, a COFINOR courier arrived at the Bettencourt mansion with a briefcase containing €400,000 in crisp new bills. That was just the first tranche. Between that date and December 2009, COFINOR made seven deliveries, totaling €4 million, all on de Maistre's personal orders.

Under questioning, de Maistre claimed that he had acted on Madame Bettencourt's instructions and that all the cash had been given to her. Inexplicably, he claimed to have "destroyed" all the receipts and told investigators he didn't know what she did with those considerable sums. An analysis of her account books and expenses for the period indicated that these Swiss funds had not been used by the heiress. So what happened to the €4 million?

The obvious suspicion was that at least some of that money went to Sarkozy. To date there had been no concrete proof, but the magistrates noted a number of intriguing co-incidences. On February 7, 2007, for example, two days after the first €400,000 delivery, de Maistre and Worth had break-fasted together. Then at 7:20 p.m. the same day, Woerth met with Sarkozy at his campaign headquarters. Later that month, in the heat of the election campaign, Sarkozy himself had made at least two visits to the Bettencourt home, feeding suspicions that he received money directly.

Some observers went as far as to speculate that the money was for Sarkozy's personal use. "For his campaign? Not at all," says Judge Isabelle Prévost-Desprez. "I am con-vinced that it had nothing to do with that. It's for his watches, his suits, all that. . . . I really think it's personal." Prévost-Desprez had no proof of this, of course, but she was not alone in thinking that perhaps some of the money wound up in Sarkozy's pocket.

Under Gentil's repeated interrogations, de Maistre never provided a clue about where the money went. For nearly three months, he stuck to his story: Claire Thibout's €50,000 claim was a "lie," and the €4 million in cash went to Madame Bettencourt. On June 14, 2012, hoping to shed some light on this murky episode, Gentil organized a confrontation between de Maistre, Merkt, and COFINOR president Vahé Gabrache via an audiovisual link between Bordeaux and Lausanne. Gabrache confirmed the seven cash deliveries, three of which went directly to de Maistre. Merkt said the requests for funds always came from de Maistre, not from Madame Bettencourt, and that he had never before been asked to send cash to the Bettencourts. Neither Merkt nor de Maistre could provide any motive for the deliveries.

Gentil became impatient with de Maistre. "Wasn't it simply because all the cash received between 2007 and 2009 was intended to be distributed secretly with total opacity?"

"No!" replied de Maistre. "The answer is no."

Gentil persisted: "At the time, Liliane Bettencourt wasn't capable of remembering her request, which is curious to say the least. Today, Liliane Bettencourt doesn't even know who you are. Didn't you simply use this system . . . to secretly obtain €4 million for your own personal ends, knowing that Madame Bettencourt would not even remember it?"

"That's absolutely wrong," de Maistre protested.

■ ■ ■ ■

Four days after this confrontation, Gentil finally ordered de Maistre's liberation. There was clearly nothing more to be gained from keeping him in prison, although the judge exacted an additional bail payment of €2 million, on top of the €2 million that he had required when de Maistre was first arrested in December. That made a nice round sum of . . . €4 million.

Though Gentil failed to break de Maistre, he had learned enough to go after the president himself as soon as time and circumstances would permit. He was still playing hardball.

CHAPTER 23
A PRESIDENT
IN THE CROSSHAIRS

Sunday, May 6, 2012. At precisely eight p.m., Daniel Pujadas, anchorman of the France 2 network, pronounced the nation's verdict while a simulated image showed a red carpet unfurling toward the entrance to the Élysée Palace: "François Hollande is elected President of the Republic with 51.9 percent of the vote . . ." As Hollande's portrait flashed on the screen, Judge Jean-Michel Gentil may well have muttered to himself the French equivalent of *gotcha*!

Nicolas Sarkozy's loss to his Socialist challenger not only put him out of a job, it also shoved him into the crosshairs of the Bordeaux-based magistrate by lifting his presidential immunity as of June 16. Sarkozy's suspected implication in the Bettencourt Affair, which had contributed at least tangentially to his loss, was about to become an even bigger problem for him.

In the meantime, the Bettencourt probes were advancing on all fronts. Since an appeals court had cleared the use of Bonnefoy's illicit recordings in January 2012, Gentil and his colleagues had shifted into high gear. With Banier, d'Orgeval, and de Maistre already designated as official targets, the Bordeaux judges put more than a dozen additional suspects under investigation between February and November. Among them: ex-minister Éric Woerth (abuse of weakness, influence peddling); ex-butler Pascal Bonnefoy and five French journalists (invasion of privacy); and lawyer Pascal Wilhelm and businessman Stéphane Courbit (abuse of weakness). And in a parallel case, Judge Isabelle Prévost-Desprez, suspected of leaking court documents to the press, was herself put under investigation for violation of professional secrets.

As for Sarkozy, Gentil strongly suspected that he had received Bettencourt money. The testimony of Claire Thibout and several Bettencourt employees and ex-employees nourished his presumptions. But no witness reported actually seeing an exchange of cash — at least not on the record. One clue came from an unlikely source: François-Marie Banier. In a notebook seized by police, the photographer had quoted Madame Bettencourt as saying, "De Maistre told me that Sarkozy had asked for money again. I said yes." Banier had written that note after meeting Liliane on April 26, 2007, the same day that a cash delivery of €400,000 arrived from Switzerland — a coincidence that the judge found "curious, to say the least."

Interrogated by Gentil, Banier backtracked, suggesting first that this was merely a study for a novel, then asserting that the money in question was within the legal limit, and finally claiming that he wasn't sure it was Sarkozy that Liliane referred to, "but it was someone important."

Exasperated, Gentil put the question bluntly: "I'll ask you one last time, in your recollection did Liliane Bettencourt evoke the name of Nicolas Sarkozy — which seems logical — or another candidate?"

Banier cut him off: "That doesn't interest me." While it's true that Banier had little interest in politics, his flippant answer was probably aimed at protecting Liliane from charges of illegal campaign financing.

On November 22, 2012, Sarkozy was summoned to Bordeaux for a marathon grilling by Gentil and his two associate judges, Valérie Noël and Cécile Romonatxo. Gentil warned the ex-president at the outset that he was suspected of "fraudulently abusing the state of ignorance or situation of weakness of Madame Liliane Bettencourt." Under the magistrates' aggressive questioning, Sarkozy denied having any special relationship with the Bettencourts and insisted that he "never asked them for a centime." He recalled dining at chez Bettencourt only once, but said he was unable to communicate with his hostess because "she heard nothing." He admitted making a single brief visit to the Bettencourt home, on February 24, 2007, which he described as a "courtesy" call on André as a respected elder statesman who supported his candidacy.

Concerning his meeting with Liliane Bettencourt and Patrice de Maistre in his Élysée office on November 5, 2008, Sarkozy denied any connection with political funding. "I gave this appointment to the main shareholder in one of France's leading companies, one of France's biggest taxpayers, and someone I knew from my days in Neuilly," he said. It was at that meeting that he had first learned of Françoise's suit and the potential threat to L'Oréal. Apart from that occasion, Sarkozy denied knowing de Maistre, the suspected conduit for funneling Bettencourt money into his campaign chest. If treasurer Éric Woerth had relations with Liliane's wealth manager, he never discussed them with Sarkozy.

Asked about his relationship with Prosecutor Courroye, Sarkozy acknowledged their long-standing friendship but insisted that they had never discussed "a single case he was working on." What about the eight meetings Sarkozy had held with Courroye between 2008 and 2011? Yes, there were meetings, but "neither Philippe Courroye nor I ever acted to slow down, modify, or complicate the Bettencourt affair. . . . There was no interference by the Élysée, no instruction on my part to quash the case." His only aim in the affair, he said, was "to obtain a mediation, a pacification" in the mother-daughter dispute.

Gentil then asked a key question: "Why would you follow a private judicial affair that at the time concerned only the acts of François-Marie Banier with respect to Liliane Bettencourt?"

"The Banier procedure doesn't interest us in any case," Sarkozy snapped. "I don't know François-Marie Banier."

The judge attempted to connect the dots. "Couldn't one imagine that . . . if an investigation [against Banier] proceeded, then all the acts, all the gifts by Madame Liliane Bettencourt would be examined. Isn't that what could worry the Élysée?"

Even in the written transcript, Sarkozy's indignation crackles. The target of Françoise Meyers's suit, he said, was "Banier, and as far as I know, exclusively Banier — the 'billion.' Why would the Élysée feel threatened? There was no [illegal] donation for me or my campaign. Why would I be concerned? Why should Nicolas Sarkozy feel threatened by such an investigation?"

At 9:10 p.m., after nearly twelve hours of inconclusive jousting, Gentil brought the interrogation to an end. Though the magistrates refrained from putting the former president under formal investigation, they assigned him the status of "assisted witness," meaning there were "plausible" reasons to suspect an infraction but not conclusive proofs. Even as Sarkozy's armored car drove away from the Bordeaux courthouse, his lawyer, Thierry Herzog, was on his cell phone assuring the press that the "affair no longer exists" as far as his client was concerned.

Wishful thinking.

On March 21, 2013, Sarkozy was summoned back to Bordeaux. This time, he was confronted by four former Bettencourt employees in order to determine whether he had made more than one visit to the Neuilly mansion during the 2007 campaign season. Sarkozy stuck to his earlier claim to have made a single short visit, on February 24, but the testimony of the witnesses convinced the judges that he had made another appearance two weeks earlier. At the end of the seven-hour session, they replaced Sarkozy's "assisted witness" status with a *mise en examen,* meaning he was now the target of a criminal investigation. Once a person is put in that category, there are only two possibilities: an indictment followed by a trial, or a *non-lieu,* which cancels the charges for insufficient evidence. Whichever outcome was reserved for Sarkozy, being named a suspect in a penal case was a major embarrassment. "For a political figure like him," says Claude Guéant, Sarkozy's former chief of staff, "the very fact that an investigation is opened is devastating for his image."

On October 7, 2013, Bordeaux judges Gentil and Valérie Noël issued a long-awaited document: a 267-page *ordonnance* summarizing the charges and evidence against all the suspects in the abuse of weakness investigation. Ten were indicted and ordered to stand trial, including the main suspects Banier, d'Orgeval, and de Maistre. But charges were dropped for Nicolas Sarkozy. The decision to give him a *non-lieu* was hardly a declaration of innocence: The magistrates accused Sarkozy of lying about the number of visits to the Bettencourts, which were indeed "intended to obtain an illegal financial support from André and Liliane Bettencourt." Though they chastised Sarkozy's "abusive behavior" in seeking funds, they lacked sufficient proof that he or his campaign had actually received any. The decision to drop charges against the former president was all the more baffling since his ex-treasurer and minister, Éric Woerth, accused of receiving Bettencourt money on Sarkozy's behalf, was himself indicted and ordered to stand trial.

■ ■ ■ ■

Sarkozy was doubtless relieved, but it was also a sobering moment. At fifty-eight, he was no longer the wunderkind effortlessly ascending the career ladder. His wavy black hair showed more than a few silver strands. The worry lines on his forehead and the creases around his prominent nose were more deeply engraved. For a time after his 2012 defeat he had abandoned politics and returned to his law practice. He even grew a beard and sported turtlenecks in an attempt to reinvent himself — or at least change his image from political carnivore to laid-back professional. But he was soon dreaming, like Napoleon on Elba, of a return to power. Getting roped into the Bettencourt Affair, even with a *non-lieu,* was an embarrassing obstacle in his path. And it was not the only one.

Nicolas Sarkozy is one of those politicians who attract scandal because they put their ambitions above the rules. Their relentless quest for power can attract devoted followers but also passionate adversaries. "I once told him that he was radioactive, and that we were all irradiated by him," says Patrick Ouart, his longtime political ally. "He crystalizes hatreds and resentments to a point that is hard to imagine. He doesn't realize how much he is detested by the average French establishment."

As it happened, Sarkozy's narrow escape from prosecution was only a brief respite in a succession of scandals that would complicate his plans for a political comeback. On July 1, 2014, he suffered the indignity of becoming the first former French president ever taken into police custody for questioning. Summoned to the headquarters of a specialized anticorruption unit in Nanterre, he was interrogated for eighteen hours about his suspected role in a quid-pro-quo scheme aimed at obtaining protected judicial information about several investigations that threatened him. In the wee hours of July 2, the magistrates put him under formal investigation for "active corruption," "influence peddling," and "receiving professional secrets."

This latest scandal grew out of allegations that Sarkozy's 2007 campaign had received an illicit donation of €50 million from Libyan strongman Muammar Gaddafi. The judge investigating those charges ordered phone taps on Sarkozy and his lawyer, Thierry Herzog, between September 2013 and March 2014. Though this surveillance turned up nothing about Gaddafi — that investigation is still ongoing — it indicated that the former French president was using a web of informants to follow the progress of certain legal cases that concerned him. Prominent among them: the Bettencourt Affair.

The main informant was Gilbert Azibert, a former Bordeaux prosecutor who then served as attorney general of the Cour de cassation, the country's highest appeal court. Though Sarkozy and Herzog took the precaution of using discreet cell phones purchased under the ridiculous name of "Paul Bismuth" — bismuth is a chemical element used in suppositories — investigators captured a series of conversations in which Sarkozy offered to get Azibert named to a prestigious judicial post in Monaco in exchange for his information on the Bettencourt case, among others. The post never materialized, but the fact that it was promised in return for Azibert's services was nonetheless illegal. In March 2016, the Paris appeals court rejected Sarkozy's challenge to the wiretap evidence, clearing the way for a possible indictment and prosecution. To date, he remains a suspect in that investigation.

There was more to come. On August 30, 2016, the Paris Prosecutor's Office called for Sarkozy to stand trial for "illegal campaign financing." One of fourteen defendants in the case — unrelated to the Bettencourt Affair — the former president was accused of participating in a fake billing scheme aimed at concealing the fact that his 2012 campaign spending was more than twice the legal limit of €22.5 million. The timing could hardly have been worse for Sarkozy, coming less than three months before the primary elections that would select his party's candidate in the May 2017 presidential contest.

At that point, it appeared that Sarkozy's only hope of avoiding the disgrace of criminal prosecution was to win back the presidency, and five more years of immunity, before the trial could be scheduled. But his chances of doing that were clouded by the scandals that swirled around him. And one of them, the famous Bettencourt Affair, seemed to stick to him like a wad of gum on the sole of his high-heeled Gucci loafers.

In an October 2016 debate among presidential hopefuls, Sarkozy denounced the use of the "sordid Bettencourt Affair" to besmirch his image. The case was hardly the only smudge on him, but the accumulation of judicial issues surrounding Sarkozy undoubtedly contributed to his defeat in the conservative primary, won by his former prime minister, François Fillon, on November 27. Sarkozy's political career appeared to be over. But the embattled ex-president had some cause for consolation three months later when Fillon himself, who had passed as a model of probity, was embroiled in a nepotism scandal involving more than a million euros in payments to his wife and children for apparently fictitious jobs as parliamentary aides. To those with long memories, the Fillon Affair recalled Mitterrand's famous injunction against "money that corrupts . . . ruins and rots the conscience of men."

CHAPTER 24
BANIER STRIKES BACK

While the Bordeaux magistrates continued to pursue their complex web of investigations, Banier's legal team was working on a defense strategy. It consisted of casting doubt on the often devastating testimony against him. As early as September 2010, the photographer had filed a complaint against Françoise Meyers for subornation — bribing a witness. That stemmed from her 2008 payment of €400,000 to Claire Thibout, ostensibly as a supplement to the accountant's severance indemnities.

But Banier had been obliged to withdraw that complaint as a condition of the December 2010 protocols that were supposed to end the whole legal case. Though the investigation continued, Banier was barred from reviving his action against Françoise. The protocols also stipulated that Françoise could no longer be a plaintiff against the photographer. She got around that by having her sons register as plaintiffs, in effect acting as surrogates in their mother's continuing vendetta against Banier. The photographer thus found himself facing the equivalent of asymmetrical warfare: He was still under attack by the Meyers camp, yet he could not counterattack directly. But he could try to undermine the credibility of her key witnesses.

The six people in question — five former Bettencourt employees, plus a close friend of Liliane's — had all given written attestations in support of Meyers's original suit and had subsequently testified against Banier before investigators in Nanterre and Bordeaux. Collectively, they painted a devastating portrait of Banier as a scheming guru who manipulated Madame Bettencourt into giving him hundreds of millions of euros, isolated her from her family, ran roughshod over the domestic staff, and, after André's death, became the de facto master of the Bettencourt household. Their descriptions of Madame Bettencourt's mental and physical disorders, moreover, reinforced the notion that she was virtually helpless in the face of Banier's demands. If their testimony stood unchallenged, Banier's chances in court were slim indeed.

On April 6, 2012, Banier's lawyers filed a perjury complaint against the six, describing them as a "clan" organized by Thibout at the behest of Françoise Meyers. Their testimony had been given undue weight, the defense team argued, since they had been deposed multiple times while other witnesses more favorable to Banier, or neutral, had been heard only once or not at all. Of all the persons interrogated, these six were the only ones who "claim to have witnessed facts that could characterize the abuse of weakness charges against François-Marie Banier." Other witnesses who criticized Banier did so on the basis of his "personality," not any verifiable facts. Thus the case against Banier, his attorneys asserted, rested mainly on the accounts of these six individuals. The bulk of the forty-five-page complaint was a point-by-point refutation of their main accusations, citing inconsistencies of dates and facts and attempting to show that much of what they claimed was based on hearsay and second-hand information.

Banier's complaint wound up on the desk of Roger Le Loire, the senior magistrate in the financial unit of the Paris criminal court. A former police detective and antiterrorist judge, Le Loire was known as a methodical, if somewhat plodding, investigator who worked alone in his white-walled office on the boulevard des Italiens, near the Paris Opéra. With his calm and courteous manner, he seemed better disposed toward the photographer than Gentil had been — "respectful" and "civilized" were the words Banier used to describe him. Claire Thibout, on the other hand, tested Le Loire's patience with her snippy answers to questions she considered repetitive or ill informed. "I have already answered that," she would tell him. "Reread your files, Monsieur. . . . The question is ridiculous."

Le Loire took his time over the case. But when he finally acted, more than two years after the complaint was filed, Banier's team began to think that the wind might be shifting a bit in their direction. On November 27, 2014, the judge put Claire Thibout under investigation for "false testimony" and "mendacious attestation." In April 2015, he did the same with four of the other witnesses named in Banier's complaint: chambermaid Dominique Gaspard, secretary Christiane Djenane, nurse Henriette Youpatchou, and Liliane's close friend Lucienne de Rozier. The only one to escape a *mise en examen* was Chantal Trovel, André Bettencourt's ex-secretary, who was named an "assisted witness," still under suspicion but, so far, not an official target of the investigation.

In September 2015, Le Loire slapped a new charge on Claire Thibout: *faux témoignage aggravé* — that is, perjury "aggravated" by a monetary payment. That left a big question mark over the head of Françoise Meyers: Would Le Loire's continuing probe support a charge of subornation? Could he logically pursue Thibout for accepting a bribe without going after the person who paid her?

Françoise was seemingly protected against that by two things: Banier had been required by the 2010 protocol to withdraw his original subornation complaint in January 2011; and the Bordeaux judges had definitively dropped the subornation charges in December of that year. But that judgment applied only to Meyers's original €400,000 payment to Claire Thibout. Since then, an important new fact had come to light.

On November 29, 2012, Françoise granted an unsecured loan of €300,000 to Thibout and her husband, Philippe Dunand. The stated reason was that the couple was facing dire financial problems resulting from Claire's role as a witness in the case. Though she had received a total of €800,000 — severance indemnities, plus the "supplement" provided by Françoise — Thibout had locked most of it up by buying an apartment in Paris and a large farmhouse in Normandy. In the meantime, she had been fired from several accounting jobs because her employers didn't appreciate the media attention she attracted. Her husband, whose computer equipment had been confiscated by investigators, had lost his one-man infotech business. To make matters worse, the couple was billed €120,000 in back taxes on the initially unreported payment from Françoise. Thibout's attempts to get a bank loan had been turned down. The couple, with two teenagers to raise, faced a critical cash crunch. In desperation, Thibout had appealed to Françoise for yet another cash injection: a €300,000 loan, duly declared before a notary and subject to interest but without collateral or other guarantees, giving the transaction the appearance of a sweetheart deal.

Banier's lawyers argued that the loan's timing was suspect, coming just two weeks after Thibout and other witnesses had testified in a confrontation with Banier. To the Banier camp, it had all the hallmarks of a payment for testimony. In May 2015, they filed new charges against Françoise for subornation. Officially, their action cited only the loan, but the earlier payment remained a troubling fact that Judge Le Loire could not ignore. Having gone after Thibout and the other witnesses, he now had to address the question of Françoise Meyers's role in soliciting their testimony. Would he go so far as to indict the future head of one of France's biggest and proudest industrial firms? Speculating on that scenario, Thibout's lawyer Antoine Gillot said it would be the "atomic bomb if the person who was presented as a victim, who supported and protected her mother, would be seen as a delinquent."

On July 6, 2015, Le Loire took a step in that direction by opening an official investigation into a possible subornation of witnesses. Françoise was not named as a target at that point, but it was clear that she was now in the gun sights. Would the judge go so far as to detonate the bomb?

CHAPTER 25
LIFE AND DEATH

Île de Boëdic, Sunday, March 17, 2013. Even on weekends, Olivier Metzner was an early riser. He usually lit the first of his half dozen daily cigars at seven a.m., while perusing the latest news on his computer. On this particular morning, though, he was not at his desk. In fact, the guardian of Metzner's private island off the coast of Brittany could not find him anywhere, and one of his two boats was missing. On the dining-room table, she found a list of his law partners with their mobile phone numbers and instructions to contact them. She called the first name on the list: Emmanuel Marsigny. "Don't touch anything, and call the gendarmes," Marsigny instructed. Moments later, the guardian's husband spotted the boat drifting in the Gulf of Morbihan with no one aboard. Metzner's body was later found near the shore.

Within hours the Agence France-Presse wire service broadcast the stunning news that Olivier Metzner was dead at age sixty-three, an apparent suicide victim.

No one had suspected that France's leading criminal lawyer contemplated such a dramatic end to his career — least of all the four associates in his law office. Metzner had left a detailed note naming Nicolas Huc-Morel as his successor at the head of the firm and exhorting his colleagues to "preserve the defense of our clients."

Prominent among those clients, of course, was Françoise Bettencourt Meyers, whose suit against Banier had become Metzner's most famous case. According to Huc-Morel, the Bettencourt Affair was also supposed to be "the last case that he would plead. He wanted to end his professional career with this case." Huc-Morel, who worked closely with Metzner for twelve years, believes that he "perhaps felt he was starting to decline" and that his "passion" for the law was waning.

Metzner's real passion was the sea. That's why he had purchased this seventeen-acre private island three years earlier — a Y-shaped expanse of emerald grass and trees surrounded by sand beaches and rocky outcroppings. Metzner spent eleven months and a small fortune restoring its structures: a stone chapel, a three-story main house, and a sizeable outbuilding. A fervent opera lover, he had converted the chapel into a concert hall with a grand piano in place of the altar.

Speakers hidden discreetly around the property dispensed classical music nonstop. Under Metzner's personal direction, the opulent interiors were fitted out with designer furniture and modern paintings. The spaces seem conceived for convivial entertaining — an immense state-of-the art kitchen with a rosewood dinner table and ten matching chairs; a clubby living room featuring an open fireplace, cozy leather armchairs, and a mahogany bar with blue backlighting; a billiard room with a rack full of pool cues.

The only thing missing was people. Metzner was a profoundly lonely soul, a homosexual with no fixed partner, few real friends, and no family apart from an estranged brother and sister. Probably his closest relationships were his professional ties to the four partners in his firm — all young, brilliant, and strikingly handsome.

An obsessive workaholic, he would spend long hours in his gilded office near the National Assembly, then carry a computer full of scanned documents back to his Paris apartment and keep working. On weekends, he would take the high-speed TVG train to Brittany and retreat to his island, usually alone. His capacity for hard work and his brilliance as a procedural strategist had catapulted him to the top of his field as a criminal lawyer, despite his limited skills as an orator. But his sharp elbows and outsize ego won him few friends in the profession.

For all his success, Metzner was not a happy man. French journalist Denis Robert recounts a moving scene that took place in 1997, while he was filming a TV interview in Metzner's Left Bank office on the rue de l'Université. They were discussing his past cases when the lawyer suddenly fell silent. "He started crying like a baby," Robert recalls. "He explained that he had ruined his life. His real happiness would have been to be a sailor and go to sea. The work of a lawyer ground him down."

Be a sailor and go to sea. That's what he had in mind when he bought his 45-meter motor-powered yacht several weeks before his suicide. He had also put the Île de Boëdic up for sale for a reported €10 million. Asked by a journalist why he wanted to give up his beloved island after working so hard to restore it, he replied, perhaps prophetically, "I have another project; I am going to discover the sea more and more."

"Just a week before this happened, he sent me a text message inviting me to join him on vacation with my children and tour the Greek islands on his boat," says Nicolas Huc-Morel, who now regrets that he didn't take Metzner up on the offer. "He had been in love with the sea ever since he was a kid. When he bought this island, and then the boat, it was a way for him to realize a dream." Huc-

Morel, forty-one, a stylish dresser who sports a neatly manicured beard, can only speculate on what happened during Metzner's solo cruise on the Mediterranean. "I think things didn't go as he had hoped, and so he decided to return to his island and do what he did."

What does all this have to do with the Bettencourt Affair? Everything.

Because Olivier Metzner *created* the Bettencourt Affair. It was Metzner who wrote the complaint that triggered the initial investigation. It was Metzner who decided to change horses and take his case directly to Judge Prévost-Desprez's court when Courroye was about to bury it. And it was Metzner who, with a Machiavellian brilliance, leaked the butler's recordings to the press and turned his flagging case into a headline-grabbing national scandal.

But if Metzner is the man who "made" the Bettencourt Affair, perhaps it was the affair that unmade him. Every suicide has complex motivations, and Olivier Metzner's lonely private life suggests reasons for his act. But to some observers, the heady vapors of the Bettencourt case must have contributed to his fatal decision. "I think he was drunk on his own success," says his friend and colleague Hervé Temime, who for a time represented Banier. "Since he was a complex personality, and probably not at all as self-satisfied as he appeared, I think he blew a fuse." Isabelle Prévost-Desprez also believes that the Bettencourt Affair was "not unrelated to Metzner's suicide. I think all these people lost their heads in the face of all the money, all the power, all the political pressures."

Metzner was not the only one who lost his head. On April 2, 2013, less than a month after Metzner's suicide, Commissaire Noël Robin was found dead in an unmarked police car, his brains blown out by his own service revolver. As deputy director of the Paris-based Financial Brigade, Robin, fifty-five, had supervised the Bettencourt investigations under both Prévost-Desprez and Courroye.

Prévost-Desprez says Robin was caught in the tug-of-war between the two rival magistrates. His apparent suicide was attributed to "personal" reasons, but who can say that the stress of the high-profile Bettencourt case did not add a dose of anxiety and despair?

On January 25, 2015, an early-morning stroller spotted a man dangling from a tree in a forest near the town of Brétigny-sur-Orge, south of Paris. Emergency workers cut him down and rushed him to the hospital hovering between life and death. It was Alain Thurin, sixty-five, Liliane Bettencourt's trusted nurse, who was scheduled to go on trial the next day for abusing the weakness of his former employer. One of ten defendants in the case, along with Banier, d'Orgeval, and de Maistre, Thurin had been overwhelmed by the affair and had not even engaged a lawyer to represent him. He had been extremely close to the heiress — he would write *"je t'aime"* on his notes to her — and she reciprocated by bequeathing him a €10 million legacy in her will (since rescinded). Married, with a daughter and an autistic son, Thurin had prepared his act in advance, as he explained in a poignant letter to the Bordeaux prosecutor.

"I adored working with Madame, it was a great honor, she is a remarkable woman," he wrote. "I am not in a position to manage my own defense, because if I verbally attack M. Banier or others, it will be my word against theirs, and being confronted by all these eminent lawyers would be very difficult, especially without proofs." He added: "My wife does not know about my decision, and it is for that reason that I must push back the hour. To be awakened in the middle of the night would not be a good thing, especially when she and my son will be sleeping. I know it will be difficult at first, but I know she will get over my absence." Thurin remained in a deep coma for weeks. He finally recovered and was acquitted in a separate trial in October 2015.

The Bettencourt Affair, it seems, was no mere struggle over jealousy, money, and power. For some, it was a matter of life and death.

Chapter 26
The Reckoning

Bordeaux, Monday, January 26, 2015. Shortly before ten a.m., two black vans with tinted windows pull up in front of the gold-tipped gates of the Palais de justice. Françoise Meyers and her two sons emerge, accompanied by two bodyguards with curlicue wires jammed in their ears, four lawyers, and two representatives of the PR firm that handles the family's press relations. Françoise, as usual, is dressed in a black pantsuit with a multicolored scarf. Staring straight ahead through her thick-framed glasses, she ignores the outstretched microphones and clicking cameras that surround her. She is protectively flanked by Jean-Victor and Nicolas Meyers, both wearing black suits and somber expressions more befitting a funeral than a court of law where their mother hopes, after eight years, to see justice done to the man she claims expropriated her mother and ripped her family apart.

Minutes later, François-Marie Banier arrives on foot, accompanied by Martin d'Orgeval and their three lawyers. Banier wears a slight smile on his thin lips, as if he were an amused spectator of this drama and not its central figure. Martin does not smile; his jaw is tightly clenched. Their fellow defendants — Liliane's former adviser Patrice de Maistre, her ex-lawyer Pascal Wilhelm, businessman Stéphane Courbit, and the notaries Patrice Bonduelle and Jean-Michel Normand — all enter the courtroom and take their place on the front benches to the right of the central aisle. Carlos Vejarano, manager of the Île d'Arros, accused of cajoling €2 million out of the heiress, is too ill to attend, as is nurse Alain Thurin, still in a deep coma after attempting suicide the day before. The last to arrive is Éric Woerth, Sarkozy's former cabinet minister and campaign treasurer. Looking strangely cheerful, Woerth goes out of his way to shake the hand of Patrice de Maistre, the man with whom he allegedly colluded over campaign cash, a prestigious medal, and a plum job for Woerth's wife.

On the plaintiffs' benches to the left of the aisle sits Olivier Pelat, Liliane Bettencourt's guardian for legal matters. Standing well over six feet, with broad shoulders, a jutting chin, and an intimidating gaze, he could be a retired rugby player, though the elegant cut of his suit and the mirror shine on his black shoes bespeak the prosperous real estate promoter that he is. Placid and stone-faced, he reveals no hint of emotion — apart perhaps from his compulsive nail-biting.

In October 2011, Pelat had filed on Liliane's behalf as a plaintiff in the action against Banier and the other defendants. That was a total turnaround from her position in 2009, when her lawyer, Georges Kiejman, registered her as a plaintiff *against* her daughter's suit. At that time, Liliane's objective was to affirm that she was not a victim of abuse and to oppose the action targeting Banier. Now, unable to voice her own wishes, she found herself on the opposite side of the dispute. Not that she knew the difference at that point. As Pelat told the court, the heiress, then ninety-two, had passed "into another world," her words "absolutely unrealistic" and her mind somewhere "out west."

The other plaintiffs against Banier were Liliane's grandsons, Jean-Victor, twenty-nine, and Nicolas, twenty-seven. As noted, Françoise had been obliged to drop charges against Banier and de Maistre as a condition of the December 2010 protocols. She got around that by having her sons file complaints in her place. Françoise herself was a plaintiff against the other defendants. Prominent among them was Pascal Wilhelm, the lawyer who had negotiated the 2010 accord — a deal that was highly favorable to the Meyerses —

but who was now accused of abusing Liliane Bettencourt in his role as her protector. Jean-Pierre Meyers, though totally supportive of his wife's action, was not a plaintiff and did not attend the trial.

The prosecution's main target was Banier himself, who faced the prospect of three years in prison, plus substantial fines and damages. The photographer was specifically accused of abusing the weakness of Liliane Bettencourt by obtaining more than €442 million worth of gifts between September 1, 2006, and October 29, 2009, the period covered by the trial. The bulk of that sum was in the form of insurance contracts that he had returned in December 2010, but some €173 million remained in his possession. The gifts he received prior to September 2006, when the heiress was considered lucid, were not in question. And though Banier's status as Liliane's *légataire universel* had since been revoked, he also had to answer for the circumstances that led to that designation, potentially worth more than €1 billion to him had the heiress died while it was still in force.

At precisely ten a.m. a bell rings and all rise as presiding judge Denis Roucou enters the courtroom through a rear door, accompanied by his associates Anne-Marie Vollette and Sylvia Pons. Arrayed before the judges' bench are the thirty-five red-bound volumes of investigative files transmitted by Judge Jean-Michel Gentil. Gentil and his associates are no longer involved in the case: In the French legal system, once the investigating magistrates send a case to court, a trio of trial judges takes charge. It is the presiding judge, in this case Roucou, who plays the lead role in interrogating defendants and witnesses. Lawyers for the various parties can make observations and question witnesses, but the presiding judge remains firmly in control. Unlike the adversarial system used in the United States and Britain, where advocates for opposing parties argue their cases before impartial judges or juries, the French practice, based on the Napoleonic Code, is an inquisitorial system in which the judges themselves pursue the truth and pronounce the verdict.

Roucou, then age fifty-five, was known as a tough, sometimes combative judge. In his previous career in the Assize tribunals — the courts that deal with violent crimes — Roucou had presided over two of France's most notorious cases: the 2009 death of an eight-year-old girl after years of brutal torture by her parents; and the rape/murder of a thirteen-year-old by her twenty-four-year-old neighbor. Roucou pulled no punches in those cases: All three defendants received thirty-year sentences. (Incompressible life terms are rare in France, and the death penalty was abolished in 1981.) François-Marie Banier was no murderer, but he and his legal team could expect no leniency from this battle-hardened jurist whose hostility to the photographer seemed evident from the beginning of the four-week trial. With his salt-and-pepper goatee and wire-rimmed glasses, Roucou regarded the defendant with the air of a disapproving schoolmaster — and Banier had never gotten along with his schoolmasters. "It is clear that Roucou cannot abide him and scarcely tries to hide the fact," observed a reporter for *Le Monde.*

Standing alone at the bar, arms folded behind his back, Banier was alternately charming, droll, flippant, and exasperated under his first six hours of questioning by Roucou. Asked to describe his background, he portrayed himself as a battered child from a modest family. "I didn't lead the life of some little marquis." Roucou interjected that he lived on the avenue Victor-Hugo, one of Paris's most fashionable streets. "Yes, but it was a tiny apartment," Banier retorted. He evoked his youthful "panache" and recited the now-familiar litany of his early triumphs as a writer, his appearance on the cover of the *Sunday Times,* his friendships with famous people, his naming of the "world's two best-selling perfumes." Rejecting the notion that he was some frivolous dandy or gigolo, he insisted that he had "always worked, morning till night" and had plenty of money before he met Liliane Bettencourt.

At times, Roucou and Banier appeared to be engaged in a sparring match. The judge asked why he had stashed away so many paintings in bank vaults. "That's a very French question," Banier retorted. "I'm not going to hang them one on top of one another. I'm not that kind of poseur." And why did Banier refer to Pierre Bergé, the lifelong partner of Yves St. Laurent, as the "dwarf Bergé" in his notebooks? "Why not?" Banier shot back. "Where is my freedom? People call Sarkozy a dwarf and that doesn't bother him." Roucou's response — "Sarkozy is no longer part of this case" — touched off peals of laughter from the packed courtroom.

Banier's mockery seemed somewhat ungracious, since Bergé had provided a letter on his behalf. It was one of a dozen attestations from his supporters — including former supermodel Inès de la Fressange and fashion designer Diane von Furstenberg — extolling Banier's generosity, charm, and creativity. Two character witnesses appeared in person. The rotund actor and theater director Jean-Michel Ribes, sporting a purple fedora with a pink headband, called Banier "sharp, intelligent, droll" — nothing like "this predator image that people try to stick on him." But wouldn't you say he is "seductive"? prompted

455

the prosecutor. "Why don't you summon the pope to your courtroom?" Ribes replied with a mocking smile. "The pope has charm, he is seductive. If seduction and charm are condemnable, then a lot of people should go to jail." More titters from the public benches.

Corinne Paradis, mother of singer/actress Vanessa Paradis, described Banier as an attentive godfather to Lily-Rose, the daughter of Vanessa and Johnny Depp. Had she ever seen Banier act violently? Only once, said Paradis, "when I lit a cigarette, he ripped it out of my mouth and crushed it." (Banier, adamantly anti-tobacco, makes a habit of doing this — even to total strangers in the street.)

Roucou was visibly unimpressed with the pro-Banier contingent, and refused to allow Corinne Paradis to read her daughter's letter in court. Nor did he give much attention to the investigative depositions that were favorable to the photographer. On the contrary, Banier was confronted with an array of hostile witnesses who either appeared at the bar or had their depositions read out loud by Judge Roucou. Collectively, they reinforced the image of Liliane as physically and mentally impaired and depicted Banier as a cynical manipulator.

Liliane's close friend Monique de Libouton, an eighty-two-year-old L'Oréal retiree, was unable to attend, but Roucou read portions of her 2010 deposition. "François-Marie Banier used violent language with Liliane, and called her *ma grosse* [fatty]. I saw him in front of me grab Liliane brusquely and the surprising reaction of my friend was to cluck like a hen. . . . I think François-Marie Banier has become a kind of guru to her. . . . [He] mixes cajolery and meanness and knows no limits." Banier sputtered with outrage: "It's slanderous! It's an absolute lie! It's a vile, ignoble testimony. . . . I was never violent with Madame Bettencourt."

Former chambermaid Dominique Gaspard repeated the claims she had made in her original 2007 attestation and subsequent interrogations: Banier ripped the lipstick out of Liliane's hands, asked her repeatedly about her checkbook, chose her clothes, told her which doctors to consult. And of course Gaspard recounted the now-famous story about overhearing Banier and Liliane discussing a plan for "simple adoption."

Roucou asked Banier what this adoption project was all about.

"It never existed," Banier scoffed. "Madame Bettencourt would never have had such an idea and me neither. We didn't have that kind of relationship . . . It's a joke." He dismissed Gaspard's claim as another of "the lies infiltrated into the procedure by all these false witnesses."

But lawyers for the Meyers side insisted the adoption story was not so easy to dismiss. How could a chambermaid invent a term like *"adoption simple,"* which has a precise legal meaning? (In an *adoption simple,* which can apply to adults as well as minors, the adoptee has all the rights of a biological child and heir without taking the name of the adopter.) Jean-Pierre Ferrandes, Banier's former notary, admitted that he might have mentioned adoption briefly while giving him an overview of succession issues but said it was never seriously discussed. "François-Marie Banier was not adopted," said Nicolas Huc-Morel, attorney for Françoise Meyers and her sons, "but we must admit that he came pretty close to it." Banier's defense team called the idea unthinkable. "In France," said Laurent Merlet, "adoption requires the accord of the family and has to go before a judge. That was impossible in this case. What professional of the law would propose such a thing?"

Other Bettencourt employees, including secretaries Christine Djenane and Claire Trovel stepped up to the bar and delivered damning accounts of Banier's behavior and Liliane's mental confusion. Banier rejected their claims as rumor-mongering by jealous underlings. "These are people seeking revenge for a life they've never had," he sneered. "You have only to read *Les bonnes* [The maids] by Jean Genet."

■ ■ ■ ■

Banier's most determined accuser was the person who had launched the suit against him in the first place: Françoise Bettencourt Meyers. Questioned as a witness, she repeated the charges she had previously aired in her public interviews and multiple depositions before the magistrates. She and her parents formed a happy and united family until Banier came along. Little by little he imposed his influence on her mother, put her under a "spell," and sought to destroy the family in order to get his hands on Liliane's fortune. "Monsieur Banier's technique was divide and conquer," she said. "As an only child, I had to rescue my mother from this hornet's nest." Under questioning, she admitted soliciting the attestations that accompanied her original complaint, but insisted that she had never "bought the testimony" of any witness.

Banier did not attack Françoise head-on, but managed to insert a few barbs over the course of the trial. "Madame Bettencourt was frightened to death at the idea of winding up in the hands of her daughter and son-in-law," he said. "It's been like that ever since their marriage." Asked why he tried to persuade Madame Bettencourt that her daughter's suit was against her, Banier again took aim at Françoise, his words dripping with irony and venom: "I think that a daughter who loves her mother so tenderly, so deeply, would have talked to her before launching this suit if it was not against her," he said. "What counts in my eyes is not what's going to happen to me, but the fact that Liliane Bettencourt has been portrayed as some laughable, grotesque personage. Of course it's a suit against Liliane Bettencourt."

Françoise could hardly have been pleased to hear Banier expound upon his intimate relationship with her mother. "She was a woman who wanted to share things with me," he said. "She gave me the possibility of doing things I could never have done without her. And with me she experienced things that she would certainly not have known. . . . There was a language I created with her that was expressed through this money that she wanted to give me."

Over and over he made this point: Money was merely the means of expressing the depth of their relationship, not the reason for it. "It gave her pleasure to give me money," he told the court. "It was a great joy for her. She said herself that I never asked for anything. There is no manipulation. There is no abuse of weakness . . . It was a game for her. She lit a fire, but she is no longer here to put it out."

And what did he do with all those millions? Roucou asked.

Banier said he spent it on improving his

properties, on artworks, on collecting rare books and manuscripts — Proust, Rimbaud, Flaubert — "things I could never have had without Liliane." Aesthetic and intellectual pursuits, not the ostentatious acquisitions of the nouveau riche. "I didn't buy a house in St. Tropez, or an airplane, or a Rolls. I won't exchange my motor scooter for a Ferrari." Still, that was a long way from Liliane's initial claim that she was helping launch Banier's career as an artist.

Didn't he ever think of refusing her gifts?

Impossible, said Banier. "When I refuse, it's like denying Liliane Bettencourt her pleasure and her desire." He insisted that it was Liliane who took the lead in their relationship, Liliane who decided. "Which one of us had control over the other? Which one is the victim of the other?"

The prosecutor and the lawyers for the Meyers side did not buy the notion that Liliane decided of her own free will to cover Banier with gold. Leaning on the reports of medical experts and the testimony of numerous witnesses from the heiress's entourage, they maintained that her declining mental state left her open to manipulation by her protégé. In particular, Banier's accusers pointed to a disturbing pattern by which the liberalities spiked at periods of Liliane's greatest weakness. It was in the wake of the Formentor ac-

461

cident in 2006, for example, that Liliane, still groggy and overmedicated by many accounts, officially designated Banier as the beneficiary of a life-insurance contract worth €262 million at the time. It was shortly after André's death that the distraught and grieving heiress named Banier her *légataire universel* in December 2007. And it was during that same period that the maid Dominique Gaspard claimed to have overheard talk of an adoption project.

Banier angrily denied any such pattern, just as he denied that Liliane's powers of decision-making were altered by her age and physical decline. "You know very well that Madame Bettencourt had full control of her mind, she was not this laughable character we are presented with," he said. "Do you think the people at L'Oréal kept a nutcase around since 2003?" he said. The insurance designation, he accurately noted, was merely the confirmation of something she had already granted him by testament in 1997, at a time when no one questioned her mental capacities. As for his *légataire universel* status, Banier claimed not to have understood what it meant, even though he himself had organized and hosted the meeting at which his lawyer and notary discussed that option. To his mind, the meeting was about ways to secure Liliane's gifts against future challenges by her daughter and son-in-law. "She told me five or six days later that she had made me her *légataire universel.* I was very upset," he told the court. "I had already had enough money in my life, I didn't need to deal with that."

In contrast to Banier's stormy performance, Martin d'Orgeval was calm and composed at the bar. Like Banier, he was accused of abusing the weakness of the aged heiress, but his gains seemed almost modest compared to Banier's: two paintings by Jean Arp and Max Ernst as reversionary property (total value €1,699,931, including gift taxes); a check for €564,853 to pay for three photographs by Eugène Cuvelier purchased at auction by d'Orgeval and Banier; and the outright gift of three Cuvelier prints (€909,164, including tax). Beyond that, he was seen to share in a lavish lifestyle, financed largely by Liliane's gifts to Banier, that was marked by expenditures averaging as much as €25,000 a day, according to the Meyerses' lawyers.

The amounts in question were substantial, but Martin appeared to have wandered into this windfall almost blindly, following the lead of his older partner. Indeed, some critics called him, uncharitably, Banier's *toutou* — or lap dog. His responses to the charges were a mixture of frankness, naïveté, and denial. He was surprised and touched by the gifts, which were thoughtfully "chosen" by Liliane as a sign of friendship and support. As a

463

specialist on Jean Arp, the subject of his art history thesis, and as an admirer of Cuvelier, an inspiration for his own photography, Martin said he was pleased by these acquisitions for reasons that had nothing to do with their monetary value. "I never saw Liliane for her money," he protested. "I never expected or demanded anything from her. Whenever she was described as a billionaire, it burned my ears. I protested before I accepted [her gifts]."

Questioned about his role as Liliane's subsidiary *légataire universel* — her backup heir if Banier died first — d'Orgeval claimed that he was unaware of his designation until he learned of it from the press. "I knew nothing about the conditions," he said, "and it was absolutely not legitimate." Like Banier, he said he was glad when that testament was annulled in 2010. On this and other points, Martin's claim of innocence and ignorance met with skepticism from the court and the plaintiffs' lawyers. But his words at the witness stand mostly gave the impression of a polite young man who had blithely accepted his good fortune without troubling too much about the details. "I knew Liliane was helping François-Marie," he said, "but I didn't get involved in the accounting."

Claire Thibout, whose whistle-blowing had triggered the whole affair, testified from Paris via an audiovisual hookup. Under psychiatric treatment and medication for nervous depression, she had obtained a doctor's certificate to avoid the stress of appearing in person. She seemed to be on the verge of a nervous breakdown, her voice rising at times to a shrill pitch. Her anxiety was understandable: Not only was she a key witness against Banier and de Maistre, she herself was under investigation by a Paris magistrate for false testimony. The obvious aim of the defense teams was to throw Thibout off balance and discredit her claims.

Almost from the beginning of her five-hour screen appearance, Thibout was grilled by Roucou and defense lawyers about her financial relations with Françoise Meyers — the €400,000 "severance" payment and the €300,000 loan. "I never negotiated for my testimony," Thibout insisted. "My lawyer negotiated an indemnity in case I was fired." Her claim contradicted earlier testimony by Eve du Breuil, de Maistre's former secretary, who called Thibout "bipolar" and said the accountant had told her "that the employees of Madame Bettencourt crossed the street to see Françoise Meyers and recount what happened in her mother's house in exchange for cash." (Thibout denied ever discussing the subject with du Breuil and called her story "nonsense.")

Thibout was also pressed to explain why in 2006 she sent Madame Bettencourt's notary the deeds to two apartments with a letter claiming the heiress wanted to gift them to her. It was all Banier's fault, said Thibout: He kept harassing her to accept Liliane's gifts in order to compromise her and shut her up. She sent the deeds to get Banier off her back, but never followed up. She described Banier as someone who was initially amusing but eventually became "omnipresent and had a terrible hold on [Madame Bettencourt]. He interfered in everything, from her employees to her guests and her friends . . . He's the one who organized the whole household." Among other accusations, she recounted the story of Banier's alleged attempt to get his hands on the heiress's jewelry collection, a claim that the photographer denied.

Thibout was no less critical of de Maistre, who she said "was not there to protect [Madame Bettencourt] but to protect Banier and his other interests." She repeated her oft-told tale of de Maistre's 2006 request for €150,000 in cash for Sarkozy's campaign treasurer Éric Woerth. She said she had provided only €50,000 and presumed, based on de Maistre's own remarks, that he had obtained the rest of the money from Madame Bettencourt's Swiss accounts. Thibout's claim, and the other elements that appeared to back it up — bank records, datebooks — was the basis for charges against both de Maistre and Éric Woerth.

De Maistre had much more to answer for than the suspected cash payment to Woerth. He was accused of abusing Liliane's weakness to the tune of €12 million. That sum consisted of the €5 million donation he solicited from the heiress to support him in his "old age," plus €3 million in gift taxes, plus the €4 million he had brought into France from Liliane's Swiss accounts. In addition, he was charged with tax fraud for moving funds from Liliane's illegal Swiss bank accounts to a tax haven in Singapore.

De Maistre's appearance on the stand was marked by a whiny self-pity — he broke down in tears no fewer than three times — that contrasted sharply with his usual air of haughty superiority. He justified the €5 million gift as a "supplementary retirement pension," and claimed that the steep hikes in his annual fees — from €500,000 to €2 million in six years — reflected his increased responsibilities. True, he had asked the heiress to buy him the "boat of [his] dreams," but finally realized it was a "bad idea" and didn't follow through. Like Banier, he denied that Liliane's declining mental state affected her discernment when it came to spending her money. "Granted, she's an elderly lady, but I didn't think she wasn't in a state to do these things."

His response to Thibout's claims about the €50,000 in cash was a petulant he-said-she-said denial of her "lying denunciations." Everybody knew the Bettencourts gave money to politicians, he said, but they themselves were never called to account for that. "It's easier to attack an underling like me," he moaned. "I'm the ideal fall guy." He accused Thibout of "inventing this story because she had nothing else and she wanted to compromise me."

Concerning the €4 million in cash that came from Switzerland, de Maistre was at a loss to explain what had happened to it. "I can't prove to you that I did not take this money, but I didn't take it." Madame Bettencourt "could have given it to lots of people" — perhaps "to politicians or others, I don't know." After rather ungallantly shifting the suspicion over possible political payments to the heiress, de Maistre insisted that he had "not given this money to Éric Woerth or to Mr. Sarkozy. The Bettencourts didn't need me for that."

That was an odd way to protect his "friend" Éric Woerth, who sat next to de Maistre on the defendants' bench. But Woerth seemed unfazed. "I never received any cash from Patrice de Maistre," he said with pokerfaced confidence during his perfunctory one-hour appearance at the bar. Under kid-glove questioning from the bench, he admitted meeting with de Maistre twice, but never to discuss campaign finance issues. Yes, there were troubling coincidences involving the timing of these encounters, but "life is made of coincidences." Though there was a strong circumstantial case against Woerth, no hard proof existed that cash had ever changed hands between the two men — it is, after all, rare that a person receiving illegal funds writes out a receipt. (The other embarrassing questions concerning de Maistre's Légion d'honneur medal and Madame Woerth's cushy job were addressed in a separate hearing a month later.)

During breaks in the proceedings, Banier seemed oddly lighthearted, even playful, as he photographed lawyers with his vintage Leica and chatted amiably with police guards and reporters in the main hall of the court-house. One evening, he attempted to climb the gates around the cathedral, damaging his shoes in the process. On another occasion, he crawled unseen into a restaurant where his lawyers were dining with several journalists, sticking his head up at the end of the table, barking like a dog, and howling with laughter. Such moments illustrated the "insouciance" that is often attributed to Banier — a sort of happy-go-lucky carelessness. But it was also his way of blowing off steam, sublimating his fear, and minimizing the danger he faced. "He told us he was in an unreal world for five weeks," recalls his lawyer, Laurent

Merlet.

By the time the trial moved into its final week, all eight of the defendants present had testified, as well as seventeen witnesses and five medical experts. Dozens of depositions were read aloud, Liliane's TV interviews were screened, and portions of the butler's secret recordings were played over loudspeakers — much to de Maistre's squirming embarrassment. It was now time for the closing arguments, a moment of great theatricality where the eminent barristers, draped in their solemn black robes with starched white collars, stand at the bar and deliver their pleas with such studied eloquence that the best among them are called "tenors" — like the operatic stars they sometimes resemble.

Benoît Ducos-Ader, looking like a Roman senator with his receding mane of silver hair, delivered a sweeping condemnation of the defendants on behalf of Liliane Bettencourt. In a deep, resonant voice, his right hand waving in the air, he depicted Banier as a cynical schemer who "perfectly meditated his acts." For proof, he cited a passage from one of Banier's confiscated notebooks: "Play on one's guilt feelings to obtain what they don't want to give." Don't be fooled by appearances, the veteran jurist intoned. Banier is "not just a charming eccentric who rides around on his motor scooter," but a "formidable" seducer with the "technique of a guru." Turning his head to glare at the photographer, he quipped, "If they handed out Oscars for fraud, Banier would certainly win one." Blasting the other defendants in turn, Ducos-Ader pronounced his conclusion with a disdainful gesture toward the eight men seated behind him: "These are the characters you will have to judge, these men who try to pull the wool over your eyes. There is no remorse among them. They're just common delinquents turning around a pile of money."

The most withering indictment came from deputy prosecutor Gérard Aldigé. A pudgy, white-haired functionary with the drooping eyes of a bloodhound, Aldigé stood at the bar for six hours and reviewed the details of the case in a droning voice until he reached a crescendo in his closing attack on the main defendant.

"Madame Bettencourt was only a marionette, with Banier holding the strings," he thundered. "He knew everything about her, to the point where he could enter her room, even lie on her bed, and make himself at home. He was fully conscious of her vulnerability. He imposed his control over her like a spider spinning its web. And once he had her in his net, he never let her go. She became his thing. He dealt with her like a vampire."

Banier's legal team had the difficult task —

some might say the mission impossible — of winning over a triumvirate of judges that seemed set against their client from the beginning and had heard nearly five weeks of damning testimony. The defense's main line of argument was to concede that Banier was an "atypical personality," and that the amounts in question were vertiginous, while insisting that he had brought happiness to a grateful woman who rewarded him of her own free will.

"One might find it shocking that a person chooses to cover a friend with gold, but that doesn't make it an abusive act," said Laurent Merlet. "That's the choice she made." The depth of the friendship between the heiress and the photographer was illustrated by the hundreds of letters they exchanged over two decades, said Merlet. The notarial acts that "regularized" Liliane's gifts were mostly "confirmations of decisions" made years earlier, not the caprices of a fragile woman under the influence.

Banier's senior attorney, the avuncular Pierre Cornut-Gentille, described his client as "an impulsive man" who could not help acting in "excessive ways." Yes, he could be "familiar" and "rude" — he was a "mad dog with the personality of a child" — but that's exactly what Liliane liked about him. All her life, the lawyer argued, Liliane had been seen only as the daughter and wife of important men, the heiress to an immense fortune. "Then one day in her life, this half-mad figure, Banier, arrives and makes everything explode: He recognizes her for what she is!" Liliane is not the "marionette" described by the prosecutor and the plaintiffs, but a free woman doing exactly what she wanted. "Respect her and her choices!"

The verdict that Roucou and his associates handed down on May 18, 2015, was harsh. Banier, guilty on all counts, was sentenced to three years in prison (of which six months were suspended), fined €350,000, and ordered to pay a staggering €158 million in damages to Liliane Bettencourt. Martin d'Orgeval was given an eighteen-month suspended sentence, a €150,000 fine, and charged €2.3 million in damages. Patrice de Maistre copped a thirty-month jail term (twelve months suspended), with a €250,000 fine and €12 million in damages. Pascal Wilhelm received the same jail sentence as de Maistre, with €3 million in damages. Four of the remaining defendants, Courbit, Normand, Bonduelle, and Vejarano, were pronounced guilty but given lesser penalties. As it commonly happens in France, and was fully expected in this case, almost all those convicted filed appeals. The single exception: Stéphane Courbit, who paid his €250,000 fine and washed his hands of the whole affair.

Only Éric Woerth was acquitted. But the judgment hardly left him unscathed: The magistrates voiced their "strong suspicion" that he had in fact received money from de Maistre, but the investigation failed to provide irrefutable proof. Following the verdict, Woerth told a TV interviewer that he had "totally recovered [his] honor" and pronounced the political angle of the Bettencourt Affair closed. Not everyone was convinced that Woerth's narrow escape amounted to an exoneration of him or Sarkozy. Antoine Gillot, attorney for Claire Thibout, Woerth's main accuser, scoffed at his claim. "Yes, he was declared not guilty, but when you read the decision I don't think 'honor' was the appropriate word," he told me. As for Sarkozy's role in the affair, Gillot's analysis is scathing: "In America, this would be a scandal. A sitting president who intervenes and violates judicial secrecy for the benefit of one party in a strictly private matter would never get away with it. He'd be gone, resigned, game over."

Banier had come to the Bordeaux courthouse that day expecting the worst. His lawyers warned him that a conviction was likely, and there were rumors that Roucou might send him immediately to prison. Cornut-Gentille told him to pack a bag just in case. Banier was somewhat relieved upon his arrival at the Palais de justice: The security guards told him not to worry; the special police unit that handles incarcerations had not been summoned. He sat stony-faced through Roucou's hour-and-a-half reading of the judgment and showed no emotion when his conviction was pronounced. "It was judged from the beginning," he says. "I understood from the first time he interrogated me that I was faced with a judge who didn't want to hear anything and had already formed his opinion."

Banier did not go to jail that day — the judges left him free on bail pending his appeal — but he had received a stunning blow. He stood convicted in a court of law of abusing a woman he considered an intimate friend, a woman who had been presented to the whole world as a batty old lady and a helpless victim of his cynical machinations. Apart from that humiliation, the court had immediately impounded one of his apartments and the proceeds of three insurance policies worth a total of some €80 million at the time. The €158 million in damages, if upheld on appeal, would leave Banier's finances as ruined as his reputation. And if he was finally sent to prison, there was no telling how he would fare. That was a grim prospect for a man nearing his seventieth year.

And yet, he was still François-Marie Banier,

the man who had rubbed shoulders with some of the most famous people of his day and was now, largely thanks to this affair, a celebrity himself. As he descended the courthouse steps, he was surrounded by a gaggle of fans — or perhaps curiosity seekers — who asked him for his autograph as if he were a rock star. Some wielded copies of his photo books. He smiled and joked with them, just as he did with the ordinary people he met while photographing in the streets of Paris. He had always considered himself a man of the streets.

Judge Roucou and his colleagues had no respite following the four-week extravaganza. Three other Bettencourt-related cases came before them in March, June, and November 2015. The defendants were Patrice de Maistre and Éric Woerth (influence peddling); Judge Isabelle Prévost-Desprez (violation of professional secrets); and ex-butler Pascal Bonnefoy and five journalists who had published excerpts of his recordings (violation of privacy). All three cases resulted in acquittals. *Mediapart* director Edwy Plenel, one of the journalists on trial, was not surprised by Éric Woerth's escape. "French justice finds it very hard to convict politicians," he said. "They find a lot of excuses for public figures."

CHAPTER 27
THE EYE OF THE BEHOLDER

While awaiting the appeal trial, Banier continued his frenetic work pace. The distractions of the Bettencourt Affair, he says, have not altered his schedule one iota — witness the publication in 2015 of his two most recent photo books: *Imprudences* and *Never Stop Dancing.* He rises early each morning, hops on his blue Peugeot motor scooter, and heads for the rougher sections of Paris looking for interesting faces to photograph with his Hasselblad. Later in the day, he will spend several hours writing in his journal or working on his latest novel, and several more hours drawing or painting in his studio. Despite his media image as a dandy and jetsetter, he is in fact an obsessed workaholic and a serious artist.

Monday, November 30, 2015. On the Place de la République, mounds of flowers, multicolored candles, and hundreds of handwritten messages surround the central monument. Its allegorical statues represent the triumph of French liberty, but the crowd milling around the square on this chilly fall day are not here to celebrate the Republic: They have come to mourn the 130 people who were mowed down at the Bataclan music hall and nearby restaurants two weeks earlier by a band of Islamist terrorists.

Many people take photos of the makeshift shrine. Some just stare silently or pray. They are a mix of tourists and Parisians — young, old, whites, blacks, Asians, Arabs. A squadron of self-appointed volunteers circles the base of the monument with brooms, clearing away debris and rotting flowers. A hand-painted banner proclaims a defiant message, même pas peur (We're not even scared) along with a smiley face. But many people in France are afraid these days, in the wake of the murderous assault on the offices of the satirical magazine *Charlie Hebdo* ten months earlier, and in anticipation of the even more horrific events to come.

A man in a black-and-white parka drives his motor scooter across the square and parks near the monument. Clutching his Hasselblad, François-Marie Banier wades into the crowd with the intense determination of a hunter. When he spots a subject that interests him, he leaps into action, usually sticking the camera right in the person's face without a word of warning or explanation. Sometimes, if he senses resistance, he might ask people if he can take their photo. The typical reaction is surprise, followed by acquiescence or, occasionally, the striking of a pose. Rarely does anyone refuse outright. Banier has that effect on people. His in-your-face boldness, often accompanied by compliments, or even kisses, seems to mesmerize his subjects.

"For me, the street is like a studio in the open air," he says. His work demands enormous concentration: He is always on the lookout for the right subject, the right moment. "You have to decide in a thousandth of a second. Between movement and immobility, you must always see who is there in front of you."

In his search for what he calls "a remarkable face, a remarkable human being," he zeroes in on atypical subjects: a well-dressed Algerian woman come to pay her respects, an elderly Chinese man in a heavy overcoat, a skinny black man wearing an imitation fur hat and holding the hand of his four-year-old son (Banier kisses both of them). Two North African youths in smart tracksuits pass by. Banier calls out to them. They turn around. Both have short beards, long black hair swept back, an imperious regard in their coal-black eyes. They are detached, neither friendly nor hostile. Banier snaps their portraits, side by side. One turns and walks away with an air of silent contempt. Banier continues to shoot the other one until he, too, turns and moves on. "There is something disturbing about these two brothers," he says. "They are like characters in a Buñuel movie. They have this sort of false virility. They may be thieves and killers, who knows?"

Some encounters are frankly hostile. A short, middle-aged man in a blue sweater and horn-rimmed glasses approaches the photographer with a smirk. "So, Monsieur Banier, you're making money?"

Banier bristles. "What?"

"You make money with your photos. You make books."

"You know where the money from my books goes? I'm stupefied by the number of people who think they know all about my finances."

His challenger, still smiling, backs away. But Banier doesn't let him off that easily.

"That's right, take off. It's best for you."

The man turns around. "No, it's best for you."

"Is that a threat?"

As the man turns and walks away, Banier shouts after him, *Collabo!* — an epithet referring incongruously to Nazi collaborationists during the Occupation.

Banier says that confrontation is unusual — though he was once slapped in the face by a Mauritanian who didn't like having his photo taken as he emerged from the Métro. In 2011, he threatened to sue a homeless man who similarly smacked him on the Champs-Élysées. Normally, he says, he is applauded and congratulated by people who recognize him. Why? "Because they like celebrity and they don't like injustice."

As a photographer, Banier specializes in black-and-white portraits. His subjects fall into two categories: the famous and the anonymous. His uncommon ability to befriend celebrities not only gives him access but allows him to win their trust and shoot them in intimate, often provocative poses: Isabelle Adjani sticking out her tongue; Mick Jagger yawning; Marcello Mastroianni dancing alone in front of a grand piano; Italian film star Silvana Mangano emerging dripping wet from the sea; French singer and actress Vanessa Paradis breastfeeding her baby. What he seeks in each subject, he says, is "their truth." *Vanity Fair* editor Graydon Carter, who has featured Banier's work on the cover of his high-profile magazine, praises him as "a hugely gifted artist and photographer."

Though he is known for his celebrity portraits, Banier is most interested in the random people he encounters in the street — bums, cripples, babies, toothless old ladies, swaggering youths, gray-bearded beggars. Humanity in all its various forms and colors remains his central subject. Writes the Belgian art historian Jan Hoet: "He tries to make contact with those who, through no choice of their own, live on the margins of society."

Banier returns home each day with up to twenty rolls of exposed Tri-X film — more than two hundred images. Once processed, the negatives and contact sheets are stored in a special climate-controlled archive on the second floor of his town house. The 750-square-foot space is equipped with rail-mounted mobile compactor shelves that provide a maximum amount of storage. "Nobody else in the world has anything like this," Banier boasts, negotiating the narrow passages between shelves lined with folders and boxes that, he says, contain more than a million images. Only a tiny fraction of them are selected for inclusion in his books or printed and framed for his exhibitions.

Many of Banier's photos have handwritten texts inscribed on them. That, in fact, is Banier's "thing" — the aspect of his work that sets it apart from conventional portrait or street photography. The words are not just decorative calligraphy; they are narratives, memories, personal essays, often philosophical reflections. For Banier is a writer and his words are as carefully chosen as his images. "The thing that marks the originality of Banier's work," says Jean-Luc Monterosso, director of the Maison européenne de la photographie (MEP), "is unquestionably the 'written' photographs, where the photographer and the writer hold a harmonious dialogue."

The MEP, an important Paris showcase, gave Banier a major exhibit in 2003. It also houses thirty-six of his photos in its permanent collection, including twenty-two donated by Liliane Bettencourt and valued at €700,000. (At least, that is the price Madame Bettencourt paid Banier's company for the works before donating them to the MEP.) Monterosso, who considers Banier "a great French artist," calls his 2003 show "one of our biggest successes of the past fifteen years" with more than 50,000 visitors and glowing press reviews.

In France, at least, such triumphs are few and far between for Banier. The 2003 MEP event was Banier's only major Paris show since 1991. (A planned second exhibition was canceled by the MEP in 2010 because of the Bettencourt scandal.) He has had numerous international shows, but they were almost all sponsored by L'Oréal as part of Banier's sweetheart contract. The accompanying books were also paid for by L'Oréal. Since Banier's contract was terminated in 2010, he himself has subsidized the production of most of his photo books by buying hundreds of copies from the publisher, as is customary for that type of work.

Relatively little of Banier's photographic

work has been sold at public auction — only eight images since 1997, according to *Le Monde* — and his gallery sales are modest. Thierry Ehrmann, director of the website artprice.com, says that "Banier does not exist in the art market; he does not exist in the big museums nor in the professional art fairs." Nor does he currently have any regular gallery representation since the Galerie Ghislaine Hussenot dropped him in 2010. Most of his sales go to a group of friends and fans, including Johnny Depp and Diane von Furstenberg, who buy his work directly. The same is true for his drawings and paintings, which attract some big American collectors but are largely absent from the commercial art venues.

The main reason for Banier's low profile on the art market, says his lawyer Laurent Merlet, is that L'Oréal subsidized his work so lavishly that he paid no attention to sales. Before the L'Oréal contract, Banier's annual revenues from photo sales and book royalties averaged some €200,000 — a respectable but hardly spectacular income. "Then all of a sudden, he didn't sell anything. In fact it was a trap — he should have continued to sell, but he no longer needed to because Liliane told him, 'Don't worry about selling. Create!' "

Banier's privileged situation, out of the rough-and-tumble commercial world, has also affected his reputation in the eyes of other working professionals. "For photographers from the agencies or fashion studios," says Guy Marineau, formerly with *Women's Wear Daily,* "he was considered a minor artist, in spite of the incredible quantity of exhibitions and photo books sponsored by L'Oréal. That had nothing to do with the way I and my colleagues worked." Marineau was particularly struck by a 2005 visit to Banier's town house. "I didn't know a single photographer capable of buying a place like that with the revenues from his work," says Marineau. "We were in a very big room, a sort of library, where I noticed a good number of master paintings on the walls. I had never considered this guy part of our 'family' of photographers, but there I had the proof that he had nothing to do with our circle."

As a novelist Banier was initially hailed as a prodigy with a brilliant future — a new Stendhal or Turgenev, as Louis Aragon put it. But his early success might be seen, in retrospect, as a flash in the pan. His biggest seller, and arguably his best book, was *Balthazar, fils de famille,* which has sold about 70,000 copies since it came out in 1985. After that, the figures plummeted. His latest novel, *Johnny Dasolo* (2008), sold fewer than 2,000 copies. Today, Banier is not even on the literary radar screen. Nonetheless, he continues to write several hours each day, scribbling in the journal he has kept since he was eighteen — always by hand — or working on his latest novel, entitled *Nineta,* about a woman in some unnamed South American dictatorship in revolt against an oppressive regime. "Writing is a necessity for me," he explains. "A single word can move me deeply. So I write pages and pages that may never be published."

Dominique Fernandez, author, editor, and member of the prestigious Académie française, thinks he knows why Banier's writing career has stagnated. Fernandez, an editor at the Grasset publishing house and a close personal friend of Banier's, considers him "a very good writer. He has spirit, clarity, vivacity, and rapidity." But instead of focusing on his writing, patiently developing his craft book after book, he allowed himself to be distracted by photography.

"He started out like a whirlwind, and then" — Fernandez shrugs. "He hasn't published anything in a long while. He threw himself into photography, that's what preoccupies him." That is a reflection of Banier's temperamental "dispersion," says Fernandez. As a photographer, he "runs through the streets chasing images. Writing requires concentration. He has a hard time concentrating." Banier hasn't grown as a writer "because he hasn't worked enough — and he knows it."

His career illustrates the dangers of being *surdoué* — supertalented — says Fernandez. "He's unpredictable, he jumps from one idea to another. And he himself has trouble knowing who he is. Sometimes he asks bizarre questions — 'Who am I?' — because there are too many things in him. He is too rich, too talented, and that's very difficult."

Fernandez doesn't use the word, but what he is really describing is a gifted dilettante. Banier takes photos, he writes, he paints, he draws; he does it all very well, but he lacks the discipline to fully develop his talent in any one field. Since all these activities are basically projections of himself — his ego, his identity — he is reluctant to commit to any one endeavor for fear, perhaps, that it would diminish his worth in the eyes of others. When *Le Monde* journalist Michel Guerrin asked him to define his real *métier,* Banier replied, "Writer." Why not photographer? "Photographer, like artist, is an inspiration. But writer is a craft." And yet, when his sixth novel, *Les femmes du métro Pompe,* came out in 2006, he didn't even want to promote it. Liliane scolded him like a schoolboy for his lack of commitment. "Promoting a book may be exhausting," she wrote him, "but is it better if no one talks about it? You should have thought about that before."

Who, indeed, is François-Marie Banier? Even

today, after so much about him has been revealed, it is impossible to answer that question with any certainty. Is he the former battered child crying out for love? Is he the charming and seductive character that so many people flocked to for his witty conversation and provocative originality? Is he the master manipulator and cynical schemer that much of the media — and the judges — have made him out to be? Or is he, as he sometimes suggests, a victim of Liliane Bettencourt's manipulation, the innocent object of her affections, and the ultimate expression of her own ego?

Banier himself can't tell you who he is: He hides as much as he reveals. The most useful insights come from the people who know him best — lovers, ex-lovers, close friends, even his lawyers. Martin d'Orgeval, who has shared Banier's life for nearly a quarter century, is a thoughtful man whose calm manner could not be more different from his partner's frenetic style. Looking younger than his forty-three years, he is tall and slender with a fashionable black stubble on his prominent chin. His large black-framed glasses give him the look of a university student, which is what he was twenty years ago when he earned his master's and began a doctorate (unfinished) in art history at the Sorbonne. Today he works as a photographer in his own right after serving for years as

Banier's assistant. His Left Bank studio on the rue Visconti, a space Banier purchased years ago from Madeleine Castaing, is filled with framed prints of his work — mostly landscapes and geometric plays on light and shadow. He consciously avoids the kind of portraiture that Banier specializes in.

"François-Marie is someone who is rather elusive," he explains. "He can be joyful, crazy, completely extravagant and funny, but inside he is dark, wounded, tortured. Often with joyful artists, there is a dark side." Banier is "someone who is free, you see that right away." But the cost of that freedom is that he is "ill-adapted" to the society around him. "He's a child. I live with a child. He fights against the reality of social, urban, and civic codes. People have this image of the man who succeeds at everything, who is very social. That image is long outdated. We never go out, we never go to dinner parties. We're pretty secretive."

Martin's uncle, Pascal Greggory, sixty-two, a veteran actor who has appeared in numerous French films, plays, and TV series, shared Banier's life for seven years from 1974 to 1981. Today, though Greggory lives in a separate building adjoining Banier's town house, the three of them are like a small family. "François-Marie is different from most people because of his sensibility," he says. "He's someone who is not in the consensus;

he lives on the margins. When you are on the margins, you need space, a lot of liberty. But he pays dearly for it."

Today, Greggory laments, Banier's image is based almost entirely on a distorted view of the Bettencourt Affair. "People see him as a crook, but he's not that. There is a Robin Hood side to him — he provokes people to see their reactions. But the aim is never financial gain. His relationship with Liliane Bettencourt is based on mutual affection. He has a phenomenal, enormous need to be loved — by Liliane or by an ordinary woman or man."

Banier has "no sense of guilt, no regret," says Greggory. "Everything is clear and sound in his mind. But he is struggling against the moral order, tilting against windmills, against very conventional people, because of these sums that are considered abnormal. But in this affair, everything is abnormal — the wealth, the characters of Liliane and François-Marie. People don't understand that. They only understand envy."

"Everybody who met François-Marie was charmed by him," says New York–based fashion designer Diane von Furstenberg, a close friend of Banier's since 1972 and one of his most ardent defenders. "He's the kind of person that exceptional people wanted to have around. It's not the other way around.

People are intrigued by him because he's very funny, and he's deep. It was his wit and his mind that were so sharp, his outlook. This wasn't just anybody."

One of the people who knows Banier best is his lawyer Laurent Merlet, who handled his copyright and libel matters for four years before becoming part of his defense team in 2010. "Everybody knows Banier is an excessive man, but excessive doesn't mean he's going to abuse anyone." Banier "explodes" but then he submerges himself in his work. "That's his personality. I think he was like that when he was twenty. In any case, you will never make him fall in line."

Merlet, a youthful-looking fifty-two-year-old with a striking resemblance to Harry Potter, admits that there is something abnormal, almost pathological, about his client's behavior. "He's hyperactive, he needs to see a doctor. He's not someone who makes plans, he's incapable of that. He's also incapable of realizing when he's in danger." Which explains, Merlet believes, why he could never say enough is enough as Liliane Bettencourt's gifts mounted into the hundreds of millions. "A rational person" would not have accepted such limitless largesse, he says, "but Banier doesn't say 'enough!' He is content. It gives him pleasure. It's easy to understand. The thing is he was not at all loved by his parents, and Liliane could not build a relationship with her daughter, so they found something to repair all that." Echoing a view that many others have voiced, including Banier himself, Merlet concludes: "He's a five-year-old child. You can do whatever you want with him. He's not someone who manipulates you."

Enigmatic, iconoclastic, eccentric, ungovernable. In the end, Banier is not someone who can be pinned down or pigeonholed. He is sui generis in the literal sense, one of a kind. Maybe that's what made him so attractive to Liliane — and so difficult to judge according to a moral code based on right and wrong, black and white, good and evil. In the complex Bettencourt saga, after all, there were strains of evil that had nothing to do with Banier.

CHAPTER 28
THE WHEELS OF JUSTICE

By the time the abuse case was reheard on appeal in May 2016, only four of the original ten defendants remained: Banier, d'Orgeval, Wilhelm, and the notary Patrice Bonduelle, accused of complicity in Wilhelm's machinations. Carlos Vejarano, ex-manager of the Île d'Arros, died of a degenerative brain disease in April 2016. Nurse Alain Thurin, who had attempted suicide on the eve of the first trial, was tried separately in October 2015 and acquitted. Patrice de Maistre and Jean-Michel Normand both abandoned their appeals after reaching agreements with the plaintiffs.

De Maistre's withdrawal followed two months of negotiations with lawyers for Madame Bettencourt. The financier's aim was to avoid the eighteen months of jail time and reduce the €12 million in damages that had been ordered at the first trial. The damages, payable to Liliane as plaintiff, were reportedly cut to €5 million. The Bettencourt camp had no authority concerning de Maistre's incarceration, but the withdrawal of their complaint against the financier led court officials to suspend the jail time. That was an immense relief to de Maistre, who had spent eighty-eight days in pretrial detention in 2013 and had no desire, at sixty-seven, to return behind bars. But he still had to pay the court a €250,000 fine and accept the shame of a definitive felony conviction. To add to his humiliation, he was officially stripped of the Légion d'honneur that had caused him such trouble, as well as the Ordre national du Mérite medal that he had received in 2000.

Curiously, the negotiations had been initiated not by de Maistre but by Olivier Pelat. While acting officially as Madame Bettencourt's legal representative, Pelat also had in mind the interests of his childhood friend Françoise Meyers. And Françoise had good reason to seek a deal with de Maistre. A key condition of the accord was the financier's abandonment of all the legal proceedings he had launched along the way, including, most significantly, his 2012 complaint for false testimony against Claire Thibout. Following on the heels of Banier's action against Thibout and five other witnesses, de Maistre's complaint had implicitly targeted Françoise. At a time when a Paris judge was looking into possible subornation charges, it was clearly in Françoise's interest for de Maistre to abandon his action. In the opinion of Patrick Ouart, Sarkozy's former adviser, that was "hardly the least important objective of this negotiation." Ouart didn't say so, but the deal also defused a possible threat to Sarkozy by effectively burying the mystery surrounding the €4 million in cash that de Maistre had brought in from Switzerland — money that he was suspected of funneling into the ex-president's campaign coffers. Now de Maistre would never have to appear in court and answer any more questions about the money trail.

The appeal hearing that began on May 10, 2016, covered much the same ground as the first trial. But the tone was markedly different. Presiding judge Michèle Esarté, though rigorous in her questioning, treated the defendants with respect. And Banier, who had undergone training sessions with a communications expert hired by his lawyers, abandoned his sarcastic, often abrasive manner in favor of an almost obsequious deference to the judges. Practically every answer he gave began with the ritual salutation "Madame la Présidente . . ." By contrast, Jean-Pierre Meyers, called as a witness by Banier, projected an air of arrogance and contempt in a three-and-a-half-hour appearance at the bar that was marked by his repeated refusals to answer questions from the defense. He pronounced the words "no comment," or variations thereof, more than twenty times. Meyers's performance won little sympathy from the court or the public, but then he was not the one on trial.

Though Judge Esarté bore in on the troubling questions — Liliane's long history of ill health and mental confusion, the murky circumstances of Banier's *légataire universel* designation, and his acceptance of the life-insurance policies — the civility from the bench gave the defense team some hope for a more lenient verdict. But their cautious optimism was tempered by lacerating final pleas from the Meyers lawyers and the prosecution's call to uphold the harsh sentences meted out at the first trial. At the conclusion of the two-week hearing, Esarté announced that the final verdict would be handed down on August 24. For the next three months, the defendants were free to go about their business — under a sword of Damocles.

Meanwhile, the wheels of justice began to turn in a different direction. On July 7, 2016, Judge Le Loire finally launched what Antoine Gillot had called "the atomic bomb" by putting Françoise Meyers under formal investigation for allegedly suborning witness Claire Thibout. Meyers had previously tried the judge's patience by refusing to answer a summons to appear before him in April. This time she did show up for questioning, under the implicit threat of being arrested and escorted to Le Loire's Paris office in handcuffs.

The judge got right to the point.

"Do you believe the testimony in your favor can be objective when [the witness] has received €700,000 from your own hand?" he demanded.

"This woman was drowning," Françoise replied, "out of work, without a salary, with two children . . ."

Le Loire then read aloud from the transcripts of wiretaps placed on the phones of the six accused witnesses. Claire Thibout had told one of her interlocutors, "The daughter comes out fine, for them everything is OK, but she needs to show more support, because I'm the one who went on the line for her, eh! And . . . uh . . . she's not exactly penniless!"

In a conversation recorded in May 2015, nurse Henriette Youpatchou is heard telling Dominique Gaspard, "We received less than . . . Claire Thibout in cash . . . and it wasn't traceable."

Le Loire asked Madame Meyers point-blank whether these witnesses had been "corrupted."

"Absolutely not!" she answered.

It was at the end of this interrogation that Le Loire officially pronounced Françoise *mise en examen* — under investigation on suspicion of bribing a witness.

Meyers's lawyer Jean Veil called the action groundless because the €300,000 in question was not a "payment" but a loan "that will be reimbursed." The judge clearly did not see things that way and continued to pursue the investigation that could possibly lead to Françoise's indictment and prosecution. Her lawyers say that's improbable. "In my opinion, no one will even be talking about this in six months," Veil predicted in August 2016. Nonetheless, Françoise's legal team was sufficiently worried to make discreet overtures to the Banier camp in hopes of inducing the photographer to withdraw his complaint against her. The initiative apparently went nowhere.

In the event that Françoise were tried and convicted, she would risk three years in prison and a €45,000 fine. It would be the greatest of ironies if the person who triggered this decadelong legal battle became its ultimate victim. It would also be a serious blow to the image of L'Oréal. Up to this point, the family firm had managed to prosper in spite of the negative publicity surrounding the daughter's suit, the mother's creeping dementia, and the lavishing of hundreds of millions of euros in L'Oréal dividends upon an eccentric photographer and artist. CEO Jean-Paul Agon shrugged off the effects of the suit in a 2009 interview, calling it "a private matter that concerns the family but in no way affects the management of the group." Indeed, the company consistently posted healthy growth figures throughout this period: an average 6.7 percent annual increase in sales between 2008 and 2015, with a surprising 15 percent jump in 2010, the year the story catapulted into the headlines. But a felony conviction of L'Oréal's future principal shareholder might be more difficult for the company to shrug off. Says former L'Oréal PR consultant Seth Goldschlager: "Françoise's legal situation is a problem, and it could become a bigger problem." Just how much of a problem, no one knows at this point.

One L'Oréal figure who made out quite well was Lindsay Owen-Jones. The dashing British-born executive, knighted by Queen Elizabeth, had led the company for eighteen years, then stayed on as president of the board of directors after handing over the top management job to Jean-Paul Agon in 2006. As OJ was preparing to step down as chief executive, Madame Bettencourt gave him a breathtaking farewell present of €100 million (on which she paid €30 million in taxes). This was in addition to his €381 million in stock options and €3.4 million annual retirement pension from L'Oréal. In her act of donation, Liliane stated that her gift to Owen-Jones was motivated by her "affection and personal gratitude for his exemplary performance in continuing the work begun by [her] father, Eugène Schueller."

The donation was supposed to remain secret, but Judge Prévost-Desprez discovered the paperwork in a July 2010 search of notary Jean-Michel Normand's bank box. Owen-Jones's acceptance of this eye-popping sum from a woman whose mental faculties were presumably declining struck Prévost-Desprez as a potential abuse of weakness. If Banier could be pursued for receiving lavish gifts from the heiress, she reasoned, why should Owen-Jones be treated differently? But Prévost-Desprez could not pursue Owen-Jones directly because she was authorized to investigate only the complaint against Banier. She says she planned to cite Liliane's gifts to Owen-Jones and others as potential abuses of weakness in her final report, but the case was wrested away from her and sent to Bordeaux before she got that far. "That way they limited the damage," she says with a sardonic laugh.

Owen-Jones's defenders point out that his gift was not comparable to Banier's take because the former L'Oréal CEO had made billions for the heiress through his brilliant stewardship of the company over nearly two decades. Sales grew sixfold during his tenure, the stock price increased twelvefold, and Liliane Bettencourt's personal fortune rose from €2.3 billion to €17 billion — an increase of

700 percent. Asked by a journalist if he had ever considered refusing the gift, Owen-Jones snapped, "On the contrary! I said thank you and I continue to say thank you. For me it was the final chapter of a fairy tale . . . I have no complex or regrets about it."

Even so, there were questions about the propriety of accepting €100 million from an aged woman who was at the center of an abuse case. One source close to the Meyers family suggests that Owen-Jones did not approve of Françoise's suit — and personally sought to broker an early peace settlement — because he was afraid of getting caught up in the investigation himself.

That didn't happen in the end, because the 2005 donation predated by sixteen months the onset of Liliane's "vulnerability" in the opinion of the court-appointed medical experts. The case that was finally brought against Banier and the others concerned only acts that occurred after September 1, 2006. Spared the indignity of a potential investigation and trial, Owen-Jones retired in 2012 to Lugano, Switzerland, in order to avoid French wealth taxes and sail Lake Maggiore on his 30-foot yacht. Standing at the bar of the Bordeaux courtroom, OJ's erstwhile friend Patrice de Maistre voiced what he considered a bitter irony: "Today, I am here, and he is in Lugano!"

■ ■ ■ ■

Even as its former CEO crossed the Alps, L'Oréal itself finally obviated the Swiss takeover threat that had hovered over it since the beginning of the affair. In February 2014, the company bought back 8 percent of its capital from Nestlé, giving the Bettencourt family a preponderant 33.1 percent of the stock to Nestlé's 23.29 percent. With Liliane under legal guardianship, L'Oréal's future is now firmly in the hands of her daughter and son-in-law. As stipulated by the December 2010 protocol, Jean-Pierre Meyers is the director general of the Thétys and Clymène holding companies that control the family's company stock and investments; Françoise is the titular president of both entities, as well as the Bettencourt Schueller Foundation. Jean-Pierre also serves as vice president of L'Oréal's board of directors, on which Françoise and her eldest son, Jean-Victor, hold seats.

Though they may weigh in on important decisions, the Meyerses will doubtless follow Liliane's example by leaving the actual management of the company in the hands of professionals like CEO Jean-Paul Agon. "This family has always delegated the direction of L'Oréal to someone outside the family," says Marie-France Lavarini, a communications advisor to the Meyerses. "That has always worked well, and they want that to continue."

What is less sure is the degree to which the Meyers sons, both unmarried, will be implicated in the firm. Though they will one day be the major shareholders, their passions do not appear to lie with the shampoos, gels, and hair sprays that made the family fortune. Jean-Victor, now thirty, is a fashion maven who designs upscale cashmere sweaters (all black or gray with prices starting at €650) for his own boutique on the rue Saint-Honoré. Nicolas, twenty-eight, who has apprenticed at Swatch headquarters in Switzerland, plans to create his own watchmaking company. For Liliane, who had L'Oréal running through her veins, the current bent of her grandsons might be disappointing — though she apparently never talked to them about their future in the company. All that matters little now: She is no longer aware of their doings.

In his eloquent final plea for Martin d'Orgeval, Richard Malka compared the Bettencourt story to the ancient Greek myth of the Atreides, the descendants of the Mycenaean king Atreus, condemned by an ancient curse to destroy one another out of jealousy, ambition, vengeance, and the quest for power. The most grisly episode was the feast to which Atreus invited his rivalrous brother, Thyestes, only to serve up his three murdered sons in a delicious meat stew. The strife ended, fittingly enough, with a public trial in which Orestes, son of Agamemnon, was acquitted for the revenge murder of his mother and her lover.

The story of the Atreides is one that Françoise Meyers knows by heart: She devoted seven chapters to it in her book on Greek mythology. One passage that jumps out is her account of Electra, sister of Orestes, who we are told nurtured "one of history's most beautiful hatreds" for her adulterous mother. Things never got quite that bad in the house of Bettencourt, but as Malka argues, "The reality of this family is not peace, it is war. You cannot grasp this affair without understanding its dimension of Greek tragedy."

If the Bettencourts were not literally a family at war with itself, they were undoubtedly a family riven by conflicting desires, jealousies, and resentments. A family of things unsaid. No one talked about Schueller's dark past — was that the original family curse? — or André's proclivities, or Liliane's discreet private life. Just as no one talked about money, or secret political payments, or Liliane's not-so-secret loathing for her son-in-law. Most of all, no one in the family talked openly about Banier's alleged machinations until Françoise finally lashed out. Following the death of the prince consort, the princess attacked the queen's jester. But perhaps her real aim was to seize the throne and the royal treasure — and to defang and humiliate the queen who had always shown her more scorn than love. All this might be just a fanciful interpretation of this complex family drama. What cannot be denied is the ineffable sadness at its heart. As Tolstoy wrote: "Every unhappy family is unhappy in its own way."

CHAPTER 29
FAREWELL TO PARADISE?

Thursday, August 11, 2016. Time was running out on François-Marie Banier. In less than two weeks, he would stand in a Bordeaux courtroom and hear the appeal verdict. If his prison sentence was upheld, court bailiffs would bundle him straight off to jail. If not, he would be a free man even if he was ordered to pay millions in damages. The final possibility was a full acquittal. In that case, Banier could walk out of the courtroom, keep what remained of Liliane Bettencourt's largesse, and put the affair behind him for good. His lawyers were not optimistic about that last scenario.

Banier was spending this time at Le Patron, his palatial retreat in the south of France, a three-story eighteenth-century Italianate villa surrounded by classical statues, gurgling fountains, manicured gardens, and nearly 1,500 acres of land. The five stone outbuildings of this former farm compound contain a garage for Banier's Mercedes and BMW (both used), guest apartments, storage areas, and, in an immense space above a disaffected stable, the painting studio where Banier spends six to eight hours a day.

Standing at the end of a long gravel driveway, clad in a rust-colored shirt with paint-stained cuffs, black-and-white plaid pants, and red slip-ons, Banier escorts me into the main house, a square stone edifice glazed with cream-colored stucco. Two gray Weimaraner dogs, Chérie and Esmeralda, follow their master everywhere.

The central gallery that cuts through the ground floor is lined with statues on marble pedestals and outsize framed prints of Banier photos — including one of Picasso's studio. Up the winding stone staircase, graced by a seventeenth-century Italian tapestry, another long gallery boasts matching canapés and armchairs from Imperial Russia, more paintings, and a baby-grand piano.

The piano prompts an anecdote. Once, when he was still young and beautiful, Banier was at a party attended by Richard Burton and Elizabeth Taylor. He spotted a piano in the drawing room and offered to play for the guests. "Oh yes, by all means," said Burton, well into his cups. Banier objected that there was no piano stool. "No problem," said Burton, who got down on his hands and knees and invited the young man to sit on his back. Banier did so and proceeded to bang on the keys with both hands. "I can't play the piano at all," says Banier, "it was a dreadful racket. But Burton howled with laughter. He loved it."

The four second-floor bedrooms, each with its own decorating theme, are voluptuous and intimate. Johnny Depp slept in this one. Liliane preferred that one. Faye Dunaway (who stayed three weeks) slept in another one. Banier's master bedroom, bathed in a Tuscan light, is on the next floor up, as are Martin's office, a dusty library, and a large open room with a full-size movie screen and projector.

Banier prides himself on the way he has fitted out the place. "Princess Caroline told me this is the most beautiful house in the south of France."

He purchased the property in 1987 with filmmaker David Rocksavage, aka Lord Cholmondeley, who was his closest friend at the time. They paid 2,650,000 francs (the equivalent of some $424,000), the bulk of which was financed by a mortgage. It was seemingly a steal at that price, but Banier says the place was a "ruin," requiring millions for restoration, landscaping, and improvements — like the 11-kilometer stone wall surrounding the compound and the swimming pool tucked into a wooded area near the main house. One of Banier's greatest coups was to persuade the local authorities to move a departmental road that cut right through the back garden.

Though the property was purchased before Liliane began raining money on him, it is clear that more than a few of her millions went into the renovations and improvements. Banier eventually bought out Rocksavage's share and is now sole owner of the estate.

The property sits on the outskirts of a sleepy village located 30 kilometers east of Nîmes in the Languedoc wine-growing region. The surrounding countryside is dominated by vineyards and gnarly scrubland — *la garrigue* to locals — nestled between wooded hills. Like the rest of the Provence region, it is hot and dry in the summer, chilled in winter by the northerly *mistral* wind, and, according to Banier, populated by some of the country's most cantankerous citizens.

Like an English squire inspecting his domains, he takes me on a tour of the grounds. At the end of the garden, we cross a stone bridge leading to an immense open field covered with scraggly grass. In a far corner, huddled around a rail fence, a half dozen longhorn bulls turn lazily to look in our direction. Banier doesn't raise them for beef; they are there to graze and keep the grass down. In another corner of the field, seven white horses stand in the shade, munching grass and flicking their tails at the flies. When he's not painting in his studio, writing, or entertaining guests, Banier likes to ride them bare-back.

He waves at a figure standing among the cattle, a man of medium height with a faded blue cloth cap, graying hair, and a perfectly round face. It's the employee who takes care of his livestock, a timeless *paysan* who might have leapt from the pages of a Marcel Pagnol novel. Cocking his head toward the horses, Banier asks him about a certain mare that has lost an eye. "You know, the one I got for my fiftieth birthday."

"*Oui,* Monsieur Banier," the man says in the lilting accent of southern France. "She's getting up in years now."

"Have a look at her. If she's suffering, I want you to put her down. I can't stand to see an animal suffer."

Banier is in his studio, surrounded by dozens of canvases large and small. The place smells of oil paint, linseed oil, and turpentine. Working frenetically, instinctively, he has lost count of how many paintings he has done since arriving here three weeks ago — fifty, eighty, a hundred? Most of them consist of stark black strokes on a white background, emblematic, he says, of the "grave" times we live in — rife with racism, poverty, violence, terrorism. There are ISIS fighters with phallic rifle barrels, frightened children running into the void, menacing skull-like faces with jagged

510

teeth. "I am very much affected by current events," he says. "The only thing that counts for me is emotion."

Louis Armstrong's gospel album is playing at almost ear-splitting volume:

Nobody knows the trouble I've seen,
    nobody knows but
Jesus . . .

Banier points to a large vertical canvas he calls *Mère et fille* — mother and daughter. It depicts a woman in a long, flowing dress who is smiling triumphantly and sitting atop another pathetic, defeated-looking woman with boxing gloves at the end of her drooping arms. He doesn't need to say who it represents.

Sometimes I'm up, sometimes I'm down,
    yes, yes, Lord,
Sometimes I'm almost to the ground, yes,
    yes, Lord . . .

"I'm always happy when I'm painting," he says. "I can't live without it. It's like breathing." He admits that his canvases have little commercial success — in fact, he has only rarely shown them.

Over a lunch of sautéed sole, served on a stone table in the shaded garden, Banier's conversation careens from painting and music to his rotten childhood, friends he's lost to the AIDS epidemic, his relationship with Liliane. As always, he talks about the famous people he has rubbed shoulders with: Rudolf Nureyev, Prince Charles, Bianca Jagger, and Vanessa Paradis, who is coming to visit in a few days. A talented mimic, he does a hilarious impression of Salvador Dalí, with a Spanish accent you could cut with a Toledo saber. One begins to understand how his verbal panache and youthful beauty once allowed him to dominate a soirée, fascinate male and female alike, suck all the oxygen out of a room. But that was then. Today he is all too conscious of the passing years. "Before I die, will I have time to accomplish all I want to do, to write and paint and photograph? I feel the urgency."

I bring the conversation back to the affair and the verdict that awaits him in Bordeaux: "You're in paradise now, but in two weeks . . . ?"

"Paradise is inside me," he replies.

What does he expect in Bordeaux? Is he afraid of going to prison?

"I was tortured by my father, I attempted suicide, what more do I have to fear?"

A long silence is broken only by the drone of cicadas and the splashing of a fountain. Banier takes a swig of Diet Coke and offers a final thought: "This affair will be judged by history. It's not my thing."

Yes, it is your thing, François-Marie. Like it or not, your place in history will be forever linked to it.

Several days later, Vanessa Paradis calls me on the phone. She is visiting Banier, trying to comfort him while he waits to hear his fate. She is fiercely devoted to him, ever since she and her then boyfriend Johnny Depp attended Banier's fiftieth birthday party at his villa back in 1997. Two years later, when the couple's daughter Lily-Rose was born, they asked him to be her godfather.

"I love him, I admire him, I feel for him. He moves me and makes me laugh," she says in a surprisingly girlish voice, something like a bubbly American teenager with a French accent. "He's as pure as a little boy. He has defects, yeah, who doesn't?" He's getting a bum rap, she says, because he's "the perfect villain — it's easy to point at him because he's not an easy one to understand. He's the ideal bad guy. He's like a figure in a novel." The amounts Liliane Bettencourt gave him might seem "disgusting" to some people, but "I totally understand that she would want to cover him with presents because she loves him. Once you love him, you love him." Right now, one week before the verdict comes down, Paradis confesses that she is worried about her friend. "The only thing we speak about is how it might come out for him," she says. "I have no idea, but I hope he's not going to prison. I don't think he'd do well in prison. Some people are more fragile than others."

CHAPTER 30
THE VERDICT

Wednesday, August 24, 2016. A relentless sun beats down on the gray stone buildings and parches the shrubbery in the little park across from Bordeaux's neoclassical courthouse. Inside the main hall, a clutch of photographers and reporters lie in wait. The atmosphere is quiet, almost sleepy. It's the middle of France's sacrosanct vacation season, a time when even the wheels of justice slow down.

Suddenly the cameras click and flash like a battery of machine guns. Banier enters the hall, followed by Martin d'Orgeval and their team of lawyers. They proceed to courtroom G, a churchlike chamber with stained-glass windows and allegorical frescoes on the ceiling. Banier, *très élégant* in a medium-gray suit with a black-and-white tie, takes his accustomed place on the defendants' bench to the right of the aisle. He adjusts his discreet behind-the-ear hearing aids, dons his blue-framed glasses, and begins to write in a black notebook. On his knees lies a paperback volume of *La Curée,* part of Émile Zola's nineteenth-century saga about the rise and fall of a wealthy French family. Martin d'Orgeval sits silently beside him, his cheeks and chin dusted by a four-day beard. To Martin's right is Pascal Wilhelm, Liliane's former lawyer and protector, tanned and fit after his vacation on the Greek islands. The fourth defendant, notary Patrick Bonduelle, is absent.

While waiting for the judges, a dozen lawyers, dressed in their long black robes, mingle and murmur. Though they fought bitterly during the hearings, the attorneys for both sides now chat with one another as easily as fellow members of an elite fraternity — which is what they are.

At two p.m., presiding judge Michèle Esarté and her two associates enter the courtroom. "You may be seated," Esarté says, and calls the defendants up to the bar.

The three men stand side by side facing the judges. Banier has his arms behind his back, his right hand clutching his left wrist. D'Orgeval folds his arms across his chest. Wilhelm, looking shorter than usual next to the six-foot d'Orgeval, clasps his hands tightly behind his back. None of the defendants moves during the reading of the verdict.

The judge pronounces all three men guilty of *abus de faiblesse* and related charges, confirming the original trial verdict. But the sentencing sends a mixed message. Instead of two and a half years hard prison time, Banier is given a suspended four-year sentence. His fine is raised from €350,000 to €375,000. The state confiscates one of his apartments and the proceeds of insurance contracts now worth €140 million. But in a major concession, the judges wipe out the €158 million in civil damages that he was initially ordered to pay to Liliane Bettencourt. As for Martin d'Orgeval, his original sentence is upheld — a suspended eighteen-month prison term and a €150,000 fine — but his €2.3 million damage payment is struck down. Wilhelm's sentence is reduced from eighteen months hard time to twelve months suspended, with €3 million in damages. The absent notary Bonduelle is acquitted.

Banier's hope of escaping conviction because of tainted testimony proved vain. Though the investigations into suspected subornation and perjury may possibly result in prosecutions down the line, the appeals court ruled that the accounts of those witnesses were not "determining" factors in light of the other testimony, recordings, and documents that were deemed sufficient to prove his guilt. On the other hand, the judges threw out the civil damages levied against Banier because they considered that the family's demand of €158 million amounted to a restitution of Liliane's donations during the period in question, whereas the December 2010 protocol specifically allowed Banier to keep all gifts prior to that date.

It is all over in fifteen minutes. Judge Esarté closes the session and quickly exits with her associates. As the lawyers gather up their papers, Banier resumes his seat on the defendants' bench, beads of sweat glistening on his creased forehead. What is he thinking at this precise moment? "I think of Liliane. Through me, she's the one whose freedom is trampled. It's a story based on morality, not law."

In the hall outside the courtroom, lawyers for both sides joust with one another before the microphones and cameras. "It's a total slap in the face for Françoise Bettencourt Meyers," says Banier's lawyer, Laurent Merlet, "because instead of the 158 million they won in the first trial, they now leave here with zero. Banier keeps his millions." Arnaud Dupin, a lawyer for the Bettencourt family, ripostes: "François-Marie Banier is a criminal; he was just declared guilty of abuse of weakness."

Liliane Bettencourt's lawyers considered her the main winner because the man who allegedly exploited her was convicted as charged. But is this what Liliane Bettencourt really wanted — this proud and feisty woman who from the beginning fought against her daughter's suit, denied her victimhood, defended Banier, and insisted for two decades that her gifts were voluntary and intentional? Surely Banier profited from her excessive largesse — for the amounts were indeed excessive, even obscene in the eyes of most observers — and he should have started saying no thanks when it became apparent that her mental faculties were slipping. And maybe he did cajole and manipulate her, as the judgment states. But whatever blame is assigned to Banier, it is quite a leap to call his conviction a victory for Liliane.

Nor was it a total defeat for Banier. Despite the opprobrium of a guilty verdict, he managed to avoid hard prison time and got to keep his €158 million. As the French say, *il a sauvé les meubles* — he saved the furniture. The downside for him is that the affair poisoned his life for a decade, blighted his reputation, and cost him millions in legal fees — even though those millions came largely from Liliane. Fairly or unfairly, terms "gigolo," "dandy," and "guru" will remain forever fixed to his name in the minds of many.

It seems that the biggest victors were Françoise and Jean-Pierre Meyers. Not only did they obtain Banier's conviction in court, but they successfully used the affair to gain control over Liliane and her fortune. Via the December 2010 protocol, Jean-Pierre took

charge of the family holding companies —
which no longer pay Liliane her dividends —
while Françoise received €300 million and
control of the family's L'Oréal shares. Not to
mention the €12 million she obtained from
her mother to pay her own lawyers. Unless
she is tripped up by the still-unresolved
subornation charges, Françoise could say she
made out quite well.

From the beginning, she insisted her suit
was about protecting her mother. But money
was always at the center of the battle. Money
heaped on Banier. Money stashed away in
Switzerland. Money allegedly slipped to the
president of France. Money paid to whistle-
blower Claire Thibout. Money raked in by
Françoise. Money bequeathed to her sons.
Money was the thing that defined the Bettencourt Affair — and the heiress herself — in
the eyes of the public. Which is why, given
the peculiar French prejudice against wealth,
popular opinion did not look on Liliane
Bettencourt as a sympathetic figure. She was
"Mamie Zinzin," a barmy old dame with
more money than she knew what to do with
— such a cruel caricature for the proud,
elegant, regal figure she had been.

The biggest loser was the heiress herself,
who now languishes in her gilded cage under
the legal guardianship of her daughter and
grandsons — exactly the fate she always
wanted to avoid. These days, she is held in

almost complete isolation: Even her closest friends are not allowed to see her. But the greatest tragedy that confronts Liliane Bettencourt is what Charles de Gaulle called the "shipwreck" of old age. Money can make it easier to deal with the material and logistical problems of aging, but it cannot solve the human condition. In a society that sees old age as something shameful and repulsive, the elderly are treated as weak, incompetent, and vulnerable even if they are sitting on one of the world's biggest fortunes. And death is, of course, the ultimate leveler.

Who can say how all this would have wound up if advancing years and creeping senility had not intervened to rob the heiress of her free will? Would a younger and more lucid Liliane Bettencourt have continued to shower gold on Banier, or would she have risen up one day and told him *"Raus"*? Would she have yanked her L'Oréal shares back from her daughter, or sold them to Nestlé? Would she have retired to the Île d'Arros and left all the emotional strife and financial wrangling behind her? We'll never know.

Lawyers for both parties have filed petitions with the *Cour de cassation,* France's highest jurisdiction, to have the judgment overturned: The Meyers side seeks to restore the damages; the Banier side wants to reverse the conviction. But the whole exercise seems like legal posturing by lawyers who don't know when to quit — as long as the meter is running. The cassation court rejects decisions only based on procedural errors, not substance, and no one seriously expects it to strike down the rigorous appeal judgment.

For Banier, the Bettencourt Affair is pretty much over. For Françoise Meyers and the witnesses who supported her, not quite. Their fate is still in the hands of a Parisian magistrate who is famous for taking his time. Ironically, in spite of her courtroom victory, Françoise and her family remain in a state of stress and uncertainty that is at least partly self-inflicted.

Saturday, September 24, 2016. Banier sits in a Left Bank café near the Luxembourg gardens. Weekend visitors to the famous Parisian park stroll among the manicured flower beds and the rows of chestnut trees while kids sail toy boats on the circular basin. Just across the street from the café sits the seventeenth-century Luxembourg Palace, home of the French Senate where André Bettencourt spent the better part of his political career. But Banier's thoughts are not on André. He is trying to put the affair behind him and look to the future.

At the age of sixty-nine, after the decade-long ordeal, he is strangely full of optimism. "I have a novel to finish before starting a new play. I have thousands of pages to revise. I get tremendous pleasure from my work." Since the legal action ended, he says he is "back in touch" with himself. "I have become what I was before all that. I am finally freed of the obligation to explain myself. My dreams are whole again."

What impact did the affair have on him? "While it was going on, it was difficult for me. Nothing next to what Liliane suffered. She still lives entirely within me. Her humor, her warmth — I remember it all like yesterday. Dear Liliane." Banier makes no mention of the fortune she bestowed upon him, or the fact that he has come out of the affair a very wealthy man.

And how does Liliane look back on it all? Her last known comment on the subject came in January 2012, when she was interrogated at her home by Judge Jean-Michel Gentil. Well into Alzheimer's by that time, she remembered nothing about de Maistre, or Wilhelm, or Stéphane Courbit, or any of the others. But when Gentil mentioned Banier's name, she said, "I don't want to talk about him." Did Banier abuse her, Gentil asked. "Surely, a bit, but I don't care. I'm not going to get sick over it. I don't have time to lose over that. I don't deny his faults, but I was a victim of my own enthusiasms. If he took money from me, I don't give a damn. I accept the consequences of my mistakes. I'm not going to sit around and cry about it."

EPILOGUE
WINGS

Friday, October 21, 2016. It is Liliane Bettencourt's ninety-fourth birthday. Françoise and
her son Jean-Victor take her to lunch at the
Ritz to mark the occasion. Elegantly coiffed,
sporting gray wool pants, a long tan coat,
and a multicolored silk scarf, she recalls the
Liliane of old. But she is visibly feeble, shuf-
fling slowly as she clutches the arms of her
daughter and grandson. She stops to say a
pleasant word to the uniformed doorman,
her social instincts still flickering like the light
of a dying candle. But she doesn't know it's
her birthday, and if someone tells her, she
immediately forgets. She is on her cloud.

Those close to Liliane say she is not unhappy. "Serene" is the word Françoise uses.
She can still walk in her garden, with assistance, and swim in her pool. She travels
with her family to Formentor, Arcouest, and
other destinations — preferably sunny ones,
though her island in the Seychelles is long
gone. Not that she remembers ever owning

it. Her mind slips in and out of time. Liliane lives with the dead souls from her past more than the people who surround her today. She doesn't always recognize her daughter. Her grandsons are strangers to her. Olivier Pelat, who has known Liliane since his childhood, says she hasn't a clue who he is. "She knows I am someone close to her, she says *tu* to me, but she couldn't tell you my name." Still, as Liliane's guardian for legal matters, Pelat considers it his duty to keep her informed about the judicial proceedings even though she understands nothing. As he prepared to take his leave after one visit, she told him, "Don't go yet, Papa will be home any minute."

And Banier? Today, Liliane doesn't even remember his name. Nor anything about him — not his witty conversation, his photos, his letters; not their trips together, or their restaurant dinners, or the gallery openings, or the hundreds of millions she showered on him. But unless Françoise has removed it, she still has a Banier painting hanging on the wall of her bedroom. It is the image of a woman, drawn with a rapid stroke that ends in a graffiti-like inscription:
With you we have wings . . .

CAST OF CHARACTERS

François-Marie Banier (1947–) Photographer-writer-artist who became Liliane Bettencourt's confidant and received hundreds of millions of euros in gifts from her over two decades.

André Bettencourt (1919–2007) Husband of Liliane Bettencourt and father of Françoise Bettencourt Meyers. Had a long political career as a deputy, senator, and minister.

Liliane Schueller Bettencourt (1922–) Daughter of L'Oréal founder Eugène Schueller, heiress to his fortune, currently the world's wealthiest woman. Her extravagant gifts to photographer François-Marie Banier prompted her daughter's 2007 suit and launched the so-called Bettencourt Affair.

Françoise Bettencourt Meyers (1953–) Daughter of André and Liliane Bettencourt. Wife of Jean-Pierre Meyers, mother of Jean-Victor (b. 1986) and Nicolas Meyers (b. 1988). Amateur pianist, author of works on the Bible and Greek mythology. Plaintiff in the 2007 suit against François-Marie Banier.

Pascal Bonnefoy (1963–) André Bettencourt's longtime valet, later served as Liliane Bettencourt's butler and secretly recorded her conversations with advisers. Currently runs a seaside hotel in Brittany.

Gilles Brücker (1946–) Professor of public health at University of Paris-Sud, cofounder and former president of Doctors Without Borders, childhood friend of François-Marie Banier, former medical adviser to Liliane Bettencourt.

Pierre (aka Pascal) Castres Saint Martin (1936–) Former L'Oréal executive who served as Liliane Bettencourt's financial adviser from 2002 to 2004.

Pierre Cornut-Gentille (1950–) Senior defense attorney for Banier.

Jacques Corrèze (1912–1990) Member in the 1930s of the pro-Fascist Cagoule movement, later active in its successor groups under the Nazi Occupation and volunteered to fight alongside the Waffen-SS. Hired by Eugène Schueller after the war, he became head of L'Oréal's US subsidiary.

Stéphane Courbit (1965–) French businessman, friend of ex-president Nicolas Sarkozy, client of attorney Pascal Wilhelm.

Philippe Courroye (1959–) Former prosecutor in the Paris suburb of Nanterre, headed the initial investigation of Banier.

François Dalle (1918–2005) Friend of François Mitterrand and André Bettencourt from their student days. Succeeded Eugène Schueller as L'Oréal's CEO in 1957 and successfully ran the company until his retirement in 1984.

Christiane Djenane (1950–) Former secretary and assistant to Liliane Bettencourt.

Benoît Ducos-Ader (1945–) Attorney for Liliane Bettencourt.

Jean Frydman (1925–) French-Israeli businessman who formed a film distribution venture with L'Oréal's ex-CEO François Dalle in 1987. Their subsequent falling-out had dramatic consequences for the company and for André Bettencourt.

Dominique Gaspard (1956–) Former chambermaid to Liliane Bettencourt.

Jean-Pierre Gentil (1961–) Bordeaux-based magistrate who took over the Bettencourt investigations in November 2010 and sent ten defendants to trial.

Antoine Gillot (1956–) Attorney for Claire Thibout and Pascal Bonnefoy.

Valéry Giscard d'Estaing (1926–) President of France from 1974 to 1981. Political ally of André Bettencourt.

Fabrice Goguel (1946–) Liliane Bettencourt's former lawyer for tax and financial matters.

Pascal Greggory (1954–) Actor, uncle of Martin d'Orgeval, and former partner of François-Marie Banier.

Claude Guéant (1945–) Former prefect and director of France's National Police, served as chief of staff under President Nicolas Sarkozy from 2007 to 2011, then as interior minister until 2012.

Thierry Herzog (1955–) Attorney for ex-president Nicolas Sarkozy.

Nicolas Huc-Morel (1975–) Attorney for Françoise Bettencourt Meyers and her two sons, former associate of Olivier Metzner.

Georges Kiejman (1932–) Former cabinet member under President François Mitterrand and a leading criminal lawyer. Represented Liliane Bettencourt in opposing her daughter's suit from 2009 to 2011.

Monique de Libouton (1922–) Close friend of Liliane Bettencourt since 1942.

Patrice de Maistre (1949–) Financier who advised Liliane Bettencourt and managed her investments from 2003 to 2010.

Richard Malka (1968–) Defense attorney for Martin d'Orgeval, novelist, graphic-novel scenarist.

Laurent Merlet (1965–) Defense and copyright attorney for François-Marie Banier.

Olivier Metzner (1949–2013) One of France's top criminal lawyers who represented Françoise Meyers in her 2007 suit against Banier.

François Mitterrand (1916–1996) French president from 1981 to 1995 and friend of André Bettencourt.

Jean-Michel Normand (1934–) Former notary for Liliane Bettencourt. Registered most of her gifts to Banier.

Martin Le Barrois d'Orgeval (1973–) Photographer and partner of François-Marie Banier since 1991.

Patrick Ouart (1959–) Former judicial adviser to President Nicolas Sarkozy.

Lindsay Owen-Jones (1946–) British-born head of L'Oréal from 1988 to 2011, yachtsman, Formula 1 driver, knighted by Queen Elizabeth in 2005.

Olivier Pelat (1958–) Real estate promoter and longtime friend of the Bettencourt family. Named Liliane Bettencourt's guardian for legal matters (*tuteur ad hoc*) in October 2011.

Georges Pompidou (1911–1974) President of France from 1969 to 1974, friend of André and Liliane Bettencourt.

Isabelle Prévost-Desprez (1959–) Former judge in the Paris suburb of Nanterre. Opened a new case against Banier in July 2009 as Prosecutor Philippe Courroye prepared to close his investigation.

Denis Roucou (1960–) Bordeaux-based judge who presided over the 2015 trial of Banier and nine other defendants on abuse of weakness charges, as well as three related hearings stemming from the Bettencourt case.

Lucienne de Rozier (1925–) Longtime friend

and neighbor of Liliane Bettencourt.

Nicolas Sarkozy (1955–) French president from 2007 to 2012 whose implication in the Bettencourt Affair hurt him politically.

Eugène Schueller (1881–1957) Founder of L'Oréal, the world's leading cosmetics firm, and of one of the world's wealthiest family dynasties. Father of Liliane Schueller Bettencourt.

Hervé Temime (1957–) Former defense attorney for Banier (2009–2010).

Claire Thibout (1958–) Former Bettencourt accountant. One of the original witnesses supporting Françoise Meyers's suit against Banier.

Alain Thurin (1960–) Liliane Bettencourt's former nurse.

Chantal Trovel (1947–) Former secretary to André Bettencourt, later assistant to Liliane Bettencourt.

Jean Veil (1947–) Attorney for Françoise Bettencourt Meyers.

Pascal Wilhelm (1961–) Former attorney for Liliane Bettencourt. Named her protector and financial manager in 2010.

Éric Woerth (1956–) Former budget and labor minister under ex-president Nicolas Sarkozy, also served as treasurer for Sarkozy's UMP Party and 2007 campaign.

Florence Woerth (1956–) Wife of Éric Woerth. Worked for the holding company that handles Liliane Bettencourt's investments from 2007 to 2010.

Henriette Youpatchou (1961–) Former nurse for Liliane Bettencourt.

ACKNOWLEDGMENTS

In addition to the sources previously named in the Author's Note, I would like to thank the following people for their time and assistance going back to 2010: Bruno Abescat, Douce de Andia, Marc Audibet, Corinne Audouin, Nicolas Banier, Jean-Marc Berlière, Claire Bommelaer, François Bonduel, Pascal Bonnefoy, François Bonnet, Marion Bougeard, Gilles Brücker, Alain Carignon, Stéphanie Carson-Parker, Pierre Castres Saint Martin, Diane de Clairval, Roland Coutanceau, Pierre Cornut-Gentille, Gilles Delafon, Brune Dircq, Renaud Donnedieu de Vabres, Christiane Dufour, Stéphane Durand-Souffland, Laura Essner, Judy Fayard, Dominique Fernandez, Diane von Furstenberg, Herré Gattegno, Antoine Gillot, Seth Goldschlager, Claude Herambourg, Evelyne Herambourg, Nicolas Huc-Morel, Georges Kiejman, Annie Lacroix-Riz, Marie-France Lavarini, Sophie Lamouroux, François Le Goarant de Tromelin, Fabrice

Lhomme, Richard Malka, Guy Marineau, Laurent Merlet, Olivier Metzner, Gérard Miller, Jean-Luc Monterosso, Nadine Morano, Janine Mossuz-Lavau, Laurent Obadia, Vanessa Paradis, Pascal Perrineau, Monique Pinçon-Charlot, Edwy Plenel, Bernard Rideau, Jean-Michel Ribes, Pascale Robert-Diard, Julian Sancton, Claire Senard, Dominique Simonnot, Jean-Marie Schmit, Hervé Temime, Patricia Topolsky, Claude Delay Tubiana, Jean-Pierre Valériola, Hubert Védrine, Jean Veil, Michel Wieriorka, and Pascal Wilhelm.

Special thanks also to my agent, Katherine Flynn, who first encouraged me to write this book; my editor at Dutton, Jill Schwartzman, whose guidance and deft touch were invaluable; and my wife, Sylvaine, who read through all the drafts and provided many useful suggestions along the way.

NOTES

Prologue: Lost in the Fog

"Is it because she has no memory": François-Marie Banier, *Balthazar, fils de famille* (Paris: Editions Gallimard, 1985), 114.

world's richest woman, worth $36.1 billion: *Forbes* website, accessed online November 14, 2016, http://www.forbes.com/pictures/heik45k/liliane-bettencourt/#3f6f27be482b.

"the odious accusations that I read": Liliane Bettencourt, *Déclaration de Madame Liliane Schueller Bettencourt,* Formentor, July 23, 2010. Distributed by her press attaché.

Perhaps it all started: Details on Arcouest house and luncheon from Marie-France Etchegoin, *Un milliard de secrets* (Paris: Robert Laffont, 2011), 67.

Banier always denied it: François-Marie Banier, interview with author, September

28, 2015; Etchegoin, *Milliard de secrets,* 101.

Meyers had formerly lived with: Pascal Greggory, interview with author, December 12, 2015; Richard Malka, interview with author, June 9, 2016; Georges Kiejman, interview with author, July 8, 2015; Stéphane Durand-Souffland, "Au procès Bettencourt, le compagnon de François-Marie Banier a adopté une posture détachée," *Le Figaro,* May 14, 2016, accessed online May 15, 2016, http://www.lefigaro.fr/actualite-france/2016/05/13/01016-2016 0513ARTFIG00312-d-orgeval-rubens-et -les-cadeaux-du-bonheur.php.

"He started speaking": "Françoise Bettencourt Meyers, l'interview vérité," *Le Figaro,* June 25, 2010.

"Banier addressed Monsieur with irony": Quoted by Hervé Gattegno, "Le majordome qui a fait trembler Sarkozy," *Vanity Fair* (French edition), June 26, 2014, accessed online June 1, 2015, http://www .vanityfair.fr/actualites/france/articles/ exclusif-affaire-bettencourt-le-majordome -bonnefoy-a-pose-un-dictaphone/14593.

Banier remembers the scene: Etchegoin, *Milliard de secrets,* 69–70.

anti-Semitic diatribes: For details on André Bettencourt's wartime articles and Eugène Schueller's collaboration see chapters 1, 2, and 6.

"pulled into a sect" . . . **"That was too much":** Françoise Bettencourt Meyers, "Je n'ai qu'un but: retrouver ma mère," *Elle,* July 9, 2010, 12.

she filed a criminal complaint: Olivier Metzner, complaint of December 19, 2007. Court document D00026.

Chapter 1: The Founder

a cook in his native Alsace: Pierre Volf, "Note pour M. Eugène Schueller," May 10, 1948, 2. Archives Nationales Z/6 NL/498 dossier 11108. This is the complete investigative file on Schueller's suspected Nazi collaboration, referred to hereafter in abbreviated form as AN Z/6.

son of a shoemaker: Bruno Abescat, *La saga des Bettencourt* (Paris: Plon, 10 2010), 62.

Schueller moved to Paris in 1871: Eugène Schueller deposition before the Cour de Justice, February 11, 1948, AN Z/6; Abescat, *La saga,* 62–63.

"Life was very rude": Schueller deposition, February 11, 1948, AN Z/6.

collapse of the Panama Canal Company: Abescat, *La saga,* 63; Schueller deposition, February 11, 1948.

"I succeeded brilliantly": Schueller deposition, February 11, 1948.

most of the lead-based concoctions:

Jacques Marseille, *L'Oréal: 1909–2009* (Paris: Perrin, 2009), 13.

"damages the brain and the eyesight": Blanche Staffe, *Usages du monde, règles du savoir-vivre dans la société moderne, par la Baronne Staffe* (Paris: Victor-Havard, 1893), quoted in Marseille, *L'Oréal,* 25.

Schueller agreed to become: Schueller deposition, February 11, 1948.

"It was a very difficult time": Ibid.

In 1909, he founded: On the early history of the company, Marseille, *L'Oréal,* 13–19.

Things moved quickly: Anouk Vincent, *Le roman vrai des Bettencourt* (Paris: City Editions, 2010), 17–19; Abescat, *La saga,* 65.

he dabbled with Socialist ideas . . . became a Freemason: Abescat, *La saga,* 65–66.

He would later become a visceral opponent: Ibid., 90–91.

He volunteered for active duty: Schueller deposition, February 11, 1948.

"peerless liaison officer": Citation of December 23, 1917, AN Z/6.

his wife, Betsy, had run the company: Schueller deposition, February 11, 1948; Vincent, *Le roman vrai,* 20.

considered a woman's place to be in the home: Ian Hamel, *Les Bettencourt: derniers secrets* (Paris: l'Archipel, 2013), 38.

the influence of Coco Chanel: Vincent, *Le*

roman vrai, 23.

By 1921, the company had permanent offices: Ibid.

Emboldened by the success: For all the details in this paragraph, see Schueller deposition, February 11, 1948, AN Z/6.

the Valstar Corporation, a manufacturer of paint: Marseille, *L'Oréal,* 42.

Invited by the new Soviet government: Schueller deposition, February 11, 1948.

he was spending 300,000 francs: Hamel, *Les Bettencourt,* 39–40.

In a pitch aimed especially at the rural population: Ibid., 42.

"tell people that they're disgusting": Schueller, quoted in Ibid., 40.

"never . . . wash with their soap themselves": Mark Twain, *The Innocents Abroad, or The New Pilgrim's Progress* (London: Collins, 1954), ch. XI.

"the indifference of public opinion on questions of hygiene": Cited in Marseille, *L'Oréal,* 39.

The results of Schueller's campaign were impressive: Schueller deposition, February 11, 1948, AN Z/6.

Schueller was way ahead of his time: Abescat, *La saga,* 31; Hamel, *Les Bettencourt,* 42; Vincent, *Le roman vrai,* 32–33.

The vacations, at least, were excellent: Marseille, *L'Oréal,* 75–85, on success of Ambre Solaire; Abescat, *La saga,* 67.

he had little use for democracy: Eugène Schueller, *La révolution de l'économie* (Paris: Ed. Robert Denoël, 1941), 122 and *passim*.

His main idea was the "proportional salary": Abescat, *La saga,* 78–79.

"illegality" and "underground action": Deloncle, quoted in Hamel, *Les Bettencourt,* 46.

Attracted by Schueller's ideas: Abescat, *La saga,* 86–88.

Among the terrorist actions: René Rémond, *La droite en France, de la Première Restauration à la Ve République* (Paris: Editions Montaigne, 1968), vol. 1, 227; Hamel, *Les Bettencourt,* 59–60.

On September 3, 1939: Jeremy D. Popkin, *A History of Modern France* (New Jersey: Prentice Hall, 2001), 229–32.

By the time the armistice was signed: Ian Ousby, *Occupation: The Ordeal of France, 1940–1944* (New York: Cooper Square Press, 2000), ch. 1.

"I know full well": Eugène Schueller, *La révolution de l'économie,* 122.

"We must rip from men's hearts": Ibid., 294.

"strong and durable government": Ibid., 372.

Schueller's book was part of a collection: Abescat, *La saga,* 81.

"our future minister of National Economy": Quoted in Ibid., 89.

"We seek to construct": Quoted in Ibid.

"blowing up the synagogues": Annie Lacroix-Riz, *Les élites françaises entre 1940 et 1944* (Paris: Armand Colin, 2016), 178.

Deloncle merged the group: Ousby, *Occupation,* 140; Abescat, *La saga,* 89.

Schueller served as president: Abescat, *La saga,* 89.

He later claimed that he had never belonged: Schueller depositions of February 18, 1948, and April 12, 1948, AN Z/6.

"None of these three peaceful revolutions": Quoted in Abescat, *La saga,* 90.

"the essential thing for us": Quoted in Ibid., 90–91.

Schueller had cause to regret: Ousby, *Occupation,* 303–310, on *épuration* details.

His troubles began: Georges Digeon deposition, January 8, 1946, AN Z/6; Marseille, *L'Oréal,* 95–101.

"all those who favored the undertakings": Raymond Marchand, *Le Temps des restrictions* (Château-Gontier: Impr. de l'Indépendant, 2000), 540.

"for advancing the enemy's designs": Abescat, *La saga,* 96.

he was formally charged: Judge Marcel Gagne and Judge M. Callaud, *Exposé,* December 6, 1948, 1, AN Z/6.

"minimal percentage of German business": Ibid.

"Schueller showed a certain activity": Ibid.

"an influential member of the M.S.R.": Report of the Renseignements Généraux [French police intelligence unit], January 26, 1942, quoted in Lacroix-Riz, *Les élites,* 174–475.

Gestapo agents burst into his apartment: Lacroix-Riz, *Les élites,* 378.

Deloncle's son Louis: Pierre Péan, *Une jeunesse française: François Mitterrand 1934–1947* (Paris: Pluriel, 2010), 522; Hamel, *Les Bettencourt,* 264.

many ex-Cagoulards who were welcomed: See Chapter 6.

One influential witness: Jacques Sadoul letter to Monsieur le Président du Comité interprofessionnel de l'épuration, June 29, 1946, AN Z/6.

Another was the Cagoulard turned Resistance leader: Pierre Guillain de Bénouville, atttestation of December 27, 1946, AN Z/6.

Not least among Schueller's defenders: André Bettencourt letters to Eugène Schueller, January 29, 1944, September 27, 1944, AN Z/6; Hamel, *Les Bettencourt,* 104–5.

His case was closed: Gagne and Callaud, *Exposé,* December 6, 1948, 6, AN Z/6.

Had he been convicted: Marie-France Etchegoin, *Un milliard de secrets* (Paris: Robert Laffont, 2011), 125.

L'Oréal's sales nearly quadrupled: Gagne and Callaud, *Exposé,* 2.

Schueller officially ceased to be the director . . . remained on the board: Rapport d'expert dans l'affaire Schueller, December 23, 1947, 51, AN Z/6. In his statement to Judges Gagne and Callaud, Schueller claimed to have left Valentine's board of directors in 1941; in fact, he remained on the board until well after the war and transferred his seat to André Bettencourt following the latter's marriage to Liliane in 1950. André Bettencourt, *Souvenirs* (Paris, 1999), vol. 1, 95, 177.

Schueller was also instrumental: Annie Lacroix-Riz, *Industriels et banquiers sous l'Occupation* (Paris: Armand Colin, 1999), 327–28.

The administrator of Neochrome: Lacroix-Riz, *Les élites,* 168–70.

"an ardent partisan": Hamel, *Les Bettencourt,* 91.

linked through a company called Alginates: Lacroix-Riz, *Industriels et banquiers,* 328; Lacroix-Riz, *Les élites,* 169; Hamel, *Les Bettencourt,* 91.

Valentine's official accounting records: Lacroix-Riz, *Les elites,* 169; Rapport d'expert dans l'affaire Schueller, December 23, 1947, 15, 30, AN Z/6.

as much as 95 percent of the company's wartime tonnage: Lacroix-Riz, *Les élites,* 169–70.

"The company Valentine": Report of Renseignements Généraux, March 24, 1945, AN Z/6.

According to the Reich's "Paint Plan": Lacroix-Riz, *Les élites,* 169; Annie Lacroix-Riz interview with author, October 21, 2015.

"augmented his fortune considerably": Lacroix-Riz interview with author, October 21, 2015.

His tax returns for the period: Rapport d'expert dans l'affaire Schueller, December 23, 1947, 15, AN Z/6. These figures are subject to caution, since the 1940 amount may be artificially low due to the disruptions caused by the war.

involved in the deportation of French Jews: Ousby, *Occupation,* 229.

he listed Schueller: Helmut Knochen deposition, November 16, 1946, cited in Lacroix-Riz, *Les élites,* 171.

French investigators discovered a list: Ibid., 159.

"At the time I knew him": Knochen deposition, November 22, 1946, cited in Ibid., 171.

designated as the future minister: Ibid., 171.

"all the members of the party": Eugène Schueller circular letter of July 29, 1941, in Archives Nationales dossier Cour de Justice contre Michel Harispé Z/6/ 698 A/B. Copy provided to the author by French historian François Le Goarant de Tromelin.

The French unit was integrated: Ousby, *Occupation*, 202–3.

Taken together with his role: Jean-Marc Berlière, email to author, June 10, 2015. Berlière, emeritus professor of history at l'Université de Boulogne, affirms that these facts could conceivably have led to Schueller's execution — by firing squad, since collaboration with the enemy was considered a military crime — though more likely would have resulted in the stripping of his civic rights.

"He was a man full of hope": Liliane Bettencourt, quoted in Franz-Olivier Giesbert, *François Mitterrand, une vie* (Paris: Seuil, 1996), 96.

Chapter 2: The Heiress and the Consort

"I was five years old": Liliane Bettencourt, interviewed by Nicole Wisniak, "A partir d'un certain Chiffre, les gens Déraillent," *Egoïste,* no. 10 (1987), 55.

"It allowed my father": Ibid.

the Dominican nuns who . . . gave her a strict education: Liliane Bettencourt interview, *Egoïste,* 55.

Schueller married the comely Nita: Bruno Abescat, *La saga des Bettencourt* (Paris: Plon, 2010), 58.

"She never, ever talked": Claude Delay, interview with author, September 10, 2015.

"What shaped me": Liliane Bettencourt, interviewed by Arnaud Bizot, "Liliane Bettencourt nous ouvre les portes de son coeur," *Paris Match,* September 30, 2010.

"6,000-hour" man: Abescat, *La saga,* 74.

he would typically rise at five a.m.: Merry Bromberger, quoted in Ibid., 74–75.

"I had a tray full of labels": Liliane Bettencourt interview, *Paris Match,* September 30, 2010.

"My father adored me": Liliane Bettencourt conversation with Jean-Michel Normand, recorded September 12, 2009, by butler Pascal Bonnefoy. The complete transcript of Bonnefoy's secret recordings is included in the investigative file. Henceforth, recorded material will be referenced simply by date.

Schueller had built a granite villa: Descriptions and history of the Arcouest property drawn from Ronan Le Flécher, "Liliane Bettencourt: l'Arcouest, parce qu'elle le vaut bien," website of Agence Bretagne Presse, July 1, 2010, accessed

online March 31, 2015, http://www
.agencebretagnepresse.com/id=18912; Abescat, *La saga,* 32–33; Marie-France Etchegoin, *Un milliard de secrets* (Paris: Robert
Laffont, 2011), 67.

**Eugène never stayed more than two
weeks:** Abescat, *La saga,* 59–60.

"It was intense": Liliane Bettencourt interview, *Paris Match,* September 30, 2010.

"Have you seen those shoes?": Liliane
Betttencourt's handwritten comment, dated
March 21, 2010, in confiscated notebook
of François-Marie Banier, included in the
investigative file.

**Bettencourt, then nineteen, had been in-
troduced:** André Bettencourt, *Souvenirs*
(Paris, 1999), vol. 1, 57.

"didn't find her extraordinary": Martin
d'Orgeval, quoted in Etchegoin, *Milliard de
secrets,* 97.

Bettencourt claimed to be a descendant:
Details on family background from Bettencourt, *Souvenirs,* vol. 1, 7–14.

André judged him a "saint": Ibid., vol. 1,
14.

The youngest of six children: Ibid., vol. 1,
39–46; also Pierre Bettencourt, *Les désordres de la mémoire* (Rouen: Bibliothèque
Municipale de Rouen, 1998), 28 and *passim.* Copy made available to author by
Bruno Abescat.

According to his own account: Bettencourt, *Souvenirs,* vol. 1, 44–49.

Mitterrand, who belonged to a group: Pierre Péan, *Une jeunesse française,* 33–34.

frequented members of the notorious Cagoule: Ibid., 384–85 and *passim.* According to Péan, refuting persistent rumors, Mitterrand never actually joined the Cagoule. Ibid., 109.

Dalle secured an invitation: Ibid., 99.

Henri d'Orléans and Charles de Gaulle: Alain Peyerefitte, *C'était de Gaulle* (Paris: Éditions de Fallois/Fayard, 1997), vol. 2, 532.

"talked all the time": Dalle, quoted in Péan, *Jeunesse française,* 99.

"Coming from the pine forest": André Bettencourt, article in *La Terre française,* October 18, 1941, quoted in Hamel, *Les Bettencourt,* 116–17.

he attempted to enlist in Normandy: Bettencourt, *Souvenirs,* vol. 1, 36, 59–61.

he also began writing for a paper: Abescat, *La saga,* 115; Hamel, *Les Bettencourt,* 120. André Bettencourt explained the circumstances surrounding his work for *La Terre française* in his *Souvenirs,* vol. 1, 62–63, and in a letter to US congressman Eliot Engel, January 25, 1995, excerpted in *Le Monde,* February 14, 1995.

"The Jews, hypocritical Pharisees":

Bettencourt, *La Terre française,* April 12, 1941, quoted in Hamel, *Les Bettencourt,* 123.

"The young must be": Bettencourt, *La Terre française,* October 11, 1941, quoted in Hamel, *Les Bettencourt,* 127–28.

"revolutionary current of the new Europe": Bettencourt, *La Terre française,* July 19, 1941, quoted in Hamel, *Les Bettencourt,* 125.

Mobilized into the army: Péan, *Jeunesse française,* 111–18.

After two failed attempts: Jean Védrine, ed., *Dossier Les prisonniers de guerre, Vichy et la Résistance, 1940–1945* (Paris: Fayard, 2013), 489–91; Péan, *Jeunesse française,* 173.

Mitterrand entered the Resistance: Védrine, *Prisonniers,* 493–94; Péan, *Jeunesse française,* 297–323.

Mitterrand enlisted Bettencourt: Védrine, *Prisonniers,* 179.

His role was to recruit Resistance members: Bettencourt, *Souvenirs,* vol. 1, 66.

Bettencourt was arrested by the Gestapo: Ibid., vol. 1, 70–73.

"the experience of the cell": André Bettencourt, letter to Eugène Schueller, January 29, 1944, AN Z/6.

François herself was jailed, tortured: Védrine, *Prisonniers,* 315.

Working in the Geneva office: Bettencourt, *Souvenirs,* vol. 1, 75–83; Péan, *Jeunesse française,* 423; Védrine, *Prisonniers,* 180–81.

impressive collection of decorations: Bettencourt, *Souvenirs,* vol. 1, 84–85; Védrine, *Prisonniers,* 182.

Bettencourt's first step: Abescat, *La saga,* 50; Hamel, *Les Bettencourt,* 178–79.

"such a good-looking guy": Georges Kiejman, interview with author, July 8, 2015.

"You have spoken to me about your fears": André Bettencourt, letter to Eugène Schueller, January 29, 1944, AN Z/6.

Schueller offered to send money: André Bettencourt, letter to Eugène Schueller, September 27, 1944, AN Z/6.

Schueller invited the young man: Bettencourt, *Souvenirs,* vol. 1, 126.

the very place where his mother had died: Pierre Bettencourt, *Désordres,* 100.

"letters and presence": Ibid., 100.

She fell in love with the country: Etchegoin, *Milliard de secrets,* 98–99.

"His mentality was too far from mine": Liliane Bettencourt conversation, as transcribed by François-Marie Banier, May 2, 2010, in Banier's confiscated notebook.

It was some years after the Moroccan romance broke off: Liliane Bettencourt conversation, as transcribed by Banier, notebook entry of December 29, 2002;

François-Marie Banier faxed letter to Liliane Bettencourt, November 22, 2008, *Correspondance échangée entre Madame Liliane Bettencourt et Monsieur François-Marie Banier pour la période allant de 1989 à 2010,* vol. 2. (Documents included in the court record.)

"I was terribly frightened of marriage": Liliane Bettencourt interview, *Egoïste,* 56.

Liliane ran ahead of everyone else: Liliane Bettencourt conversation, as transcribed in Banier's confiscated notebook, July 12, 2010; Pierre Bettencourt, *Désordres,* 190.

Liliane later insisted: Banier notebook, July 12, 2010.

Liliane kept up her ties to Morocco: Bettencourt, *Souvenirs,* vol. 1, 129.

"Of course Bettencourt did political financing": Georges Kiejman, interview with author, July 8, 2015.

"I was happy for him": Liliane Bettencourt interview, *Paris Match,* September 30, 2010.

"Liliane didn't want me to enter politics": André Bettencourt, interview filmed October 10, 1992, included in documentary *"Liliane Bettencourt: dans l'intimité d'une milliardaire,"* broadcast by France 2, August 7, 2014. This documentary is accessible online at: https://www.youtube.com/watch?v=JN60_O2QvqE.

The couple made a groundbreaking trip: Hamel, *Les Bettencourt,* 29.

"He really liked me": Liliane Bettencourt interview, *Paris Match,* September 30, 2010, 72.

"What could André Bettencourt have done but politics?": Author interview with source speaking on condition of anonymity.

Former colleagues describe him: Renaud Donnedieu de Vabres, interview with author, September 30, 2015; Alain Carignon, interview with author, November 27, 2015.

"I did not adore Giscard": Bettencourt, *Souvenirs,* vol. 2, 324.

"I could only say bad things about him": Valéry Giscard d'Estaing, comment relayed to author by his office, September 23, 2015.

"After all, André, you are not lacking for bread": Bettencourt, *Souvenirs,* vol. 2, 327.

It was restored in the 1980s: Claude Herambourg, interview with author, July 16, 2015.

"With the people of the village": Ibid., for all quotes in this paragraph.

"To tell you the truth": Jean-Pierre Valériola, telephone interview with author, November 6, 2015.

"One does not become a general": Eugène Schueller, *Théorie du deuxième salaire* (Paris, 1939), 23.

even he admitted: Bettencourt, *Souvenirs,* vol. 1, 110.

Schueller's handpicked choice: François Dalle, *L'Aventure L'Oréal* (Paris: Odile Jacob, 2001); Jacques Marseille, *L'Oréal,* 147–57.

Dalle, in turn, lobbied: Péan, *Jeunesse,* 503–4.

increased annual sales more than forty-fold: Sales increased from 421 million francs in 1966 to 16.4 billion francs in 1985, according to L'Oréal annual reports for those years. (Figures are not publicly available before 1966.)

"On the really important matters": Jean-Pierre Valériola, telephone interview with author, November 6, 2015.

"She did public relations": Author interview with source speaking on condition of anonymity, September 9, 2015.

Schueller built them a two-story . . . mansion: Bettencourt, *Souvenirs,* vol. 1, 106. Details about the Bettencourt mansion: "Dans les secrets de la maison Bettencourt," *Capital,* September 2010, 86–89; Anouk Vincent, *Le roman vrai des Bettencourt* (Paris: City Editions, 2010), 82.

the highest median per capita income: Elodie Buzeaud, "Le revenu des Français, ville par ville," Cadremploi.fr website, July 18, 2013, accessed online November 1, 2016, https://www.cadremploi.fr/editorial/

actualites/actu-emploi/detail/article/salaire
-combien-gagne-t-on-ville-par-ville-en
-france.html.

At home in Neuilly: Etchegoin, *Milliard de secrets,* 201–9; Abescat, *La saga,* 37; Antoine Gillot, interview with author, July 20, 2015.

"Liliane was a brilliant woman": Georges Kiejman, interview with author, July 8, 2015.

"She was not arrogant": Pascal Greggory, interview with author, December 12, 2015.

In 1988, he was elected: Bettencourt, *Souvenirs,* vol. 2, 355–64.

joking in his acceptance speech: André Bettencourt, "Notice sur la vie et les travaux de M. Michel Fare," November 30, 1988, on the website of the Académie des Beaux-Arts, accessed online on November 17, 2016, http://www.academie-des-beaux-arts .fr/membres/actuel/libres/Bettencourt/ Discours_hommage_Fare.htm.

"He was anything but stupid": Diane de Clairval, interview with author, October 31, 2015.

Chapter 3: Poor Little Rich Girl

"My mother is dead": Liliane Bettencourt to François-Marie Banier, March 8, 2005, *Correspondance échangée entre Madame Liliane Bettencourt et Monsieur François-Marie*

Banier pour la période allant de 1989 à 2010, vol. 2.

Suffered a relapse of the tuberculosis: Judge Michèle Esarté, medical report read in Bordeaux appeals court, May 12, 2016, from author's trial notes.

"She had to leave for a sanatorium": Lucienne de Rozier deposition, September 6, 2010.

"a mussel on a rock": Françoise Meyers, interviewed by Raphaëlle Bacquet, "Françoise Bettencourt Meyers: 'Allons-y, mieux vaut tout purger,' " *M Le Magazine du Monde,* March 10, 2012, 45.

"I think that the relationship": Isabelle Prévost-Desprez, interview with author, September 24, 2015.

"manage her hygiene issues": Alain Caillol, quoted in "En enlevant Empain, on s'est trompé sur toute la ligne," *Le Figaro,* January 13, 2012.

"had more means to exert pressure": Alain Caillol, quoted in "Alain Caillol, l'un des ravisseurs du Baron Empain, se confie à VSD," *VSD,* November 24, 2009, accessed online December 11, 2016, http://www.vsd.fr/les-indiscrets/alain-caillol-l-un-des-ravisseurs-du-baron-empain-se-confie-a-vsd-3714.

"La belle Lili had a close call": Alain Caillol, quoted in Patricia Tourancheau, "Remords postbaron," *Libération,* January

14, 2012.

"formed a close-knit family": Françoise Meyers interview, "Françoise Meyers se confie," *Elle,* July 8, 2010.

"I was always very close to my parents": Françoise Meyers, quoted in Bacquet, "Françoise Bettencourt Meyers," 45.

"It's a failure with my daughter": Liliane Bettencourt, quoted in Jean-Marie Pontaut and Pascal Ceaux, "Bettencourt mère et fille: chronique d'une relation houleuse," *L'Express,* July 21, 2010, accessed online June 15, 2016, http://www.lexpress.fr/ actualite/societe/justice/bettencourt-mere-et -fille-chronique-d-une-relation-houleuse_ 907417.html.

"I told you she was not happy": Liliane Bettencourt, interviewed by Arnaud Bizot, "Liliane Bettencourt nous ouvre les portes de son coeur," *Paris Match,* September 30, 2010, 73.

"She never kisses me": Liliane Bettencourt to François-Marie Banier, December 10, 1997, *Correspondance,* vol. 1.

"She keeps them on a leash": Liliane Bettencourt to François-Marie Banier, May 31, 1997, *Correspondance,* vol. 1.

Françoise "has annihilated me": Liliane Bettencourt to François-Marie Banier, July 15, 2000, *Correspondance,* vol. 1.

"The mother massacred the daughter": Richard Malka, interview with author, July

9, 2016.

a "conciliator": André Bettencourt, *Souvenirs,* vol. 2, 344.

"joyous, docile, and emotive": Ibid., vol. 1, 132; vol. 2, 344.

Some have speculated: Jean-Michel Normand deposition, November 6, 2012.

"hard to wear and hard to look at": Liliane Bettencourt to François-Marie Banier, July 12, 2000, *Correspondance,* vol. 1.

"It's a story of jealousy between women": Liliane Bettencourt to François-Marie Banier, October 8, 2008, *Correspondance,* vol. 1.

"Music is my oxygen": Françoise Meyers, interview with Bacquet, "Françoise Bettencourt Meyers," 46.

"From the beginning, our common sensibility": Arielle Dombasle, interview with Gérard Miller, June 9, 2016. Transcript made available to the author by Gérard Miller.

"I am too eccentric for her": Liliane Bettencourt to François-Marie Banier, August 17, 2007, *Correspondance,* vol. 2.

"Françoise was a somber little girl": Arielle Dombasle, interview with Gérard Miller, June 9, 2016.

Françoise first laid eyes on Jean-Pierre Meyers: Raphaëlle Bacquet and Béatrice Gurrey, "Quand François-Marie Banier tentait une conciliation," *Le Monde,* August 30, 2010.

Françoise and Jean-Pierre got to know each other: Ibid.

"was not an easy thing to contemplate": Bettencourt, *Souvenirs,* vol. 2, 343.

Jean-Pierre Meyers was living with Agnès Greggory: Stéphane Durand-Souffland, "Au procès Bettencourt, le compagnon de François-Marie Banier a adopté une posture détachée," *Le Figaro,* May 14, 2016.

"Agnès learned of the [impending] marriage": Pascal Greggory interview, December 12, 2015.

"I wouldn't have prevented it": Liliane Bettencourt to François-Marie Banier, May 4, 2001, *Correspondance,* vol. 2.

"It was a marvelous wedding": Françoise Meyers interview, *Elle,* July 8, 2010.

"an affectionate son": Bettencourt, *Souvenirs,* vol. 2, 343.

"She always blamed Françoise": Lucienne de Rozier deposition, September 6, 2010.

"He never lost sight of the prize": Liliane Bettencourt conversation with Patrice de Maistre, recorded November 30, 2009.

"In 50 years, my daughter has never talked": Liliane Bettencourt to François-Marie Banier, October 8, 2008, *Correspon-*

dance, vol. 2.

five-volume study of the Bible: Françoise Bettencourt Meyers, *Les trompettes de Jéricho: regard sur la Bible: mieux se comprendre entre juifs et catholiques* (Paris: L'Oeuvre, 2008).

"I suppose, since I know Françoise": Bernard-Henri Lévy, "Lectures de Noël: Françoise Bettencourt Meyers et la Bible," *Le Point,* December 11, 2008.

Françoise's other published work: Françoise Bettencourt Meyers, *Les dieux grecs: généalogies* (Paris: Christian, 1994).

"Françoise doesn't like luxury": Arielle Dombasle, interview with Gérard Miller, June 9, 2016.

"frozen in the 1970s": Pascal Wilhelm, interview with author, June 24, 2016.

it is Françoise who opens the door: "Les petits secrets de Françoise Bettencourt-Meyers, la future madame L'Oréal," *Capital,* November 24, 2014, accessed online June 24, 2015, http://www.capital.fr/enquetes/hommes-et-aaires/les-petits-secrets-de-francoise-bettencourt-meyers-la-future-madame-l-oreal-645533.

actively supports a research institute: Caroline Pigozzi, "La revanche de l'héritière," *Paris Match,* September 2, 2010.

Friends describe him in bland terms:

David Le Bailly et François Labrouillère, "Affaire Bettencourt. Le discret mari de Françoise Meyers," *Paris Match,* June 26, 2011.

"never intervened very directly": Jean-Pierre Valériola, telephone interview with author, November 6, 2015.

"a prince consort": Pierre Castres Saint Martin, interview with author, September 22, 2015.

Liliane Bettencourt gifted the bulk: Anouk Vincent, *Le roman vrai des Bettencourt* (Paris: City Editions, 2010), 161–62; Olivier Metzner, *Plainte,* December 19, 2007, 3.

the gifted stock was worth some €2.5 billion: Calculation based on stock price data provided by the L'Oréal financial department.

stock dividends that currently average over a million euros a day: François Krug, "Liliane, héritière, 34 millions d'euros par mois," *Le Nouvel Observateur,* July 5, 2010, accessed online November 17, 2016, http://rue89.nouvelobs.com/2010/07/05/liliane-heritiere-34-millions-deuros-par-mois-157580.

"That's my margin of freedom": Liliane Bettencourt to Jean-Michel Normand, October 16, 2002, quoted in Pierre Cornut-Gentille and Laurent Merlet, *Conclusions* *subsidiaires au fond aux fins de relaxe* [brief filed on Banier's behalf], January 26, 2015, 6.

"If you had made this donation": Liliane Bettencourt to François-Marie Banier, July 19, 1996, *Correspondance,* vol. 1.

it was surprising to publicist Seth Goldschlager: Seth Goldschlager, interview with author, November 13, 2015.

Chapter 4: Portrait of the Artist

"The most important thing": François-Marie Banier, interview with Michel Guerrin, "Il y a toujours eu du vacarme derrière moi," *Le Monde,* September 12, 2009, 21.

François-Marie Michel Banier was born: Biographical details from François-Marie Banier, interview with author, September 28, 2015. Unless otherwise indicated, all Banier quotes in this chapter are from this interview.

A childhood friend: Gilles Brücker, interview with author, July 19, 2016.

"He practically lived at our house": Douce de Andia, quoted in Marie-Dominique Lelièvre, "Le bouquet de Narcisse," *Libération,* August 4, 1997.

Banier has undergone three psychoanalyses: François-Marie Banier, interview with author, October 25, 2016.

"François-Marie is someone who has a

desire to be loved": Pascal Greggory, interview with author, December 12, 2015.

"believed in nothing": Banier, quoted in Amy Fine Collins, "Enfant Terrible," *Vanity Fair,* December 2006, accessed online February 27, 2015, http://www.vanityfair .com/culture/2006/12/enfant-terrible -200612.

"I remember one time": Gilles Brücker, quoted in Ibid.

"When he comes here": Jean-Michel Ribes, interview with author, November 18, 2015.

"I called him up": François Bonduel, telephone interview with author, November 25, 2015.

"Young man, your line is too large" . . . **"His suite was always full":** Banier, quoted in Collins, "Enfant Terrible."

Banier quit school at seventeen: François-Marie Banier, telephone interview with author, August 9, 2016.

"They were one personality split": Valérie Lalonde, quoted in Collins, "Enfant Terrible."

Marie-Laure invited Banier to lunch: François-Marie Banier, interview with author, June 23, 2016.

"Monsieur Pélissier arrived": François-Marie Banier, *Les résidences secondaires,* *ou La vie distraite* (Paris: Gallimard, 1969), 11.

"the exaltation caused by the sudden possession": Banier, *Les résidences,* 20.

"You represented a lot of things": Ibid., 112.

press magnates Hélène Lazareff: François-Marie Banier, interview with author, September 28, 2015.

Banier has always scoffed at this story: Marie-France Etchegoin, *Un milliard de secrets* (Paris: Robert Laffont, 2011), 101; François-Marie Banier, interview with author, September 28, 2015.

"without ambiguity": Banier testimony, January 28, 2015, Tribunal correctionnel de Bordeaux, *Note d'audience,* 26.

"I have absolutely no memory of that": Liliane Bettencourt, interviewed by Arnaud Bizot, "Liliane Bettencourt nous ouvre les portes de son coeur," *Paris Match,* September 39, 2010, 72.

Banier met him by chance one night in 1968: Louis Aragon, "Un inconnu nommé Banier," *Lettres françaises,* June 2, 1971, 5; François-Marie Banier, interviews with author September 28, 2015, and December 1, 2015.

"[Banier] is the craziest": Aragon, "Un inconnu nommé Banier," 6.

"exaggerated by older admirers": Quoted in Anouk Vincent, *Le roman vrai des Betten-*

court (Paris: City Editions, 2010), 103.

"It presented me as a dandy": François-Marie Banier, interview with author, December 1, 2015.

"So tell me, joker, is it true": Nicole Wisniak, quoted in Jean-Marc Roberts, *François-Marie* (Paris: Gallimard, 2011), 62

She reportedly put 350,000 francs: Jérôme Dupuis, Boris Thiolet, and Gilles Gaetner, "François-Marie Banier: un ami qui vous veut du bien," *L'Express,* January 16, 2009; Vincent, *Le roman vrai,* 104.

Among the two hundred guests: François-Marie Banier, interview with author, November 3, 2016.

"I'm not sure that the theater": Jean-Michel Ribes, interview with author, November 18, 2015.

"We danced together": Pascal Greggory, conversation with author, December 6, 2015.

"It was all done in an amicable way": Ibid.

"In the homosexual milieu": Pascal Greggory, interview with author, December 15, 2015.

After one dispute: Cited in Vincent, *Le roman vrai,* 104.

he allegedly snatched her wig: Christophe d'Antonio, *La lady et le dandy* (Paris: Éditions Jacob-Duvernet, 2010), 30.

When Castaing refused to let him in: Ibid.

"We were two monsters": Banier, quoted in Etchegoin, *Milliard de secrets,* 59.

Banier sued for defamation: Laurent Merlet (Banier's lawyer), interview with author, August 3, 2015.

"Madeleine was very stingy": Pascal Greggory, conversation with author, December 6, 2015.

"You're cheeky, but it's good": Quoted in *François-Marie Banier* (Paris: Gallimard, 2003), 320.

"the dwarf Bergé": Banier notebook, December 29, 2002.

"You think he sucks well?" . . . **"He wanted to be saucy"**: Pierre Bergé, *Les jours s'en vont, je demeure* (Paris: Gallimard, 2003), quoted in Vincent, *Le roman vrai,* 107.

"main quality is to seduce old people": Bergé, *Les jours,* quoted in Michel Guerrin, "Francois-marie Banier le mauvais génie," *M Le Magazine du Monde,* October 16, 2010.

"a *tour de force* of marketing": Alicia Drake, *The Beautiful Fall: Fashion, Genius and Glorious Excess in 1970s Paris* (London: Bloomsbury, 2006), 251.

Banier named Dior's Poison: François-Marie Banier, interview with author, October 25, 2016.

in 1987 Banier was able to buy: Ibid.;

Banier enquête patrimoniale, June 4, 2009, in investigative dossier.

"The fashion world exploded at this time": Judy Fayard, interview with author, October 3, 2015.

published a photo book on Le Palace: Guy Marineau and Jean Rouzaud, *Le Palace: Remember* (Paris: Hoëbeke, 2005).

"Banier had become excellent in the art of creating friendships": Guy Marineau, email to author, October 26, 2015.

didn't really like hanging out in "homo places": François-Marie Banier, interview with author, October 26, 2015.

"an absolute nonconformist": Arielle Dombasle, quoted in Michel Guerrin, "François-Marie Banier le mauvais génie," *M Le Magazine du Monde,* October 16, 2010.

"extraordinary personage she was" for him: François-Marie Banier, *Balthazar, fils de famille* (Paris: Gallimard, 1985), 167.

"she's the one who pays": Ibid., 169.

"I saw in her falsely distracted eyes": Ibid., 222; quoted in Nicolas Huc-Morel and Cédric Labrousse, *Conclusions de parties civiles* [brief filed on behalf of Jean-Victor Meyers and Nicolas Meyers], January 2015, 38.

"part of the woodwork": Christianne Dufour, interview with author, September 29, 2015.

"Mitterrand was amused by him": Hubert Védrine, interview with author, September 21, 2015.

Reportedly at Mitterrand's urging: Michel Guerrin, "François-Marie Banier le mauvais génie," *M Magazine du Monde,* October 16, 2010; Guy Marineau, email to author, October 26, 2015.

landed a rare interview: Liliane Bettencourt, "A partir d'un certain Chiffre, les gens Déraillent," *Egoïste,* no. 10 (1987), 55–57.

"The first time I saw you": Liliane Bettencourt to François-Marie Banier, October 11, 1994, *Correspondance échangée entre Madame Liliane Bettencourt et Monsieur François-Marie Banier pour la période allant de 1989 à 2010,* vol. 1.

Chapter 5: Such Good Friends

"With you, I am like a mother, a lover": Liliane Bettencourt to François-Marie Banier, August 20, 2007, *Correspondance échangée entre Madame Liliane Bettencourt et Monsieur François-Marie Banier pour la période allant de 1989 à 2010,* vol. 2.

"good thing I never intended": Liliane

Bettencourt, recording of September 7, 2009.

Liliane longed for more physical closeness: Banier notebook, December 29, 2002.

"She fell in love with François-Marie . . . She was fascinated by him": Lucienne de Rozier depositions, September 6, 2010, and February 13, 2008.

"not only in love with Banier": Gilles Brücker, interview with author, July 19, 2016.

"never in love": François-Marie Banier trial testimony, February 3, 2015, *Note d'audience* [transcript of Banier's first trial], 87.

"my beautiful child": Liliane Bettencourt to François-Marie Banier, May 2006, *Correspondance,* vol. 2.

was fed a diet of fresh fish: Olivier Bouchara and Olivier Druin, "Dans les secrets de la maison Bettencourt," *Capital,* September 2010, 88.

"ma petite chérie": François-Marie Banier to Liliane Bettencourt, September 29, 2006, *Correspondance,* vol. 2.

"I kiss you tenderly": Liliane Bettencourt to François-Marie Banier, March 11, 1995, Ibid., vol. 1.

"That's when we realized": Jean-Pierre Meyers testimony before the Bordeaux appeals court, May 18, 2016, *Procès verbal d'audition de témoin,* 3.

"Liliane was rich": Georges Kiejman, interview with author, July 9, 2015.

"grave depression": Lucienne de Rozier deposition, February 23, 2008.

"My health was bad for ten years": Liliane Bettencourt to François-Marie Banier, February 7, 1995, *Correspondance,* vol 1.

"he renovated me": Liliane Bettencourt conversation with Patrice de Maistre, recording of September 7, 2009.

"You do not raise your voice at my table": André Bettencourt, quoted in Banier notebook entry of March 18, 2007.

attended the International Film Festival: Claire Thibout deposition, September 18, 2008, 2.

danced on the famous Piazza San Marco: Monique de Libouton deposition, September 6, 2010.

"She wore a bright orange scarf": Diane von Furstenberg, interview with author, December 23, 2015.

Banier insists that Liliane was not a stand-in mother: François-Marie Banier, interview with author, September 28, 2015.

"Through me there was a vision": Ibid.

"You have two people who meet": Diane von Furstenberg, interview with author, December 23, 2015.

She came two or three times a month:

Banier testimony before Bordeaux appeals court, May 11, 2016, from author's notes.

bread and cheese that she always brought: François-Marie Banier, interview with author, June 14, 2016.

"François-Marie, you need more space": Dialogue as recounted by Banier in interview with Christophe Barbier and Jean-Marie Pontaut, "La générosité de Liliane Bettencourt est voulue," *L'Express,* July 14–20, 2010, 57.

Good as her word: Anouk Vincent, *Le roman vrai des Bettencourt* (Paris: City Editions, 2010), 142; Marie-France Etchegoin, *Un milliard de secrets* (Paris: Robert Laffont, 2011), 82.

Between 1994 and 1999: Vincent, *Le roman vrai,* 152.

she accompanied Banier to the offices of her notary: François-Marie Banier, interview with author, November 3, 2016.

"I have decided to give you the paintings": Barbier and Pontaut, "La générosité."

The collection, which included canvases by Picasso: Tribunal de Grande Instance de Bordeaux, *Jugement correctionnel* [court ruling in Banier's initial trial], May 28, 2015, 92; Etchegoin, *Milliard de secrets,* 161.

currently estimated at €90 million: Laurent Merlet, conversation with author, January 17, 2017.

"She knew exactly what she wanted": Jean-Michel Normand deposition, November 6, 2012.

"token of my gratitude": Quoted in Etchegoin, *Milliard de secrets,* 161.

she named Banier in her will as the beneficiary: Pierre Cornut-Gentille, Laurent Merlet, and Daniel Lasserre, *Conclusions subsidiaires au fond aux fins de relaxe,* January 26, 2015, 4.

he purchased four apartments: *Banier enquête patrimoniale,* June 4, 2009.

Liliane cashed in a life-insurance contract: *Jugement correctionnel,* May 28, 2015, 15.

He immediately put the funds: Ibid., 108–9.

he drew large sums: Banier deposition, January 30, 2013.

Liliane arranged for L'Oréal to grant two generous contracts: Zineb Dryef and François Krug, "Affaire Bettencourt: comment L'Oréal finance Banier," *Rue89,* September 23, 2010, accessed online March 3, 2015, http://tempsreel.nouvelobs.com/rue89/rue89-nos-vies-connectees/20100 723.RUE7695/affaire-bettencourt-comment-l-oreal-finance-banier.html.

were eventually worth €710,000: Ibid.

"I make money for Liliane": Owen-Jones, quoted in Etchegoin, *Milliard de secrets,* 192; Jean-Michel Normand deposition, February 21, 2008.

"I am well aware": Banier to Lindsay Owen-Jones, quoted in Etchegoin, *Milliard de secrets,* 168.

"L'Oréal could be something other": Banier testimony, February 2, 2015, *Note d'audience,* 69.

"What I want is for you to be known": Liliane Bettencourt to François-Marie Banier, March 23, 1996, *Correspondance,* vol. 1.

"we" are putting on an exhibition: Louis Abel (Madame Bettencourt's former osteopath) deposition, March 24, 2009.

"She was intelligent enough to realize": Claude Delay Tubiana, interview with author, September 10, 2015.

"She's a woman who imposes": Banier testimony, quoted in Michel Deléan, "Procès Bettencourt: la faute de Liliane," *Mediapart,* February 3, 2015, accessed online October 8, 2016, https://www .mediapart.fr journal/france/030215/proces -bettencourt-la-faute-de-liliane.

"It is Madame Bettencourt who takes the lead": Jean-Michel Normand deposition, February 21, 2008.

"Each one got what they needed": Ibid.

described her as "stingy": Monique de Libouton deposition, September 15, 2010.

"Liliane was quite miserly": Lucienne de Rozier deposition, September 6, 2010.

"detests overpaying": Liliane Bettencourt interview, *Egoïste*, no. 10 (1987).

"I don't like blandness": Ibid.

"Haut les cœurs": Banier to Liliane Bettencourt, September 17, 2006; May 30, 2007.

"It's obvious that you're part crazy": Liliane Bettencourt to François-Marie Banier, August 15, 2003, *Correspondance,* vol. 2.

"I spoke to François-Marie as I spoke to my father": Liliane Bettencourt to Jean-Michel Normand, May 23, 2003, cited in Cornut-Gentille, Merlet, and Lasserre, *Conclusions,* 14.

"I got along very well with my mother": Françoise Meyers testimony, January 30, 2015, *Note d'audience,* 61–62.

"There was no incident!": François-Marie Banier, interview with author, September 28, 2015.

He says he got along fine: Details of 1993 Arcouest luncheon from Etchegoin, *Milliard de secrets,* 69–70.

The two first crossed paths in 1981: Arielle Dombasle, interview with Gérard Miller, June 9, 2016.

She took more notice of him when he showed up: Françoise Meyers testimony,

January 30, 2015, *Note d'audience,* 60.

Françoise and Banier met again: Ibid.

the heiress would rise at seven a.m.: Louis Abel (Liliane's former osteopath) deposition, March 24, 2009; details on her daily schedule in Etchegoin, *Milliard de secrets,* 42–43; Bouchara and Drouin, "Dans les secrets," 88.

One thing Liliane never wore was perfume: Bouchara and Drouin, "Dans les secrets," 86; Banier notebook entry of December 29, 2002.

no more than forty-five minutes: François-Marie Banier, interview with author, September 28, 2015.

"I visited her four times a month": Banier testimony before Bordeaux appeals court, May 11, 2016, from author's trial notes.

"Claire is someone who can be off-putting": Antoine Gillot, interview with author, August 4, 2015.

"never laughed so much": Thibout, quoted in Etchegoin, *Milliard de secrets,* 200.

"They would go to restaurants": Claire Thibout, interviewed on "Liliane Bettencourt: dans l'intimité d'une milliardaire," *Complément d'enquête,* France 2, broadcast November 17, 2013.

According to official court records: *Jugement correctionnel,* May 28, 2015, 91.

"What's this all about?": Dialogue as recounted by Antoine Gillot, interview with author, August 4, 2015.

"Monsieur Bettencourt did not know everything": Chantal Trovel testimony, February 4, 2015, *Note d'audience,* 105.

"wasn't he himself supported": Georges Kiejman, interview with author, July 8, 2015.

Claire telephoned Banier: Dialogue and scene as recounted in Banier's notebook, December 29, 2002. Thibout also testified on this encounter, February 10, 2015, *Note d'audience,* 136.

The heiress confessed she'd made a mistake: Claire Thibout testimony, February 10, 2015, *Note d'audience,* 136.

she changed her mind again: *Jugement correctionnel,* May 28, 2015, 95.

the most exotic was the Seychelles island of d'Arros: Hervé Gattegno, "L'île maudite des Bettencourt," *Vanity Fair* (French edition), February 9, 2015, accessed online May 29, 2015, http://www.vanityfair.fr/ actualites/france/articles/ile-darros-paradis -maudit/1641.

Françoise and her family were never once invited: Jean-Pierre Meyers trial testimony, *Procès verbal d'audition de témoin,* May 18, 2016, 4.

"In no case did she want the island to go

to her daughter": Fabrice Goguel, quoted in Gattegno, "L'île maudite des Bettencourt."

Goguel created a Lichtenstein-based foundation: Ibid.

finally sold in 2011: Ibid.

"I detest this island": Banier deposition, July 16, 2010.

Chapter 6: Dark Roots

Seth Goldschlager was awakened: Quotes and scene description from Seth Goldschlager, interview with author, November 13, 2015.

It all started in September 1987: Details on Paravision and the Frydman-Dalle-L'Oréal dispute from Jacques Marseille, *L'Oréal, 1909–2009* (Paris: Perrin, 2009), 255–65; Ian Hamel, *Les Bettencourt: derniers secrets* (Paris: l'Archipel, 2013), 251–62; Bruno Abescat, *La saga des Bettencourt* (Paris: Plon, 2010), 98–100.

"the personification of horror": Jean Frydman, quoted in "La Guerre de l'ombre," *Le Point,* May 13, 1991.

perpetrator of some of the group's bloodiest terror attacks: Michel Bar-Zohar, *Une histoire sans fard: L'Oréal, des années sombres au boycott arabe* (Paris: Fayard, 1996), 50–51.

served as an officer in his collaboration-

ist groups: Marseille, *L'Oréal,* 261; Hamel, *Les Bettencourt,* 255–57.

Corrèze took part in the expropriation of Jewish properties: Annie Lacroix-Riz, *Les élites françaises entre 1940 et 1944* (Paris: Armand Colin, 2016), 177–78.

He swore allegiance to Hitler: Abescat, *La saga,* 101.

"Before we knew it": Seth Goldschlager, interview with author, November 13, 2015.

Frydman appeared on a popular French TV show: *Le Droit de savoir,* TF1, May 1991, cited in Abescat, *La saga,* 104.

One especially despicable character: Hamel, *Les Bettencourt,* 264–65.

"systematically sheltered criminals": Jean Frydman, quoted in Ibid., 266.

"The Cagoule were the storm troopers": Author interview with source requesting anonymity.

"When the affair exploded, he was stunned": Jean-Pierre Valériola, telephone interview with author, November 6, 2015.

Owen-Jones was a wunderkind: Marseille, *L'Oréal,* 245–51.

"the booster of sales": Dalle, quoted in Anouk Vincent, *Le roman vrai des Bettencourt* (Paris: City Editions, 2010), 117.

"a bundle of energy": Seth Goldschlager, interview with author, November 13, 2015.

"no longer played any operational role":

Abescat, *La saga,* 103.

"the slightest attack against the Jews": Jacques Corrèze, quoted in Marie-France Etchegoin, *Un milliard de secrets* (Paris: Robert Laffont, 2011), 138.

"man with no character": Liliane Bettencourt, quoted in Ibid., 138.

"I cannot change what happened": Corrèze, quoted in Vincent, *Le roman vrai,* 121.

Aided by Klarsfeld: Hamel, *Les Bettencourt,* 133; Christophe d'Antonio, *La Lady et le dandy* (Paris: Éditions Jacob-Duvernet, 2010), 92.

***Le Monde* published a full page on its revelations:** Edwy Plenel, "L'affaire L'Oréal se transforme en affaire Bettencourt," *Le Monde,* February 12, 1995.

she had invited Banier and d'Orgeval: Etchegoin, *Milliard de secrets,* 146–47; Liliane Bettencourt to François-Marie Banier, March 26, 1998, *Correspondance échangée entre Madame Liliane Bettencourt et Monsieur François-Marie Banier pour la période allant de 1989 à 2010,* vol. 1.

Liliane was furious: Banier notebook, March 14, 2010.

"apologies" . . . "youthful error": André Bettencourt, interview with Stéphane Durand-Souffland and Jean-Alphonse Richard, "André Bettencourt: Je ne suis pas antisémite," *Le Figaro,* February 15, 1995.

"After fifty years of existence": André Bettencourt, quoted in Abescat, *La saga,* 119.

Serge Klarsfeld flew to New York: Edwy Plenel, "M. Klarsfeld a saisi les autorités américaines des révélations sur le passé de M. Bettencourt," *Le Monde,* February 14, 1995.

the US Commerce Department fined L'Oréal: Pierre Angel Gay, "Les États-Unis condamnent L'Oréal à une amende pour le boycottage d'Israël," *Le Monde,* August 31, 1995.

"available evidence did not support": Justice Department spokesman's email to author, September 2, 2015.

a scathing review: Stéphanie Marteau, "André Bettencourt: mémoires d'un prince consort," *M Magazine du Monde,* May 3, 2013, accessed online September 23, 2015, http://www.lemonde.fr/societe/article/2013/ 05/03/memoires-d-un-prince105-consort _3169507_3224.html.

"In the Catholicism of my childhood": André Bettencourt, *Souvenirs* (Paris, 1999), vol. 1, 63.

"a very violent episode for my family": Jean-Pierre Meyers testimony before the Bordeaux appeals court, May 18, 2016, *Procès verbal d'audition de témoin,* 2.

Chapter 7: A Generous Man

"I hope your future wife": Victor Bettencourt, quoted in André Bettencourt, *Souvenirs* (Paris, 1999), vol. 1, 111.

Thierry Coulon, the Bettencourts' chef: Thierry Coulon deposition, August 30, 2010.

Enrico Vaccaro . . . to whom she bequeathed: "Thomas, le chien de Liliane Bettencourt," *Nouvel Observateur,* May 9, 2011, accessed online November 30, 2016, http://tempsreel.nouvelobs.com/societe/ 20110508.OBS2642/thomas-le-chien-de -liliane-bettencourt.html.

Born in the central French city of Châteauroux: Hervé Gattegno, "Le majordome qui a fait trembler Sarkozy," *Vanity Fair* (French edition) website, June 26, 2014, accessed online June 1, 2015, http:// www.vanityfair.fr/actualites/france/articles/ exclusif-aaire-bettencourt-le-majordome -bonnefoy-a-pose-un-dictaphone/14593. This is my source for all quotes and details in this chapter regarding Bonnefoy, unless otherwise specified.

"I think André was seduced": Antoine Gillot, interview with author, July 20, 2015.

It was a large room, bathed in light: Details from Gattegno, *Vanity Fair;* Marie-France Etchegoin, *Un milliard de secrets*

(Paris: Robert Laffont, 2011), 11, 20; and photographs made available to author by Bruno Mouron, December 22, 2016.

Among the bric-a-brac, one object stood out: Olivier Bouchara and Olivier Druin, "Dans les secrets de la maison Bettencourt," *Capital,* September 2010, 86.

"humoristic gift, an allusion to their vigor": "La vérité sur la sculpture coquine de Liliane Bettencourt," *Capital,* September 2, 2010, accessed online July 4, 2015, http://www.capital.fr/a-la-une/actualites/la-verite-sur-la-sculpture-coquine-de-liliane-bettencourt-526854.

It was Claire who made regular runs to the BNP bank: Claire Thibout deposition, July 5, 2010.

"I've been drained dry": Anouk Vincent, *Le roman vrai des Bettencourt* (Paris: City Editions, 2010), 130.

"He had always financed the right": Claire Thibout, quoted in Ibid., 130.

"My father was already doing it before I was married": Liliane Bettencourt, quoted in Etchegoin, *Milliard de secrets,* 286.

Alain Juppé was convicted: Gilles Gaetner and Jean-Marie Pontaut, "L'Affaire Juppé," *L'Express,* February 2, 2004, accessed online August 1, 2016, http://www.lexpress.fr/informations/l-affaire-juppe_654940.html.

Chapter 8: The Christmas Visitor

A man in a tan trench coat: Details from Pierre Castres Saint Martin, interview with author, September 22, 2015.

"It was a modern painting": Ibid.

"Please show him all the documents": Liliane Bettencourt to Jean-Michel Normand, June 24, 2002.

When Castres pored over the papers: Castres Saint Martin, interview with author, September 22, 2015.

"Madame, this is madness": Castres Saint Martin, quoted in Marie-France Etchegoin, *Un milliard de secrets* (Paris: Robert Laffont, 2011), 173.

"She gave me her permission": Castres Saint Martin, interview with author, September 22, 2015.

"You're mad to seek such sums from Liliane": Dialogue as recounted in Etchegoin, *Milliard de secrets,* 171–72.

"He was trembling with rage as he spoke": Nicole Gilbert attestation of December 27, 2002, cited in Pierre Cornut-Gentille, Laurent Merlet, and Daniel Lasserre, *Conclusions subsidiaires au fond aux fins de relaxe,* January 26, 2015, 8.

He was sure that Castres had been sent by Françoise: Banier testimony, February 2, 2015, *Note d'audience,* 77, 80.

"Castres told you he was linked with the

584

Chapon": Liliane Bettencourt fax to François-Marie Banier, December 25, 2002, *Correspondance échangée entre Madame Liliane Bettencourt et Monsieur François-Marie Banier pour la période allant de 1989 à 2010,* vol. 1.

"This incident with Castres drove me mad": François-Marie Banier, interview with author, September 28, 2015.

Banier was tempted to file a suit: Banier trial testimony, February 2, 2015, *Note d'audience,* 76, 80.

"the affection that I have": Liliane Bettencourt to Jean-Michel Normand, February 10, 2003, cited in Cornut-Gentille and Merlet, *Conclusions,* 10.

"My dear François-Marie, I am leaving a considerable fortune": Liliane Bettencourt to François-Marie Banier, quoted in Etchegoin, *Milliard de secrets,* 175.

hire a lawyer to "secure" the donations: Laurent Merlet plea at Bordeaux appeal trial, May 24, 2016, from author's notes.

"[Banier] had told Madame Bettencourt": Castres Saint Martin, interview with author, September 22, 2015.

"The real reason behind the suit": François-Marie Banier, interview with author, December 1, 2015.

"He didn't realize the risk": Castres Saint Martin, interview with author, Septemer

22, 2015.

Chapter 9: The Ambitious Monsieur Sarkozy

"ambition was a little engine": William Herndon, *Herndon's Lincoln, the True Story of a Great Life* (Chicago: Belford, Clarke & Company, 1889).

Sarkozy, the son of a Hungarian immigrant: Biographical details from an undated article on Sarkozy on the Politique.net website, accessed online November 22, 2016, http://www.politique.net/nicolas-sarkozy.htm.

working as an ice-cream vendor: Ian Hamel, *Sarko & cie* (Paris: Archipel, 2011), 4.

he outmaneuvered the Gaullist heavyweight Charles Pasqua: Politique.net, http://www.politique.net/nicolas-sarkozy.htm.

At one dinner at chez Bettencourt: Sarkozy deposition, March 21, 2013, reprinted on *Vanity Fair* (French edition) website, March 21, 2013, accessed online May 29, 2015, http://www.vanityfair.fr/actualites/france/articles/pv-audition-sarkozy-affaire-bettencourt-herzog-lantuas-youpatchou/122.

Liliane was put off: Marie-France Etchegoin, *Un milliard de secrets* (Paris: Robert Laffont, 2011), 286.

A former financial consultant: Éric Woerth, *Dans la tourmente* (Paris: Plon, 2011), 22–27.

Woerth organized an elite group: Raphaëlle Bacquet and Pascale Robert-Diard, "Les riches heures de l'affaire Bettencourt," *Le Monde Mensuel,* August 2010, 34; Fabrice Arfi, Fabrice Lhomme, with staff of *Mediapart, L'Affaire Bettencourt: un scandale d'état* (Paris: Don Quichotte, 2010), 139–50.

the Sarkozy campaign received €9,125,105: Arfi and Lhomme, *L'Affaire Bettencourt,* 141.

A descendant of Joseph de Maistre: Biographical details on de Maistre from Mélanie Delattre, "La face cachée de Patrice de Maistre," *Le Point,* July 1, 2010, 52; Nicolas Cori, "Amateur de chasse et de sloop," *Libération,* March 24, 2012.

€30 million stake in Bernie Madoff's notorious Ponzi scheme: "Fraude Madoff: Maistre entendu comme témoin," *Challenges,* September 10, 2010, accessed online September 10, 2010, http://www.challenges.fr/monde/20100910.CHA0651/fraude-madoff-maistre-entendu-comme-temoin.html; Pierre Castres Saint Martin, interview with author, September 22, 2015.

"Count Patrice de Maistre": Etchegoin, *Milliard de secrets,* 219.

African network: François Krug, "Affaire Bettencourt-Woerth: les secrets de Patrice de Maistre," *Rue89/Obs,* November 24, 2010, accessed online October 20, 2015, http://rue89.nouvelobs.com/2010/11/24/a aire-bettencourt-woerth-les-secrets-de -patrice-de-maistre-176081.

"With high-placed people": Author interview with source requesting anonymity.

de Maistre walked right past André: Antoine Gillot, interview with author, August 4, 2015.

"Patrice de Maistre quickly attracted notice": Woerth, *Tourmente,* 118–19.

André Bettencourt had asked him: Patrice de Maistre, interview with Laurent Valdiguié, "Il faut que tout cela s'arrête!" *Journal du Dimanche,* July 25, 2010, 2.

they legally gave €30,000 to the campaign: Ibid.

Éric Woerth wrote personally to candidate Sarkozy: "De nouveaux documents embarrassants pour Eric Woerth," *Le Monde,* August 31, 2010, accessed online April 27, 2016, http://abonnes.lemonde.fr/ societe/article/2010/08/31/une-lettre-qui -contredit-les-declarations-d-eric-woerth _1404753_3224.html.

He celebrated his victory with a gala dinner: Michel Pinçon and Monique Pinçon-Charlot, *Le président des riches* (Paris: Éditions de la Découverte), 15–19.

ex-girlfriend of Mick Jagger and Eric Clapton: Maureen Orth, "Paris Match," *Vanity Fair,* July 28, 2008, accessed online September 12, 2016, http://www.vanityfair.com/news/2008/09/bruni200809.

"Look at my watch": Michel Wieviorka, interview with author, November 6, 2015.

Carla, though, reinforced the image: J.M., "Carla Bruni obsédée par l'argent?" *Closer,* September 27, 2016, http://www.closermag.fr/article/carla-bruni-obsedee-par-l-argent-l-ex-premiere-dame-dans-le-viseur-de-l-ancien-conseiller-de-nicolas-sarkozy-672075.

de Maistre hired Woerth's wife: Etchegoin, *Milliard de secrets,* 292.

Chapter 10: The Whistle-blower

"But one can't be shaken up all the time": Liliane Bettencourt to François-Marie Banier, August 20, 2006, *Correspondance échangée entre Madame Liliane Bettencourt et Monsieur François-Marie Banier pour la période allant de 1989 à 2010,* vol. 2.

She was gripped by anxiety: Ibid.

the couple remained sprawled on the floor: Chantal Trovel deposition, January 24, 2008.

"She thought she was going to die": Françoise Mauclère deposition, March 31, 2010.

Rushed back to Paris: Jean-Pierre Meyers testimony, *Procès verbal d'audition de témoin,* May 18, 2016, 4.

"When are we going back to Neuilly?": Christiane Djenane deposition, February 7, 2008, cited in Pierre Cornut-Gentille, Laurent Merlet, and Daniel Lasserre, *Conclusions subsidiaires au fond aux fins de relaxe,* January 26, 2015, 78.

called the Bettencourt home at eight a.m.: Details and dialogue from Banier notebook entry of February 17, 2008; Banier testimony, February 2, 2015, *Note d'audience,* 71.

Banier and Brücker had known each other: Gilles Brücker, interview with author, July 19, 2016.

At Banier's urging: All details in this paragraph from Brücker interview with author, July 19, 2016, and Brücker deposition, July 29, 2010.

"It was totally abnormal": Gilles Brücker, interview with author, July 19, 2016.

"light coma" and "severe dehydration": Patrick de Rohan Chabot deposition, January 31, 2008, cited in Cornut-Gentille and Merlet, *Conclusions,* 78.

too heavily dosed for a woman of her age: Gilles Brücker, interview with author, July 19, 2016.

"Madame Meyers forbids Monsieur

Banier": Martin d'Orgeval testimony, May 13, 1996, from author's trial notes.

"I hope there's no checkbook in her purse": Banier testimony, May 11, 2016, from author's trial notes.

said she was "surprised" to find Vaccaro: Françoise Meyers deposition, February 1, 2010.

"Come sit next to me": Gilles Brücker, interview with author, July 19, 2016.

"She was transformed": Ibid.

"Christiane has betrayed me": Banier testimony, May 11, 2016, from author's trial notes.

had already been attributed to Banier: Tribunal de Grande Instance de Bordeaux, *Jugement correctionnel,* May 28, 2015, 93–94.

"in no case to my address in Neuilly": Liliane Bettencourt to Arcalis insurance company, September 14, 2007, cited in *Jugement correctionnel,* May 28, 2015, 94.

"going through a phase of dementia": Lucienne de Rozier deposition, February 13, 2008.

"She asked me what country she was in": Henriette Youpatchou deposition, October 24, 2011.

found her "shocked": Bruno Lantuas deposition, February 13, 2008.

she gave €500,000 to the daughter: *Jugement correctionnel,* May 28, 2015, 101.

she declared an additional €33,519,852: Ibid., 98.

she was gifting him a painting by Max Ernst: Ibid., 112.

"I am in such a state of rage": Liliane Bettencourt to François-Marie Banier, November 28, 2006, *Correspondance,* vol. 2.

"Weeks, perhaps months": Françoise Meyers deposition, February 1, 2008.

In April 2007, Françoise had an accident: Jean-Pierre Meyers testimony, May 18, 2016, 4.

blamed Banier for intentionally taking: Françoise Meyers to Liliane Bettencourt, January 14, 2008. Copy provided by Meyers's attorney Nicolas Huc-Morel.

Banier and d'Orgeval claimed: Banier testimony, May 11, 2016, from author's trial notes.

"You stay here if you want": Ibid., also Martin d'Orgeval testimony, May 13, 2016, from author's notes.

set back her recovery: Nicolas Huc-Morel and Cédric Labrousse, *Conclusions de parties civiles,* January 2015, 70.

call her black female nurse "André": Henriette Youpatchou deposition, October 24, 2011.

cut up food in the dog's bowl: Pascal Bonnefoy deposition, July 23, 2010.

turned violently against a dinner guest:

Judgment correctionnel, May 28, 2015, 58, 63.

kept up a busy schedule of meetings: Liliane Bettencourt's confiscated appointment books, included in investigative file.

met at least once a month with Lindsay Owen-Jones: Cornut-Gentille and Merlet, *Conclusions,* January–February 2015, 68–69.

her husband deferred to her decisions: Ibid., 85–86.

as many as fifty-six pills a day: Doreen Carvajal, "In Case of L'Oréal Heiress, a Private World of Wealth Becomes Public," *New York Times,* February 25, 2015.

the somnifer Stilnox and the tranquilizer Lexomil: Enrico Vaccaro deposition, March 24, 2009.

"a certain medical nomadism": Christian de Jaeger, cited in *Dossier Liliane Bettencourt* [medical experts' report], September 16, 2011.

fifty-seven different doctors: Liliane Bettencourt's confiscated address books, included in investigative file.

Banier denies claims by some: Banier deposition, January 26, 2012.

"I saw that there were many doctors": Gilles Brücker, interview with author, July 19, 2016.

"How's it going, Claire?": Dialogue as recounted in Anouk Vincent, *Le roman vrai* *des Bettencourt* (Paris: City Editions, 2010), 179. Françoise's version of this exchange appears in her typed summary of events leading up to the suit, included in investigative file. Claire Thibout's version appears in her deposition of July 5, 2010.

"I told her everything": Claire Thibout, interviewed in documentary "Liliane Bettencourt: dans l'intimité d'une milliardaire," *Complément d'enquête,* France 2, broadcast November 17, 2013.

One episode that had especially shaken Claire: Antoine Gillot, interviews with author July 21, 2010, and August 4, 2015.

Claire claimed that Banier was behind this: Huc-Morel and Labrousse, *Conclusions,* January 2015, 53.

She was so stressed: Ibid.

Claire went to the bank: Antoine Gillot, interview with author, August 4, 2015.

"It was Ali Baba's cave": Ibid.

"You have absolutely no right to do that": Jean-Michel Normand deposition, November 6, 2012; also Huc-Morel and Labrousse, *Conclusions,* 53.

"Very well. I'll throw them out the window": François-Marie Banier, quoted in Marie-France Etchegoin, *Un milliard de secrets* (Paris: Robert Laffont, 2011), 229.

"Would you be willing to testify": Françoise Meyers, quoted in Antoine Gillot, interview with author, August 4, 2015.

"What is going on there is not at all normal": Ibid.

Claire had already worked it out: Ibid.

"We can imagine the delicate situation": Françoise Meyers to Claire Thibout, November 11, 2007, included in investigative file.

"It was unthinkable for me not to respect": Françoise Meyers deposition, July 20, 2010, quoted in Fabrice Arfi and Fabrice Lhomme, with staff of *Mediapart, L'Affaire Bettencourt: un scandale d'état* (Paris: Don Quichotte, 2010), 79.

she had received a donation of €50,000: Claire Thibout testimony, February 10, 2015, *Note d'audience,* 133.

"François-Marie, you are going to laugh": Liliane Bettencourt to François-Marie Banier, March 20, 2006.

"As agreed, I am sending": Thibout to Jean-Michel Normand, November 17, 2006, quoted in Etchegoin, *Milliard de secrets,* 247.

"He told me Madame Bettencourt wanted": Claire Thibout testimony, February 10, 2015, *Note d'audience,* 133.

"Let's say, for the sake of argument": Antoine Gillot, interview with author, August 4, 2015.

Castres Saint Martin had told André as

early as 2004: Castres Saint Martin, interview with author, September 22, 2015.

"I didn't realize it was so terrible": André Bettencourt, as quoted by Antoine Gillot, interview with author, August 4, 2015.

"My wife is sick": Etchegoin, *Milliard de secrets,* 263.

"Ah, the bastard!": Chantal Trovel, quoted in Huc-Morel and Labrousse, *Conclusions,* 76.

"Banier is a crook": Françoise Meyers testimony, January 30, 2015, *Note d'audience,* 62.

"he did not react in front of the others": Pascal Bonnefoy, quoted in Huc-Morel and Labrousse, *Conclusions,* 76.

"I think he sensed the problem": Liliane Bettencourt, interviewed by Arnaud Bizot, "Liliane Bettencourt nous ouvre les portes de son cœur," *Paris Match,* September 30, 2010, 73.

"It's shameful to make the dead speak": François-Marie Banier, interview with author, September 28, 2015.

"If he had something to say": Ibid.; Banier email to author, December 12, 2016. Banier said essentially the same thing in court on January 28, 2015, *Note d'audience,* 30.

Pascal Bonnefoy took his leave of André: Hervé Gattegno, "Le majordome qui a fait trembler Sarkozy," *Vanity Fair* (French edition), June 26, 2014.

It was Martin d'Orgeval who got: Martin d'Orgeval testimony, May 13, 2016, from author's trial notes.

"Françoise has to see his body": Banier testimony, May 12, 2016, from author's notes.

Françoise and her mother clashed over the organization: Françoise Meyers testimony, January 30, 2015, *Note d'audience*, 63.

"As long as Papa was alive": Dialogue as recounted by Pascal Bonnefoy to Gattegno, "Le majordome."

"The casket was in Monsieur's office": Pascal Bonnefoy, conversation with author, November 4, 2015.

"She didn't understand what was going on": Olivier Pelat, conversation with author, November 4, 2015.

"she didn't understand why she went to the church": Jean-Victor Meyers, cited in *Jugement correctionnel,* May 28, 2015, 65.

The funeral was held in Neuilly's Saint-Pierre Church: Details of funeral service from Etchegoin, *Milliard de secrets,* 17–19, and accounts of various attendees.

he dined with Liliane beforehand: François-Marie Banier, interview with author, December 6, 2015.

"Liliane took off her wedding ring": Monique de Libouton, cited in *Jugement cor-*

rectionnel, May 28, 2015, 65.

but admits to giving Liliane an expensive diamond ring: François-Marie Banier, interview with author, July 18, 2016.

"I wanted to preserve the presence of Monsieur": Pascal Bonnefoy testimony, November 3, 2015, from author's trial notes.

"Concerning the adoption": Dominique Gaspard, attestation included in Françoise Meyers's original complaint, December 19, 2007.

"a dam that collapsed": Françoise Meyers, interviewed by Cyrille Louis, "Françoise Bettencourt Meyers: l'interview vérité," *Le Figaro,* June 25, 2010, accessed online August 2, 2010, http://www.lefigaro .fr/actualite-france/2010/06/24/01016 -20100624ARTFIG00581-francoise-betten court-l-interview-verite.php.

"I never wanted to adopt a son": Liliane Bettencourt, interviewed by Michel Deléan, "Liliane Bettencourt: 'Je n'ai plus envie de voir ma fille,' " *Journal du Dimanche,* December 21, 2008.

"There were six lawyers": Lucienne de Rozier deposition, quoted in Laurent Valdiguié, "L'autre affaire Bettencourt qui menace Françoise Meyers-Bettencourt," *Journal du Dimanche,* May 8, 2016.

Chapter 11: The Opening Salvo

Philippe Courroye received a phone call: Philippe Courroye, interview with author, August 28, 2015.

had risen to prominence: Stéphane Arteta, "Olivier Metzner, le roi de la place," *Nouvel Observateur,* March 17, 2013, accessed online September 15, 2015, http://tempsreel .nouvelobs.com/justice/20130317.OBS 2177/olivier-metzner-le-roi-de-la-place .html.

he had defended rock singer Bertrand Cantat: Flore Galaud, "Kiejman et Metzner: le duel féroce de deux ténors," *Le Figaro,* June 30, 2010, accessed online July 1, 2010, http://www.lefigaro.fr/actualite -france/2010/06/30/01016-20100630ART FIG00746-kiejman-vs-metzner-le-duel -feroce-de-deux-tenors.php.

"The hysterical fury of women": Georges Kiejman, quoted in Bastien Bonnefous, "Kiejman — Metzner, poings de droit," *Slate* (French edition), September 14, 2010, accessed online September 16, 2010, http://www.slate.fr/story/27227/bettencourt -kiejman-metzner-poings-de-droit.

"he left the land of human beings": Philippe Courroye, interview with author, August 28, 2015.

he was gay himself: Vincent Monnier,

"Olivier Metzner, histoire d'un héritage impossible," *Nouvel Observateur,* April 20, 2014, accessed online May 14, 2015, http://o.nouvelobs.com/people/20140418.OBS 4484/olivier-metzner-histoire-d-un-heritage-impossible.html.

the Bettencourt Affair as his last great case: Nicolas Huc-Morel, interview with author, November 26, 2015.

the *juge d'instruction* has extensive powers: Guillaume Perrault, "Le juge d'instruction, l'homme le plus puissant de France," *Le Figaro,* March 13, 2014.

Courroye had been an aggressive investigator: François Koch, Jean-Marie Pontaut, et al., "Philippe Courroye, un procureur très en cour," *L'Express,* November 12, 2009, accessed online August 28, 2015, http://www.lexpress.fr/actualite/societe/justice/philippe-courroye-un-procureur-tres-en-cour_827998.html.

personal friend of President Nicolas Sarkozy: Gérard Davet and Fabrice Lhomme, "Philippe Courroye: 'Nos relations ne sont pas amicales, mais personnelles,' " *Le Monde,* October 12, 2012.

"knowingly abused the state of weakness": Olivier Metzner, *Plainte,* December 19, 2007, 2.

his own *enquête préliminaire:* Gérard Davet, "L'autodéfense du procureur," *Le Monde,*

July 13, 2010, 3.

he turned to the *brigade financière:* Philippe Courroye, interview with author, August 28, 2015.

Metzner's dossier was "well supported": Ibid.

was more than €500 million: Metzner, *Plainte,* 6.

"Banier harassed Madame Bettencourt": Dominique Gaspard attestation, included with Metzner's complaint of December 19, 2007, *Certificats et attestations,* 18–25.

"That's much too much!": Henriette Youpatchou attestation, included in Ibid., 5–10. Parentheses in the original.

"At the end of 2005, Monsieur Banier telephoned": Claire Thibout attestation, included in Ibid., 12–16.

"First, we had to verify": Philippe Courroye, interview with author, August 28, 2015.

Owen-Jones proposed for Liliane to cede: Lindsay Owen-Jones to Liliane Bettencourt, November 19, 2007, cited in Pierre Cornut-Gentille, Laurent Merlet, and Daniel Lasserre, *Conclusions au fond aux fins de relaxe,* May 10, 2016, 101; Laurent Merlet, interview with author, August 3, 2015.

"life expectancy was not more than five years": Liliane Bettencourt to Jean-Michel

Normand, November 15, 2005, cited in Cornut-Gentille, Merlet, and Lasserre, *Conclusions,* January 26, 2015, 5.

"he was merely awaiting my death": Liliane Bettencourt to Jean-Michel Normand, June 26, 1999. Copy provided to the author by Georges Kiejman.

she decided to change her will: Banier testimony, February 2, 2015, *Note d'audience,* 84; Merlet interview with author, August 3, 2015.

Liliane had already granted: *Procès verbal de synthèse,* April 16, 2008, 2.

she officially named Banier as the heir: *Testament authentique de Liliane Bettencourt,* December 11, 2007, included in investigative file.

making the photographer the owner of 1.2 percent of the firm: Nicolas Huc-Morel and Cédric Labrousse, *Conclusions de parties civiles,* January–February 2015, 35, 66; Nicolas Huc-Morel, interview with author, November 26, 2015.

Not to mention the buildings: Olivier Metzner, interview with author, July 20, 2010; Tribunal de Grande Instance de Bordeaux, *Jugement correctionnel,* May 28, 2015, 105.

"an act of pure violence": Jean-Michel Normand testimony, February 2, 2015, *Note d'audience,* 84.

"I was gutted": Banier testimony, February 2, 2015, *Note d'audience,* 84.

"I'm not crazy": Banier testimony, May 12, 2016, from author's trial notes.

jurists later told investigators: *Jugement correctionnel,* May 28, 2015, 103–4.

"never understood that I was to be [Liliane's] heir": Banier testimony, May 12, 2016, from author's trial notes.

"I know ahead of time": Françoise Meyers to Liliane Bettencourt, January 14, 2008. Copy provided to author by Nicolas Huc-Morel.

"Your letter is absurd": Liliane Bettencourt to Françoise Meyers, January 16, 2008, cited in Cornut-Gentille, Merlet, and Lasserre, *Conclusions subsidiaires,* January 26, 2015, 16.

"I really cannot digest your letter": Liliane Bettencourt to Françoise Meyers, January 18, 2008, cited in Ibid., 16.

"It's thanks to him": Liliane Bettencourt to Françoise Meyers, February 2008, quoted in Béatrice Gurrey, "Cette lettre est un dernier avertissement," *Le Monde,* December 20, 2008.

"put an end to this procedure": Liliane Bettencourt to Procureur de la République [Courroye], January 30, 2008.

"I turned white as death": François-Marie Banier, interview with author, June 14, 2016; Banier testimony, February 2, 2015,

Note d'audience, 86.

"It's a story of mother-daughter jealousy": Martin d'Orgeval journal, January 17, 2008, included in investigative file.

"It was horrible": Martin d'Orgeval, interview with author, December 15, 2015.

the photographer had a complete record: *Jugement correctionnel,* May 28, 2015, 81.

claimed that Liliane had insisted: Banier testimony, May 11, 2016, from author's trial notes.

"I didn't want my action to further weaken": Françoise Meyers deposition, February 1, 2008.

"a professional of manipulation": Ibid.

Other employees, however: Cornut-Gentille, Merlet, and Lasserre, *Conclusions,* May 10, 2016, 55–56.

"This was an elderly person": Philippe Courroye, interview with author, August 28, 2015.

"I have known Monsieur François-Marie Banier for twenty-five years": Liliane Bettencourt deposition, May 13, 2008, cited in Cornut-Gentille, Merlet, and Lasserre, *Conclusions,* January–February 2015, 2.

she didn't "want to see a doctor": Philippe Courroye, interview with author, August 28, 2015.

"after her hospitalization": Youpatchou attestation, included with Metzner's complaint of December 29, 2007, *Certificats et attestations.*

"extremely fragile": Chantal Trovel attestation, included in Ibid.

"[Liliane] had completely lost her head": Nicole Berger attestation, included in Ibid.

serious health challenges: Details from résumé read in court by Judge Michèle Esarté, May 12, 2016, from author's trial notes; also in report on Liliane's medical history by Dr. Philippe Azouvi, April 7, 2008.

"My head is OK": Banier testimony, May 12, 2016, from author's trial notes.

a brain scan revealed a "hemispheric leukoaraiosis": Christophe d'Antonio, *La Lady et le dandy* (Paris: Éditions Jacob-Duvernet, 2010), 25.

"like a zombie": Claire Thibout deposition, cited in *Jugement correctionnel,* May 28, 2015, 79.

"persistent memory problems": Philippe Koskas deposition, January 17, 2008.

"alteration of her mental faculties": Michel Kalafat deposition, November 28, 2011.

"no difficulties of intellectual strategy": Yves Agid, cited in d'Antonio, *La Lady,* 26; also *Jugement correctionnel,* May 28, 2015, 75.

"the possibility of an organic intellectual

deterioration": Philippe Azouvi, cited in *Jugement correctionnel,* 76. Parentheses in original.

"disposes of her total will": Hubert Rémy, certificate, February 19, 2009, 4.

"not the same person": Rémy, cited in *Jugement correctionnel,* 76.

destroyed all records: Ibid.

proposed a reconciliation: Anouk Vincent, *Le roman vrai des Bettencourt* (Paris: City Editions, 2010), 196–97.

spoke for his wife's interests: Maurice Lévy deposition, January 18, 2013.

According to one version: d'Antonio, *La Lady,* 166–67.

"I don't even dare imagine the risk": Liliane Bettencourt to Françoise Meyers, quoted by Béatrice Gurrey, "Cette lettre est un dernier avertissement," *Le Monde,* December 20, 2008.

"the choice of guardian would be made by her daughter": Maurice Lévy deposition, January 18, 2013.

"she only wanted to see Jean-Victor": Xavier Fontanet, cited by Cornut-Gentille, Merlet, and Lasserre, *Conclusions subsidiaires,* January 26, 2015, 18.

"I don't want to see you anymore": Nicolas Meyers testimony, January 30, 2015, *Note d'audience,* 68.

"We crossed paths some fifteen years

ago": François-Marie Banier to Françoise Meyers, July 1, 2008, quoted in "Quand François-Marie Banier tentait une conciliation," *Le Monde,* August 28, 2010.

"Monsieur, do not expect me to believe": Françoise Meyers to François-Marie Banier, July 16, 2008, quoted in Ibid.

Chapter 12: Sibling Rivals

"You will shed tears of blood": François-Marie Banier, interview with author, August 11, 2016.

Liliane told those around her: Georges Kiejman, interview with author, July 8, 2015; Jean-Michel Normand deposition, November 6, 2012, 13.

Françoise was slow, passive, lacking in energy: Liliane Bettencourt to François-Marie Banier, August 17, 2007, *Correspondance échangée entre Madame Liliane Bettencourt et Monsieur François-Marie Banier pour la période allant de 1989 à 2010,* vol. 2; Arielle Dombasle interview with Gérard Miller, June 9, 2016.

never talked about her grandfather: Liliane Bettencourt to François-Marie Banier, December 14, 2008, *Correspondance,* vol. 2.

"Our attachment is real": Liliane Bettencourt to François-Marie Banier, October 8, 2008, *Correspondance,* vol. 2.

Liliane sometimes described herself: Liliane Bettencourt to François-Marie Banier, August 20, 2008, *Correspondance,* vol. 2.

"the son she never had": Pascal Bonnefoy deposition, quoted in Tribunal de Grande Instance de Bordeaux, *Jugement correctionnel,* May 28, 2015, 71.

"he was in a way the son she would have wanted": Jean-Michel Normand deposition, November 6, 2012, 21.

"She is crazy": Liliane Bettencourt to François-Marie Banier, December 28, 1994, *Correspondance,* vol. 1.

"Your mother makes me furious": Liliane Bettencourt to François-Marie Banier, July 15, 2000, *Correspondance,* vol. 1.

"I have no confidence in your mother": Liliane Bettencourt to François-Marie Banier, March 8, 2005, *Correspondance,* vol. 2.

"For 20 years I've been telling you": Banier notebook entry, April 6, 2010, 16.

"Who abandoned the other?" Ibid., 17.

"You don't understand": Liliane Bettencourt entry in Banier notebook, Ibid.

"I think I eliminated Françoise": Ibid., April 25, 2010, 35.

In his 1941 book: Edmund Wilson, *The Wound and the Bow: Seven Studies in Literature* (New York: Houghton Mifflin, 1941).

she has recorded a CD: André Bettencourt,

Souvenirs (Paris: 1999), vol. 2, 342.

"an extraordinary virtuosity": Arielle Dombasle, interview with Gérard Miller, June 9, 2016.

Hélène Ahrweiler: Françoise Bettencourt Meyers, *Les dieux grecs: géneaologies* (Paris: Editions Christian, 2001), i–iii.

"I talked to my father": Banier testimony, May 12, 2016, from author's trial notes.

Chapter 13: Sarkozy Joins the Fray

Jean-Pierre Meyers was also a member: Nicolas Sarkozy deposition, November 22, 2012, 4.

The president had accorded this rendez-vous: Ibid., 6.

"I see this grande dame arrive": Ibid., 8.

Ouart had held high positions: "Patrick Ouart, portrait du conseiller justice de Nicolas Sarkozy," Politique.net, March 12, 2009, accessed online September 7, 2015, http://www.politique.net/2009031204 -portrait-patrick-ouart.htm.

"The discussion was led by Madame Bettencourt": Patrick Ouart, interview with author, November 10, 2015.

"I supported you for your election": Dominique Gaspard, quoted in Anouk Vincent, *Le roman vrai des Bettencourt* (Paris: City Editions, 2010), 199.

Nestlé might be tempted to set aside:

Patrick Ouart, interview with author, November 10, 2015; Patrice de Maistre testimony, January 29, 2015, *Note d'audience,* 51.

"The president was very upset": Patrick Ouart, interview with author, November 10, 2015.

Today the company boasts 82,000 employees: L'Oréal 2015 Annual Report.

The firm's future seemed solidly in the hands: Details on L'Oréal–Nestlé alliance in Jacques Marseille, *L'Oréal: 1909–2009* (Paris: Perrin, 2009), 213–17.

It was renewed for five years: Fabrice Arfi and Fabrice Lhomme, with staff of *Mediapart, L'Affaire Bettencourt: un scandale d'état* (Paris: Don Quichotte, 2010), 267.

The danger, Ouart explained: Patrick Ouart, interview with author, November 10, 2015.

Liliane had always sworn: Jean-Pierre Valériola, telephone interview with author, November 6, 2015.

"I don't want [L'Oréal] to piss off": Nicolas Sarkozy, quoted in Arfi and Lhomme et al., *Affaire Bettencourt,* 264.

a personal friend of Sarkozy's: Philippe Courroye, interview with author, August 28, 2015.

Ouart met no fewer than five times: De Maistre testimony, January 29, 2015, *Note* *d'audience,* 51.

"I quoted to both parties this aphorism": Patrick Ouart, interview with author, November 10, 2015.

"the instincts of a hunting dog": Ibid.

Since the beginning of their friendship: Philippe Courroye, interview with author, August 28, 2015.

met with Sarkozy at least eight times: Gérard Davet and Fabrice Lhomme, "Philippe Courroye: 'Nos relations ne sont pas amicales, mais personnelles,' " *Le Monde,* October 12, 2012.

"Never about cases": Philippe Courroye, interview with author, August 28, 2015.

Courroye, who craved the Paris job: Alain Carignon (former minister of communication, political ally of Sarkozy), interview with author, November 27, 2015.

"People reproach the fact": Sarkozy, quoted in Raphaëlle Bacqué, "Les réseaux du procureur," *Le Monde,* May 17, 2009.

a seven-page report: d'Antonio, *La Lady,* 12, 36–37; *Journal du Dimanche,* December 6, 2009.

"body of presumptions": Gérard Davet and Jacques Follorou, "Les policiers sont à la recherche des 'petits papiers' de Mme Bettencourt," *Le Monde,* September 1, 2010.

"It's always dangerous to offer an opinion": Courroye interview with author,

August 28, 2015.

Hervé Gattegno broke the story: Hervé Gattegno, "La milliardaire et le 'favori,' " *Le Point,* December 18, 2008, accessed online September 1, 2015, http://www .lepoint.fr/actualites-societe/2008-12-18/la -milliardaire-et-le-favori/920/0/300908.

his "instructions" to journalists: Stéphane Arteta, "Olivier Metzner, le roi de la place," *Nouvel Observateur,* March 17, 2013, accessed online September 15, 2015, http:// tempsreel.nouvelobs.com/justice/20130317 .OBS2177/olivier-metzner-le-roi-de-la -place.html#.

"What on earth has gotten into my daughter?": Liliane Bettencourt, interviewed by Michel Deléan, "Liliane Bettencourt: 'Je n'ai plus envie de voir ma fille,' " *Journal du Dimanche,* December 21, 2008.

"I am totally indifferent to criticism": "Le procureur Courroye estime n'avoir 'ni à se justifier ni à se défendre,' " *Nouvel Observateur,* July 12, 2010, accessed online July 15, 2010, http://tempsreel.nouvelobs .com/politique/20100712.OBS7019/le -procureur-courroye-estime-n-avoir-ni-a-se -justifier-ni-a-se-defendre.html.

"I studied all the elements": Courroye interview with author, August 28, 2015. 172

"I don't see how you can send Banier to trial": Marie-Christine 175 d'Aubigney, as quoted by Courroye, Ibid.

612

"I wanted to let you know": Courroye, Ibid.

Chapter 14: Metzner's End Run

The papers were already drawn up: Nicolas Huc-Morel, interview with author, November 26, 2015.

Metzner cited Banier: Oliver Metzner, *Citation directe devant le Tribunal correctionnel de Nanterre,* July 15, 2009.

a long-standing rivalry: Isabelle Prévost-Desprez, interview with author, September 24, 2015; Philippe Courroye, interview with author, August 28, 2015.

Some said the bad blood: Gérard Davet and Fabrice Lhomme, *Sarko m'a tuer* (Paris: J'ai Lu, 2011), 129.

several motions to nullify: Nicolas Huc-Morel and Cédric Labrousse, *Conclusions de parties civiles,* 5–6.

changed all the locks: Prévost-Desprez, interview with author, September 24, 2015.

"I was under surveillance": Ibid.

"I thought it was a joke": François-Marie Banier, interview with author, August 16, 2016.

a state of uncontrolled anger: Hervé Temime, interview with author, November 20, 2015.

"a confident and free relationship": Ibid.

brought Georges Kiejman on board:

Georges Kiejman, interview with author, July 8, 2015.

"oratory cruelty": Pascale Robert-Diard, *La Déposition* (Paris: L'Iconoclaste, 2016), 6.

"someone brilliant and original": Georges Kiejman, email to author, November 7, 2016.

"She explained that it was unacceptable": Georges Kiejman, interview with author, November 9, 2016.

"She never varied on that point": Georges Kiejman, interview with author, July 8, 2015.

That first encounter: Details in this paragraph from Georges Kiejman, interview with author, November 9, 2016; Kiejman emails to author, November 7 and 8, 2016.

"too Jewish": Liliane Bettencourt, conversation with Patrice de Maistre, recorded November 19, 2009.

asked whether Françoise's lawyer: Liliane Bettencourt, conversation with Fabrice Goguel, recorded May 27, 2009.

"A daughter can't accept": Françoise Meyers interviewed by Hervé Gattegno, "Interview Françoise Bettencourt-Meyers," *Le Point,* July 16, 2009, accessed online March 15, 2016, http://www.lepoint.fr/actualites-societe/2009-07-16/interview-francoise-bettencourt-meyers/920/0/361839.

"a gift for encounters": François-Marie Banier, interviewed by Michel Guerrin, "Il y a toujours eu du vacarme derrière moi," *Le Monde,* September 12, 2009, 20–21.

"I understand that you are shocked": François-Marie Banier to Liliane Bettencourt, December 5, 2009, *Correspondance échangée entre Madame Liliane Bettencourt et Monsieur François-Marie Banier pour la période allant de 1989 à 2010,* vol. 2.

Françoise petitioned a civil judge: Tribunal de Grande Instance de Bordeaux, *Jugement correctionnel,* May 28, 2015, 40.

"My dear mother": Françoise Meyers to Liliane Bettencourt, December 2, 2009, published by *Le Figaro,* December 3, 2009.

In the absence of a medical certificate: *Jugement correctionnel,* May 28, 2015, 40.

"It was the only way to express": Georges Kiejman, email to author, November 2, 2016.

The brief he filed: Georges Kiejman, *Conclusions d'intervention volontaire,* December 11, 2009. Copy provided to the author by Georges Kiejman.

"I don't always follow": Isabelle Prévost-Desprez, as quoted by Georges Kiejman in interview of November 9, 2016.

"didn't have the necessary elements": Isabelle Prévost-Desprez, interview with author, September 24, 2015.

did not claim any monetary damages: Olivier Metzner, interview with author, July 20, 2010.

"In my opinion": Hervé Temime, interview with author, November 20, 2015.

"What I think is horrible": Karl Lagerfeld, quoted in Bob Colacello, "The Bettencourt Affair, Part II: The Gilded Friendship," *Vanity Fair,* November 2010, accessed online February 27, 2015, http://www.vanityfair.com/style/2010/11/bettencourt-part-2-201011.

"beyond our comprehension": Seynur de Gramont de Guiche deposition, September 14, 2010.

"People who stood to inherit money": Hervé Temime, interview with author, November 30, 2015.

Chapter 15: The Butler Did It

"The atmosphere among the personnel": Liliane Hennion deposition, August 2010, cited in Pierre Cornut-Gentille, Laurent Merlet, and Daniel Lasserre, *Conclusions subsidiaires au fond aux fins de relaxe,* January 26, 2015, 60.

"a basket of crabs": Alain Thurin deposition, October 21, 2010.

The personnel were divided into clans: Tribunal de Grande Instance de Bordeaux, *Jugement correctionnel,* May 28, 2015, 5.

"Madame Gaspard often adopted": Thierry Coulon deposition, August 27, 2010, cited in Cornut-Gentille, Merlet, and Lasserre, *Conclusions subsidiaires,* January 26, 2015, 58.

"profoundly hysterical and jealous": Françoise Mauclère deposition, October 26, 2006, appended to Banier's complaint of April 6, 2012.

showed up drunk: Jérôme Sarran deposition, October 20, 2010, 3; Banier refers to this "unqualifiable" incident in a letter to Liliane Bettencourt, May 30, 2007, *Correspondance échangée entre Madame Liliane Bettencourt et Monsieur François-Marie Banier pour la période allant de 1989 à 2010,* vol 2.

one staffer reportedly threatened: Banier journal entry, March 28, 2007.

After André's death, some concluded: Antoine Gillot, interview with author, July 20, 2014.

the "charming" bodyguard Vaccaro: François-Marie Banier to Liliane Bettencourt, May 30, 2007, *Correspondance,* vol. 2.

another rift opened up: Françoise Meyers testimony, January 30, 2015, *Note d'audience,* 63.

Madame Bettencourt fired most of those: Nicolas Huc-Morel and Cédric Labrousse,

Conclusions de parties civiles, January–February 2015, 36.

When she was fired in November 2008: Antoine Gillot, interview with author, July 20, 2015.

she didn't even report it to tax authorities: Antoine Gillot, interview with author, August 4, 2015.

he might be the next victim: Pascal Bonnefoy testimony, November 3, 2015, from author's trial notes.

urinating on the plants: Pascal Bonnefoy deposition, cited in Huc-Morel and Labrousse, *Conclusions,* January–February 2015, 51.

"Madame is not your wife": Pascal Bonnefoy deposition, quoted in Ibid., 50.

"Madame frowned and ignored me": Ibid., 49.

"I know you suspect me of testifying": Pascal Bonnefoy, quoted in Hervé Gattegno, "Le majordome qui a fait trembler Sarkozy," *Vanity Fair* (French edition), June 26, 2014.

"Madame Bettencourt needs to know": Lindsay Owen-Jones, as quoted by Bonnefoy in Ibid.

"I wanted to know what was going on": Bonnefoy, in Ibid.

Patrice de Maistre arrived: Recording transcript, May 25, 2009.

having security experts sweep the office:

Patrice de Maistre, conversation with Liliane Bettencourt, recorded January 6, 2010.

"After serving the drinks": Bonnefoy, in Gattegno, "Le majordome."

he decided to consult a lawyer: Antoine Gillot, interview with author, July 21, 2010.

"It was the atom bomb": Antoine Gillot, interview with author, August 4, 2015.

"what you have done is a crime": Dialogue as recounted in Antoine Gillot, interview with author, July 21, 2010.

Bonnefoy turned to Philippe Dunand: *Jugement correctionnel,* May 28, 2015, 44.

He was determined to capture: Pascal Bonnefoy testimony, November 3, 2015, from author's trial notes.

decided to give his notice: Ibid.

crossed the rue Delabordère: Details from Gattegno, "Le majordome"; Bonnefoy testimony, November 3, 2015, from author's trial notes.

"How did you get them?": Dialogue as recounted in Françoise Meyers's typed summary of events, included in investigative file.

Bonnefoy asked Françoise to wait: Bonnefoy testimony, November 3, 2015.

"We have to be transparent": Olivier Metzner, interview with author, July 20, 2010.

they took the CDs to the office of Jérôme Cohen: *Jugement correctionnel,* May 28,

2015, 40–41.

he called Judge Prévost-Desprez: Isabelle Prévost-Desprez, interview with author, September 24, 2015.

"You will have them": Dialogue as recounted by Prévost-Desprez, Ibid.

Françoise sent a courier: *Jugement correctionnel,* May 28, 2015, 40–41.

contacted Nanterre prosecutor Courroye: Ibid.

The first violation he targeted: Philippe Courroye, interview with author, August 26, 2015.

ordered a complete transcription: Ibid.

provided Prévost-Desprez with copies: Prévost-Desprez, interview with author, September 24, 2015.

"explosive document": Stéphane Arteta, "Olivier Metzner, le roi de la place," *Nouvel Observateur,* March 17, 2013.

"Metzner had a reputation": Pascale Robert-Diard, interview with author, October 8, 2015.

"the collusion between the summit of political power": Edwy Plenel, interview with author, July 14, 2010.

"The courtroom was as full as a beehive": Prévost-Desprez, interview with author, September 24, 2015.

"Now he's looking for it": Exchange between Kiejman and Metzner as recounted by Bastien Bonnefous, "Kiejman — Metzner, poings de droit": *Slate* (French edition), September 14, 2010, accessed online September 16, 2010, http://www .slate.fr/story/27227/bettencourt-kiejman -metzner-poings-de-droit.

"I warn you, gentlemen": Prévost-Desprez, interview with author, September 24, 2015.

"the methods used by the plaintiff": Hervé Temime, quoted in Karl Laske, "Le procès Banier s'empare des écoutes," *Libération,* July 2, 2010.

"You can no longer render a credible decision": Georges Kiejman, as quoted in Ibid.

"an aged little girl 57 years old": Ibid.

suspended the session: Prévost-Desprez, interview with author, September 24, 2015.

"in a confrontation with Sarkozy": Ibid.

Chapter 16: Behind Closed Doors

"I'm going to the Élysée this afternoon": Patrice de Maistre, conversation with Liliane Bettencourt, recording of June 12, 2009.

"Sarkozy's adviser, whom I see regularly": Patrice de Maistre, recording of July 21, 2009.

a charge that Sarkozy, Courroye, and Ouart deny: Philippe Courroye, interview with author, August 26, 2015; Patrick Ouart, interview with author, November 10, 2015.

"[Ouart] wanted to see me": Patrice de Maistre, recording of April 23, 2010.

de Maistre had recruited: "Florence Woerth s'explique sur ses conditions d'embauche," *Le Monde,* July 21, 2010.

"friend Éric Woerth": Patrice de Maistre, recording of October 27, 2009.

"the one who oversees your taxes": Patrice de Maistre, recording of October 29, 2009.

"pushy" and "tiresome": Ibid.

"it's only 7,500": Patrice de Maistre, recording of March 4, 2010.

"arranging to send [the funds]": Patrice de Maistre, recording of November 19, 2009.

"several things to discuss": Patrice de Maistre, exchange with Liliane Bettencourt, September 7, 2009.

"I sign at the bottom?": Liliane Bettencourt, exchange with Jean-Michel Normand, September 9, 2009.

only de Maistre was designated: Tribunal de Grande Instance de Bordeaux, *Jugement correctionnel,* May 28, 2015, 118.

buy him a sailboat as a "gift": Patrice de Maistre, recording of October 22, 2009.

"When I cut off the onboard engine": Patrice de Maistre, recording of October 29, 2009.

"Oh yes, I understand": Liliane Bettencourt, recording of October 22, 2009.

"Do you still want to offer me a gift?": Patrice de Maistre, exchange with Liliane Bettencourt, recorded October 23, 2009.

talked Liliane into giving him €5 million: *Jugement correctionnel,* May 28, 2015, 120.

bumped up by 60 percent: Ibid., 117–21.

"pluck the feathers": Antoine Gillot, interview with author, July 20, 2015.

"imbecile" who "throws oil on the fire": Patrice de Maistre, recording of November 30, 2009.

"Your notary tells me": Patrice de Maistre, exchange with Liliane Bettencourt, recorded March 4, 2010.

"Banier wants you to change": Jean-Michel Normand, exchange with Liliane Bettencourt, March 12, 2010.

"he doesn't know how to behave": Liliane Bettencourt, exchange with Patrice de Maistre, recorded October 29, 2009.

"I just hope he doesn't kill me": Liliane Bettencourt, exchange with Patrice de Maistre, recorded April 7, 2010.

Île d'Arros, the private island: Details on the Bettencourts' acquisition and use of d'Arros from Hervé Gattegno, "L'île maudite des Bettencourt," *Vanity Fair* (French edition), February 9, 2015, accessed online May 29, 2015, http://www.vanityfair.fr/actualites/france/articles/ile-darros-paradis-maudit/1641.

"What island?": Liliane Bettencourt, exchange with Patrice de Maistre, recorded May 11, 2010.

"For 2006, you have to find something": François-Marie Banier, recorded May 11, 2010.

"things will turn out fine": Ibid.

"With your letters, thanks to your ear": Ibid.

"If [Sarkozy] had been spattered": Philippe Courroye, interview with author, August 26, 2015.

Another possible interpretation: Antoine Gillot, interview with author, July 21, 2010.

"everything spun out of control": Patrick Ouart, interview with author, November 10, 2015.

Chapter 17: The Woerth Affair

Sarkozy might even name him: Éric Woerth, *Dans la tourmente* (Paris: Plon, 2011), 69.

had filed a complaint: Fabrice Arfi and Fabrice Lhomme, with staff of *Mediapart, L'Affaire Bettencourt: un scandale d'état* (Paris: Don Quichotte, 2010), 62.

Courroye had his detectives interrogate

Thibout: Ibid., 61–66.

"the affair turned political": Antoine Gillot, interview with author, July 21, 2010.

"The Accountant Accuses": Fabrice Arfi and Fabrice Lhomme, "L'ex-comptable des Bettencourt accuse: des enveloppes d'argent à Woerth et à Sarkozy," *Mediapart,* July 6, 2010, accessed online July 16, 2010, https://www.mediapart.fr/journal/france/060710/lex-comptable-des-bettencourt-accuse-des-enveloppes-dargent-woerth-et-sarkozy. All Thibout quotes in this and the following three paragraphs are from this source.

"Sometimes it is useful": Tribunal de Grande Instance de Bordeaux, *Jugement correctionnel,* May 28, 2015, 131.

Thibout's interview triggered: Claude Guéant, interview with author, December 15, 2015.

"I'm starting to get sick and tired": Nicolas Sarkozy, quoted in Woerth, *Tourmente,* 138.

Guéant had organized a nucleus: Arfi and L'homme, *Affaire Bettencourt,* 253–57.

"light counter-fires": Claude Guéant, interview with author, December 15, 2015.

Guéant called an emergency meeting: Ibid.

One participant suggested: Details on the meeting from Nadine Morano, telephone interview with author, November 17, 2015;

Antoine Guiral, "La cellule Guéant, défense immunitaire contre les affaires," *Libération,* September 3, 2011.

UMP party leader Xavier Bertrand: " 'Méthodes fascistes': Mediapart va attaquer Xavier Bertrand en diffamation," *L'Express,* July 7, 2010.

***Mediapart* lost the 2013 ruling:** "Xavier Bertrand relaxé pour ses ptopos sur les 'méthodes fascistes' de Mediapart," *Le Monde,* March 26, 2013, accessed online January 25, 2017, http://www.lemonde.fr/actualite -medias/article/2013/03/26/xavier-bertrand -relaxe-pour-ses-propos-sur-les-methodes -fascistes-de-mediapart_3148213_3236 .html.

Courroye ordered his detectives to re-interrogate: Arfi and Lhomme, *Affaire Bettencourt,* 67–71.

"the real truth comes out!": Ibid., 256.

confronted her face-to-face: Deposition de Maistre–Thibout confrontation, July 8, 2010.

"I felt they were treating me": Thibout, quoted in Arfi and Lhomme, *Affaire Bettencourt,* 72.

"ceaselessly told the truth": Antoine Gillot, interview with author, July 21, 2010.

the president took to the airwaves: All Sarkozy quotes in this paragraph are from Sophie Landrin, "Nicolas Sarkozy joue la réforme contre les affaires," *Le Monde,* July 14, 2010, 10.

Woerth's wife, Florence, resigned: "Florence Woerth s'explique sur ses conditions d'embauche," *Le Monde,* July 21, 2010.

she told a different story: Ibid.

didn't think much of her work: Patrice de Maistre, recording of October 29, 2009.

called her "pushy": Ibid.

Woerth's "Achilles' heel": "Portrait: Florence Woerth, une femme de tête qui ne voulait pas être une 'femme de . . .' " *La Dépêche du Midi,* July 1, 2010.

"an original and trendy way": Paul Warguin, "Le haras qui rit de Florence Woerth," *L'Express,* July 7, 2010, accessed online April 27, 2016, http://www.lexpress.fr/actualite/politique/le-haras-qui-rit-de-florence-woerth_904667.html.

Florence Woerth was elected: "Portrait: Florence Woerth."

His public statements on the subject: "Eric Woerth: Tout cet acharnement, c'est fait pour tuer,' " *Le Parisien,* August 30, 2010.

Woerth was interrogated: Éric Woerth deposition, July 29, 2010.

Woerth had personally written to Sarkozy: *Jugement correctionnel contradictoire,* May 28, 2915, 6. (Ruling in the influence peddling case against de Maistre and

Woerth.)

tax returns had not been audited: Arfi and Lhomme, *Affaire Bettencourt,* 66.

The in-house report: Sophie Fay, "Un rapport en terrain miné," *Le Nouvel Observateur,* July 22–28, 2010, 37.

made him go ballistic: Gérard Davet, "L'audition de Patrice de Maistre met Eric Woerth en difficulté," *Le Monde,* July 17, 2010.

Sarkozy ordered chief of staff Claude Guéant: Gérard Davet and Fabrice Lhomme, *Sarko m'a tuer* (Paris: Editions Stock, 2011), 21–39.

removed from his Justice Ministry post: Ibid., and David Sénat, *La république des conseillers* (Paris: Grasset, 2015), ch. 10.

"Sarkozy doesn't mess around": Isabelle Prévost-Desprez, interview with author, September 24, 2015.

Chapter 18: Filthy Rich

One skit showed Sarkozy's allies: This and other Mamie Zinzin skits are viewable on YouTube, https://www.youtube.com/watch?v=FhGwRlXtK2U.

"we didn't talk about money": Françoise Meyers, interviewed by Raphaëlle Bacquet, "Françoise Bettencourt Meyers: 'Allons-y, mieux vaut tout purger,' " *M Magazine du Monde,* March 10, 2012, 45.

"My only adversary": Charles de Gaulle, quoted in Pascal Bruckner, *La Sagesse de l'argent* (Paris: Grasset, 2016), 62.

"money that corrupts": François Mitterrand, quoted in Ibid., 62.

"I don't like the rich": François Hollande, quoted in Ibid., 66.

"president of the rich": Michel Pinçon and Monique Pinçon-Charlot, *Le président des riches* (Paris: Zones, 2010).

to live happily, live hidden: Liliane Bettencourt quoted this traditional saying in a letter to François-Marie Banier, November 18, 1994, *Correspondance échangée entre Madame Liliane Bettencourt et Monsieur François-Marie Banier pour la période allant de 1989 à 2010,* vol. 1.

72 percent of the respondents: IFOP poll, October 2012. On French attitudes toward money: Janine Mossuz-Lavau, *L'Argent et nous* (Paris: Editions de La Martinière, 2007).

"reticence to talk about money": Janine Mossuz-Lavau, interview with author, July 7, 2015.

"For those who wanted to show": Michel Wieviorka, interview with author, November 26, 2015.

"We did not fully appreciate the extent": Éric Woerth, *Dans la tourmente* (Paris: Plon, 2011), 127.

Liliane herself was widely seen: Janine Mossuz-Lavau, interview with author, July 7, 2015.

One website invited users to compare: See https://www.mataf.net/en/lab/liliane.

"They massacred François-Marie": Richard Malka (attorney for Martin d'Orgeval), interview with author, June 9, 2016.

"A rich woman": Liliane Bettencourt interviewed by Nicole Wisniak, "A partir d'un certain Chiffre, les gens Déraillent," *Egoïste,* no. 10 (1987), 55.

"There are a lot of jealous people": Ibid.

created the Bettencourt Schueller Foundation: Bruno Abescat, *La saga des Bettencourt* (Paris: Plon, 2010), ch. 4.

Liliane donated €552 million: Ibid., 42.

"43 years of social and professional activity": Anouk Vincent, *Le roman vrai des Bettencourt* (Paris: City Editions, 2010), 156.

choice for master of ceremonies: Ibid.

Chapter 19: Banier's *Année Terrible*

wrote down their exchanges: The notebooks containing their written exchanges during this period are contained in the investigative dossier. The written dialogue quoted here is from an entry of July 6, 2010.

Madame "did not wish to speak" to him:

François-Marie Banier testimony, February 18, 2015, *Note d'audience,* 212.

"tender and dear" friendship: François-Marie Banier to Liliane Bettencourt, August 17, 2010, *Correspondance échangée entre Madame Liliane Bettencourt et Monsieur François-Marie Banier pour la période allant de 1989 à 2010,* vol. 2.

"didn't batter down the doors": François-Marie Banier testimony, May 12, 2016, from author's trial notes.

"The summer of 2010 was extremely hard": Hervé Temime, interview with author, November 20, 2015.

exchange with Barbier: François-Marie Banier, interviewed by Christophe Barbier and Jean-Marie Pontaut, "Francois-Marie Banier: 'La générosité de Liliane est voulue, décidée, calculée," *L'Express,* July 14, 2010, 54–59.

Liliane received her lawyer Georges Kiejman: Georges Kiejman interview with author, July 8, 2015, and November 9, 2016.

"too much is too much": Georges Kiejman, quoted in "M. Banier n'est plus légataire universel de Mme Bettencourt," *Le Monde,* August 28, 2010.

a *Paris Match* interview that read like a farewell letter: Liliane Bettencourt, interviewed by Arnaud Bizot, "Liliane Bettencourt nous ouvre les portes de son cœur," *Paris Match,* September 30, 2010, 71–74.

coached and edited: Marion Bougeard of the agency Opus Conseils: Tribunal de Grande Instance de Bordeaux, *Jugement correctionnel,* May 28, 2015, 169; Marion Bougeard, interview with author, August 10, 2010.

"the media noise": François Krug, "Affaire Bettencourt: L'Oréal lâche Banier, question d'image," *Nouvel Observateur,* September 20, 2010, accessed online March 3, 2015, http://tempsreel.nouvelobs.com/rue89/ rue89-politique/20100920.RUE8588/ affaire-bettencourt-l-oreal-lache-banier -question-d-image.html.

Banier liquidated his company: See http:// www.societe.com/societe/hericy-410235501 .html.

personally telephoned Jean-Paul Agon: Françoise Meyers deposition, August 17, 2010, 7.

"The current climate is not favorable": Jean-Luc Monterosso, quoted in "François-Marie Banier déprogrammé à Paris," *AFP,* October 7, 2010.

The same reasoning: François-Marie Banier, interview with author, October 25, 2016.

"He tries not to show it": Pascal Greggory, quoted in Michel Guerrin, "François-Marie

Banier le mauvais génie," *M Le Magazine du Monde,* October 16, 2010.

on the verge of suicide: François-Marie Banier, interview with author, June 8, 2016.

"He placed himself in a kind of theater": Jean-Michel Ribes, interview with author, November 18, 2015.

Chapter 20: The Fixer

"descent into hell": Patrice de Maistre testimony, February 11, 2015, *Note d'audience,* 154.

de Maistre's personal lawyer since 1996: Tribunal de Grande Instance de Bordeaux, *Jugement correctionnel,* May 28, 2015, 163.

no real friendship: Pascal Wilhelm, interview with author, June 23, 2016.

son of a Jewish clothier: Franck Johannès, "Procès Bettencourt #17. Relaxe générale, pour la défense," *Le Monde* website, February 25, 2015, accessed online March 1, 2015, http://libertes.blog.lemonde.fr/2015/02/25/proces-bettencourt-17-relaxe-generale-pour-la-defense.

not sailing, but judo: Alain Pénin, *Expertise Psychologique/Wilhelm,* December 4, 2012, 6.

A specialist in conflict resolution: Pascal Wilhelm, interview with author, June 23, 2016.

a man of "strong temperament": Wilhelm

testimony, February 11, 2015, *Note d'audience,* 149.

published a biography: Pascal Wilhelm, *Camille Desmoulins: le premier républicain de France* (Paris: Grancher, 2015).

"like the queen of England:" Pascal Wilhelm, interview with author, June 23, 2016.

"What should we do?" Dialogue as recounted by Wilhelm, Ibid.

Wilhelm contacted the Finance Ministry: Details of Wilhelm's dealings with tax authorities from interview of June 23, 2016, and Wilhelm's testimony, February 11, 2015, *Note d'audience,* 153.

Liliane invited Wilhelm: Pascal Wilhelm, interview with author, June 23, 2016.

"I can't continue": Dialogue as recounted by Wilhelm, Ibid.

The idea had been bandied about: Recording of September 7, 2009.

she found it "too violent": Wilhelm testimony, February 11, 2015, 147.

"It's too dangerous for L'Oréal": Laurent Valdiguié, "Affaires Bettencourt: Les dessous d'un arrangement," *Le Journal du Dimanche,* December 12, 2010.

Wilhelm contacted Didier Martin: Pascal Wilhelm, interview with author, June 23, 2016.

left out of the loop: Ibid.

de Maistre sought Wilhelm's help: Pascal

Wilhelm, interview with author, June 28, 2016.

"the recordings did not reflect": Laurent Obadia deposition, cited in *Jugement correctionnel,* May 28, 2016, 169.

a whopping monthly fee of €80,000: Gérard Davet and Fabrice Lhomme, "Voyages, encadrement des interviews: comment travaillait le 'communicant' de Liliane Bettencourt," *Le Monde,* October 27, 2011.

directly involved in editing: Marion Bougeard, email to Pascal Wilhelm, cited in *Jugement correctionnel,* May 28, 2015, 18.

"reworked and amended": Bougeard deposition, cited in *Jugement correctionnel,* May 28, 2015, 179; Marion Bougeard, interview with author, August 10, 2010.

"Madame is not interested in that": Patrice de Maistre, quoted in Michel Guerrin, "21 minutes avec Liliane Bettencourt," *Le Monde,* June 19, 2010.

"looking over [her] shoulder": Marion Bougeard, email to Michel Guerrin, cited in *Jugement correctionnel,* May 28, 2015, 179.

***Le Monde* published the interview:** Guerrin, "21 minutes."

It was later revealed: *Jugement correctionnel,* May 28, 2015, 179.

"You want me to take it all back?": Liliane Bettencourt, interview with Claire

Chazal, TF1, July 21, 2010.

"must have taken German lessons": Breitou [screen name], "Le Raus des Bettancourt [*sic*] et les juifs," Harissa.com, July 25, 2010, accessed online October 17, 2016, http://www.harissa.com/forums/read.php?56,84067.

Prévost-Desprez first learned the details: Isabelle Prévost-Desprez, interview with author, September 24, 2015.

indemnity "poses a problem": Ibid.

a police search of the Meyers apartment: Françoise Meyers to Claire Thibout, July 11, 2007, included in investigative file.

Banier's lawyers filed a complaint: *Jugement correctionnel,* May 28, 2015, 34.

Kiejman phoned Courroye: Georges Kiejman interview with author, November 9, 2016.

complaint for "violation of professional secrets": Ibid.

fifty-seven text messages: Philippe Courroye, interview with author, August 26, 2015.

"the Nanterre tribunal had become a boxing ring": Patrick Ouart, interview with author, November 10, 2015.

the cases were transferred: *Jugement correctionnel,* May 28, 2015, 47.

"So I would stop the investigations": Isabelle Prévost-Desprez, interview with author, September 24, 2015.

Courroye would be demoted: Philippe Courroye, interview with author, August 26, 2015; "La mutation forcée de Courroye désormais officielle," *Le Figaro,* August 3, 2012, accessed online May 15, 2016, http://www.lefigaro.fr/politique/2012/08/03/01002-20120803ARTFIG00277-la-mutation-forcee-de-courroye-desormais-officielle.php.

promoted in August 2016: Isabelle Prévost-Desprez, email to author, December 1, 2016.

Wilhelm retaliated: Pascal Wilhelm to Philippe Courroye, October 20, 2010; *Jugement correctionnel,* May 28, 2015, 46.

"You want war, you'll get war": Pascal Wilhelm, interview with author, July 28, 2016.

a second citation: Olivier Metzner, *Citation directe devant le Tribunal Correctionnel de Nanterre,* November 3, 2010.

pressure from L'Oréal management: Raphaëlle Bacqué and Pascale Robert-Diard, "Les dessous de la réconciliation des Bettencourt," *Le Monde,* December 7, 2010.

But both sides would have to make concessions: Pascal Wilhelm, interview with author, June 23, 2016.

"Your daughter is like Prince Charles": Ibid.

"family coexistence": Wilhelm testimony, *Jugement correctionnel,* May 28, 2015, 167.

she mandated Wilhelm: Ibid.

It was Metzner's task to negotiate: Bacqué and Robert-Diard, "Les dessous."

the whole family gathered: Laurent Valdiguié, "Affaires Bettencourt: Les dessous d'un arrangement," *Journal du Dimanche,* December 12, 2010.

"happy about the reconciliation": Françoise Meyers testimony, January 29, 2015, *Note d'audience,* 64.

"not apt to perform legal acts": Christian de Jaeger deposition, October 8, 2012; cited in *Jugement correctionnel,* May 28, 2015, 165.

The eight-page protocol: *Protocole d'accord,* December 6, 2010, included in investigative file.

a separate agreement: Franck Johannès, "Procès Bettencourt #2. La défense échoue à renvoyer l'audience," *Le Monde,* February 3, 2015, accessed online March 2, 2015, http://libertes.blog.lemonde.fr/2015/02/03/proces-bettencourt-2-la-defense-echoue-a-renvoyer-laudience/.

Liliane has not received a dime: Jean-Pierre Meyers testimony, May 18, 2015, from author's trial notes; Jean-Victor Meyers testimony, January 30, 2015, *Note* *d'audience,* 67.

there wasn't much room to negotiate: Pierre Cornut-Gentille, interview with author, May 31, 2016.

giving up more than €600 million: Marie-France Etchegoin, *Un milliard de secrets* (Paris: Robert Laffont, 2011), 333. By the time the case went to trial in 2015, the contracts were worth more than a billion euros: *Jugement correctionnel,* May 28, 2015, 197.

could have cashed in the contracts: Laurent Merlet, interview with author, June 2, 2016.

On the afternoon of December 6: Ibid.

the return of "family harmony": Bacqué and Robert-Diard, "Les dessous."

"Didier Martin called me": Pascal Wilhelm, interview with author, June 23, 2016.

"I was in a rage": Georges Kiejman, interview with author, July 8, 2015.

ten times more: Ibid.

"how could she sign this protocol?": Ibid.

"It's incomprehensible": Richard Malka, interview with author, June 9, 2016.

Ouart privately questions: Patrick Ouart, interview with author, November 10, 2015.

"I think those people": Pascal Wilhelm, interview with author, June 23, 2016.

"No comment": Jean-Pierre Meyers testimony, May 18, 2016, from author's trial notes.

denying that she had played any direct role: Françoise Meyers testimony, January 30, 2015, *Note d'audience,* 64–65.

"The family never considered": Nicolas Huc-Morel, interview with author, November 26, 2015.

the direct financial benefit: Pierre Cornut-Gentille, Laurent Merlet, and Daniel Lasserre, *Conclusions subsidiaires au fond aux fins de relaxe,* January 26, 2015, 22–23.

became her testamentary executor: *Jugement correctionnel,* May 28, 2015, 196.

"assumed most of these tasks": Wilhelm deposition, June 12, 2012, cited in Ibid., 165–66.

billed €200,000 per month: Wilhelm testimony, February 11, 2015, *Note d'audience,* 155.

Wilhelm was to manage the capital: *Jugement correctionnel,* May 28, 2015, 142.

claimed it was Liliane herself: Wilhelm testimony, February 16, 2015, *Note d'audience,* 207–8.

Wilhelm's intervention: *Jugement correctionnel,* May 28, 2015, 182–95.

a personal friend of President Sarkozy: Renaud Revel, "Stéphane Courbit, la roue de la fortune," *L'Express,* January 16, 2013, accessed online, December 9, 2016, http://www.lexpress.fr/actualite/medias/stephane

-courbit-la-roue-de-la-fortune_1210300 .html.

mistook him for a pop singer: *Jugement correctionnel,* May 28, 2015, 190. Wilhelm insisted in court that Liliane had indeed "understood the nature of the investment." Wilhelm testimony, February 16, 2015, *Note d'audience,* 206.

The initial agreement with Courbit: *Jugement correctionnel,* May 28, 2015, 192.

"it was a good investment": Pascal Wilhelm, interview with author, July 28, 2016.

billed Courbit's company €150,000: Wilhelm testimony, February 16, 2015, *Note d'audience,* 211.

241 **Thurin acted as a conduit:** *Jugement correctionnel,* May 28, 2015, 142.

Wilhelm would send Thurin the texts: Ibid., 166.

purloin her letterhead stationery: Claire Thibout depositions, cited by Nicolas Huc-Morel and Cédric Labrousse, *Conclusions de parties civiles,* January–February 2015, 41–42; Nicolas Huc-Morel, interview with author, November 26, 2015.

"Thurin's role went beyond": Wilhelm testimony, February 18, 2015, *Note d'audience,* 212.

Madame Bettencourt revised her will: "L'ancien infirmier de Liliane Bettencourt mis en examen," *Le Monde,* October 17, 2010.

in spite of the local prosecutor's call: Procureur Claude Laplaud, *Communiqué,* March 23, 2011.

the withdrawal of complaints: Author interviews with Nicolas Huc-Morel, November 26, 2015; Georges Kiejman, July 7, 2015; Laurent Merlet, August 3, 2015.

For Georges Kiejman, though, it was over: Georges Kiejman, interview with author, November 9, 2016.

Chapter 21: Bordeaux

"Bordeaux has always been a snake pit": Patrick Ouart, interview with author, November 10, 2015.

The son of a Mercedes dealer: Details on Gentil's background from François Labrouillère and David Le Bailly, "Jean-Michel Gentil: un juge apolitique et inflexible," *Paris Match,* April 27, 2012; Gérard Davet and Fabrice Lhomme, "Jean-Michel Gentil, juge intransigeant et solitaire," *Le Monde,* March 22, 2013.

a manner some described as haughty: Nicolas Cori, "Jean-Michel Gentil, un 'justicier' dans l'affaire Bettencourt," *Libération,* January 19, 2010, accessed online January 9, 2016, http://www.liberation.fr/france/2012/01/19/jean-michel-gentil-un

-justicier-dans-l-affaire-bettencourt _789421.

Starting salary for a French judge: Article on French magistrates, cidj.com, accessed online September 1, 2016, http://www.cidj .com/article-metier/magistrat-magistrate.

divided them into eight separate cases: Tribunal de Grande Instance de Bordeaux, *Jugement correctionnel,* May 28, 2015, 48.

withdrew their respective complaints: Ibid., 49.

Accompanied by the judge and two police officers: Details on medical experts' examination of Liliane Bettencourt and conclusions from Sophie Gromb et al., *Rapport d'experts,* September 28, 2011, included in investigative file.

critics hotly disputed the validity: *Jugement correctionnel,* May 28, 2015, 85; Bernard Laurent testimony, February 16, 2015, *Note d'audience,* 192.

Demands by Banier, de Maistre, and others: "Bettencourt: la cour d'appel valide l'ensemble de la procédure," *Nouvel Observateur,* September 24, 2013, accessed online August 15, 2016, http://tempsreel .nouvelobs.com/justice/20130924.OBS 8147/bettencourt-la-cour-d-appel-valide-l -ensemble-de-la-procedure.html.

she filed a petition to investigate Pascal Wilhelm's conduct: Nicolas Huc-Morel and Cédric Labrousse, *Conclusions de parties civiles,* January–February 2015, 9–10.

Françoise justified her initiative: Gérard Davet and Fabrice Lhomme, "Affaire Bettencourt: Françoise Bettencourt-Meyers saisit à nouveau la juge des tutelles," *Le Monde,* June 8, 2011.

she wanted to keep Wilhelm: Liliane Bettencourt, quoted in Franck Johannès, "Procès Bettencourt #13. Liliane Bettencourt n'est plus dans le même monde," *Le Monde* website, February 18, 2015, accessed online March 1, 2015, http://libertes .blog.lemonde.fr/2015/02/18/proces -bettencourt-13-liliane-bettencourt-nest -plus-dans-le-meme-monde.

"That's how it is": Ibid.

Kass-Danno handed down her decision: *Jugement correctionnel,* May 28, 2015, 49; Huc-Morel and Labrousse, *Conclusions,* 49.

"I raised her and yet": Liliane Bettencourt, interviewed by Laurent Valdiguié, "Bettencourt: 'Si ma fille gagne, je pars à l'étranger," *Journal du Dimanche,* October 16, 2011.

"What's the matter, *Grand-mère?*": Dialogue as recounted by a source close to the Meyers family who wishes to remain anonymous; Jean-Victor Meyers described the same scene more succinctly in his testimony of January 30, 2015, *Noted'audience,* 66.

Judge Kass-Danno named real estate developer Olivier Pelat: *Jugement correctionnel,* May 28, 2015, 49.

Liliane Bettencourt's godson: François Vidal, "Olivier Pelat, le discret ange gardien de Liliane Bettencourt," *Les Echos,* April 29, 2016, accessed online April 30, 2016, http://www.lesechos.fr/29/04/2016/Les EchosWeekEnd/00029-011-ECWE_olivier -pelat-le-discret-ange-gardien-de-liliane -bettencourt.htm.

Chapter 22: Hardball

Monday, December 12, 2011: Unless otherwise indicated, all details of the arrest and incarceration of François-Marie Banier and Martin d'Orgeval from police reports labeled *Mandat d'amener François-Marie Banier,* December 9–12, 2011; also Martin d'Orgeval's unpublished notes, made available to the author by Martin d'Orgeval.

kept in the so-called VIP wing: Martin d'Orgeval, interview with author, December 15, 2015.

helped a friend arrange: "Affaire Bissonnet: Le vicomte d'Harcourt libéré," *France Soir,* May 18, 2012, accessed online September 3, 2016, http://archive.francesoir.fr/ actualite/justice/affaire-bissonnet-le-vicomte -d-harcourt-libere-227341.html.

"It was a violent experience": Martin d'Orgeval, interview with author, December 15, 2015.

gifts worth more than €3 million: Tribunal de Grande Instance de Bordeaux, *Jugement correctionnel,* May 28, 2015, 19.

the judge was hostile: François-Marie Banier, telephone conversation with author, September 2, 2016.

they were *mis en examen:* *Procès verbal de première comparution,* December 14, 2011.

bail in the amount of €10 million: *Jugement correctionnel,* May 28, 2015, 3, 7.

"the extremely brutal way": *Procès verbal de première comparution,* December 14, 2011, 3.

"absolutely no reason": Pierre Cornut-Gentille, interview with author, May 31, 2016.

"you become an obstacle, or you lie down": Pascal Wilhelm, interview with author, June 23, 2016.

"I was on the wrong side": Patrice de Maistre testimony, January 29, 2015, *Note d'audience,* 52.

the prosecutor had specifically instructed: Isabelle Prévost-Desprez, email to author, November 29, 2015; Isabelle Prévost-Desprez, interview with author, September 24, 2015.

She and other jurists: Hervé Temime,

interview with author, November 20, 2015.

Courroye did have de Maistre briefly detained: Philippe Courroye, email to author, January 14, 2016.

Wednesday, December 14, 2011: Details of de Maistre's arrest and detainment from police reports labeled *Mandat d'amener DE MAISTRE Patrice,* December 14, 2011.

The judge laid out the charges against him: *Réquisitions aux fins de placement sous contrôle judiciaire,* December 15, 2011.

Judge Gentil had him locked up: "Affaire Bettencourt: Patrice de Maistre en détention provisoire," *Le Monde,* March 23, 2012.

What Gentil really wanted: Patrice de Maistre testimony, February 18, 2015, *Note d'audience,* 214; Pascal Wilhelm, interview with author, June 28, 2016.

Sarkozy summoned his key advisers: Judge Jean-Michel Gentil and Judge Valérie Noël, *Ordonnance de non-lieu partiel et de renvoi devant le tribunal correctionnel,* October 7, 2013, 153–54.

Sarkozy's crusade to abolish: "Nicolas Sarkozy confirme qu'il veut supprimer le juge d'instruction," *Le Monde,* January 7, 2009.

"hatred of rare intensity": "Sarkozy et les juges: chronique d'une guerre sans merci," *Nouvel Observateur,* March 23, 2013, ac-

cessed online June 9, 2016, http://temp sreel
.nouvelobs.com/societe/20130323.OBS
2839/sarkozy-et-les-juges-chronique-d-une
-guerre-sans-merci.html.

their chance to exact revenge on a president: Ibid.

According to accountant Claire Thibout:
See chapter 17.

de Maistre and Woerth met in a café:
Jean-Michel Gentil and Cécile Romonatxo,
Procès-verbal de diligences et d'analyse,
March 27, 2013, 2–3.

he had flown to Geneva: Chronology cited
by Judge Gentil in his interrogation of
Nicolas Sarkozy, November 22, 2012, 17.

COFINOR made seven deliveries: *Jugement correctionnel,* May 28, 2015, 127;
Procès verbal de confrontation, June 14,
2012.

**he claimed to have "destroyed" all the
receipts:** *Jugement correctionnel,* May 28,
2015, 138.

An analysis of her account books: Ibid.,
139.

The obvious suspicion: Ibid., 140.

Woerth met with Sarkozy at his campaign headquarters: Ibid., 134; Gentil
and Romonatxo, *Procès-verbal,* 3.

**Sarkozy himself had made at least two
visits:** Gérard Davet and Fabrice Lhomme,
"Affaire Bettencourt: non-lieu pour
Sarkozy," *Le Monde,* October 7, 2013.

"For his campaign? Not at all": Isabelle Prévost-Desprez, interview with author, September 24, 2015.

she was not alone in thinking: *Jugement correctionnel,* May 28, 2015, 127; *Procès verbal de confrontation,* June 14, 2012.

Claire Thibout's €50,000 claim was a "lie": *Jugement correctionnel,* May 28, 2015, 129.

Gentil organized a confrontation: Details of the confrontation from *Procès verbal de confrontation,* June 14, 2012.

the judge exacted an additional bail payment: "Affaire Bettencourt: Patrice de Maistre libéré contre une caution de 2 millions d'euros," *Le Monde,* June 18, 2012.

Chapter 23: A President in the Crosshairs

51.9 percent of the vote: the actual result was 51.64 percent for Hollande and 48.36 percent for Sarkozy, according to the official figures of the French Interior Ministry.

cleared the use of Bonnefoy's illicit recordings: Tribunal de Grande Instance de Bordeaux, *Jugement correctionnel,* May 28, 2015, 50.

"Sarkozy had asked for money": Quoted in Gérard Davet and Fabrice Lhomme, "L'affaire Bettencourt se rapproche de Nicolas Sarkozy," *Le Monde,* March 27, 2012.

a coincidence that the judge found "curious": Jean-Michel Gentil interrogation of Nicolas Sarkozy, *Procès verbal de première comparution,* November 22, 2012, 22.

"but it was someone important": François-Marie Banier deposition, quoted in Davet and Lhomme, "L'Affaire Bettencourt."

"That doesn't interest me": Ibid.

Gentil warned the ex-president at the outset: *Procès verbal,* November 22, 2012, 2.

"never asked them for a centime": Sarkozy, Ibid., 17.

"she heard nothing": Ibid., 4.

"I gave this appointment to the main shareholder": Ibid., 6.

never discussed "a single case": Ibid., 25.

"to obtain a mediation, a pacification": Ibid., 28.

"Why would you follow a private judicial affair": Gentil, Ibid., 28.

"The Banier procedure doesn't interest us": Sarkozy, Ibid., 30.

"Couldn't one imagine": Gentil, Ibid., 30.

"Banier, and as far as I know, exclusively Banier": Sarkozy, Ibid., 31.

they assigned him the status of "assisted witness": Ibid., 33.

the "affair no longer exists": "L'affaire Bettencourt 'n'existe plus' selon Thierry Herzog, avocat de Nicolas Sarkozy," *Huff-*

ington Post (French edition), November 23, 2012, accessed online September 9, 2016, http://www.huffingtonpost.fr/2012/11/23/affaire-bettencourt-terminee-selon-thierry-herzo-avocat-nicolas-sarkozy_n_2176596.html.

Sarkozy stuck to his earlier claim: The entire transcript of Sarkozy's confrontation with ex-butlers Pascal Bonnefoy and Bruno Lantuas; former nurse Henriette Youpatchou; and former chambermaid Dominique Gaspard was published on the website of *Vanity Fair*'s French edition: "Sarkozy face aux employés de maison: le texte intégral des confrontations," February 17, 2015, accessed online July 21, 2015, http://www.vanityfair.fr/actualites/france/articles/pv-audition-sarkozy-aaire-bettencourt-herzog-lantuas-youpatchou/122.

"For a political figure like him": Claude Guéant interview with author, December 15, 2015.

267-page *ordonnance* summarizing the charges: See Jean-Michel Gentil and Valérie Noël, *Ordonnance de non lieu partiel de requalification et de renvoi devant le tribunal correctionnel,* October 7, 2013, for all details in this paragraph.

"I once told him that he was radioactive": Patrick Ouart, interview with author, November 10, 2015.

interrogated for eighteen hours: Dan Bilefsky and Maïa de la Baume, "French Ex-Leader Questioned in Graft Inquiry, Imperiling Comeback Hopes," *New York Times,* July 1, 2014.

This latest scandal grew out of allegations: Jonathan Parienté, Maxime Vaudano, and Samuel Laurent, "Affaire des écoutes: ce qui est reproché à Nicolas Sarkozy," *Le Monde,* March 13, 2014.

The main informant was Gilbert Azibert: Ibid.

the Paris appeals court rejected Sarkozy's challenge: Paul Gonzales, "La justice valide des écoutes de Nicolas Sarkozy," *Le Figaro,* March 22, 2016, accessed online March 22, 2016, http://www.lefigaro.fr/actualite-france/2016/03/22/01016-20160322ARTFIG00259-la-justice-valide-des-ecoutes-de-nicolas-sarkozy.php.

the Paris Prosecutor's Office called for Sarkozy to stand trial: "Affaire Bygmalion: le parquet demande le renvoi de Sarkozy en correctionnelle," *Le Parisien,* September 5, 2016.

"sordid Bettencourt Affair": Nicolas Sarkozy, primary debate broadcast October 13, 2016, by TF1.

"money that corrupts": François Mitterrand, quoted in Pascal Bruckner, *La Sagesse de l'argent* (Paris: Grasset, 2016), 62.

the photographer had filed a complaint: Tribunal de Grande Instance de Bordeaux, *Jugement correctionnel,* May 28, 2015, 45.

they painted a devastating portrait of Banier: See summary of their original attestations in chapter 11.

Banier's lawyers filed a perjury complaint: See Pierre Cornut-Gentille and Laurent Merlet, *Plainte pour faux témoignages et attestations inexactes,* April 6, 2012, for all details in this paragraph.

Banier's complaint wound up on the desk of Roger Le Loire: David Bensoussan, "Roger Le Loire, l'atypique juge de l'affaire de la caisse noire de l'UIMM," *Challenges,* October 4, 2013, accessed online September 13, 2016, http://www.challenges.fr/economie/20131003.CHA5 095/atypique.html; Simon Piel, "La tentation politique du juge Le Loire," *Le Monde,* August 6, 2016.

"respectful" and "civilized": François-Marie Banier, interview with author, July 18, 2016.

put Claire Thibout under investigation: Affaire Bettencourt: l'ex-comptable poursuivie pour faux témoignages," *L'Obs,* November 28, 2014, accessed online September 15, 2016, http://tempsreel .nouvelobs.com/justice/20141128.OBS6

503/affaire-bettencourt-l-ex-comptable
-poursuivie-pour-faux-temoignages.html.

In April 2015, he did the same: Pascal
Ceaux, "Affaire Bettencourt: soupçons sur
les témoins," *L'Express,* January 14, 2016,
accessed online September 15, 2016, http://
www.lexpress.fr/actualite/societe/justice/
affaire-bettencourt-soupcons-sur-les
-temoins_1753103.html.

Le Loire slapped a new charge: "Affaire
Bettencourt: Claire Thibout mise en examen," *Le Figaro,* September 29, 2015, accessed online September 29, 2015, http://
www.lefigaro.fr/flash-actu/2015/09/28/
97001-20150928FILWWW00368-aaire
-bettencourt-claire-thibout-mise-en
-examen.php.

dropped the subornation charges: *Jugement correctionnel,* May 28, 2015, 34.

Françoise granted an unsecured loan:
Antoine Gillot, interviews with author, July
20, 2015, and August 4, 2015; Claire Thibout testimony, February 10, 2015, *Note
d'audience,* 134.

Thibout had appealed to Françoise: Antoine Gillot, interview with author, August
4, 2015.

the loan's timing was suspect: Pierre
Cornut-Gentille, interview with author,
May 31, 2016.

filed new charges against Françoise:

Pierre Cornut-Gentille, email to author, September 14, 2016.

it would be the "atomic bomb": Antoine Gillot, interview with author, December 11, 2015.

Le Loire took a step in that direction: "Le procès Bettencourt manipulé?" *Le Point,* October 3, 2015, accessed online October 3, 2015, http://www.lepoint.fr/justice/le -proces-bettencourt-manipule-03-10-2015 -1970386_2386.php.

Chapter 25: Life and Death

On this particular morning: Details from Vincent Monnier, "Olivier Metzner, histoire d'un héritage impossible," *Nouvel Observateur,* April 20, 2014, accessed online September 16, 2016, http://o.nouvelobs.com/ people/20140418.OBS4484/olivier-metzner -histoire-d-un-heritage-impossible.html.

"preserve the defense of our clients": Ibid.

"the last case that he would plead": Nicolas Huc-Morel, interview with author, November 26, 2015.

Metzner spent eleven months: Details from Stéphane Durand-Souffland, "L'avocat Olivier Metzner vend son île bretonne," *Le Figaro,* November 20, 2012, accessed online September 15, 2016, http:// immobilier.lefigaro.fr/article/l-avocat-olivier

-metzner-vend-son-ile-bretonne_bca3eb2c
-3325-11e2-8b8c-bebc0bbc3090/; also,
online video of the island and its structures:
http://iledeboedic.fr.

An obsessive workaholic: Pascale Robert-
Diard, "Olivier Metzner, derrière l'avocat,
l'homme secret," *Le Monde,* March 19,
2013, 11.

"He started crying like a baby": Denis
Robert, Facebook post, March 13, 2011,
accessed online September 15, 2016,
https://www.facebook.com/search/top/
?q=olivier%20metzner.

put the Île de Boëdic up for sale: Durand-
Souffland, "L'avocat Olivier Metzner."

"I have another project": Olivier Metzner,
quoted in Ibid.

"Just a week before this happened":
Nicolas Huc-Morel, interview with author,
November 26, 2015.

"drunk on his own success": Hervé
Temime, interview with author, November
30, 2015.

"not unrelated to Metzner's suicide":
Isabelle Prévost-Desprez, interview with
author, September 24, 2015.

Noël Robin was found dead: "Suicide d'un
haut-fonctionnaire, sous-directeur des affaires financières de la PJ parisienne," *Le
Monde,* April 2, 2013.

an early-morning stroller spotted a man:
"L'ex-infirmier de Bettencourt, prévenu au

procès, a tenté de se suicider," *L'Express,* January 26, 2015, accessed online March 1, 2015, http://www.lexpress.fr/actualite/ societe/l-ex-infirmier-de-bettencourt -prevenu-au-proces-a-tente-de-se-suicider _1644579.html.

"I adored working with Madame": Alain Thurin to Bordeaux prosecutor Gérard Aldigé, January 26, 2015, quoted in Franck Johannès, "Procès Bettencourt #3. La lettre d'Alain Thurin," *Le Monde,* February 4, 2015, accessed online March 2, 2015, http://libertes.blog.lemonde.fr/2015/02/04/ proces-bettencourt-3-la-lettre-dalain -thurin/.

He finally recovered and was acquitted: "L'ex-infirmier de Liliane Bettencourt relaxé," *Le Figaro,* October 26, 2015, accessed online October 26, 2015, http://www .lemonde.fr/societe/article/2015/10/26/ abus -de-faiblesse-l-ex-infirmier-de-liliane -bettencourt-relaxe_4797180_3224.html.

Chapter 26: The Reckoning

accused of cajoling €2 million: Tribunal de Grande Instance de Bordeaux, *Jugement correctionnel,* May 28, 2015, 16.

Pelat had filed on Liliane's behalf: Laurent Merlet, interview with author, November 7, 2016.

Liliane's objective: Georges Kiejman, email

to author, November 7, 2016; Georges Kiejman, interview with author, November 9, 2016.

passed "into another world": Olivier Pelat testimony, February 16, 2015, *Note d'audience,* 200–1.

having her sons file complaints: Nicolas Huc-Morel and Cédric Labrousse, *Conclusions de parties civiles,* January–February 2015, 8.

Françoise herself was a plaintiff: *Jugement correctionnel,* May 28, 2015, 2.

accused of abusing the weakness of Liliane Bettencourt: Ibid., 100.

€173 million remained in his possession: Huc-Morel and Larbousse, *Conclusions,* 35.

that designation, potentially worth more than €1 billion: Ibid., 35.

a tough, sometimes combative judge: Details on Roucou from "Denis Roucou, l'homme qui devra juger de la moralité de l'entourage de Liliane Bettencourt," *Le Figaro,* January 26, 2015.

"Roucou cannot abide him": Franck Johannès, "Procès Bettencourt #8. Bilan à mi-parcours," *Le Monde,* February 10, 2015, accessed online March 1, 2015, http://libertes.blog.lemonde.fr/2015/02/10/proces-bettencourt-8-bilan-a-mi-parcours/.

"I didn't lead the life of some little mar-

quis": All quotes in this paragraph from François-Marie Banier testimony, January 28, 2015, *Note d'audience,* 27–30.

"That's a very French question": Ibid., 29.

"Where is my freedom?": Ibid., 36.

"sharp, intelligent, droll": Jean-Michel Ribes testimony, January 28, 2015, 33.

"Why don't you summon the pope": Jean-Michel Ribes, interview with author, November 18, 2015.

"when I lit a cigarette": Corinne Paradis testimony, January 28, 2015, 32.

Nor did he give much attention: Pierre Cornut-Gentille, interview with author, July 18, 2016.

"Banier used violent language": Monique de Libouton deposition, September 15, 2010, read aloud in court on February 4, 2015, *Note d'audience,* 99.

"It's slanderous!": François-Marie Banier testimony, February 4, 2015, *Note d'audience,* 99.

Gaspard repeated the claims: Gaspard testimony, February 2, 2015, Ibid., 88–92.

"It never existed": François-Marie Banier testimony, February 2, 2015, Ibid., 86–87.

In an *adoption simple:* Nicolas Huc-Morel, interview with author, November 26, 2015.

he might have mentioned adoption: *Jugement correctionnel,* May 28, 2015, 71.

"Banier was not adopted": Nicolas Huc-More, quoted in "Liliane Bettencourt est une 'victime' ni plus ni moins, selon ses avocats," *L'Express,* February 2, 2015, accessed online October 5, 2016, http://www.lexpress.fr/actualites/1/societe/liliane-bettencourt-est-une-victime-ni-plus-ni-moins-selon-ses-avocats_1653327.html.

"adoption requires the accord of the family": Laurent Merlet, interview with author, June 6, 2016.

"These are people seeking revenge": François-Marie Banier testimony, January 28, 2015, *Note d'audience,* 37.

she repeated the charges: Françoise Meyers testimony, January 29, 2015, *Note d'audience,* 61–65.

"a daughter who loves her mother so tenderly": François-Marie Banier testimony, February 16, 2015, *Note d'audence,* 217.

"a woman who wanted to share things with me": François-Marie Banier testimony, February 2, 2015, 70–71.

"It gave her pleasure to give me money": François-Marie Banier testimony, January 28, 2015, *Note d'audience,* 36.

"things I could never have had": François-Marie Banier testimony, February 2, 2015, *Note d'audence,* 72.

"When I refuse, it's like denying": Ibid., 80.

in the wake of the Formentor accident: *Jugement correctionnel,* May 28, 2015, 14.

shortly after André's death: Ibid., 154.

"Madame Bettencourt had full control": François-Marie Banier testimony, quoted in "Procès Bettencourt: le truculent François-Marie Banier à la barre," Bfmtv .com, January 28, 2015, accessed online October 8, 2016, http://www.bfmtv.com/ societe/proces-bettencourt-le-truculent -francois-marie-banier-a-la-barre-860087 .html#.

"Do you think the people at L'Oréal kept a nutcase around": François-Marie Banier testimony, February 2, 2015, *Note d'audience,* 75.

the confirmation of something she had already granted him: Pierre Cornut-Gentille and Laurent Merlet, *Conclusions subsidiaires au fond aux fins de relaxe,* January 26, 2015, 4.

"She told me five or six days later": François-Marie Banier testimony, February 3, 2015, *Note d'audience,* 84.

two paintings by Jean Arp and Max Ernst: Inventory of gifts received by Martin d'Orgeval in *Jugement correctionnel,* May 28, 2015, 19.

as much as €25,000 a day: Nicolas Huc-Morel courtroom commentary, May 20, 2016, from author's trial notes.

Banier's *toutou:* Monique de Libouton deposition, September 15, 2015.

"I never saw Liliane for her money": Martin d'Orgeval testimony, January 28, 2015, *Note d'audience,* 40.

"I knew nothing about the conditions": Martin d'Orgeval testimony, February 3, 2015, Ibid., 98.

"I knew Liliane was helping François-Marie": Ibid., 97.

Under psychiatric treatment: Claire Thibout testimony, February 10, 2015, *Note d'audience,* 137.

"I never negotiated for my testimony": Thibout testimony, February 10, 2015, *Note d'audience,* 141.

called Thibout "bipolar": Eve du Breuil testimony, January 29, 2015, *Note d'audience,* 53.

called her story "nonsense": Thibout testimony, February 10, 2015, 136.

It was all Banier's fault: Ibid., 133.

"omnipresent and had a terrible hold": Ibid., 133, 135.

"not there to protect [Madame Bettencourt]": Ibid., 139.

She repeated her oft-told tale: Ibid., 134–35.

That sum consisted of a €5 million donation: *Jugement correctionnel,* May 28, 2015, 18.

charged with tax fraud: Ibid., 140–41.

He justified the €5 million gift: Ibid., 120–23.

finally realized it was a "bad idea": Patrice de Maistre testimony, February 16, 2015, *Note d'audience,* 201–3.

"Granted, she's an elderly lady": Patrice de Maistre testimony, February 4, 2015, quoted in Michel Deléan, "Procès Bettencourt: les enregistrements refont surface," *Mediapart,* February 10, 2015, accessed online October 6, 2016, https://www .mediapart.fr/journal/france/050215/proces -bettencourt-les-enregistrements-refont -surface?onglet=full.

denial of her "lying denunciations": Patrice de Maistre testimony, February 18, 2015, *Note d'audience,* 213.

"It's easier to attack an underling": Ibid.

"I can't prove to you that I did not take this money": Patrice de Maistre testimony, February 16, 2015, *Note d'audience,* 202.

"not given this money to Éric Woerth": Patrice de Maistre testimony, February 18, 2015, *Note d'audience,* 214.

"I never received any cash from Patrice de Maistre": Éric Woerth testimony, February 10, 2015, *Note d'audience,* 142–45.

"he was in an unreal world": Laurent

Merlet, interview with author, August 3, 2015.

seventeen witnesses and five medical experts: *Jugement correctionnel,* May 28, 2015, 13–19.

delivered a sweeping condemnation: Benoît Ducos-Ader plea, quoted in Franck Johannès, "Procès Bettencourt #14. Les parties civiles et les énergumènes," *Le Monde* website, February 19, 2015, accessed online March 1, 2015, http://libertes .blog.lemonde.fr/2015/02/19/proces-betten court-14-les-parties-civiles-et-les-energu menes/.

The most withering indictment: Gérard Aldigé summation, quoted in Franck Johannès, "Procès Bettencourt #15. Le réquisitoire du parquet en ses tunnels," *Le Monde* website, February 21, 2015, accessed online March 1, 2015, http://libertes .blog.lemonde.fr/2015/02/21/ proces -bettencourt-15-le-requisitoire-du-parquet -en-ses-tunnels/.

"One might find it shocking": Laurent Merlet plea, quoted in "Procès Bettencourt: Pour la défense de Banier, la milliardaire a décidé 'de le couvrir d'or,' " 20minutes.fr, February 25, 2015, accessed online March 1, 2015, http://www.20minutes.fr/bordeaux/ 1549787-20150225-proces-bettencourt

-defense-banier-milliardaire-decide-couvrir
-or.

"an impulsive man": Pierre Cornut-Gentille plea, quoted in Aude Courtin, "Procès Bettencourt: le 'brillant' De Maistre et 'l'excessif' Banier," *Sud Òuest,* February 25, 2015.

The verdict that Roucou and his associates handed down: Sentencing details from *Jugement correctionnel,* May 28, 2015, 269–82.

The magistrates voiced their "strong suspicion": Ibid., 161.

"totally recovered [his] honor": Éric Woerth, quoted in Franck Johannès, "Procès Bettencourt: relaxe pour Eric Woerth, prison pour François-Marie Banier," *Le Monde,* May 29, 2015.

"Yes, he was declared not guilty": Antoine Gillot, interview with author, July 20, 2015.

Cornut-Gentille told him to pack a bag: Laurent Merlet, interview with author, August 3, 2015.

"judged from the beginning": François-Marie Banier, interview with author, July 18, 2015.

Banier's finances as ruined as his reputation: Laurent Merlet, interview with author, August 3, 2015.

As he descended the courthouse steps: Scene as described in Ibid.; François-Marie Banier, telephone conversation with author,

November 3, 2016.

All three cases resulted in acquittals: In an unusual move, the Bordeaux prosecutor appealed the acquittals of Bonnefoy and the journalists, as well as that of Prévost-Desprez. Both cases are scheduled for retrial in 2017.

"French justice finds it very hard to convict politicians": Edwy Plenel, conversation with author, November 4, 2015.

Chapter 27: The Eye of the Beholder

his two most recent photo books: *Imprudences* (Göttingen: Steidl, 2015); *Never Stop Dancing* (Göttingen: Steidl, 2015).

Monday, November 30, 2015: From author's notes taken on the Place de la République.

"the street is like a studio": François-Marie Banier, conversation with author, November 30, 2015.

"There is something disturbing": Ibid.

"So, Monsieur Banier, you're making money?": Dialogue from author's notes, November 30, 2015.

he was once slapped in the face: François-Marie Banier to Liliane Bettencourt, December 29, 2003, *Correspondance échangée entre Madame Liliane Bettencourt et Monsieur François-Marie Banier pour la période allant de 1989 à 2010,* vol. 2.

"Because they like celebrity": François-Marie Banier, conversation with author, August 11, 2016. Jean-Marc Roberts recounts scenes of passersby cheering and encouraging Banier, in *François-Marie* (Paris: Gallimard, 2011), 46.

"their truth": François-Marie Banier, interview with author, September 28, 2015.

"a hugely gifted artist": Graydon Carter, "Editor's Letter: Paris Is Burning," *Vanity Fair,* November 2010.

"He tries to make contact": Jan Hoet, postscript to Banier, *Imprudences.*

"Nobody else in the world": François-Marie Banier, conversation with author, July 18, 2016.

"The thing that marks the originality": Jean-Luc Monterosso, email to author, October 11, 2016.

gave Banier a major exhibit: Ibid.

the price Madame Bettencourt paid: Liliane Bettencourt to Jean-Luc Monterosso, April 11, 2007, in investigative file; Michel Guerrin, "L'exposition Banier aura-t-elle lieu?" *Le Monde,* February 11, 2016.

"a great French artist:" Jean-Luc Monterosso, email to author, October 11, 2016.

"one of our biggest successes": Guerrin, "L'exposition Banier."

second exhibition was canceled: Jean-Luc

Monterosso, email to author, October 11, 2016.

buying hundreds of copies: Guerrin, "L'exposition Banier."

"all of a sudden, he didn't sell anything": Laurent Merlet, interview with author, August 3, 2015.

"For photographers from the agencies": Guy Marineau, email to author, October 26, 2015.

sold about 70,000 copies: Laurent Merlet, interview with author, August 3, 2015.

fewer than 2,000 copies: Michel Guerrin, "François-Marie Banier le mauvais génie," *M Magazine du Monde,* October 16, 2010.

"Writing is a necessity for me": François-Marie Banier, interview with author, September 28, 2015.

"a very good writer" . . . "has trouble knowing who he is": Dominique Fernandez, interview with author, October 31, 2015.

Banier replied, "Writer": François-Marie Banier, interview with Michel Guerrin, "Il y a toujours eu du vacarme derrière moi," *Le Monde,* September 12, 2009, 21.

"Promoting a book may be exhausting": Liliane Bettencourt, fax to François-Marie Banier, September 30, 2006, *Correspondance,* vol. 2.

"someone who is rather elusive": Martin d'Orgeval, interview with author, December

15, 2015.

"different from most people": Pascal Greggory, interview with author, December 12, 2015.

"Everybody who met François-Marie": Diane von Furstenberg, telephone interview with author, December 23, 2015.

"Banier is an excessive man": Laurent Merlet, interview with author, August 3, 2015.

Chapter 28: The Wheels of Justice

died of a degenerative brain disease: Corinne Audouin, "Mort de Carlos Vejarano, l'ex-gestionnaire de l'île d'Arros," FranceInter.fr, April 19, 2016, accessed online April 19, 2016, https://www.franceinter.fr/justice/mort-de-carlos-vejarano-l-ex-gestionnaire-de-l-ile-d-arros.

was tried separately: "L'ex-infirmier de Liliane Bettencourt relaxé," *Le Figaro,* October 26, 2015, accessed online October 26, 2015, http://www.lefigaro.fr/actualite-france/2015/10/26/01016-20151026ART FIG00010-l-ex-infirmier-de-liliane-bettencourt-attend-son-jugement.php.

both abandoned their appeals: "Un notaire de Liliane Bettencourt renonce à faire appel de sa condamnation," *France Soir,* May 8, 2016, accessed online May 9, 2016, http://www.francesoir.fr/societe-faits-divers/

un-notaire-de-liliane-bettencourt-renonce -faire-appel-de-sa-condamnation.

De Maistre's withdrawal followed two months of negotiations: "De Maistre conclut un accord avec la famille Bettencourt et renonce à son appel," *Le Point,* October 29, 2015, accessed online October 30, 2015, http://www.lepoint.fr/societe/ patrice-de-maistre-conclut-un-accord-et -juridique-avec-la-famille-bettencourt-29 -10-2015-1977867_23.php.

reportedly cut to €5 million: Lauren Valdiguié, "Banier, condamné heureux," *Journal du Dimanche,* August 28, 2016, 16.

he was officially stripped of the Légion d'honneur: *Journal Officiel,* no. 0280, December 2, 2016.

negotiations had been initiated: "De Maistre conclut un accord," *Le Point,* October 29, 2015.

"hardly the least important objective": Patrick Ouart, interview with author, November 10, 2015.

de Maistre would never have to appear in court: Valdiguié, "Banier, condamné heureux," 16.

training sessions with a communications expert: Richard Malka, interview with author, June 9, 2016.

He pronounced the words "no comment": Jean-Pierre Meyers, *Procès verbal* *d'audition de témoin,* May 18, 2016.

putting Françoise Meyers under formal investivation: Dominique Simonnot, "Bettencourt et ses témoins piégés," *Canard Enchaîné,* July 20, 2016, 6.

"Do you believe the testimony in your favor": Exchange between Judge Le Loire and Françoise Meyers, as reported in Ibid.

"The daughter comes out fine": Claire Thibout, quoted in Ibid.

"We received less": Henriette Youpatchou, Ibid.

called the action groundless: Jean Veil, telephone interview with author, August 25, 2016.

Françoise's legal team was sufficiently worried: Information from persons involved in the discussion who spoke to the author on condition of anonymity.

three years in prison and a €45,000 fine: Article 434-15 of the French *Code pénal.*

"a private matter": Jean-Paul Agon, interviewed by Mélanie Delattre, "Les femmes vont gagner dix ans de jeunesse," *Le Point,* November 19, 2009, 90.

6.7 percent annual increase in sales: L'Oréal annual reports from 2008 through 2015.

"Françoise's legal situation is a problem": Seth Goldschlager, telephone conversation with author, October 31, 2016.

a breathtaking farewell present: *Donation*

par Madame Bettencourt au profit de Monsieur Owen-Jones, May 9, 2005, in investigative file.

in addition to his €381 million in stock options: Marie-France Etchegoin, *Un milliard de secrets* (Paris: Robert Laffont, 2011), 195; Fabrice Arfi and Fabrice Lhomme, with staff of *Mediapart, L'Affaire Bettencourt: un scandale d'état* (Paris: Don Quichotte, 2010), 261.

"affection and personal gratitude": Liliane Bettencourt, *Donation par Madame Bettencourt.*

discovered the paperwork: Isabelle Prévost-Desprez, interview with author, September 24, 2015.

"they limited the damage": Ibid.

Sales grew sixfold during his tenure: Based on figures provided by L'Oreal's financial department and L'Oréal annual reports, 1988–2006.

Liliane Bettencourt's personal fortune rose: Arfi, Lhomme, et al., *Affaire Bettencourt,* 260.

Asked by a journalist: Lindsay Owen-Jones, inverviewed by Hervé Gattegno, "Affaire Bettencourt: Lindsay Owen-Jones parle," *Le Point,* September 30, 2010, accessed online February 14, 2017, http://www.lepoint.fr/economie/affaire-bettencourt-lindsay-owen-jones-parle-30-09-2010

-1246321_28.php.

One source close to the Meyers family: Author interview with source requesting anonymity.

acts that occurred after September 1, 2006: Tribunal de Grande Instance de Bordeaux, *Jugement correctionnel,* May 28, 2015, 3.

Owen-Jones retired in 2012 to Lugano: Bruno Abescat, "Exil fiscal: ils font le grand saut," *L'Expansion,* October 4, 2012, accessed online September 26, 2016, http://archive.wikiwix.com/cache/display.php?url=http://lexpansion.lexpress.fr/economie/exil-fiscal-ils-font-le-grand-saut_343631.html.

"Today, I am here, and he is in Lugano!": Patrice de Maistre, quoted in Michel Deléan, "Procès Bettencourt: où l'on reparle de Nicolas Sarkozy," *Mediapart,* February 18, 2015, accessed online October 6, 2016, https://www.mediapart.fr/journal/france/180215/proces-bettencourt-ou-l-reparle-de-nicolas-sarkozy?onglet=full.

bought back 8 percent: "L'Oréal rachète 8% de son capital à Nestlé," *Le Monde,* February 11, 2014.

"This family has always delegated": Marie-France Lavarini (vice president of the communications agency Ella Factory), interview with author, September 9, 2015.

Jean-Victor, now thirty, is a fashion ma-

ven: Nicole Vulser, "Jean-Victor Meyers, un héritier pur cachemire," *Le Monde,* January 5, 2015.

Nicolas, twenty-eight, who has apprenticed at Swatch headquarters: Ibid.

never talked to them about their future: Jean-Victor Meyers testimony, January 30, 2015, *Note d'audience,* 68.

In his eloquent final plea: Richard Malka plea, May 24, 2016, from author's trial notes.

"one of history's most beautiful hatreds": Françoise Bettencourt Meyers, *Les dieux grecs: généalogies* (Paris: Editions Christian, 2001), 145.

"The reality of this family is not peace": Richard Malka plea, May 24, 2016, from author's trial notes.

Chapter 29: Farewell to Paradise?

Banier was spending this time at Le Patron: Unless otherwise indicated, all quotes and descriptions in this chapter are from the author's visit and conversations with François-Marie Banier, August 11, 2016.

They paid 2,650,000 francs: *Banier enquête patrimoniale,* June 4, 2009.

Vanessa Paradis calls me on the phone: Vanessa Paradis, telephone conversation with author, August 17, 2016.

Chapter 30: The Verdict

The judge pronounces all three men guilty: Sentencing details from Cour d'appel de Bordeaux, Arrêt N° 714, August 24, 2016, 77–90.

not "determining" factors: Ibid., 58.

the judges threw out the civil damages: Ibid., 84.

"I think of Liliane": François-Marie Banier, conversation with author, August 24, 2016.

"It's a total slap in the face": Laurent Merlet declaration, August 24, 2016, from author's notes.

"Banier is a criminal": Arnaud Dupin declaration, August 24, 2016, from author's notes.

held in almost complete isolation: Georges Kiejman, telephone conversation with author, January 19, 2017; Claude Delay Tubiana, interviews with author, September 10, 2015, and January 19, 2017.

no one seriously expects: Pierre Cornut-Gentille, telephone interview with author, October 6, 2016.

"I have a novel to finish": Quotes in this paragraph are from author interview with François-Marie Banier, September 24, 2016.

"I don't want to talk about him": Liliane Bettencourt deposition, January 19, 2012.

Epilogue: Wings

Françoise and her son Jean-Victor take her to lunch: Details based on photographs taken October 21, 2016, by Paul Hubble for Getty Images, accessed online October 23, 2016, http://www.gettyimages .fr/photos/paul-hubble-bettencourt?ex cludenudity=true&family=editorial&page= 1&phrase=paul%20hubble%20betten court&sort=best#license.

"Serene": Françoise Meyers, interviewed by Raphaëlle Bacquet, "Françoise Bettencourt Meyers: 'Allons-y, mieux vaut tout purger,' " *M Magazine du Monde,* March 10, 2012, 42.

Liliane lives with the dead souls from her past: Details and quotes in this paragraph from Olivier Pelat, interviews with author, November 4, 2015, and August 24, 2016.

ABOUT THE AUTHOR

Tom Sancton was a longtime Paris bureau chief for *Time* magazine, where he wrote more than fifty cover stories. He first broke the Bettencourt affair for many American readers with his feature piece in *Vanity Fair* in 2010. Sancton coauthored the *New York Times* (and international) bestseller *Death of a Princess,* a probing investigation of the murky circumstances behind Princess Diana's death. He has also written for *Fortune, Reader's Digest, Newsweek,* and other leading magazines. A Rhodes scholar who studied at Harvard and Oxford, he is currently a research professor at Tulane University in New Orleans, where he spends part of the year. In 2014, the French government named Tom Sancton a Chevalier (knight) in the Order of Arts and Letters.